Broadway Yearbook, 1999–2000

1999 2000

BROADWAY YEARBOOK

Steven Suskin

OXFORD
UNIVERSITY PRESS

2001

OXFORD
UNIVERSITY PRESS

Oxford   New York
Athens   Auckland   Bangkok   Bogotá   Buenos Aires   Calcutta
Cape Town   Chennai   Dar es Salaam   Delhi   Florence   Hong Kong   Istanbul
Karachi   Kuala Lumpur   Madrid   Melbourne   Mexico City   Mumbai   Nairobi
Paris   São Paulo   Shanghai   Singapore   Taipei   Tokyo   Toronto   Warsaw

and associated companies in
Berlin   Ibadan

Copyright © 2001 by Steven Suskin

Published by Oxford University Press, Inc.
198 Madison Avenue, New York, New York 10016

Oxford is a registered trademark of Oxford University Press

ISBN: 0-19-513955-0; ISSN: 1473-933X

9 8 7 6 5 4 3 2 1

Printed in the United States of America
on acid-free paper

For

Helen, Johanna,

and Charlie

Contents

The Curtain Rises, xi

The Shows

August 12   **Voices in the Dark**, 5

August 19   **Kat and the Kings**, 11

September 10   **The Scarlet Pimpernel**, 17

September 30   **Epic Proportions**, 23

October 17   **Dame Edna: The Royal Tour**, 29

October 21   **Saturday Night Fever**, 35

October 29   **Wise Guys**, 41

November 3   **Sail Away**, 47

November 4   **Dinner with Friends**, 52

November 8   **Morning, Noon, and Night**, 57

November 11   **The Rainmaker**, 63

November 15   **The Price**, 68

November 17   **Tango Argentino**, 75

November 18   **Kiss Me, Kate**, 80

November 21   **Putting It Together**, 87

December 2   **Marie Christine**, 94

December 8   **Minnelli on Minnelli**, 101

December 9   **Swing!**, 108

December 15   **Amadeus**, 114

December 16   **Waiting in the Wings**, 119

December 30   **Jackie Mason: Much Ado About Everything**, 126

January 11   **James Joyce's The Dead**, 132

January 13   **Wrong Mountain**, 139

February 10   **On a Clear Day You Can See Forever**, 144

February 17   **Saturday Night**, 151

February 29   **Squonk**, 157

March 7   **Porgy and Bess**, 162

March 9   **True West**, 169

March 16   **Riverdance on Broadway**, 175

March 19   **A Moon for the Misbegotten**, 181

March 23   **Aida**, 188

March 23   **Tenderloin**, 195

March 30   **Contact**, 201

April 9   **The Ride Down Mt. Morgan**, 209

April 11   **Copenhagen**, 215

April 12   **Rose**, 222

April 13
(& February 24)   **Two Wild Parties**, 227

April 16   **Jesus Christ Superstar**, 237

April 17   **The Real Thing**, 243

April 18   **The Green Bird**, 249

April 24   **Taller Than a Dwarf**, 256

April 27   **The Music Man**, 262

April 30   **Uncle Vanya**, 270

May 1   **Dirty Blonde**, 275

May 4   **Wonderful Town**, 281

Curtain Calls

Honorable Mention, 291

Tony Wrap-Up and Other Awards, 295

Holdovers, 307

Shows That Never Reached Town, 313

Long-Run Leaders, 317

The Season's Toll, 321

Index, 329

The Curtain Rises

The reader of these pages is no doubt familiar with the two long-existing series chronicling the Broadway theatre. Burns Mantle's *Best Plays*, offering intensive statistics and abridged versions of ten selected plays, began following the 1919–1920 season. Daniel Blum's *Theatre World*, a comprehensive pictorial record, began with the 1944–1945 season. Both are invaluable and much-thumbed reference sources.

A third Broadway annual existed for a decade. George Jean Nathan began his *Theatre Book of the Year* with the 1942–1943 season (predating *Theatre World*). Rather than simply reporting the season's activities, Nathan presented what he termed "a record and an interpretation." *Best Plays* reliably tells you what the shows were about, while *Theatre World* provides a fascinating visual picture. Nathan, though, gave you an idea of what the shows were *like*, and whether you would have enjoyed them. In a nutshell: Were they any good?

Nathan's series ended with his retirement in 1951, when he was nearing seventy. There have since been two other notable books of seasonal Broadway analysis. Jack Gaver examined the 1965–1966 season in his highly informative *Season In—Season Out*. Two years later, William Goldman took on 1967–1968 in *The Season*, which remains one of the finest books about the Broadway theatre.

I have always found the *Theatre Book of the Year* series of inestimable value in compiling research or simply sating curiosity. (Nathan's thirty other books also make for enjoyable, if idiosyncratic, reading.) I do not necessarily agree with his opinions, but that is of little matter; to begin with, the man could barely tolerate musicals. Of course, it is unlikely for any theatregoer to find a critic with whose opinions he *always* agrees. Taste is individual, or at least it should be. What is important, I think, is that critics be consistent in their opinions and that they support their arguments, in the nonargumentative sense of the word. It is one thing to turn thumbs up or thumbs down. It is another, and more valuable, thing to explain *why* the imperial thumb is nudged toward the heavens or the opposite. Or someplace in between.

Criticism, by nature, is personal and colored by the critic's experience. I am the first person to agree that no critic is infallible, present company included. My aim has been to keep things informative and instructive; hence, the discussion is laced with examples from general Broadway history (and my checkered twenty-five years on and around Forty-fourth Street).

Nathan described his series as "a complete and detailed history of the theatrical year illuminated by critical comment that rids statistics of their conventional dryness and translates bald factual information into stimulating reading." That sounds pretty good to me, and it is in this vein that I have undertaken the new *Broadway Yearbook* series. What were the shows like? How were they received, by both the critics and the audiences? What other factors contributed to the shows' success or failure?

It is in hopes of answering these questions, for today's theatregoers and tomorrow's readers, that we offer *Broadway Yearbook*.

Broadway Yearbook 1999–2000 presents an analytical discussion of each show that opened on Broadway between May 31, 1999, and May 28, 2000. I have also deemed it fitting to include certain non-Broadway productions of importance, relevance, or general interest. These include an occasional off-Broadway production, like the year's Pulitzer Prize winner; so-called concert versions of old Broadway musicals, presented with full casts and orchestras; and even a "special workshop presentation" that was too important, historically, to omit. (The inclusion of all off-Broadway shows would make this book unwieldy, alas.) The shows are discussed in chronological order; an alphabetical arrangement might make it easier to browse through to find a specific show, but it seems pertinent to have the reader discover each show in the same order as the critics and theatregoers. As we'll see, timing—that is, the competition on the date of opening—was a significant factor in the reception and fate of some of this season's offerings.

The opening night credits and cast list are followed by a discussion of the production. There follows a section of related data, starting with dates and length of run. Performance and preview totals have been compiled using information from the League of American Theatres and Producers. In some cases these differ from the "official" counts distributed by press agents; I consider the League tabulation—reported week by week, along with the grosses—to be more accurate. Profit/loss information comes from a variety of sources, including the invaluable *Variety*. Shows from nonprofit organizations have been similarly classified where applicable, based on an estimate of surplus income generated by the production. It should be understood that a show that ends its Broadway run with a loss might well make up the difference from post-Broadway income. Conversely, it is not unknown for a show to have recouped its costs but—due to an overextended run or unforeseen touring costs—to slip back into a deficit.

Shows that were still running on May 29, 2000—the first day of the 2000–2001 season—are so indicated. (For the sake of completeness, closing dates and performance totals are included for shows that ran into 2000–2001 but closed before this book went to print.) Next comes the critical scorecard, which gives the reader a general idea of the critical reception of each production. The scorecards are based on the opinions of seven to ten critics from major newspapers and magazines. The number of reviews varies; not all attractions were covered by all the critics. (In a few "special" cases, productions discussed herein were reviewed by only a handful of critics.) The scorecards reflect the opinions of the critics from the *New York Times*, the *Daily News*, the *New York Post*, the *Newsday*, *Associated Press*, *Variety*, the *Village Voice*, and *New York Magazine*. Weekly magazines that offer occasional reviews, such as *Newsweek*, *Time*, and the *New Yorker*, were also included in some of the tabulations.

Reviews have been rated in five categories:

Rave Overwhelmingly positive, enthusiastically indicating that the show should be seen

Favorable Positive, indicating that the show is good though not outstanding; or that the show is good despite minor flaws

Mixed Positive and negative aspects are presented, with no overall recommendation; sometimes the reviewer is simply unclear

Unfavorable	Negative, indicating that the show doesn't work—often despite positive elements or good intentions
Pan	Overwhelmingly negative, indicating—often with a hint of annoyance—that the show was downright bad

Quite a few of the reviews fall somewhere between two categories. I have called 'em like I see 'em, although a pollster would probably say that there is a two-point margin of error. No recounts, please.

A brief financial section gives the reader an idea of the show's economic performance. Figures, again, have been compiled using information from the League of American Theatres and Producers. Finally, Tony Awards (and nominations) received by the show and its personnel are listed, along with other major awards.

Following the main body of the book are six appendixes that, it is hoped, will prove a useful supplement to the discussion of the season.

And so the curtain rises, as they say, on the premier edition of *Broadway Yearbook*.

See you at the theatre.

Broadway Yearbook, 1999–2000

The Shows

Voices in the Dark

The new Broadway season. Excitement reigns along Shubert Alley; enthusiasm and expectations run rampant. Critics and autograph hounds sharpen their pencils, usherettes air out their white collars, and theatre lobby bartenders practice their noise-making techniques. Car service limos barricade the sidewalks, pushcart men dust off their pretzels, ticket scalpers dance in the streets on their cell phones, and eager out-of-work actors crowd the Equity lounge hoping to scare up complimentary tickets. The lights slowly dim as the curtain rises on a brilliant new American play.

Well, maybe next year.

Not this year, certainly. *Voices in the Dark* was one of those secluded-house-in-the-country plays, featuring an imperiled-but-plucky heroine — "It takes a lot to scare me," she says — and a psychopathic murderer on the loose. But a psychological thriller — even a psychological thriller about a psychologist — needs to have some psychology. *Voices in the Dark* hadn't much of anything; it was simply a noncredible, thrill-less thriller. The audience was greeted by a curtain with a high, oblong window, within which was painted a moody forest scene strangely reminiscent of Vincent van Gogh's *Undergrowth with Two Figures*, painted right before he sliced off his ear. (Knives and blades were to play an important part in the imagery of the evening.) As the lights dimmed, a disembodied voice over the loudspeaker welcomed us and warned: "If you rattle your candy wrappers, you will be shushed. If you allow your cell

> **A psychological thriller—even a psychological thriller about a psychologist—needs to have some psychology.**

LONGACRE THEATRE
A Shubert Organization Theatre

Gerald Schoenfeld, *Chairman*   **Philip J. Smith,** *President*

Robert E. Wankel, *Executive Vice President*

BEN SPRECHER
WILLIAM P. MILLER NEIL HIRSCH AND AARON LEVY
IN ASSOCIATION WITH MINDY UTAY & STEVEN RAPPAPORT
PRESENT

JUDITH IVEY
IN

VOICES IN THE DARK
BY JOHN PIELMEIER

WITH

JOHN AHLIN PETER BARTLETT
LENNY BLACKBURN NICOLE FONAROW
ZACH GRENIER RAPHAEL SBARGE
TOM STECHSCHULTE

SCENIC DESIGN	COSTUME DESIGN	LIGHTING DESIGN	SOUND DESIGN
DAVID GALLO & LAUREN HELPERN	DAVID C. WOOLARD	DONALD HOLDER	T. RICHARD FITZGERALD

ORIGINAL MUSIC BY	FIGHT STAGING BY	SPECIAL EFFECTS
ROBERT WALDMAN	B.H. BARRY	GREGORY MEEH

CASTING BY	SHOW PROMOTIONS	TECHNICAL SUPERVISION
PAT McCORKLE, C.S.A.	PRISM PRODUCTION SERVICES, LLC	UNITECH II, CORP.

GENERAL MANAGER	PUBLIC RELATIONS	PRODUCTION STAGE MANAGER
PETER BOGYO	JEFFREY RICHARDS ASSOC.	JOHN M. GALO

	ASSOCIATE PRODUCERS		
TANA KOMMER	DONALD L. OLESEN	FRANK VALENZA	GEORGE FORBES

DIRECTED BY
CHRISTOPHER ASHLEY

PRE-BROADWAY TRYOUT RICH FORUM, STAMFORD CENTER FOR THE PERFORMING ARTS

ADDITIONALLY PRODUCED BY GEORGE STREET PLAYHOUSE
BY SPECIAL ARRANGEMENT WITH BEN SPRECHER, WILLIAM P. MILLER,
AARON LEVY AND THE SHUBERT ORGANIZATION

VOICES IN THE DARK WAS ORIGINALLY COMMISSIONED AND PRODUCED BY
A CONTEMPORARY THEATRE, SEATTLE, WASHINGTON

THE PRODUCERS WISH TO EXPRESS THEIR APPRECIATION TO THEATRE DEVELOPMENT FUND
FOR ITS SUPPORT OF THIS PRODUCTION.

Caller No. 1 Nicole Fonarow
Lil Judith Ivey
Hack Peter Bartlett
Bill Tom Stechschulte
Caller No. 2 ?
Owen Raphael Sbarge
Red Lenny Blackburn
Blue John Ahlin
Egan Zach Grenier

The play takes place in a radio sound studio and in a cabin in the Adirondacks over a November weekend.

phone to ring, you will be asked to leave. And if you reveal the ending of the show, you will be killed." The first line of the 1999–2000 season got a big laugh, only it was the best line of the evening. Then they raised the curtain.

Within minutes, our heroine was all alone in this suspiciously spooky house in the middle of the woods, perilously secluded from the world. But she wouldn't be alone for long. Mind you, she had already received a threatening phone call from some muffled fellow threatening to kill her; she was there in the middle of the woods, in the middle of the Adirondacks, in the middle of nowhere; and this overdesigned vacation house set was so ominous that there wasn't a person in the theatre who didn't know that it was going to start storming and thundering and raging as soon as the heroine's wisecracking agent drove away to his beach house in the Hamptons. Yet this primal reality therapist, with the number one radio show in the country—we know she has the number one radio show in the country because her agent says, "No wonder you're the number one radio show in the country"—she didn't say hey, get me outta here. She didn't say don't leave me alone, please stay until my lousy-husband-who-I'm-breaking-up-with shows up. What she said was: "It takes a lot to scare me." So she sent her agent away, the only character in the play who could possibly help her or tell us a few more waspish jokes, leaving her stranded there all alone with nobody to keep her company but a maniacal psychopath or three. This is one of those plays in which everyone is painted as a suspect, which seems to be the only way playwright John Pielmeier knows how to paint.

Pielmeier then brought on the natives, and you wondered what TV sitcom he did his sociological research on. They seemed to be right off the old hayseed comedy *Green Acres*, which went out to pasture some twenty-eight years ago. One of these boys, who was mentally challenged, was rather offensively drawn. That's a minor complaint, given the rest of the evening. His buddy was an oafish sort with a literary bent; he gabbed on about "Stevie" King and "Johnny" Grisham, which gives you an idea of the verbal humor of the evening. He was also a fan of "Ernie" Hemingway. (How many Stephen King fans read Hemingway, I wonder?) Anyway, as the bump-kin chopped vegetables beside the prominently placed Cuisinart, he told us, "I lost the tip of my finger in the soup once. We had to throw the whole thing out."

Now, when you have a fellow walking around waving a knife in a mystery thriller with a heroine who has already been bombarded with death threats and he says something like "I lost the tip of my finger in the soup once" while chopping up vegetables beside the onstage Cuisinart—well, this pretty clearly telegraphs that the fellow's intestines are going to end up in the veal marengo.

Yes, a playwright needs to do a bit of foreshadowing, but Pielmeier stacked his play all too baldly with conspicuously pertinent bits of information. The heroine was reminded, early on, that if the power goes out in the sure-to-materialize storm, the cordless phones won't work; but don't forget, *there's a rotary phone upstairs on the balcony.* Now, would any character or playwright think to say such a thing if there were to be *no* storm, *no* power outage, and *no* reason for our put-upon heroine to desperately grapple her way up the stairs, in the dark, through flashes of lightning, to that rotary phone? Later, our heroine went into the guest bathroom to change her clothes. She didn't change in the onstage bedroom, or even in the living room of her empty house; no, she went into the offstage guest bathroom—but somehow managed to bring her lingerie back onstage and leave it on a table by the front door. Was this just an absentminded character at work? Or was the playwright clumsily setting up a piece of clumsy business for later?

This expensive-looking house had an outdoor shed offering free access to the house through the kitchen pantry, making it possible for the murderer to steal into the house without a key. Pielmeier had one of his characters tell us this, thereby informing us that some scare or other was going to intrude from the kitchen pantry. And what about that big, gray circuit-breaker box lying along the kitchen steps? It contained special high-power lines that would work even if the storm knocked out the rest of the power, we were told. Now, why on earth would there be a circuit-breaker box with special high-power lines lying on the kitchen steps—and why would this be so carefully explained to us—unless the playwright was going to use those very same power lines to electrocute the villain in the Jacuzzi? Pielmeier elaborately labored to set up everything with which he intended to scare us, but his labors revealed the sweat of his brow. It is a time-honored device in thrillers to cleverly plant bits of information that serve to purposely throw you off the track. Pielmeier didn't throw us off the track; he laid out the track for us with tape that glows in the dark.

This was one of those plays where everyone's a suspect. Like the detective who knew a little too much about our heroine, eventually flipping out right before our eyes (aha!!) and chasing her around the house until he ended up with a knife in his back. Turned out he was not the killer; he was just a flipped-out detective who perfectly fit the profile of the play's psychotic killer and just happened to stumble upon our heroine the same night that the actual psychotic killer lunged after her, too. Just moments before the other killer bounded in, actually.

Pielmeier is known along Broadway for his 1982 mystery thriller *Agnes of God*. This was a dead-baby-in-the-nun's-trash can play in which the primary mystery was which of the three characters—Liz Ashley, Gerry Page, or Amanda Plummer—would chew up the most scenery. The ladies provided entertainment, at least, and managed to keep it running profitably for six hundred performances. Pielmeier's subsequent Broadway visits came with the 1985 Vietnam drama *The Boys of Winter*, which folded after nine performances, and the 1987 "suspense thriller" *Sleight of Hand*, which also lasted nine performances. *Voices in the Dark* forced itself through eight underattended weeks before calling it quits.

Historical note: This was the first show in Broadway history, as far as I can tell, that incorporated a real live porno movie on stage. *Forrest Hump*, according to the leading lady. The TV set was slanted toward the wings, but it was clearly viewable from where I was sitting. Poor Judith Ivey, who starred in this mess of porridge, is one of those accomplished performers who manage to keep your attention no matter what; but forty-five seconds of *Forrest Hump* were a whole lot livelier than *Voices in the Dark*.

They were selling not only a *Voices in the Dark* T-shirt and a *Voices in the Dark* coffee mug, but a *Voices in the Dark* shot glass as well.

Let it also be noted that they were selling, in the lobby, not only a *Voices in the Dark* T-shirt and a *Voices in the Dark* coffee mug, but a *Voices in the Dark* shot glass as well. Real collector's items by now, I imagine.

Some commentators commented that stage thrillers were no longer possible in our special effects–surfeited world; the sky was the limit in films, and you simply couldn't pull that sort of thing off onstage anymore. To which I say, no. You don't need machinery to surprise the audience, to bring them to the edge of their seats. Just engage the imagination. Others concluded that the only mystery of the evening was why anyone bothered to produce this play. That's simple, folks. They thought they'd make a lot of money, like the producers of *Angel Street*, *Sleuth*, *Deathtrap*, and even *Agnes of God*. There is an immense audience for a good Broadway thriller, even a mediocre Broadway thriller. But *Voices in the Dark* was not a good mediocre thriller, not by half, just a contrived attempt at manufactured scare tactics.

And yes, I heard voices in the dark, all right. Midway through the first act, a fellow behind me said, "Well I guess we can leave at intermission."

"Hell," said his companion, "why wait?"

And they beat it up the aisle.

Kat and the Kings

Back in 1982 I was working in a theatrical office in the Paramount Building. At 11:00 every morning, in would pop a short, ancient man with a scrawny mustache in a dirty apron—a bootblack, I guess, is what you'd have called him. (In the South they'd have called him a shoeshine boy.) If you'd called central casting for a bootblack, this fellow is what you'd have gotten. He was already obsolete, but there he was in our series of interlocking rooms, moving door to door offering a "shine, sir" or "shine, ma'am."

This fellow had a good thing going, at least in our office. I'm a sneaker man myself, but this place was run by two highly successful producers who I think kind of liked the idea of having their very own bootblack "do" their pumps and heels every morning; it certainly impressed people who might be

As the evening ground on it lost all sense of purpose, dissolving into a bunch of songs about this girl and that girl and don't get married, pal, who needs a wife.

coming in for meetings, whom they would offer a shine. The office contained a bunch of bright young preppyish types working for next to nothing, who also felt half dressed without that daily shine on their shoes.

One morning I had my papers spread out on the conference room table when in walked the bootblack with five pairs of shoes. He knew that I wasn't one of his customers, but I don't think he especially liked the big shot producer ladies or the young preppyish types who handed him their scuffed loafers as if he were a servant.

The office was just then producing a new musical revue consisting of 1950s rock and roll songs, which was in preview hell on the way to surefire

Kat Diamond   Terry Hector
Lucy Dixon   Kim Louis
Young Kat Diamond   Jody J. Abrahams
Bingo   Loukmaan Adams
Ballie   Junaid Booysen
Magoo   Alistair Izobell

Time: 1999 and 1957–1959
Place: Cape Town and Durban, South Africa

Original London Cast Album: First Night/Relativity 1809 (featuring four Broadway cast members)

CORT THEATRE
Ⓢ A Shubert Organization Theatre
Gerald Schoenfeld, *Chairman*   **Philip J. Smith,** *President*

Robert E. Wankel, *Executive Vice President*

HARRIET NEWMAN LEVE JUDITH AND DAVID ROSENBAUER

In Association with

RICHARD FRANKEL MARC ROUTH WILLETTE KLAUSNER KARDANA-SWINSKY PRODUCTIONS
DAVID KRAMER TALIEP PETERSEN RENAYE KRAMER

By Special Arrangement with
PAUL ELLIOTT NICK SALMON LEE MENZIES

Present

KAT AND THE KINGS

Book And Lyrics   Music and Arrangements
DAVID KRAMER   TALIEP PETERSEN

With

JODY J. ABRAHAMS LOUKMAAN ADAMS JUNAID BOOYSEN
TERRY HECTOR ALISTAIR IZOBELL KIM LOUIS

Set and Costume Design   Lighting Design   Sound Design
SAUL RADOMSKY   HOWARD HARRISON   ORBITAL SOUND/SEBASTIAN FROST

Music Supervision   Music Director   Music Coordinator
GARY HIND   JEFF LAMS   JOHN MILLER

US Casting   Technical Supervision   Production Stage Manager
JAY BINDER   TECH PRODUCTION SERVICES   PAT SOSNOW
PETER FULBRIGHT

General Management   Press Representative   Associate Producer
RICHARD FRANKEL PRODUCTIONS   HELENE DAVIS   PATRICK MOLONY
DAVID W. CALDWELL

Choreography
JODY J. ABRAHAMS AND LOUKMAAN ADAMS

Direction and Musical Staging
DAVID KRAMER

The Producers wish to express their appreciation to Theatre Development Fund for its support of this production.

---

flopdom. The stage manager came in to ask me something or other. The little old man piped in, as he slapped Griffin wax to the leather, that he, too, used to be in show business. With a top act, back in the 1950s. Me, I've always been quick to listen to old show business stories.

The Will Mastin Trio was his act. As it happened, I had actually heard of the Will Mastin Trio. (That surprised him.) They were popular on the nightclub circuit, specializing in energetic tap dancing mixed with song. They headlined at places like the Copacabana in New York, the Sands in Las Vegas, and the Fontainebleau in Miami Beach (back in the days when, as black men, they actually needed a pass to walk the streets of Miami Beach). The Will Mastin Trio even starred in a Broadway musical custom written around their act, which is why I had heard of them. Mastin was the nominal head of the act, accompanied by a guy named Sam and Sam's young son.

"You're not Will Mastin?" I asked.

"No, no, Will's dead." He told me his name, which was unfamiliar. But then, why would I know it? I supposed he must have filled in when one of the three had to miss a date. Or maybe he was part of their traveling company. Anyway, he sure looked like an ex-dancer (or an ex-jockey). There's something about show people that doesn't rub off.

Will Mastin's bootblack had totally slipped my mind long before I sat down at the Cort Theatre to see a final preview of *Kat and the Kings*. The curtain rose, and after a brief overture out bounded a charming middle-aged actor with a shoeshine kit, who informed us that he did shoeshines on the streets of Cape Town. But back in the 1950s he had been Kat, of the singing group *Kat and the Kings*. They had started small and grown to fame, but always in the shadow of apartheid, so much so that when they headlined at the posh Claridge's Hotel in Durban, they were forced to simultaneously serve as bellhops. The group finally disbanded, and Kat ended up performing shoeshines on the streets of Cape Town.

The show displayed great promise as the first act progressed, kind of like *Dreamgirls* but with friendlier material. As the evening ground on, though, it lost all sense of purpose, dissolving into a bunch of songs about this girl and that girl and don't get married, pal, who needs a wife. By the time they got around to the song about walking the invisible dog (and sprayed the good folks sitting in the front rows with noninvisible water), you realized that all they were interested in was a good-natured show with pretty singing and gimmicky staging. There is no reason that, once having brought up the question of apartheid, they needed to make something of it. But it seemed like a waste.

Kat and the Kings arrived on Broadway, in September 1999, with a 1999 Olivier Award for Best Musical. (That's the West End equivalent of the Tony.) This accolade—pasted across the ads and billboards— might have worked against the show's chances. For *Kat* was sweet, good-natured, and enjoyable in a lightweight sort of way. But Best Musical?? Broadway has seen inferior shows receive Tony Awards, for sure; "best" doesn't indicate

> The 1999 Olivier Award for Best Musical—pasted across the ads and billboards—might have worked against the show's chances. For *Kat* was sweet, good-natured, and enjoyable in a lightweight sort of way. But Best Musical??

"good," simply "better" than the competition. By prominently labeling *Kat and the Kings* "best new musical," the producers were consciously raising our expectations. We went in expecting to see something important. It turned out to be mere fun, and we ended up disappointed.

This was a miscalculation, folks, compounded by recent history: Conor McPherson's Irish play *The Weir* arrived on Broadway in April 1999, prominently labeled as the 1998 Olivier Award winner for Best Play. *The Weir* needed something to help sell it perhaps, as it knocked Martin McDonagh's superior Irish play *The Beauty Queen of Leenane* out of the Walter Kerr Theatre. *The Weir* received a staggeringly favorable review from the critic of the *New York Times*, but a majority of the critics looked at it and said: What? This was a play of great depths, depths so deep that many viewers decided that deep down underneath there was no there there. Again, the Olivier Award for Best Play raised expectations, perhaps too high; more than one critic wondered whether London audiences were simply taken in by all that boozy blarney masking a vacuum.

This is relevant in that two of the main *Kat and the Kings* producers also coproduced *The Weir*. For that matter, three of the *Kat* producers coproduced *Stomp*, a plotless revue from 1994 that's still going strong off-Broadway and around the world. Two of the same producers coproduced *Smokey Joe's Cafe*, a plotless revue from 1995 that amassed a sub-

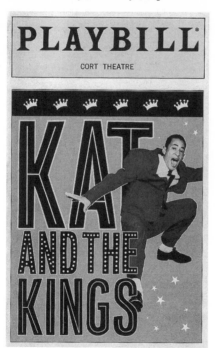

stantial 2,036-performance run before closing in January 2000 (a week after *Kat*). *Smokey Joe* wasn't much of an entertainment, simply a market-driven commodity that managed to more or less find a market. *Kat and the Kings* was far more enjoyable, filled with an upbeat score (with original songs, unlike those in *Smokey Joe*) and an energetically likable cast. It simply wasn't in any way important, nor did it have one of those supertheatrical effects, like a falling chandelier or an onstage helicopter, that can make a British import run for years and years and years. All *Kat* had to sell, in effect, was its Olivier for best new musical, which turned out to be not much of a selling point. The show never counteracted its lackadaisical reception as the poorly received *Smokey Joe's Cafe* did, and it closed after New Year's weekend.

As for that singing and dancing elder Kat at the Cort, the role was played with great energy and charm by an actor named Terry Hector. The

Kat and the Kings
Opened: August 19, 1999
Closed: January 2, 2000
157 performances (and 15 previews)
Profit/Loss: Loss
Kat and the Kings ($75 top) was scaled to a potential gross
of $506,927 at the 1,084-seat Cort. Weekly grosses
averaged about $159,000, with the show breaking
$200,000 on three holiday weeks. Total gross for the run
was $3,418,286. Attendance was about 51 percent, with
the box office grossing about 31 percent of potential
dollar-capacity.

*Critical
Scorecard*

Rave 1
Favorable 1
Mixed 2
Unfavorable 1
Pan 2

show was based on the experiences of a fellow named Salie "Kat" Daniels, of the 1950s singing group the Rockets. Daniels himself played the elder Kat in London; thus the former headliner-turned-shoeshine boy found himself back in the limelight, playing a fictionalized version of himself on the West End stage. Not only did "his" story win the Best New Musical Olivier, but he won one, too. (The entire six-person cast shared the Olivier for Best Actor in a Musical Award; Daniels, the four singing boys—who re-created their roles on Broadway—and Mandisa Bardill, who played the songwriting sister of one of the boys and will no doubt go down in history as the only actress to win a Best Actor Olivier.) Salie Daniels was set to repeat his role on Broadway, but illness forced his withdrawal; he died of cancer three weeks before the show opened here. At least he ended his life back onstage, with the roar of the crowd and the smell of the greasepaint and all that, rather than in an apron smeared with shoe wax and cream.

Which brings me back to that Paramount building bootblack. There he was, day after day, cheerfully offering spitshines to a building full of businesspeople in the entertainment business. Was he resigned to his lot? Or did he dream of a comeback? Would he have believed it if we told him that Salie Daniels of Kat and the Kings—an act that faced walls of prejudice similar to those scaled by the Will Mastin Trio—would have ended up starring in his own Broadway musical, if he hadn't died first?

I left that office almost twenty years ago and never saw that ancient little man again. Never even thought of him, either, until the night I sat watching *Kat and the Kings*. He presumably ended his days as a bootblack, and when he died—which he presumably has by now—there was no obituary in *Variety* to let me know. I never saw an obituary of Will Mastin either, although he sure didn't wind up on the street with a shoeshine kit. Neither did his partner Sam. They both earned millions, though not from tap dancing. Rather, they signed a split-it-up-in-thirds partnership contract with Sam's kid, who fought his way from the hard time to the big time and became one of the biggest stars of them all. But, then, Sammy Davis Jr. was born in segregated America, not segregated South Africa.

SEPTEMBER 10

The Scarlet Pimpernel

The Scarlet Pimpernel originally opened to a scathing critical reception on November 9, 1997. "If it's pulse-racing suspense and derring-do you're after," advised Ben Brantley in the *New York Times*, "you would be better off watching tourists crossing against the lights in Times Square."

The following spring, as the Tony Award nominations came along, Broadway producer Pierre Cosette made explicitly derogatory remarks about the show to the press; this was quite remarkable because Cosette was the producer of *The Scarlet Pimpernel*. I found his assessment rather severe. *Pimpernel* was pretty dreary, all in all, but it wasn't absolutely awful. But I suppose Cosette knows a bad show when he sees it. He also produced *The Civil War*. (Not the one in which the armies of the Union and the Confederacy slaughtered each other by the thousands; the one with songs, which was slaughtered by the critics and dropped millions.)

Within weeks of losing three Tony Awards, Cosette sold off his rights in the show to Cablevision Systems Corporation, one of those giant media conglomerates that buy up little mom-and-pop companies like Madison Square Garden and Radio City Music Hall. Cablevision's Music Hall Division took over *The Scarlet Pimpernel* and devised a campaign with which to reconstitute it as a major Broadway musical hit capable of running now and forever. They brought over one of their in-house staffers, a director-choreographer with the unlikely name of Robert Longbottom, to "fix" the show. Longbottom had only one Broadway show to his credit, the 1997 musical *Side Show*; a disappointing failure, but at least it failed nobly.

NEIL SIMON THEATRE

RADIO CITY ENTERTAINMENT   TED FORSTMANN
PRESENT

RON BOHMER
CAROLEE CARMELLO   MARC KUDISCH

 THE SCARLET PIMPERNEL

BOOK AND LYRICS BY   MUSIC BY
NAN KNIGHTON   **FRANK WILDHORN**
BASED ON THE NOVEL 'THE SCARLET PIMPERNEL' BY BARONESS ORCZY

WITH

KIRK McDONALD

DAVID CROMWELL   HARVEY EVANS   PETER FLYNN   RUSSELL GARRETT
DREW GERACI   DANNY GURWIN   CYNTHIA LEIGH HEIM   JAMES HINDMAN
EMILY HSU   ALICIA IRVING   ELIZABETH WARD LAND   KEN LAND   DAVID MASENHEIMER
ROBB MCKINDLES   KATIE NUTT   ELIZABETH O'NEILL   JESSICA PHILLIPS   TERRY RICHMOND
LAURA SCHUTTER   MATTHEW SHEPARD   JENNIFER SMITH   STEPHONNE SMITH
DAVID ST. LOUIS   JAMES VAN TREUREN   CHARLES WEST

SCENERY BY   COSTUMES BY   LIGHTING BY
ANDREW JACKNESS   **JANE GREENWOOD**   **NATASHA KATZ**

SOUND BY   HAIR DESIGN BY   PRODUCTION STAGE MANAGER   SPECIAL EFFECTS
KARL RICHARDSON   **PAUL HUNTLEY**   **BONNIE L. BECKER**   **JIM STEINMEYER**

ORCHESTRATIONS   MUSICAL SUPERVISION   VOCAL ARRANGEMENTS   MUSIC COORDINATOR
KIM SCHARNBERG   **JASON HOWLAND**   **RON MELROSE**   **JOHN MILLER**

CASTING DIRECTOR   ASSISTANT CHOREOGRAPHERS   DANCE ARRANGEMENTS
MARK SIMON, CSA   **TOM KOSIS &**   **DAVID CHASE**
DARLENE WILSON

GENERAL MANAGER   PRESS REPRESENTATIVE   PRODUCTION MANAGER
101 PRODUCTIONS, LTD.   **BARLOW•HARTMAN**   **PETER FULBRIGHT**
public relations

EXECUTIVE PRODUCER   FIGHT DIRECTOR
TIM HAWKINS   **RICK SORDELET**

DIRECTED AND CHOREOGRAPHED BY
ROBERT LONGBOTTOM

Marguerite Carolee Carmello
Chauvelin Marc Kudisch
Percy Ron Bohmer
Marie Elizabeth Ward Land
Armand Kirk McDonald
Tussaud David Masenheimer
Coupeau Stephonne Smith
Mercier David St. Louis
Ozzy Harvey Evans
Elton Russell Garrett
Dewhurst Ken Land
Jessup Charles West
Ben James Hindman
Farleigh Matthew Shepard
Hal Danny Gurwin
Robespierre David Cromwell
Prince of Wales David Cromwell
Opera Dancers, Soldiers, Prisoners, British Guests and Servants:
   Emily Hsu, Alicia Irving, David Masenheimer, Robb McKindles, Katie Nutt, Elizabeth O'Neill, Jessica Phillips, Terry Richmond, Laura Schutter, Charles West

Time: May into July, 1794
Place: England and France

Original Broadway Cast Albums:
   Atlantic Theatre 83079 (version 1.0), Atlantic Theatre 83265 ("Encore" version 2.0)

Longbottom oversaw a drastic reformatting of the show—rehearsing by day while the original version continued by night. The results (*Pimpernel* 2.0) were unveiled in September 1998, and they were a definite improvement. The original appeared to have been assembled from a how-to-write-a-hit-Broadway-operetta primer, circa 1922. Longbottom seems to have stuck a sign on the wall of the rehearsal room saying, "It's the story, stupid!" Out went the frills, out went the trimming, out went all the other French Revolution junque. *Pimpernel* 2.0 started with the heroine giving her final performance at the Comédie-Française—she's a singing star at the Comédie-Française, but we'll let that pass—and within the very first number we were introduced to the three sides of the triangle that was at the heart of the plot. (As opposed to version 1.0, which started with a cheesy production number about the guillotine, entitled "Madame Guillotine.") We never lost sight of the central triangle in 2.0; the revised book focused on the trio so closely that at times we seemed to be watching a three-character play. The merry band of English fops was still there, although they were toned down to the extent that they appeared to be typical, decent men risking their lives in a noble cause. They also all appeared to have the same bootmaker. The large chorus was still there, too, but much of its material had happily disappeared.

The strength of 2.0 was in the playing of the leading actors. Douglas Sills had been the only positive asset of 1.0; the Broadway newcomer displayed a winning manner, a pleasing personality, and an indication that he knew the show was substandard, but it was his big break so he was going to try to entertain you anyway. By the time 2.0 opened, Sills—with a great set of 1.0 personal reviews and a Tony nomination under his belt —no longer needed to *try* to entertain you; he demonstrated that special sort of stage authority which comes from knowing that you know what you're doing and you know how to do it. The big surprise in the new version was Rex Smith as Chauvelin. Terrence Mann originated the role with plenty of grimaces and eye rolling, no doubt in self-preservation when he realized he was signed to a run-of-the-play contract in a stinker of a show. (Ten years after creating Javert in the Broadway company of *Les Misérables*, he was back on Forty-fifth Street in far more misérable straits.) Smith

Most official communiqués from the production tacitly implied that *The Scarlet Pimpernel* was, indeed, a poorly received, ill-assembled show clearly in need of improvements.

played Chauvelin straight and serious, with an undertone of in-character humor, bringing some of the dash of villainous Basil Rathbone in those old Errol Flynn–Warner Bros. swashbucklers. Sills and Smith, along with the personable Rachel York (in an impossibly unsympathetic role), managed to make version 2.0 bearable.

The improvements, though, weren't enough to counteract a year's worth of poor business and bad word of mouth. The new producers spent a fair fortune on the expensive process of renovating the show from 1.0 to 2.0; on the massive operating losses suffered by 1.0 while preparing 2.0

(you have to expect a certain drop-off in business when you continue to sell tickets to a show which you have already announced is so bad that you're totally revising it); on the extensive marketing campaign heralding the arrival of 2.0; and, ultimately, on the operating losses of 2.0.

Meanwhile, the theatre owners decided that their real estate was underutilized and booked *Saturday Night Fever* into the Minskoff for the fall of 1999. Radio City Entertainment, somehow reasoning that a closed show with a big deficit was less desirable than a running show with a growing loss, decided to keep the show alive (as it were) and transfer it to another Broadway house. The Nederlander Organization, operators of the Minskoff, were glad to oblige with the Neil Simon.

Now, such a move required severe alterations to the show. The Simon stage could not accommodate the massive *Pimpernel* set, nor could the potential Simon box office receipts accommodate the large cast and stage-hand costs encountered at the Minskoff. The rules of Actors' Equity specifically prohibit a reduction of the number of Equity members working on a Broadway show. The only way to accomplish this is to close down the show altogether, wait six weeks, and then start all over again. This is precisely what *Pimpernel* did, scheduling a three-city tryout tour before returning to Broadway. So 3.0, which some might see as a mere continuation of the original run, was technically considered a new production.

The Scarlet Pimpernel had always been overblown in cast and scenery, so artistically this didn't seem like such a bad idea. Financially, though, it seemed almost as ludicrous as the transformation from 1.0 to 2.0. Clearly, Radio City was pouring out millions and millions of dollars with no practical hope of success.

And so it was that on September 10, 1999, *The Scarlet Pimpernel* 3.0 rode into the fire, as they say in one of the bouncier songs, and braved Broadway once more. The new show began with the 2.0 opening, which handily introduced the three main characters and got the plot off and running. It quickly became apparent that we would be faced with less stage-hogging scenery than at the Minskoff. For example, there had formerly been a heavy, stage-darkening prison set stretching across the wide Minskoff stage; at the Simon, the lower lever of the guillotine unit became the prison, much narrower but perfectly sufficient for the purpose. And there's something to be said for bare stage space, especially in a suffocating show. The library scene—in which the hero transformed his foppish friends into freedom fighters—played far better with less stuff on the stage.

It was also clear that there was a significantly smaller acting company, with forty-one card-carrying Equity members reduced to twenty-nine. This was no detriment at all. The original company, in 1.0, was stocked with folks who stood around like an old-fashioned operetta chorus singing bad songs; with less operetta-style numbers in 2.0—and no way, union-wise, to reduce their number—they had simply filled the large stage like cardboard cutouts. The 3.0 cast was unobtrusive, at least. There was also a reduction in the size of the orchestra, from twenty-five to nineteen pieces. Mr. Wildhorn's music, it turned out, sounded every bit as good with fewer musicians.

The *Pimpernel* publicity trumpeted the theory that the smaller stage of the Neil Simon proscribed these changes. This new downsized show was the perfect *Pimpernel*, according to Mr. Longbottom: "The up close and personal version because we're in a smaller theatre, which would always have been my choice." It is interesting to note that most official communiqués from the production tacitly implied that *The Scarlet Pimpernel* was, indeed, a poorly received, ill-assembled show clearly in need of improvements.

As act 2 of version 3 came into view, though, it became clear that the new scenic concept was not all that conceptual; rather, it was simply cheap. Less scenery to build, fewer stagehands to maneuver it. The backstage area at the Simon is far smaller than that of the Minskoff, but there is plenty of room to shoehorn in a standard-sized musical. The final seaside scene, as presented in 3.0, was simply tacky.

But all the scenery in the world—or no scenery, for that matter—would not have made much of a difference. The show was, from the first, uninspiring and uninspired. The material, even with two major revisions, was pretty bad; while the scenery was no longer clunky, the score was. The dialogue? Well, the book uses words like "nincompoop" and April Fools' jokes as supposed laugh lines. (The action takes place in 1794, back during George Washington's first term as president.) And there's no point in going into the lyrics, although one can't help noting couplets like "I wasn't born to walk on water / I was born to rape and slaughter."

There was a cut in the size of the orchestra, from twenty-five to nineteen pieces. Frank Wildhorn's music, it turned out, sounded every bit as good with fewer musicians.

If 2.0 was better than 1.0, 3.0 was a step backward, defeated by the absence of Douglas Sills (and Rex Smith). Ron Bohmer—a road company *Phantom of the Opera*—sang Sills's songs well but made for a rather humorless hero in a show, and a role, that needed all the charm they could get. All hopes were dashed without a dashing Pimpernel. The unanswerable question, though, is why anyone would buy a hopelessly unworkable musical and attempt to rework it. The initial producers of *The Scarlet Pimpernel*—or any new, previously unstaged musical—had no way of knowing it would turn out so badly, other than maybe by reading the script and listening to the score before plunking down millions. The Radio City people, though, were able to see it on the stage, survey the disgruntled audience members, and read the packet of devastatingly bad reviews. For the sort of money ultimately spent on *The Scarlet Pimpernel*, they might just as well have produced a new show from scratch. If you're determined to produce a bad musical, I suppose, it might as well be your own.

Epic Proportions

A new farce comedy helmed by Broadway's funniest director, Jerry Zaks, starring Broadway's newest, darling-est
comic discovery, Kristen Chenoweth. Sounds like this one could be good,
yes? Especially when one of the authors is cocreator of that phenomenal
television comedy hit *Friends*.

So much for expectations.

Yes, *Epic Proportions* was written by David Crane, of *Friends*. (I feel
compelled to admit that I've never seen *Friends*; but friends of mine—
real, died-in-the-wool theatre folk—swear by it.) This fellow successfully
entertains millions and gazillions of people each and every week, plus re-
runs; some of it, you might think, would rub off on *Epic Proportions*. Only
thing is, *Epic Proportions* was originally produced in 1986, before Mr.
Crane went on to fame and fortune in Hollywood. Back then, he was just
another struggling off-Broadway playwright.

Kristen Chenoweth rode into *Epic Proportions* on a wave of great publicity, heralded as Broadway's newest star. Ms. Chenoweth arrived on
Forty-sixth Street from Tulsa in the spring of 1997, to make her debut as
a Mormon soprano in the ill-fated *Steel Pier*; gave a flashy performance as
a pert ingenue in City Center Encores! production of *Strike up the Band* in
the winter of 1998; moved on to Bill Finn's ill-fated *A New Brain* in the
spring of 1998, as a singing waitress delivering calamari; and won a Best
Supporting Actress Tony Award for her whirlwind of a performance as
Sally Brown in the ill-fated revival of *You're a Good Man, Charlie Brown*
in the winter of 1999. All this, plus *Epic Proportions* and a clutch of recordings as well, in little more than two years.

But how does this impressive activity—resulting in plenty of goodwill

THE HELEN HAYES THEATRE

MARTIN MARKINSON   DONALD TICK

BOB   BRENT   ROBERT   MATTHEW   MARK
CUILLO   PEEK   BARANDES   FARRELL   SCHWARTZ

with

PHILIP & PATRICIA BARRY PRODUCTIONS and ROBERT DRAGOTTA

present

by
LARRY COEN *and* DAVID CRANE

starring
KRISTIN CHENOWETH
JEREMY DAVIDSON   ALAN TUDYK

also starring
TOM BECKETT   ROSS LEHMAN   RICHARD B. SHULL
RUTH WILLIAMSON   RICHARD ZIMAN

scenery   *costumes*   *lighting*
DAVID GALLO   WILLIAM IVEY LONG   PAUL GALLO

sound   *casting*   *fight director*
AURAL FIXATION   STUART HOWARD   RICK SORDELET
AND AMY SCHECTER, CSA

technical director   *press representative*   *marketing*
PETER FULBRIGHT   PETE SANDERS GROUP   PRO-MARKETING

executive producer   *production stage manager*   *associate director*
MARK SCHWARTZ   RICK STEIGER   BT McNICHOLL

general management   *associate producer*
BRENT PEEK PRODUCTIONS   WILLIAM K. EHRENFELD

directed by
JERRY ZAKS

The Producers wish to express their appreciation to Theatre Development Fund for its support of this production.

Narrator   Michael Carroll
Conspirators   Richard Ziman, Ross Lehman, Ruth Williamson
Octavium   Tom Beckett
Louise Goldman   Kristin Chenoweth
Benny Bennet   Alan Tudyk
Phil Bennet   Jeremy Davidson
Jack   Richard Ziman
Shel   Ross Lehman
Slavemaster   Tom Beckett
Extras   Richard Ziman, Tom Beckett, Ross Lehman
Extra Extra   Ruth Williamsom
First General   Richard Ziman
Second General   Ross Lehman
Egyptian Dancing Girl   Ruth Williamson
Egyptians   Tom Beckett, Ross Lehman, Richard Ziman
The Queen   Ruth Williamson
Queen's Attendant   Tom Beckett
Guards   Ross Lehman, Richard Ziman
D. W. DeWitt   Richard B. Shull
Executioner   Ross Lehman
Brady   Richard Ziman
Cochette   Ruth Williamson
Cochette's Assistant   Tom Beckett
Gladiators   Richard Ziman, Tom Beckett, Ross Lehman

Time: The early 1930s
Place: The Arizona desert

and one memorable nonstar turn in a failed revival of an off-Broadway revue—make her a Broadway star? The question doesn't have to do with Chenoweth's talent, of which she has oodles. And I am not referring to a star's supposed box office draw. But part of what a star needs to do is carry her show on her shoulders; the weaker the material, the stronger the need. *The Lion King* or *Rent* didn't need a star to gain acceptance, just performers wearing the costumes and giving sturdy performances. The haphazard 1999 revival of *Annie Get Your Gun*, on the other hand, needed Bernadette Peters lobbing her songs to the balcony to keep the audience from minding how dreary the rest of the enterprise was.

Yes, Chenoweth gave a cyclonic performance in *Charlie Brown*, but that in itself didn't quite make her ready to hold together an entire, flimsy *Epic*. Put someone bigger-than-life in the role assigned to Chenoweth and you'd have a chance—Whoopi Goldberg, say, or for that matter Nathan Lane. An outsized ham might have compensated for the material, providing B_{12} shots of energetic entertainment. But that was an impossible task to ask of Ms. Chenoweth at this stage of her career.

The key ingredient in the *Epic Proportions* mix, though, was Broadway comedy king Jerry Zaks. A former actor, Zaks made an impressive Broadway directing debut in 1986 with a revival of John Guare's fine play *The House of Blue Leaves*. His 1987 revival of Cole Porter's *Anything Goes* made him the director to watch; his 1990 production of Guare's *Six Degrees of Separation* cemented his reputation; and the 1992 revival of Frank Loesser's *Guys and Dolls* made him Broadway's undisputed golden boy.

Since that time, though, things have not been quite so golden. Zaks tried two new plays in 1993: David Henry Hwang's *Face Value* closed during previews, while *Laughter on the 23rd Floor* had a decent run —thanks to Neil Simon's name on the marquee—but was an artistic and commercial disappointment. After *Laughter*, Zaks seems to have become gun-shy. In 1995, he stepped in as replacement director of the musical revue *Smokey Joe's Cafe*—an unlikely Zaks project, certainly —and helped fashion it into a long-running hit (despite dismal reviews). In 1996, he directed a revival of the Sondheim-Shevelove-Gelbart farce musical *A Funny Thing Happened on the Way to the Forum*, which was successful but not nearly as successful as *Guys and Dolls* had been. (People seeing *Forum* for the first time enjoyed it; those who had seen the 1962 original or the 1972 revival weren't quite so thrilled.) In 1998, Zaks stepped in—with no billing but plenty of publicity—to take over Paul Simon's terminally ill musical *The*

Capeman. In the spring of 1999 came Frank Wildhorn's *The Civil War*, yet another enormous failure that Zaks joined during the tryout. What Zaks might have hoped to do for *The Civil War* is unclear; certainly, the Jerry Zaks touch was not in evidence.

All of which is to say, since 1993 Zaks has not developed and directed a new show from inception. Taking over as a replacement means, among other things, that you inherit certain personnel, decisions, and already-written material that the authors might not be willing to change. (The last new musical that Zaks originated was Stephen Sondheim and John Weidman's *Assassins*, which disbanded after a developmental production at Playwrights Horizons in 1991.) Neither has Zaks done anything recently displaying the fresh inventiveness of *Blue Leaves*, *Anything Goes*, or *Six Degrees*. This is not to say that the man doesn't have talent; he does. But he appears to have what one might call a fear of commitment. Tell an egoist that he's a genius enough times, and he will become a monster; tell a sensible man like Jerry that he's a genius, and he'll just smile pleasantly. After a couple of failures, though, he might well develop an overly cautious approach to new projects. And caution is not necessarily prudent in an ever-changing world like today's Broadway.

So Jerry turned to *Epic Proportions*, five months after *The Civil War* began (and four months after it ended). This appeared to be Zaks's first new Broadway play since 1993; in fact, it was yet another revival. Larry Coen and David Crane's comedy had been produced at the Judith Anderson Theatre off-Broadway in 1986, disappearing after twenty-six performances. But Crane was now a Hollywood genius, giving *Epic Proportions* a second shot at the big time. (How many off-Broadway flops end up on Broadway, anyway?) The producers and investors surely must have assumed that the combination of Emmy Award–winning comedy king Crane and Tony Award–winning comedy king Zaks was sure to even out the admittedly slight script. But then, *Laughter on the 23rd Floor* was surely more surefire, with Zaks and Simon and Nathan Lane.

A colleague of mine accompanied friends of the director to the first preview. His report was that it was already pretty funny, "but it's going to get a lot better because they say Jerry always fixes his shows during previews." Not this time, he didn't.

The show began with the lights going up on a richly handsome gold-tasseled curtain. A friendly narrator said a thing or two, after which the gold tassels rose to reveal—nothing, just a bare desert. The curtain lowered, prompting a laugh, then rose again on a DeMille-ish movie set.

Now if this seems familiar, dear reader, there's a reason; the revival of *Forum* began with the very same gag. "Open up the curtain," sang the narrator Prologus during the opening number, "Comedy Tonight." The curtain rose, taking a row of stuffed legs and shoes up into the flies with it. The curtain lowered, prompting a laugh, then rose again. This interrupted the flow of the musical number and indicated to me —at least—that Zaks was going to graft unnecessary gags onto a well-considered and time-tested farce. Zaks used the curtain joke once more in the *Forum* opening number, to diminished effect, revealing Mary Testa playing Medea; so it was disheartening to see it, yet again, at the theatre next door.

Things went downhill from there.

Epic Proportions had goodwill going for it, though; it was one of those shows that you for some unknown reason *wanted* to like. The authors displayed a lovely sense of the ridiculous and provided a barrage of funny lines in this tale about the making of one of those all-encompassing biblical epics of the silent era. The heroine—the aforementioned Ms. Chenoweth—played the film's assistant director in charge of extras, all thirty-four hundred of them (with only two bathrooms). The play was full of exchanges like the following:

Chenoweth: "Who is he without sin?"

Offstage voice: "I am."

Chenoweth: "Go to props and pick up the first stone."

Unlikely lines—like "Everybody, meet me in Mesopotamia in fifteen minutes" or, from a besieged extra, "Yesterday was the last day of Pompeii, and I for one am not sorry to see it go"—were funny at first, but by the time they got around to "I was with the Sabine women until two o'clock," there was not a laugh to be had. The folks in charge cut the intermission—thus making it more difficult to walk out—but that, in itself, was a clear sign of desperation. After hoping and hoping that things would get better, one finally sat resigned, realizing that *Epic Proportions* was simply hopelessly lame.

Critics who saw the final previews reported that the show ran between eighty and ninety minutes. I clocked the show at a mere seventy-one minutes, without laughs. And I mean without laughs.

There have been stage satires on motion pictures since the advent of motion pictures, practically; most have failed. George S. Kaufman and Moss Hart's *Once in a Lifetime* and Sam and Bella Spewack (and George Abbott's) *Boy Meets Girl* were both Depression-era hits. The scattershot *Epic Proportions* was more reminiscent of the old Carol Burnett TV show —except that Carol's sketches were fast and funny, running less than ten minutes. Critics who saw *Epic Proportions* at the final previews on Tuesday and Wednesday reported that the show ran between eighty and ninety minutes. I clocked the show, that Saturday afternoon, at a mere seventy-one minutes without laughs. And I mean without laughs.

Dame Edna: The Royal Tour

The big question, I suppose, was whether mainstream Broadway audiences were ready to flock to see a middle-aged man in a dress. This isn't England, after all. That sort of thing is quite popular across the sea; there's a whole tradition of men in gowns over there. Broadway audiences have become more and more accepting of attractions that blur the gender line over the last fifteen years or so. But *Dame Edna: The Royal Tour* wasn't a serious problem play, wasn't about an important social issue, and only briefly touched on sexual matters. It was simply a man playing a woman, in a dress. (And what a dress!)

The producers came up with a very clever preopening campaign. Dame Edna wrote folksy notes to be included in the advertisements; Dame Edna sent clever e-mails to the press. Dame Edna was presented, all in all, as a famous world-renowned celebrity; if you had never heard of her, well, that was your loss, but please don't be uncivil enough to mention it.

In all this, not a word was said that would imply to the average ticket buyer that Dame Edna Everage was not, technically, a dame. Yes, the artwork gave away the joke to many prospective patrons; but you'd have to think that others took Edna on face value. Most shows with non-star authors and directors arrange interviews with, and stories about, their cast. *Dame Edna*'s campaign featured pieces on Edna, herself. Not the star,

The producers came up with a very clever pre-opening campaign, with Dame Edna presented as a famous world-renowned celebrity. In all of this, not a word was said that would imply to the average ticket buyer that Dame Edna Everage was not, technically, a dame.

Dame Edna Everage   Dame Edna
The Fingers on the Keyboards
Andrew Ross
The Gorgeous Ednaette # 1   Roxane
Barlow
An Equally Gorgeous Ednaette # 2
Tamlyn Brooke Shusterman

BOOTH THEATRE
Ⓢ A Shubert Organization Theatre
Gerald Schoenfeld, *Chairman*   Philip J. Smith, *President*
Robert E. Wankel, *Executive Vice President*

LEONARD SOLOWAY, CHASE MISHKIN, STEVEN M. LEVY and JONATHAN REINIS
present

Australia's First Lady
DAME EDNA EVERAGE
in

DAME EDNA
The Royal Tour
"The Show that Listens"

Devised and Written by
BARRY HUMPHRIES

Additional Material by
IAN DAVIDSON

with the fingers of
ANDREW ROSS
on keyboards

and introducing
The Gorgeous Ednaettes
ROXANE BARLOW   TAMLYN BROOKE SHUSTERMAN

Scenic Design   *Costume Design*   *Lighting Design*   *Sound Design*
KENNETH FOY   STEPHEN ADNITT   JASON KANTROWITZ   PETER FITZGERALD

Production Manager   *Production Stage Manager*   *Marketing*
ARTHUR SICCARDI   JAMES W. GIBBS   THE KARPEL GROUP

General Management   *Press Representative*
SOLOWAY/LEVY   KEVIN P. McANARNEY

Artistic Associate
CYNTHIA ONRUBIA

Associate Producers
SKYLIGHT PRODUCTIONS   ADAM FRIEDSON
DAVID FRIEDSON   ALLEN SPIVAK/LARRY MAGID   RICHARD MARTINI

This lovely program contains no marsupial products.

The producers wish to express their appreciation to
the Theatre Development Fund for its support of this production.

but the character. (Just what sort of coverage do you think they'd have gotten for Barry Humphries, an Australian character actor with little American exposure?) This, presumably, helps explain the outsize coverage the show received. It's one thing to talk an editor into running a feature on the Tony Award–winning stars of *Voices in the Dark* or *Epic Proportions*, or the Olivier-winning stars of *Kat and the Kings*, or even the hopeful star-in-the-making of *Saturday Night Fever*. But a personal audience with the glamorous Dame Edna—well, that promised to be what is referred to in some circles as a "hoot." So Dame Edna wafted through a series of tongue-in-cheek preliminary press interviews—all stressing the fact that she was, in her own words, "the most gifted and popular woman in the world today"; embarked on a series of low-priced previews, resulting in many repeat customers and wonderful word of mouth; and opened at "the lovely little Booth (rhymes with smooooth) Theatre" to smash reviews. Which, as often as not, accepted Ms. Everage on her own terms. Would mainstream Broadway audiences support a man in a dress? It appears so.

The thing is, *Dame Edna* was one of the most uproarious Broadway attractions in memory. Not the funniest, not the finest, not the most rewarding; but uproarious. Mr. Humphries provoked wave upon wave of laughter, thunderclaps of the stuff. People will laugh warmly, or gently, when they are amused and entertained. Startle them out of the blue with something incredibly funny, and they'll explode with laughter all out of proportion; this is what Humphries did, again and again. More often than not these laugh lines were impolite and impolitic; when faced with something of the sort, you either take offense or give yourself over wholeheartedly. By dressing up in a pink gown with pink fur fringe and a pink hairdo, Humphries was able to get away with stuff that otherwise might have brought out pickets.

The performance began as cleverly as the show's publicity campaign. After the typical announcement asking patrons to turn off their cellular phones, watch alarms, and pacemakers (pacemakers?), on came ten minutes' worth of videotape, encapsulating Dame Edna's journey from Australian housewife to worldwide superstar—leaving uninformed theatregoers to wonder "Is this for real?" There, on the big screen, was Dame Edna with Rudolf Nureyev, Elton John, Barry Manilow, Burt Reynolds, Liza Minnelli, George Hamilton, Charlton Heston—now, there's a good combination—Robin Williams, Chevy Chase, Roseanne, Lauren Bacall, Richard Gere, Sean Connery, Luke Perry, and Mel Gibson. All this

was clearly authentic footage. (There was also a shot of the Dame and the pope, which was clearly not so authentic.)

It was not until then, with all this buildup both on- and offstage, that Dame Edna came into view, high kicking her way past a pot full of pink gladiolas, down a grand staircase with her pink hair and her pink mink. A man in a dress? Of course; or maybe not, maybe just a bigboned gal of the sort that frequents the tall woman shops.

Humphries entered and went right into a song and dance, entitled "Look at Me When I'm Talking to You." (The first line of the opening verse: "I'm only sorry your applause has ended.") The number climaxed with him doing a sidestep like a sixty-year-old imitating a twenty-year-old 1920s flapper—the sort of kick with the foot hinging out parallel to and up toward the ears. You wonder, "Where have I seen that before?" and then it hits you: It's a manic, menopausal Carol Channing.

Humphries then glided into his program, which turned out to be the equivalent of a TV talk show without "special guests." The guests were drafted from the audience, and woe to you if you happened to be sitting in the first five rows. "I don't think of this as a show," he explained. "This is more like a conversation between two people, one of whom is a lot more interesting than the other."

Humphries pulled his material out of people who had paid sixty-five bucks a seat, which is a neat trick in itself. And he was clearly aware of those ticket prices, making a running joke of the poor people upstairs in the cheap seats. ("My paupers," he lovingly called them; or "Mizzies," derived from that familiar French word for "miserable.")

Humphries started out by explaining that he—or she—was a "hands-on megastar," reaching out to shake hands with the people in the first row. He then stopped, grimacing, and looked down upon the poor unfortunate (who had paid sixty-five bucks for the privilege). "What have you been handling? Is it fish, or is it cheese?" This set the pattern for the evening. Humphries could be more than a little rough on occasion, but almost always very funny. He made a big deal about a latecomer, stopping the show so we all could watch him clumsily climb over the knees of the people seated along the way. ("I came all the way from Australia," Edna said politely, "and I managed to get here on time.") The show appeared to be wildly improvised, but it was carefully scripted; the ushers were instructed not to seat latecomers until the proper moment, so there was always bound to be someone skittering down the aisle on cue.

In the opening sequence Humphries greeted the audience, asking how they got to the theatre and poking good-natured fun at the folks in the steep, cheap seats who had arrived by bus. All the while, he was casing the joint—the first five rows, at least—for unsuspecting foils to play straight men and women to his raving Edna. For example, he sought out a good-natured couple who, he informed us, looked hungry. (At both performances I attended, they were a pair of suburban, middle-aged women.) He turned back to them from time to time, expressing concern that the poor things looked like they were fading away. Late in the first act he turned to them again, tsk-tsked, and called for one of his two dancer-assistants ("The Gorgeous Ednaettes" is their billing) to bring out a menu. He then rang up Barrymore's, a restaurant down the block, and ordered a light supper.

This set up a set piece in the second act, when an authentic Broadway waiter/out-of-work actor rolled on a table for two with a red-and-white-check tablecloth. Pasta, salad, wine. Humphries dragged his hungry couple out of their $65 seats, placed them downstage in a follow spot, and forced them to eat spaghetti while insulting them with eight hundred people watching. (At the second performance I attended, when Humphries called up his hungry couple, he discovered that they had left during intermission, presumably tipped off about the humiliation in store for them. He quickly recovered, drafting a different couple of middle-aged women who also "looked hungry.")

More often than not these laugh lines were impolite and impolitic. By dressing up in a pink gown with pink fur fringe and a pink hairdo, Barry Humphries was able to get away with stuff that might otherwise have brought out pickets.

During his first-act audience ramble, Humphries also selected a couple who had left a baby-sitter at home and mined them for information. (Did you leave a snack for the baby-sitter? What kind of snack? Where did you leave it? Do you pay the baby-sitter enough?) This led to another tour de force when he phoned the baby-sitter from the stage on a speakerphone, the audience eavesdropping on the call at the expense of the unsuspecting and presumably undereducated baby-sitter.

All this was very funny, mind you, and made for a delightful evening.

But Humphries grew a wee bit nasty in places, so much so that even his flamboyant rhinestone eyeglasses didn't quite excuse him. He prided himself on being politically incorrect, which is fine to a point. ("I was born with a priceless gift: the ability to laugh at the misfortunes of others.") But there is a line past which it becomes cruelty. He went out of his way, seemingly, to poke fun at "seniors" and Alzheimer victims; for some, this might hit too close to home. He blithely dismissed the disabled with a long and not especially funny piece about what goes on in those handicapped rest room stalls. This sort of thing did not ruin the evening; it just made it sag unevenly. Why did Humphries—whose material was otherwise so uproariously effective—feel that he had to resort to picking on defenseless targets? Five of his "victims" from the first act were brought up onstage at the end of the second, as part of a rather ponderous spoof on the royal family. (This might be funny in England, but it sorely missed here.) He dressed one of them in a mock "Fergie" costume and presented her with an enormous box of Toblerone. At both performances I attended, he selected the fattest and most slovenly woman he could spot from the stage; maybe this was a coincidence, but these girls were so overweight that you wonder whether the box office was instructed to hold house seats for the fattest person who approached. Humphries displayed himself as a wickedly funny satirist throughout most of the evening, and he deserves to be his own arbiter of taste; but must he pull a grotesquely overweight person out of the audience and hang a box of chocolates around her neck?

> You wonder, "Where have I seen that before?" and then it hits you: It's a manic, menopausal Carol Channing.

These are minor quibbles, though. Most of *Dame Edna: The Royal Tour* was so very funny that more than a few theatregoers happily returned again and again, bringing along friends (at sixty-five bucks a pop). Who'd have guessed that *Dame Edna* would do big business and become the first hit of the season?

For his finale, Humphries tossed stalk after stalk of gladiolas to everyone within reach; brought the audience to their feet; and instructed them to join in his song—written by himself—"Come on, Possums, Wave Your Gladiolas." And they did—row upon row of generally sophisticated, generally upper-middle-class types bouncing around with green and pink stalks quivering in the air. Certainly not the sort of thing you've come to expect on Broadway, and therein lay the magic and the success of *Dame Edna.*

Saturday Night Fever

B ack in the dark ages of American musical comedy, the chorus would come on and do a production number, then the actors would come out and read a book scene, then a principal or two would do a song and dance, then another book scene, and so on. All these songs and scenes and tunes and jokes were often turned out by a dozen or more writers; ideally, enough stuff "scored" to make the audiences happy. The more accomplished writers eventually insisted that collaborators be limited, but there was still, typically, a gulf between what happened in the songs and what happened when the actors started talking.

Now, once upon a time a fellow got bothered by the fact that the words the actors said and the words the actors sang were only tangentially related. What concerned him especially was that he, himself, was steadily employed writing both the words the actors said *and* the words the actors sang, in what then passed for book musicals. Shouldn't a character speak the same language, as it were, whether he or she is talking or singing?

Cast

Tony Manero   James Carpinello
Stephanie Mangano   Paige Price
Annette   Orfeh
Bobby C   Paul Castree
Joey   Sean Palmer
Double J   Andy Blankenbuehler
Gus   Richard H. Blake
Monty   Bryan Batt
Frank Manero   Casey Nicholaw
Flo Manero/Lucille   Suzanne Costallos
Frank Junior   Jerry Tellier
Fusco/Al   Frank Mastrone
Jay Langhart/Becker   David Coburn
Chester   Andre Ward
Cesar   Michael Balderrama
Vinnie   Chris Ghelfi

Sal   Danial Jerod Brown
Dino   Brian J. Marcum
Lou   Rick Spaans
Dom   Miles Alden
Roberto   Ottavio
Antonio   Drisco Fernandez
Ike   David Robertson
Shirley   Karine Plantadit-Bageot
Maria   Natalie Willes
Connie   Jeanine Meyers
Doreen   Angela Pupello
Linda Manero/Patti   Aliane Baquerot
Gina   Rebecca Sherman
Sophia   Paula Wise
Donna   Shannon Beach
Rosalie   Deanna Dys
Lola   Jennifer Newman
Inez   Danielle Jolie
Lorelle   Stacey Martin
Kenny   Kristoffer Cusick
Nick   Karl duHoffmann
Rocker   Roger Lee Israel
Natalie   Anne Nicole Biancofiore
Ann Marie   Marcia Urani
Angela   Gina Philistine

The time is 1976 . . . or whenever you were 19.

The place is New York City (Brooklyn & Manhattan)

Original London Cast Recording:
Polydor 557 932

MINSKOFF THEATRE

UNDER THE DIRECTION OF JAMES M. NEDERLANDER AND MYRON A. MINSKOFF

ROBERT STIGWOOD
presents

SATURDAY NIGHT FEVER THE MUSICAL

BASED ON THE PARAMOUNT/RSO PICTURE
BASED ON A STORY BY NIK COHN
SCREENPLAY BY NORMAN WEXLER

STAGE ADAPTATION BY NAN KNIGHTON

IN COLLABORATION WITH
ARLENE PHILLIPS, PAUL NICHOLAS & ROBERT STIGWOOD

FEATURING SONGS BY
THE BEE GEES

STARRING
JAMES CARPINELLO
PAIGE PRICE
ORFEH

WITH
BRYAN BATT
RICHARD H. BLAKE   ANDY BLANKENBUEHLER   SEAN PALMER
AND
PAUL CASTREE
AS 'BOBBY C.'

| SCENIC DESIGNER | COSTUMES DESIGNED BY | LIGHTING DESIGNED BY |
| ROBIN WAGNER | ANDY EDWARDS | ANDREW BRIDGE |

| BROADWAY COSTUMES BY | DANCE & VOCAL ARRANGEMENTS BY | SOUND DESIGN BY |
| SUZY BENZINGER | PHIL EDWARDS | MICK POTTER |

| ORCHESTRATIONS BY | MUSICAL SUPERVISION BY | MUSICAL DIRECTOR | MUSIC COORDINATOR |
| NIGEL WRIGHT | PHIL EDWARDS | MARTYN AXE | WILLIAM MEADE |

| PRODUCTION SUPERVISOR | FIGHT DIRECTOR | CASTING BY | RESIDENT CHOREOGRAPHER |
| ARTHUR SICCARDI | J. ALLEN SUDDETH | BERNARD TELSEY CASTING | JAMES WALSKI |

| ASSOCIATE CHOREOGRAPHER | ASSISTANT DIRECTOR | PRODUCTION STAGE MANAGER |
| KAREN BRUCE | TONY EDGE | PERRY CLINE |

| GENERAL MANAGER | PRESS REPRESENTATIVE | PUBLIC RELATIONS | EXECUTIVE PRODUCER |
| NIKO ASSOCIATES JEFFREY CHRZCZON | BILL EVANS & ASSOCIATES | RUBENSTEIN ASSOCIATES | PATRICK BYWALSKI |

ASSOCIATE PRODUCERS
MANNY KLADITIS   DAVID ROCKSAVAGE

DIRECTED & CHOREOGRAPHED BY
ARLENE PHILLIPS

Originally produced in London's West End by
ROBERT STIGWOOD,
PAUL NICHOLAS AND DAVID IAN

So this guy sat down and wrote *Show Boat*. I am simplifying things here, needless to say, but Oscar Hammerstein—with composer Jerome Kern—started something right then and there, which Hammerstein went on to develop (with Richard Rodgers) into the model of the well-made modern-day American musical.

Movie musicals have been adapted into Broadway musicals, at an increasing rate, since the early 1970s. Alan Jay Lerner and Frederick Loewe, who knew a thing or two about writing for Broadway, were prevailed upon to take their near-perfect film *Gigi* and expand it for the stage in 1973. Lerner did the adaptation himself, with Loewe coming out of retirement to compose a handful of new songs to fill out the film score. It turned out that the slight story—which on the screen was whipped into a delectable Parisian soufflé—was all too earthbound without the scenery and editing. And despite the presence of the same songwriters, the original material—written just after *My Fair Lady*—was of a distinctly higher quality than the songs they came up with sixteen years later.

Other classic film musicals have experienced the same trouble—or perhaps even more, as the original songwriters weren't around to create necessary material to fill out the scores: *Seven Brides for Seven Brothers*, *Singin' in the Rain*, *Meet Me in St. Louis*, *Hans Christian Andersen* (in London), *High Society*, and even—so help us—*The Red Shoes*.

Hollywood, meanwhile, stopped producing movie musicals, although a minigenre developed of youth-oriented dramas laced with frenetic dancing to pop music sound tracks. Of late, some Broadway producers— recognizing the box office marketability of familiar film titles, chart-topping song hits, and baby boomer nostalgia—have turned to stage adaptations of these non-musical movies with music. First came *Fame*, which has been kicking around the world, literally, since a 1988 tryout in Miami and at this writing is still hoping to make its way to Broadway. Next came *Footloose*, which stormed the town in 1998 and managed a twenty-month run despite critical jeers. This season's entry was *Saturday Night Fever*, based on the landmark 1977 film.

> On the screen, the songs were used as mood enhancers, only peripherally germane to the story. On stage, the familiar characters must of necessity sing these songs—whether the lyrics make sense in the context of the story or not.

In this new type of stage musical, the plots and characters are familiar to the audience, or at least to the audience that goes to see these shows.

The song hits are familiar, too, but there's a difference. On the screen, the songs were used as mood enhancers, only peripherally germane to the story. On the stage, the familiar characters must of necessity sing these songs, whether or not the lyrics make sense in the context of the story. Thus, right at the top of *Saturday Night Fever* the leading man sings "Whether you're a brother / Or whether you're a mother / You're stayin' alive." Now that song is well-known to most of the audience, and they don't stop to consider it for a second; but tell me, what is he talking about? This guy has a mother (who, in a different wig, doubles as a girl at the disco) and a brother (who quits the clergy and hangs up his frock), but I don't think he's talking about them. This is not all that much of a problem, as most of the lyrics were unintelligible. But you realize that the creators of this new *Saturday Night Fever* had their hands tied: If it's from the movie, if it's a hit song, then it must be used and can't be altered. So what does it matter if the words the actors say and the words the actors sing have little in common? (Parenthetical note: Delving through the small print in the back of the program, I counted sixteen songwriters, authors, and "collaborators"—not including the screenwriter whose original dialogue makes up much of the stage script.)

That this was an audience show for a different type of audience became clear even before it began. I noticed by the accents on the escalator that most of the people were foreigners, from France and Germany and New Jersey. People were disco dancing to the overture; one fellow seated in the front row was doing a kind of hand-snap, head-whip step. Poor guy almost poked his eye out.

Some observations of the evening: Early on, leading man James Carpinello stripped off his shirt to catcalls from the audience, revealing big biceps, a big crucifix, and the wire from his microphone to the battery pack hidden in a bulge in his trousers. . . . Sample dialogue: "Awright, awright, awright.". . . In the third scene, the boys stood around outside the disco talking about nothing until it was clear that they were staying there—instead of just going inside—for one reason only: waiting for a production number to begin. . . . Even the dancers who didn't seem to be singing had to wear those headset microphones, looking like skinny telephone operators in bad clothes. . . . At

> That this was an audience show for a different type of audience became clear even before it began. I noticed by the accents on the escalator that most of the people were foreigners, from France and Germany and New Jersey.

the end of an early production number, everybody moved upstage and
formed a line just before the finish so they could do a big finale step where
they all rushed down to the footlights. . . . The dancing got so frenetic and
aerobic—with occasional balletlike moves thrown in, for laughs—that
you wished Mr. Carpinello would just stand there and sing. . . . There was
a production number called "Disco Duck"—retained from the film
score—which just might mark a new low in musical theatre. This number brought to mind *Got Tu Go Disco*, a 1979 mishmash that inhabited,
albeit briefly, the very same Minskoff stage. . . . A girl named Orfeh, who
acquitted herself well in the frighteningly conceived Gershwin revue *Fascinating Rhythm* just six months earlier, was good here, too, singing a song
called "If I Can't Have You." Only, as I understood the story, she'd had
only one date with this guy. Why so overwrought, unless it's because they
placed her way upstage as if she was walled into a box? . . . By 9:00, there
was still no story to speak of. . . . Something called "It's My Neighborhood" had very good lighting. It was also the third song in the first act to
end with the big finale step where everyone rushed down to the footlights
in a line. . . . Intermission talk: "Travolta was a little taller." The celebri-
ties of the night were baseball's Cal Ripken Jr. and football's Mark
Gastineau—not together—both of whom were mobbed by autograph
seekers. I had to ask a high school kid who these guys were. (Ripken
talked politely to the people but wouldn't sign.) . . . The only believable
song was "Tragedy," in which the nebbish of the group sang about his
woman and then killed himself by jumping off the bridge. Paul Castree—
who played similarly out-of-place kids in *Footloose* and Tommy Tune's
Grease—sang the song extremely well, only this highly dramatic solo was

about an offstage character we never met. . . . At one point, the orchestra —out of the blue—started playing Mussorgsky's "Night on Bald Mountain." . . . By midway through the second act, it became clear that instead of reprising the songs they were simply reprising the choreography. You also realized that the disco dancers—who had nothing to do other than disco dance—didn't dance very well. But enough of this, and enough of *Saturday Night Fever*.

Other musicals—*Footloose*, for instance—have come to town fairly certain that they will receive pretty horrible reviews. But they, typically, at least *hoped* that the reviews wouldn't be too harsh. The *Saturday Night Fever* people pretty much knew what was in store; but they knew, too, how to sell tickets regardless. (Quote from the opening number: "We can try to understand / The *New York Times*'s effect on man.") You're talking about Robert Stigwood here, a fellow who knows something about selling pop music. He's the guy who signed up young Brits Andrew Lloyd Webber and Tim Rice, producing the original New York and London companies of *Jesus Christ Superstar* and *Evita*; he also produced the film version of *Grease* and the original *Saturday Night Fever*.

> People were disco dancing to the overture; one fellow seated in the front row was doing kind of a hand-snap, head-whip step. Poor guy almost poked his eye out.

So the stage adaptation of *Saturday Night Fever* was unquestionably a poorly assembled, highly unsatisfying musical that was deservedly trounced by the critics. It also—unlike *Putting It Together, Marie Christine, The Wild Party, Kat and the Kings,* and even *James Joyce's The Dead*—sold scads of tickets, at least for the first seven months. So does that make Mr. Stigwood a lousy producer or a wise producer?

Wise Guys

It is against all rules of civilized society to review *Wise Guys*, which was presented as a "special workshop" at the New York Theatre Workshop for three weeks in November 1999. This was a work in progress, presented with no scenery, no costumes, and a minimal band of three pieces. The full show was only barely presented; audiences attending the first week saw the first act; half of the second act was added sometime later; and the whole show—at least as much as was finished, in the preliminary sense of the word—was presented to the final audiences.

Tickets were impossible to buy; that is, they were free. But they were offered solely to NYTW subscribers and were not available to the theatregoing public at large. Friends of the performers, friends of the staff, and a certain amount of press also managed to get in. I attended two performances, the first night—with only the first act—and a later showing that included some but not all of the second.

Stephen Sondheim's work is of the utmost importance, and presumably of great interest to readers of this book; and *Wise Guys*, despite its incomplete state, was arguably the best score of the 1999–2000 season. Thus, it seems proper to devote at least some space to the piece.

The reason for this virtual freeze-out of the unwashed public was not unfounded. Sondheim's previous musical, *Passion* (1994), had opened cold—which is to say, without an out-of-town tryout—after fifty-two previews. In its finished state, *Passion* was quite a stunning artistic experience; during previews, though, it was not in its finished state. And in its unfinished state, *Passion* was a baffling combination of wonderful things mixed with sections that weren't as yet fully realized.

The initial word of mouth was dire. Broadway insiders like to gloat

Wilson Mizner   Victor Garber
Reporter   Christopher Fitzgerald
Addison Mizner   Nathan Lane
Papa   William Parry
Mama   Candy Buckley
A Prospector   Kevin Chamberlin

Poker Players   William Parry, Ray Wills, Kevin Chamberlin, Brooks Ashmanskas
Assayer   Clarke Thorell
Ticket Seller   Ray Wills
Business Man # 1   Michael Hall
Business Man # 2   Nancy Opel
Solicitor   Brooks Ashmanskas
Chinese Warlord   Kevin Chamberlin
Plantation Owner   William Parry
Doorman   Kevin Chamberlin
Mrs. Myra Yerkes   Jessica Molaskey
Paul Armstrong   Brooks Ashmanskas
Stanley Ketchel   Ray Wills
Flatbush Phil   Clarke Thorell
Newsboy   Christopher Fitzgerald
Gladys   Jessica Boevers
Paris Singer   Michael Hall
Mrs. Eva Stotesbury   Nancy Opel
Mr. Stotesbury   William Parry
Mrs. Lily Cosden   Lauren Ward
Mr. Cosden   Ray Wills
Mrs. Trumbauer   Jessica Boevers
Mr. Trumbauer   Brooks Ashmanskas
Mrs. Wanamaker   Jessica Molaskey
Mrs. DuPont   Candy Buckley
Gwen   Lauren Ward
Souvenir Sellers, Club Patrons, and Millionaires   Brooks Ashmanskas, Jessica Boevers, Kevin Chamberlin, Christopher Fitzgerald, Michael Hall, Jessica Molaskey, Nancy Opel, William Parry, Clarke Thorell, Lauren Ward, Ray Wills

A Special Workshop Presentation of

WISE GUYS

Book by
John Weidman

Music & Lyrics by
Stephen Sondheim

with

Brooks Ashmanskas   Jessica Boevers   Candy Buckley
Kevin Chamberlin   Christopher Fitzgerald   Victor Garber   Michael Hall
Nathan Lane   Jessica Molaskey   Nancy Opel   William Parry
Clarke Thorell   Lauren Ward   Ray Wills

Directed by...Sam Mendes
Choreographed by..Jonathan Butterell
Music Director ....Ted Sperling
Scenery Designed by ....Mark Thompson
Costumes Designed by ....Santo Loquasto
Lighting Designed by .... Jules Fisher &
Peggy Eisenhauer
Sound Designed by ....Jonathan Deans
Musical Supervisor ....Paul Gemignani
Orchestrations ....Jonathan Tunick
Casting ....Jim Carnahan
Production Stage Manager...Bonnie Panson
Production Manager...David Bradford
General Press Representation ....Barlow•Hartman public relations

about other people's troubles, and the show received microscopic attention. In such cases, most everybody accentuates the negative. By the time
Passion opened, it had failure written all over it. I'm not saying that the
early attendees were to blame, mind you, but in-town previews can put
the artists in a compromising position. They are being given the time and
resources to investigate the work on its feet, as they must, only they are

doing it directly in front of the people who, under the circumstances, are likely to pounce. (It is impolite for people with comps to bad-mouth a show, especially during the performance. But anyone who buys their own ticket is entitled to have their say, preview or no.)

This type of play surgery used to transpire in Boston, Philly, or Washington. Each tryout city had its own shakedown previews; its own opening night, complete with newspaper reviews that often provided guidance; and time to work and revise. Then it was on to the next city, with another chance to gauge reaction to the fixes. The cost of pre-Broadway tryouts has become prohibitive, which is why *Passion* was forced into reconstruction on West Forty-fifth Street, pardon our dust.

Sondheim's *Merrily We Roll Along* (1981) had an even more damaging experience, rolling through fifty-two previews as well. Early performances revealed major conceptual flaws. In came a new choreographer, a new set of costumes, a new leading man—all too visibly, before paying customers. Audiences were just as aware of *Merrily's* problems as the producers were, and vociferously resentful that they had spent their dollars on a mess of a show.

The *Wise Guys* plan was to assemble and rehearse what would presumably become the Broadway company, but to first try it out before nonpaying (and therefore not vicious) audiences. After a period for readjustment and rewrites, the show would go back into full-scale rehearsals in late winter, preview in March, and open April 27, 2000, as the "big" musical of the season.

By the time *Merrily's* flaws were displayed, most of the multi-million-dollar budget had already been spent on sets, advertising, and the rest. When the NYTW workshop revealed that *Wise Guys* was not, indeed, ready to spring forward in April, the wise producers had the **Despite its incomplete state, this was arguably the best score of the 1999–2000 season.** luxury of postponing the Broadway date. Or simply calling the whole thing off.

Wise Guys was long in preparation. The Kennedy Center for the Performing Arts commissioned Leonard Bernstein's *Mass* for its opening attraction in 1971. With its twenty-fifth anniversary approaching, it seemed only natural to offer another commission—and who more fitting to ask than Stephen Sondheim? Sondheim was approached back in 1993, when he was still in the throes of *Passion*. The composer had no interest in writing a celebratory piece in hybrid form, like Lenny's *Mass*; Kennedy Cen-

Wise Guys
Began: October 29, 1999
Ended: November 20, 1999
Wise Guys played 22 workshop performances before
    subscribers and invited audiences at the 199-seat New
    York Theatre Workshop. There was no official opening,
    and critics were not invited.

ter said he could write whatever he wanted. "What if I woke up some morning and wanted to write something like *Forum?*" asked the composer. "Anything you write will be fine with us," was the response.

Sondheim turned to an idea he'd played with back in the mid-1950s, about the semifabled brothers Wilson and Addison Mizner. Wilson was a sometime playwright, sometime prizefight promoter, and full-time con man; Addison was a self-trained architect. The then-unknown Sondheim attempted to get the rights to Alva Johnston's 1953 joint biography *The Legendary Mizners*, only to find that David Merrick had secured them for over-the-hill old-timers Irving Berlin, Sam Behrman, and George S. Kaufman. Berlin wrote at least three songs for *The Mizner Story*—also announced as *Wise Guy* and *Sentimental Guy*—but the show was never completed. Forty years later, Sondheim returned to the Brothers Mizner with librettist John Weidman, his collaborator on *Pacific Overtures* and *Assassins*.

Kennedy Center announced *Wise Guys* as the main attraction of its 1996–1997 season, but the show wasn't ready. The production was pushed back to 1997–1998, and then to 1998–1999. Private readings of the work in progress, though, displayed the high quality of the slowly developing material.

In 1998, the innovative British director Sam Mendes stormed Broadway with his production of *Cabaret*. Mendes, who had directed well-received productions of *Assassins* (1992) and *Company* (1996) at the Donmar Warehouse in London, became attached to *Wise Guys*. (He first had to finish filming *American Beauty*.) The decision was made to bypass Kennedy Center for the fall 1999 NYTW workshop, with a Broadway opening just before the 2000 Tony Awards eligibility deadline.

In *Passion*, Sondheim wove a fascinating tapestry of music. Sections of melody returned, again and again, in different guises, for different purposes. The misfortunes of the show's original Broadway production prevented the score from having its full effect at the time, although I'd guess that by 2008 or so *Passion* will be rediscovered and properly appreciated.

In *Wise Guys*, Sondheim seems to have set a similarly innovative but altogether different course. First, he gave his characters a song to sing, a simple enough, pleasant song. The scene progressed, with a plot element occurring that somewhat changed the situation. The character then sang the song again, with the altered lyric reflecting the changed meaning. More plot ensued. The scene climaxed with the final section of the song—with quite a different meaning than it had originally—and led directly into the next section of the episodic show.

Let me give an example. And mind you, I'm basing this on one hearing when I was too engrossed by the work to take detailed notes. Early in the second act, Addison (Nathan Lane) met a like-minded stranger on a train. Paris Singer was his name, a black sheep member of the sewing machine family. Singer had bought up acres of desolate land in Florida, with the hopes of starting an artists' colony. We see him trying to convince a millionaire couple to build on some of his land. Addison steps into the conversation, introducing himself as Singer's partner, and—bluffing his way through a grand description of what he will build—talks the people into going ahead. Watching Addison's performance in amazement, the heretofore unsuccessful Singer sings "Where Have You Been All My Life?" The scene continues as more millionaires commission mansions on Paris's land, allowing Addison to design a wonderland of his own (with "indoor trees and outdoor stairs"). Singer handles the business dealings, causing the heretofore unsuccessful Addison to sing "Where Have You Been All My Life?" The scene continues, with

> Kennedy Center said Sondheim could write whatever he wanted. "What if I woke up some morning and wanted to write something like *Forum*?," asked the composer. "Anything you write will be fine with us," was the response.

Singer and Addison's little project having developed into Palm Beach, Florida. Paris and Addison join once more to sing "Where Have You Been All My Life?", although this time it seems to be building itself into a glorious love song. Unfortunately, the last performance of *Wise Guys* I attended ended on that note.

Fans might recognize this structure from one of Sondheim's finest songs, "A Bowler Hat," from the 1976 musical *Pacific Overtures*. A Japanese observer comments on the new Western diplomats, contrasting their new ideas (and bowler hats) with those of the natives. By the time the song is over, the observer has become one of "them"; he has his own bowler hat and monocle, divorces his wife, and reads Spinoza every day.

In *Pacific Overtures*, this song was isolated; *Wise Guys*, as presented, already had four or five such musical sequences. These numbers built in layers. The initial layers seemed sturdy, if unexceptional; the second layers brought us further into the scenes—as opposed to the songs; and the final, many-layered versions were glorious. (In the days before computers, didn't architects layer drawings over drawings as they designed their edifices?) Was Sondheim aiming to develop a new method of musical theatre storytelling? It is hard to say based on limited and incomplete hearings of the score, but what I heard was certainly intriguing.

> **Sondheim's latest score is a treasure that is far too valuable to remain unheard.**

It is somewhat inapt to judge performances at this early state. The cast was packed with familiar musical theatre actors, most of whom were underutilized. I feel impelled, though, to say that Nathan Lane was sensitive, sympathetic, and controlled as Addison Mizner. This was perhaps the best performance I've seen from him, principally because he didn't seem to be "performing." He was acting a role believably, and it was a lovely thing to see. Michael Hall—who spent most of the season at Studio 54 as the Emcee in Mendes's *Cabaret*—was especially strong as Singer.

At this writing, it remains questionable whether *Wise Guys* will ever see the lights of Broadway. Word is that it will be remounted, possibly in the fall of 2001, with Sondheim's long-ago collaborator Hal Prince replacing Mendes as director. Let us hope so, as Sondheim's latest score is a treasure that is far too valuable to remain unheard.

Sail Away

Norman Nadel, the musically perceptive drama critic of the old *World-Telegram & Sun*, remarked that Noël Coward's 1961 musical *Sail Away* "easily could have qualified as the musical of the year if it had opened in 1936." Performed on the cusp of Sir Noël's hundredth birthday, it seemed to be at least 101 years old. This was a concert version not unlike those at City Center Encores!, but very much unlike those at Encores! While the two annual series seem to have started with the same mission, City Center's relatively enormous size—in both capacity and stage space—has encouraged Encores! to move toward fully staged and choreographed shows, with stylish set pieces and increasingly complex costuming. Carnegie Hall's rooftop Weill Recital Hall has a tiny stage that is necessarily crammed by a full-sized Broadway pit orchestra, leaving the cast lined up in a row of chairs along the apron. No wings, here; the actors use the aisles of the auditorium to enter and exit. No room for choreography; everybody sits politely and listens to the dance sections of the score. Under these circumstances, the concentration is mostly on the music, the orchestrations, and the performers who read their abridged parts from loose-leaf binders.

The overall air was that of a festive farewell benefit for Elaine Stritch, although the lady is clearly not ready to pack it in and move to a retirement community in Boca Raton.

Which is not to say that the Carnegie Hall series can't compete with Encores!; it simply offers a very different and more traditional kind of concert version. Carnegie Hall's Musical Theatre Program began in 1985, nine years before Encores! It generally presents one production a year.

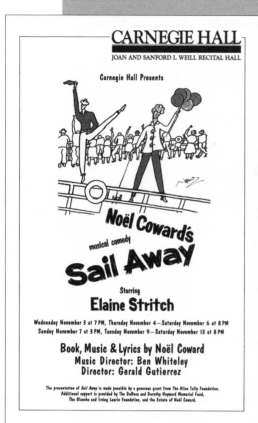

Joe, the ship's purser   Jonathan Freeman

Mimi Paragon   Elaine Stritch

Elmer Candijack   Bill Nolte

Mamie Candijack, his wife   Anne Allgood

Alvin Lush   Paul Iacono

Mrs. Lush, his mother   Alison Fraser

Sir Gerard Nutfield   Herb Foster

Lady Nutfield   Gina Ferrall

Johnny Van Mier   Jerry Lanning

Mrs. Van Mier, his mother   Jane White

Barnaby Slade   James Patterson

Mrs. Sweeney   Jane Connell

Mr. Sweeney   Gordon Connell

Elinor Spencer Bollard   Marian Seldes

Nancy Foyle, her niece   Andrea Burns

Passengers, Stewards, etc.   Danny Burstein, Tony Capone, Dale Hensley, Jennifer Kathryn Marshall, Bill Nolte

The Little Ones   Tanya Desko, Paul Iacono, Alexandra Jumper

Adlai, a dog   Phyllis Gutierrez

Place: mostly aboard the SS *Coronia*

John McGlinn conducted the first several seasons, followed by Rob Fisher and—presently—Ben Whiteley. Carnegie Hall's 1996 production of Irving Berlin's *Louisiana Purchase*, for one, was as polished as a typical Encores! production and resulted in an invaluable cast album.

Sail Away seemed an odd candidate for resuscitation, but the choice was apparently dictated by the combination of the Coward centennial and the availability of seventy-five-year-old leading lady Elaine Stritch. (She originated the role more than half a lifetime ago, when she was thirty-six.) While some might see the negligible *Sail Away* as a waste of Carnegie Hall's resources, the audiences assembled seemed to enjoy themselves for the ten sold-out performances (at 268 seats per). The overall air was that of a festive farewell benefit for Ms. Stritch, although the lady is clearly not ready to pack it in and move to a retirement community in Boca Raton.

Ms. Stritch did not disappoint her fans, and she was clearly the only reason to attend this event. She seemed shaky at first. Part of the Carnegie series attraction is that the shows are performed without amplification, and Stritch needed it; she was clearly inaudible during her opening number. She grew better as the first act wore on, although she spent a good deal of the time fumbling with her glasses and trying to focus on the words in her script. But she always got the jokes out, all right; while she seemed to have forgotten most of the forgettable *Sail Away*—which she played in both New York and London—Stritch clearly remembered her laugh lines. Her big ballad, "Something Very Strange," was totally memorized (and very effective), as was her closing number, "Why Do the Wrong People Travel?" She had this one down pat, complete with two encores; she even threw down her script and did what was presumably the original musical staging, punctuated by her pocketbook.

Stritch in some ways seemed to be acting in a different show than everybody else. The cast included such familiar faces as Jane and Gordon Connell, Marian Seldes, Jane White, Jerry Lanning, Alison Fraser, and Jonathan Freeman. While they were conscientiously acting the script, Stritch seemed to be breezing through, waiting for the good parts. By the end of the second act, Stritch was fighting off laughs while the rest of them seemed to be fighting off sleep.

In addition to writing plays, novels, autobiographies, and miscellanea, England's prolific actor-writer was also credited with a dozen musicals and revues, leaving behind a handful or two of somewhat brittle, semiclassic song hits (like "Poor Little Rich Girl," "I'll See You Again," "Mad Dogs and Englishmen," and "Someday I'll Find You"). His only successful book musical was his first operetta, *Bitter Sweet*, in 1929; the reception of his musicals grew poorer and poorer. This makes it somewhat surprising that Coward—whose musicals had never done well on Broadway, and who hadn't had a box office hit here since 1941—suddenly turned up in the early sixties with *two* new musical comedies written specifically for Broadway. "New" is the operative word here, though. The supposedly contemporary *Sail Away* seemed awfully dated (as per Mr. Nadel above); and *The Girl Who Came to Supper*, in 1963, took place during the coronation of King George VI in 1911 and would have seemed tame even back then. Coward's ability to mount two new musicals here was tied to his highly successful Las Vegas

> **By the end of the second act, Stritch was fighting off laughs while the rest of the cast seemed to be fighting off sleep.**

Sail Away
Opened: November 3, 1999
Closed: November 13, 1999
10 performances (and 0 previews)
Profit/Loss: Nonprofit
Sail Away ($61 top) played the 268-seat Weill Recital Hall.
  Box office figures not available.

Critical Scorecard

Rave 3
Favorable 3
Mixed 0
Unfavorable 1
Pan 0

appearance in 1956, which brought him new celebrity in the United States.

Sail Away had a long and troubled history. Coward originated the idea of a cruise ship musical back in the 1930s. The project was apparently intended, at different times, for Ethel Merman, Rosalind Russell, Marlene Dietrich, and Judy Holliday. (The song "Sail Away," which ultimately became the title song, was originally heard in Coward's 1950 London musical *Ace of Hearts*.) *Sail Away* underwent the usual out-of-town turmoil, although this is the only case I can think of where a show fired one of its two stars in Philly and simply excised the role, shifting the material over to the remaining star. Opera singer Jean Fenn played an "older" woman who had a shipboard romance with a twenty-six-year-old and then attempted suicide. Faced with disgruntled audiences, the romantic story line—sans suicide—was switched to Stritch, who was playing the comedy role of the shipboard social director. Thus it became even more of a Stritch vehicle than originally intended, and she did her best to entertain the ticket buyers while *Sail Away*'s ship—the *Coronia*—foundered.

Coward's libretto was curiously fragmented. The various cast members seemed to come on in pairs, deliver a joke, and move on like couples at a cocktail party. Coward's jokes were somewhat quaint: one old broad said, "My mother went to school with Edith Wharton. They used to always get into mischief together." Another old broad asked a third, "Is your husband alive?" the answer being "Yes and no." And when the girl asked the boy what was playing in the shipboard movie theatre, he replied, "It's Josh Logan's *Fanny* on a wide screen." This kind of humor and this kind of musical

Coward surely never supposed that his May-December love song, "Later than Spring," would be performed in the context of the show by a lovestruck lad of fifty-six.

were almost passable in 1961, but they were a great stretch in 1999. Coward surely never supposed that his May-December love song "Later Than Spring" would be performed in the context of the show by a lovestruck lad of fifty-six, but that's what we had at Carnegie Hall. Jerry Lanning, best known for his role as the grown-up Patrick Dennis in *Mame*, hit all the notes, and nicely, too; but the whole thing looked strange—especially as he was chased around all evening by his dominating mother.

The Weill Recital Hall audiences seemed to love it and to especially love Stritch, so a good time was had by (almost) all. But I don't suppose we'll be revisiting *Sail Away* soon. At least, not until Sir Noël's 150th.

Dinner with Friends

The 2000 Pulitzer Prize for Drama was awarded, shockingly, to an off-Broadway play. Or not so shockingly, perhaps.

Since 1988, when the award went to Alfred Uhry's off-Broadway play *Driving Miss Daisy*, the winners have been *The Heidi Chronicles, The Piano Lesson, Lost in Yonkers, The Kentucky Cycle, Angels in America: Millennium Approaches (Part One), Three Tall Women, The Young Man from Atlanta, Rent, How I Learned to Drive*, and *Wit*. Five of the eleven were, by any definition, off-Broadway plays. Another three, *The Piano Lesson, Angels in America*, and *Rent*, won just before their Broadway openings, based on prior productions. *Kentucky Cycle* and *Young Man from Atlanta* won long before their (unsuccessful) Broadway productions were planned. Of the lot, only *The Heidi Chronicles* and *Lost in Yonkers* were traditional new plays produced, specifically, for Broadway. So maybe it wasn't quite so surprising that the 2000 award once again went off-Broadway, to Donald Margulies's *Dinner with Friends*.

People tend to compare the Pulitzer winner with the Tony Award winner, but this is a faulty comparison. The Pulitzer is awarded to "a distinguished play by an American author, preferably original in its source and dealing with American life." The Tony is awarded to the best play of the Broadway season, no matter how bad it — the season and/or the play — is.

Compare *Dinner with Friends* to the Broadway competition. The Tony nominees were *Copenhagen*, a fine British play and therefore ineligible for the Pulitzer; *True West*, a 1980 play and therefore ineligible; *Waiting in the Wings*, a 1960 British play and therefore ineligible; and *Dirty Blonde*, which was presumably eligible based on its January 6, 2000, opening at the New York Theatre Workshop. (The Pulitzer cutoff date was March 1, two months before the Tony deadline.) The other more or less eligible Broadway plays—*Voices in the Dark, Epic Proportions, Wrong Mountain,* and *Taller Than a Dwarf*—were so poor that even the Tony nominators overlooked them. Joining *Dinner with Friends* as finalists for this year's Pulitzer were *In the Blood* by Suzan-Lori Parks, which opened October 26, 1999, at the New York Shakespeare Festival's Public Theatre; and *King Hedley II* by August Wilson, which opened December 15, 1999, at the Pittsburgh Public Theatre. Musicals have won Pulitzers from time to time, but the 1999–2000 season had little to offer except *Contact*—and I don't suppose the Pulitzer folks were ready to give an award to a show without words.

Although the members of the Pulitzer board try to attend performances of the nominated plays, this is not necessarily possible; in this year's case, only one of the plays was still running when the nominations were made. The rules state that the board members must read the scripts and have "attended the performances or seen videos where possible," which means that unlike the Tonys, the Pulitzer can be awarded based solely on the script and not the production. (Does that explain the award to *The Kentucky Cycle,* which presumably read much better than it played?)

The other major difference between the two awards is that the Pulitzer people can, and sometimes have, determined that there ain't no best play at all. There has been no award fourteen times in the Pulitzer's eighty-four-year existence, which comes to once every six years. Imagine the Broadway establishment admitting that. (Into the 1960s, the Pulitzer was given to "the original American play performed in New York which shall best represent the educational value and power of the stage in raising the standard of good morals and good manners." This knocked out plays like *Who's Afraid of Virginia Woolf?* If these criteria were still in effect, there would probably be no award ever.)

> The play veers into familiar ground, which grows more and more sitcom-like as the minutes pass. But that's part of the playwright's craft; he uses deft dialogue and unending humor to examine marriage, and relationships, and suburban-boomers' failed expectations.

Which brings us to *Dinner with Friends.* Donald Margulies had been up for two previous Pulitzers, in 1991 (for *Sight Unseen*) and 1997 (for *Collected Stories*). His one stab at Broadway—and I use the word "stab" advisedly—was the 1994 supposed-comedy *What's Wrong with This*

Gabe Matthew Arkin
Karen Lisa Emery
Beth Julie White
Tom Kevin Kilner

VARIETY ARTS THEATRE
Under the direction of BEN SPRECHER and WILLIAM P. MILLER

MITCHELL MAXWELL   MARK BALSAM   TED TULCHIN
VICTORIA MAXWELL   MARI NAKACHI   STEVEN TULCHIN

present

MATTHEW ARKIN   LISA EMERY   KEVIN KILNER   JULIE WHITE

in

dinner with friends

by
DONALD MARGULIES

Set Design by   Costume Design by   Lighting Design by
NEIL PATEL   **JESS GOLDSTEIN**   **RUI RITA**

Sound Design by   Music & Sound Score by   Casting by
PETER FITZGERALD   **MICHAEL ROTH**   **STEPHANIE KLAPPER, CSA**

Production Stage Manager   Press Representative   General Management
R. WADE JACKSON   **BARLOW•HARTMAN**   **RICHARDS/CLIMAN, INC.**
                        public relations

Associate Producers
FRED H. KRONES   BOB CUILLO

Directed by
DANIEL SULLIVAN

Commissioned by and premiered at ACTORS' THEATRE OF LOUISVILLE
Subsequently produced by South Coast Repertory

Picture? *Dinner with Friends*, even before the Pulitzer arrived, had surely been Margulies's most commercially successful work. It is, all told, a pretty good play, which I'd place midway on the list of previous Pulitzer winners at the top of the previous page.

Dinner with Friends started out on a breezy note, with a forty-something couple (Gabe and Karen) feeding dinner to their friend Beth, who is clearly disinterested in their trip to Italy and the open-air market at Campo de' Fiori. (This is the sort of conversation apt to draw in forty-something theatregoers; my wife and I spent our honeymoon on a rooftop terrace just off the sixteenth-century Campo de' Fiori, with a friendly caffè downstairs and a filettaro di baccalà just across the piazza.) As the conversation continued, Gabe and Karen learned that Beth's absent husband, Tom—whose dinner plate sits empty—has left his wife for a young airline stewardess. The play veers onto familiar ground, which grows more and more sitcom-like as the minutes pass. (The adults kept yelling offstage to the kids in the TV room, watching a video of *The Aristocats*.) But that's part of the playwright's craft; he uses deft dialogue and unending humor to examine marriage, relationships, and suburban boomers' failed expectations. The characters are interesting, the comedy is comic, and everything is enhanced by a thought-provoking undercurrent of truth.

Tom and Beth break up seemingly out of the blue, which greatly affects their best friends. ("We were supposed to grow old and fat together, the four of us," Gabe complains.) Gabe and Karen are even more disturbed, though, when both Tom and Beth quickly hook up with new (and exciting) lovers. Here are people they depended on, people they knew as well as themselves; but they apparently didn't know them well at all.

Margulies uses his secondary characters to hold up an examining glass to his main couple. Gabe and Karen's marriage is not all that different than Tom and Beth's; all the strains that appear in one relationship are clearly evident in the other. Tom acts on them, though, by leaving (as opposed to "sticking in miserable marriages for fifty years like our parents"). We learn that Beth, too, has had an affair. (Karen: "We saw them practically every weekend. When would she have had time for an affair?" Gabe: "I don't know, during the week?") Beth and Tom, separately, tell their friends of the lack of intimacy and desire in their marriage; Gabe and Karen clearly know about this all too well. The two couples are the same, and the cracks in the mirror of their marriages are the same. But Gabe and Karen have determinedly stuck to their marriage. Or have they? When Beth tells Karen that Tom is having an affair, Gabe sits frozen at the dinner table looking guilty as hell—in thought if not in body. Similarly, there is a moment in a flashback when Tom passes behind Karen standing at the kitchen counter, stops, and momentarily touches the back of her neck. She shakes him away after an instant, and we never do learn what that means. Did they have an affair—or something—before she married Gabe? What would that mean, in relation to the rest of the play? Margulies made little suggestions throughout the evening but left them hanging, tantalizingly, content to leave us uncertain, in the same way that the characters themselves are uncertain. How well do you know your best friend?

What remains unspoken is how well do you know your best friend when your best friend is your spouse? Gabe and Karen can't face this, although beneath the surface the prospect has them recoiling in terror. Margulies managed to express this with great skill, leaving much of the subtext implied but unspoken. He couldn't have done it alone, of course. These moments were presumably written into the stage direc-

The characters are interesting, the comedy is comic, and everything is enhanced by a thought-provoking undercurrent of truth.

Dinner with Friends
Opened: November 4, 1999
Still playing May 29, 2000
To date: 259 performances (and 15 previews)
Profit/Loss: Profit
Dinner with Friends ($50 top) played the 498-seat Variety
  Arts Theatre. Box office figures not available.

PULITZER PRIZE
Donald Margulies (WINNER)

Critical Scorecard

Rave 7
Favorable 1
Mixed 1
Unfavorable 1
Pan 0

tions, but many of them are specifically *not* in the dialogue. Which is to say that director Daniel Sullivan did an enormously effective job with his actors.

Most of the inner anguish of the piece seemed to come from Gabe. Was it the actor? Matthew Arkin seemed to be constantly offering support to the other characters—except when his character thought nobody was looking at him, when he underwent intense self-evaluation. Was it the director? Sullivan knows his way around and has an especially fine hand with serious comedy. (He also staged Wendy Wasserstein's Pulitzer winner *The Heidi Chronicles*, this season's *Moon for the Misbegotten*, and the Manhattan Theatre Club's off-Broadway spring hit, *Proof*.) Or was it Margulies himself, who indicated in interviews that the subject of middle-aged marital malaise was chosen from personal experience? At any rate, it's safe to say that *Dinner with Friends* would have been equally successful had it been mounted on Broadway. Safe to say now, anyway; I don't know how it might have looked

> **Donald Margulies made little suggestions throughout the evening but left them hanging, tantalizingly, content to leave us uncertain, in the same way that the characters themselves are uncertain. How well do you know your best friend when your best friend is your spouse?**

to potential investors in the spring of 1999, although I suppose that at this late date the backers of *Voices in the Dark*, *Epic Proportions*, and *Waiting in the Wings* would much rather have spent their money on *Dinner*.

Morning, Noon, and Night

The addition of children to a household makes a profound difference in the life of the parents. This is even more the case, perhaps, with parents of middle age, who are apt to be more set in their ways than younger parents. The change in lifestyle can be even more pronounced when a set-in-his-ways middle-aged parent is a self-employed writer who works at home. Or what used to be home but has slowly been transformed into one-third nursery, one-third playground, one-third storage space for kidstuff, and two-fifths battlefield. Self-absorbed monologist Spalding Gray discovered a new world at the age of fifty-six, when he found himself waking up every four hours like clockwork to make sure his infant son was still breathing. This change in lifestyle was reflected in Gray's performance piece *Morning, Noon, and Night*.

Gray has become a periodic visitor to Lincoln Center Theater with his series of personal monologues. (*Morning, Noon, and Night* was scheduled on Sunday and Monday evenings, when the Beaumont's main attraction was dark.) Past monologues include *Sex and Death to Age 14*, about Gray's boyhood; *Swimming to Cambodia*, about Gray's experiences while acting in the film *The Killing Fields*; *Monster in a Box*, about Gray's attempt to write a novel; *Gray's Anatomy*, about—well, about, Gray's anatomy; and *It's a Slippery Slope*, about Gray's adultery while skiing. Now came *Morning, Noon, and Night*, in which Gray-watchers readily discerned

A loyal, assured audience can be problematic for a self-defined maverick like Spalding Gray; at some point, your creativity can become tailored to what you know your listeners will laugh at.

Spalding Gray

a major difference: Instead of talking solely about himself, Gray spent a good deal of the time focusing attention on his two sons.

It's a Slippery Slope described how Gray fathered a child with Kathy Russo while both were otherwise married. (I did not see *It's a Slippery Slope*, having found both *Swimming to Cambodia* and *Monster in a Box* interesting but eventually wearying.) *Morning* describes a day—October 8, 1997, specifically—in the life of playwright Gray; Forrest, the two-and-a-half-year-old child born of the *Slope* love match; and Theo, Gray's newborn, second son. Making somewhat subsidiary appearances in the narrative are Kathy, a theatrical agent for performance artists who is the boys' mother; and Marissa, Kathy's eleven-year-old daughter from the broken marriage.

The narrative is framed by the house in which Gray's unconventional family lives, in the old Long Island whaling village of Sag Harbor. His window faces an 1844 church in a style he considers "Colonial Egyptian Revival." (It looks like "Edith Wharton and King Tut buried side by side.") From his window overlooking the graveyard, Gray ponders his life as heretofore, except this time his customary self-examination is continually interrupted by thoughts of Theo (who looks like a "little old Italian winemaker") and the precocious Forrest. The boys have added a heart-warming sentimentality to Gray's work, and no one seems more surprised than Gray himself; he sounds like a father pretty much in love with his children and everything they think or do. And what's wrong with that? The day in question began at 6:40, with Gray walking "crunching across the Cheerios" as Forrest cried that he was "terrified of the grass." It ended late at night, with Theo kicking him in the stomach as he fell asleep. "And we've got to get up tomorrow and start all over again."

Mind you, the morning of the night that I saw Gray, I myself had been up at 5:30, serenaded over the transom with "Skin-a-ma-rink a dink-a-dink" from my two-and-a-half-year-old daughter. I was immediately thereafter summoned with the dangerous words "I'm naked, but I have my diaper on 'cause it's leaking." And I, too, had gone to sleep the night before with my four-month-old son digging his fragile but deceptively razorlike toenails into my stomach. Which is to say I was, all in all, receptive to Gray's edgy elegy.

But I found a strange problem with it. The overriding theme of his oeuvre seems to be that he is presenting himself to our gaze just as he is. This is real life, here, and if his inner thoughts at times strike us as inappropriate, politically incorrect, or downright offensive, so be it; this is who he is, the unvarnished Gray, and that's what you are going to get in his monologues.

This is fine with his audience, a loyal subset of the Lincoln Center Theater subscription list (including a wide swath of middle-class baby boomers and their parents). But as I watched Morning, Noon, and Night, I couldn't help but notice glimpses of a contrived phoniness. Gray's discourse was filled with personal truths—sometimes highly unflattering—about himself and his subsidiary subjects; yet he never hesitated to throw in impersonal, easy jokes lobbed at his audience for surefire laughs. Sag Harbor's "evacuation plan for nuclear disaster" is the

The kids keep coming up with snappy lines, too snappy for comfort. The outspoken Forrest is a regular baby Beckett, through his father's mouth.

Long Island Expressway; the understocked local general store carries "one of some things." Through years of what surely must have been hard work, Gray has developed a performance artist persona that provides him with a loyal, assured audience up at Lincoln Center and elsewhere. (Morning, Noon, and Night was commissioned by the Kravis Center, in Palm Beach.) But a loyal, assured audience can be problematic for a self-defined mav-

Morning, Noon, and Night
Opened: November 8, 1999
Closed: January 10, 2000
17 performances (and 3 previews)
Profit/Loss: Nonprofit [Profit]
Morning, Noon, and Night ($45 top) was scaled to a
   potential gross of $88,490 per two-performance week at
   the 1,068-seat Vivian Beaumont. Attendance was about
   77 percent. Complete box office figures not available.

*Critical
Scorecard*

Rave 1
Favorable 5
Mixed 0
Unfavorable 0
Pan 2

erick like Gray; at some point, your creativity can become tailored to
what you know your listeners will laugh at.

Thus the kids keep coming up with snappy lines, too snappy for comfort. The outspoken Forrest is a regular baby Beckett, through his father's
mouth. "Elves don't have armpits," he states. "How do flies celebrate?" he
asks. "I am so glad you met mom," he says, "or I would have been stuck in
sperm forever." This is a kid who goes to the store and orders an Orangina
instead of a Coke, explaining that he doesn't want to be hyper. Marissa,
for her part, chimes in that "people can change. Look at the Unabomber.
He was a professor, now he's a bomber." Gray is very good at what he does,
and he displays a fair amount of charm (he describes himself as "a dressed-
down Ozzie Nelson, always on the verge of going to work"), but at times
you feel like he's simply telling jokes. And his chronology at times is way
out of whack. Forrest is two and a half on the morning, noon, and night
of the title, but at some points in the narrative he is suddenly five. Theo,
too, seems to age a couple of years, resulting in a rather alarming moment
when it appears that he is suddenly breast-feeding at three. Marissa remains eleven throughout, but then she's a girl.

A bit of uncomfortable nastiness also creeps in. Gray is perfectly entitled to discuss the ins and outs of his own life, but how much privileged
information do we want to know about the others? Gray's lover, Kathy
Russo, had already been stripped pretty bare in *It's a Slippery Slope;* here
he discusses her sex drive, among other things (in a story that climaxes
with a "Tickle Me Elmo" doll). Of course, Russo might well be a willing
participant in Gray's monologues. But he tells a story of walking along a
beach with Forrest, when a stranger approaches. "Is that the woman you
had the baby with when she was married to someone else?" the man asks,
pointing to Forrest's mother. And then, "Is that the boy?" Now maybe I
overreact, but is it fair to subject a five-year-old to that sort of comment

from strangers? If Forrest is anything like papa Spalding, he doesn't care what people say and will hit the kiddy monologue circuit by the time he's ten. But if he's a sensitive child, how many years of analysis will he need to overcome his father's public pronouncements—for laughs and money —about his conception? And what of Theo, who will presumably read *Morning, Noon, and Night* someday or see it on DVD and learn that his father wanted him aborted? (Kathy agreed that she would abort the child as soon as Gray underwent a vasectomy, and that was the end of that.) Gray is outspoken on the subject of Kathy's ex-husband, the father of his stepdaughter, Marissa, and that is perfectly fine. But he then starts reporting on Marissa's private relationship with her father, and it begins to sound like Gray is using Marissa and Kathy and his sons to get laughs and sympathy.

And then there was the matter of the water. One might expect an actor delivering a seventy-minute monologue to have a glass on hand, just in case. By about the fourth sip, I began to get a little suspicious; was he so very thirsty? I watched the next two sips, which curiously enough came at clear breaks in the action. Stop everything, take a drink of water, and then on to the next section of the narrative. By the seventh sip I realized that it was all meticulously planned, gulp by gulp. How many ounces in a gulp? Would he have enough water to make it through the play?

Around about the ninth gulp of water, I noticed Gray looking through the glass—as it were —as he sipped. Casing the audience, gearing their reactions, savoring their laughter under cover of his prop. Now, we ac-

cept that this nonstop talker might get thirsty, and we'd gladly allow him to take a drink (while we would be appalled if Brian Dennehy in *Death of a Salesman* stopped midmonologue for a swig of Evian). But when the nonstop Gray premeditatedly plots out his ten ounces of water, saving it for strategic spots—well, that's phony theatricality that you wouldn't expect from a guy who purposely eschews stagecraft and pretense. Granted, this is all rather silly as analysis goes; but I contend that something is wrong if an audience member sits there wondering how many ounces of water you get per gulp.

Reservations aside, Gray managed to make *Morning, Noon, and Night* a tender and enjoyable discourse, leaving us with his realization that "it's a fearful thing to love what can be touched by death." That is a chastening thought, certainly, and one that might never occur to you until you rock your trembling child in your arms late on a storm-filled night. For a self-absorbed, middle-aged, professional egoist like Spalding Gray, it can't help but have a warming effect.

> **If Forrest is a sensitive child, how many years of analysis will he need to overcome his father's public pronouncements—for laughs and money—about his conception?**

On February 3, 2000—three weeks after *Morning, Noon, and Night* closed at the Beaumont—it was announced that the show would reopen February 20 at the Union Square Theatre, for ten two-performance weeks (on the dark nights of *Wit*). On February 10, the whole thing was called off due to "scheduling," and that was that.

The Rainmaker

The Miracle Worker. Requiem for a Heavyweight. Twelve Angry Men. Marty. The Days of Wine and Roses. Man of La Mancha. Judgement at Nuremberg. There is a common denominator here: All these properties began life as television plays, back in the 1950s when television was live and talented young writers had a place to showcase their wares. (Television needed product, and the movie studios—which saw the new form as competition—were not yet ready to provide programming to the enemy.) One of the earliest to make the transfer was N. Richard Nash's *The Rainmaker*, which appeared on the *Philco Playhouse* in the summer of 1953.

The play—about a handsome con man who arrives in a hot and steamy Midwest town, stirs up things, seduces the daughter of the house, and invites her to leave with him—arrived on Broadway in October 1954. Unfortunately, William Inge's *Picnic*—about a handsome con man who arrives in a hot and steamy Midwest town, stirs up things, seduces the daughter of the house, and invites her to leave with him—had just finished a highly successful run. So the far less flashy *Rainmaker* was somewhat old hat before it arrived. The reviews were generally favorable, in a pleasant sort of way; most of the praise went to budding star Geraldine Page, who brought life, humor, and sympathy to the role of the spinsterish heroine. *The Rainmaker* is remembered mostly for the 1956 film version, which

A con man barnstorming the drought-stricken Midwest selling people false miracles would need to appear believable, at least. Woody Harrelson's Starbuck might as well have been from the moon; he jumped and flitted around like Jiminy Cricket.

⇒N⇐ **BROOKS ATKINSON THEATRE**
UNDER THE DIRECTION OF THE MESSRS. NEDERLANDER

ROUNDABOUTTHEATRECOMPANY

TODD HAIMES, Artistic Director
ELLEN RICHARD, Managing Director
JULIA C. LEVY, Executive Director, External Affairs

Presents

Woody Harrelson   Jayne Atkinson

THE RAINMAKER

by
N. Richard Nash

with David Aaron Baker   Jerry Hardin   John Bedford Lloyd
Bernie McInerney   Randle Mell

Eric Axen   Scott McTyer Cowart   David Harbour   Brian Ibsen   Rey Lucas
Donovan McGrath   Dustin Tucker   Jason Winther

Set Designer	Costume Designer	Lighting Designer
James Noone	Jess Goldstein	Peter Kaczorowski

Sound Designer	Special Effects Designer	Original Music	Fight Choreographer	Hair Designer
Brian Ronan	Gregory Meeh	Louis Rosen	David Leong	David Brian Brown

Director of Production	Technical Supervision	Production Stage Manager	Casting by	Founding Director
Nancy Harrington	Unitech	Lori M. Doyle	Jim Carnahan	Gene Feist
			Amy Christopher	

Associate Artistic Director	Director of Artistic Development	Press Representative	Director of Marketing
Scott Ellis	Jim Carnahan	Boneau/Bryan-Brown	David B. Steffen

Directed by
Scott Ellis

Support for this production provided by The Blanche and Irving Laurie Foundation.
The Williamstown Theatre Festival presented a production of *The Rainmaker* **in July 1998, under the direction of Scott Ellis.**
Roundabout Theatre Company is a member of the League of Resident Theatres.
www.roundabouttheatre.org

starred Katharine Hepburn and Burt Lancaster.

N. Richard Nash, who died on December 11, 2000, made something of a career out of *The Rainmaker*. ("N. Richard Nash" sounds a little too asymmetric, doesn't it? It turns out his real name was Nat Nussbaum.) In addition to writing the *Rainmaker* teleplay, play, and screenplay, Nash adapted the piece into a musical. Two musicals, you might say. In 1960, he more or less borrowed the character of his rainmaker—complete with that big bass drum he uses to drum up thunderclaps—and turned him into an oil prospector. Bill Starbuck became Wildcat Jackson, played not by Burt Lancaster but by Lucille Ball. (*Wildcat*, which Nash coproduced, ran into all sorts of storm clouds and soon went bust.) The official musical adaptation of *The Rainmaker*, 1963's *110 in the Shade*, turned out far better. While only a moderate hit in its day, it is one of the better-written musicals of the decade. (It is also, as far as I can tell, Nash's one and only Broadway effort to actually turn a profit.) Nash's other stage credits include *The Happy Time*, a 1968 musical that became the first Broadway show to lose a million dollars, and *Sarava*, a 1979 musical that lost considerably more.

110 in the Shade featured a wonderfully spare book, along with a highly effective and atmospheric score by Harvey Schmidt and Tom Jones (direct from *The Fantasticks*). Watching the 1999 revival of *The Rainmaker*, audience members familiar with the musical were no doubt struck by how much more concise Nash was in his libretto than in his play; things move along swiftly, with none of the bloated stage waits of the dramatic version. (Perhaps this overwriting occurred when Nash originally transformed his sixty-minute teleplay into three acts for Broadway.)

The new *Rainmaker* started with the sound of a far-off train—just like *Picnic*—on the house right loudspeakers. The train noise then moved across the rear of the house, around to the house left speakers, then to the upstage speakers behind the cyclorama. This created an unintended effect, as if the locomotive was circling around us. As the play lumbered to a start, I wondered whether things would ever start moving. I couldn't help but recall that the last production of *110 in the Shade* I saw—the 1992 New York City Opera production—was disappointingly lifeless; and I became rather concerned when I realized that this new *Rainmaker* was directed by the same fellow, the Roundabout Theatre Company's associate artistic director, Scott Ellis. I needn't have worried, as it turns out. Ellis did a

much better job here, helping his actors—some of whom appeared in his 1998 production of *The Rainmaker* at the Williamstown Theatre Festival—probe beneath the surface. Most of the actors, that is.

Unfortunately, there was a problem—a big one—with Woody Harrelson in the title role. Harrelson is a talented screen actor, but he gave a mighty quirky performance here. His Starbuck wasn't a strong, powerful type like Darren McGavin (who originated the role) or Burt Lancaster. He was more like Kevin Spacey, only Kevin Spacey without the stage savvy. A con man barnstorming the drought-stricken Midwest selling

The Rainmaker
Opened: November 11, 1999
Closed: January 23, 2000
82 performances (and 25 previews)
Profit/Loss: Nonprofit [Profit]
The Rainmaker ($65 top) was scaled to a potential gross of
$327,614 at the 998-seat Brooks Atkinson. Weekly grosses
averaged about $248,000, with the show maintaining a
fairly steady pace. (These figures are not indicative, as the
potential was calculated at the top ticket price, but
subscribers paid less.) Total gross for the run was
$3,321,242. Attendance was about 83 percent, with the
box office grossing about 76 percent of potential dollar-
capacity.

TONY AWARD NOMINATION
Best Performance by a Leading Actress: Jayne Atkinson

*Critical
Scorecard*

Rave 0
Favorable 2
Mixed 1
Unfavorable 3
Pan 4

people false miracles would need to *appear* believable, at least; folks don't
give away their money and their dreams to obvious fools. Harrelson's Starbuck might as well have been from the moon; he jumped and flitted
around like Jiminy Cricket. (During the love scene in the second act, we
heard the sound of a cricket—or was it someone's cell phone? The audience turned around glaring angrily at the interruption, but I do kind of
think it was a sound cue.) When Starbuck's rainmaking techniques were
questioned and he answered that they're all "bunk and hokey-pokey,"
Harrelson raised his leg and shook it, dancing a bit of the hokey-pokey
for us. That's the kind of performance it was, not exactly suitable to the
milieu.

Harrelson's lapses were more than compensated for by Jayne Atkinson,
as the spinster not quite ready to give up on life. Atkinson is not exactly
unknown; she acquitted herself well as Kevin Kline's wife in Lincoln
Center Theater's 1997 production of *Ivanov*. She is quite an actress, and
it's fair to say that she made this *Rainmaker* well worth viewing despite
her costar. Lizzie Curry is unhappy and unfortunate and awkward, an ungainly woman in a world where she can't hope to be appreciated. (*The
Rainmaker* is, at heart, a Cinderella story.) Atkinson acted with her wrists;
she seemed not to use her clumsy fingers, awkwardly rubbing her nose
with the hem of her sleeve, drying her hands on her dress as if she were
wearing mittens. Seventy minutes into the first act, she suddenly smiled
and then laughed; the whole stage lit up, and the audience too. In the

second act Atkinson finally let herself dream aloud, about children and family; it was almost as if the wind kicked up a cool breeze, offering promise of relief from the torrid August drought. I never saw Gerry Page's performance in this role, although she once spilled a bottle of red wine on me in a hotel room in Philadelphia. I'm sure she was very good, and made the play seem far more substantial than it is. But I imagine that Ms. Atkinson's work was comparable; and oh, if she only had a Starbuck to act against.

> **In the second act, Jayne Atkinson finally let herself dream aloud, about children and family; it is almost as if the wind kicked up a cool breeze, offering promise of relief from the torrid August drought.**

Yes, this *Rainmaker* was a museum piece; you always felt you were watching a play. But all in all, Ms. Atkinson—aided by Mr. Ellis and some of the featured players—made it a thing to see, despite the hole at its center.

The Price

Attention must be paid, as the man once wrote.

What struck me most, watching this 1999 revival of Arthur Miller's 1968 play, was how carefully the people sitting around me were listening to the dialogue. Totally rapt they were, as if afraid to miss a word. Which is, for sure, uncommon in this day and age. And I wondered why. Due to the acclaim of the previous season's award-winning *Death of a Salesman*, which finished its successful run the week before *The Price* opened? Perhaps. Certainly they didn't listen this closely to *The Price* when it was last revived here, in 1992; nor did they pay much attention at all to Miller's last Broadway play, the underappreciated and quickly shuttered *Broken Glass*, in 1994.

Not that *The Price* is unworthy of attention. It is an unusual play; unusual in construction and—for Miller—unusual in its moral ambiguity and its lowbrow comedy quotient. Two men from two different worlds— Victor, a scrimping-and-saving blue-collar policeman, and Walter, a highly successful white-collar surgeon—are brought together by an attic full of old furniture. They are long-estranged brothers, oddly enough, meeting to liquidate the estate of their long-dead father, and the socio-economic gulf between them is tied directly to the manipulative old man.

Rather than getting into it head-on, though, Miller chose to keep the successful Walter offstage for a full hour, bringing him on midway through the play. (In this production he entered just before the first-act curtain, although *The Price* was originally performed without an intermission.) A third character, whose questions and comments allow the brothers to describe their pasts and presents, is Victor's wife, Esther. The final character is pulled from another world altogether: a little old Jewish man, eighty-nine years old, a secondhand furniture dealer named Solomon (i.e., the judge). The play begins with the policeman's entrance; the wife appears just long enough to get the exposition out of the way. After this, on comes Solomon, who proceeds to do about forty minutes' worth of little old man Jewish jokes. (Many of the reviewers greeted *The Price* as "Arthur Miller's funniest play." Well, yes, it is; but "funny" is not the point.) As the price for the sale of the family's possessions is set and agreed upon, Walter enters, and we enter a rather different sort of play, dealing with choices and sacrifices and recriminations and such. At this point, Miller finally gets down to it, with the truth about the brothers and their manipulative father revealed. And revealed and revealed; the truth, it seems, is a slippery proposition.

But Solomon sets up the brothers' confrontation, enlightening and informing us of the price one can pay today for yesterday's choice. This oblique method of information transmittal makes for interesting drama, but I wonder if this is not a case where circumstance and practicality led Miller to a course even more oblique than anticipated. Miller, along with his original producer and director, chose to cast *The Price* with three accomplished dramatic actors. Walter, for example, was played by Arthur Kennedy, who created the roles of Chris in *All My Sons*, Biff in *Death of a Salesman*, and John Proctor in *The Crucible*. For the key role of Solomon, though, they turned to musical comedy and cast one of the funniest funnymen in the business, David Burns. Best known as Horace Vandergelder, Carol Channing's

prey in *Hello, Dolly!*, Burns had won Tony Awards as the mayor in *The Music Man* and as the dirty old man in *A Funny Thing Happened on the Way to the Forum*. His occasional nonmusical credits included two George S. Kaufman plays, *Dinner at Eight* and *The Man Who Came to*

ROYALE THEATRE
Ⓢ A Shubert Organization Theatre
Gerald Schoenfeld, *Chairman*   Philip J. Smith, *President*

Robert E. Wankel, *Executive Vice President*

David Richenthal

presents

Jeffrey DeMunn   Bob Dishy   Lizbeth Mackay   Harris Yulin

in

Arthur Miller's

Scenic Design   Costume Design   Lighting Design   Sound Design
Michael Brown   Laurie A. Churba   Rui Rita   Jerry M. Yager

Casting   Production Stage Manager   Technical Supervision
Amy Christopher   Grayson Meritt   Gene O'Donovan

Press Representative   Company Manager   General Management   Executive Producer
Richard Kornberg   Lisa M. Poyer   Robert Cole Productions   Robert Cole
Don Summa   Steven Chaikelson

Directed by
James Naughton

This production was first presented by the Williamstown Theatre Festival.
Michael Ritchie, Producer   Deborah Fehr, General Manager   Jenny C. Gersten, Associate Producer

The producer wishes to express his appreciation to Theatre Development Fund for its support of this production.

Victor Franz   Jeffrey Demunn
Esther Franz   Lizbeth Mackay
Gregory Solomon   Bob Dishy
Walter Franz   Harris Yulin

The action takes place in the attic of a brownstone on the West Side of Manhattan, mid-afternoon on a Saturday in winter, 1966.

Dinner (in which he created the role of the Harpo Marx–inspired Banjo).

With Davey Burns in the play, Miller's judicial character Solomon couldn't help but grow funnier and funnier. Burns couldn't walk across the stage without getting a laugh, and *The Price* featured forty straight minutes of Burns walking across the stage. An authoritative author and a strong director can keep things in control, of course, but three not-so-funny things happened on the way to the Morosco (which is where the original *Price* opened). As the play was about to open in Philadelphia, the actor playing Victor—Jack Warden, who had created Marco in Miller's 1955 play, *A View from the Bridge*—was replaced. Pat Hingle, a fine actor who had played important roles for Tennessee Williams and William Inge and the title character of Archibald MacLeish's *J.B.*, was rushed to Philadelphia to learn the role virtually overnight. And this was no small role, carrying the burden of the piece for a full hour until Walter's entrance.

So what Miller had in Philadelphia was this main character learning the role onstage, in front of paying audiences. (Not the lines themselves, but the inner life of the character.) And what was expert scene-stealer Davey Burns, who had already spent a month in rehearsal, doing onstage while Hingle was figuring out Victor's motivations? Getting laughs, I'd guess. Helpful laughs. More and more and more laughs, from night to night. While all this was going on, director Ulu Grossbard was fired and replaced by Miller. Under other circumstances, Miller might have been doing some rewriting and putting a cap on the somewhat underwritten resolution of the brothers' relationship. But the author had his hands full.

And then, two nights before the Broadway opening, David Burns—the oxygenated life support of *The Price*—was rushed to the hospital for emergency abdominal surgery. The show must go on, so on went the understudy. Harold Gary was also from the world of musical comedy but was not a star like Burns; he was a bit player, the sort of actor who played a crony of the star comedian and had solo lines in a song or two. (Burns eventually rejoined the cast of *The Price*. Two shows and four years later, back in Philadelphia, Burns suffered a fatal heart attack onstage.)

Gary, who had presumably been studying Burns closely, gave a pretty good performance; but what you had in *The Price* when it opened in New York was a director-less new Arthur Miller play, with two replacements holding the stage for an hour, before Arthur Kennedy entered and the fireworks began. The play in its final form was not necessarily what Miller had wanted it to be; rather, it was what it turned out to be under the circumstances.

The original production was respectfully received, although it was somewhat unclear as to what Miller intended the audience to go away with. Which brother prevails? The answer seems to be that there is no answer, that both of them were right and wrong in their decisions. Miller named his secondhand man Solomon, as his clear purpose is to serve as judge. What, then, was his purpose in calling the policeman brother Victor? If he is meant to be the victor (i.e., winner), then it is unclear in the writing. (The choice of name couldn't be merely coincidental, not with a writer like Arthur Miller.)

Many of the reviewers greeted *The Price* as "Arthur Miller's funniest play." Well, yes, it is; but "funny" is not the point.

The Price was Miller's last successful Broadway play, running 426 performances. I saw it at the time, while a high school student, and found it engrossing if inconclusive. It was revived, with a problematic cast, in 1992 by the Roundabout Theatre. I remember having little interest in the characters—despite the presence of the always interesting Hector Elizondo—but being intrigued by the writing of the latter half.

The 1999 revival—which, like this season's Roundabout revival of
The Rainmaker, originated at the Williamstown Theatre Festival—received the best batch of reviews of all three; it seemed that many of the
critics were overwhelmed by the previous season's *Death of a Salesman*.
The audience with which I attended the play was, as indicated, hanging
on Miller's every word. I was not. As the play reached its climax, with the
two brothers topping each other with perceived truths, I was concentrating on everything they had to say, but I wasn't with them, wrapped in the
action like I'd been at *Death of a Salesman* and the recent *The Iceman
Cometh*. Clearly, I was sitting in the auditorium at the Royale, wondering
why I was removed from the emotion. I admired the playing of Jeffrey
DeMunn and Harris Yulin as the two brothers, although I found Lizbeth
Mackay's Esther somewhat too hysterical. The Solomon of Bob Dishy was
a laugh a minute, to the point where you almost thought he was the leading character of the play (stemming, I suppose, directly from the Davey
Burns situation). But ultimately he seemed to be giving a comic performance, as opposed to playing a character. And wasn't some of his farcical
business borrowed from Larry Gelbart's *Sly Fox*, in which he memorably
chewed up the scenery back in 1976?

And then there was the Vietnam thing. I try never to read so-called
think pieces beforehand, but I thought it might be enlightening to hear
what Mr. Miller had to say in the Arts and Leisure section of the *New
York Times* the Sunday before the opening, about why he wrote *The Price*.

"As the dying continued in Vietnam with no adequate resistance to it
in the country, the theater, so it seemed to me, risked trivialization by failing to confront the bleeding. . . . As the corpses piled up, it became cru-

elly impolite if not unpatriotic to suggest the obvious, that we were fighting the past; our rigid anti-Communist theology, born of another time two decades earlier, made it a sin to consider Vietnamese Reds as nationalists rather than Moscow's and Beijing's yapping dogs. . . . And so 50,000 Americans, not to mention millions of Vietnamese, paid with their lives to support a myth and a bellicose denial."

I thought the play was about two brothers selling some old furniture. So I sat in the theatre determined to see *The Price* for what it really was, as per Mr. Miller. And paid attention to every word—attention must be paid, as they say—and I just simply did not get Vietnam. And I'm afraid this could have tilted my attention from where it would otherwise have been.

Walking home from the theatre, I delved further into the question—and, yes, I finally got it. The brothers Franz based their beliefs on truths from yesterday; these not necessarily still valid truths overpowered their reason, and so they paid the price. When Miller wrote the play, America's political leaders were in the very same way fighting Communism in Vietnam based on the truths from yesterday—the post–World War II era—and refusing to consider that those truths might have changed. Of course, I'd never have come up with this—in 1968 or 1999—without Miller spelling it out. When Miller starts talking about Communism, I listen.

But then I started to wonder. In *The Price*, Miller condemned Vietnam hawks who were attacking Communist ideology born of another time two decades earlier. Okay. Now, go back to the House Un-American Activities Committee, which had such a profound effect on Miller's life. There you had people on trial whose crime was, in some cases, merely having sympathized with the Communist Party back in the meager days of the Depression; that is, people who were defending Communist ideology born of another time two decades earlier,

What you had in *The Price* when it originally opened in New York was a director-less play, with two replacements holding the stage for the first hour. The play in its final form was not necessarily what Miller wanted it to be; it was what it turned out to be under the circumstances.

a behavior that Miller seems, precisely, to have been criticizing in *The Price*. Certain people went before the committee and recanted, on the grounds that the Party of the 1950s was not the same as the one they viewed idealistically in the 1930s. Does this make them—people who have gone down in history as self-serving stool pigeons, most notably

Miller's former colleague Elia Kazan—heroes in Miller's eyes? Isn't this the same logic Miller was using against involvement in Vietnam?

But enough of this. As for *The Price*, audiences did not flock to it despite an enthusiastic set of notices. Lightning—as in the unparalleled success of the Brian Dennehy *Death of a Salesman*—does not strike again so easily. But there was already a revival of another Miller play en route.

Which brother prevails? The answer seems to be that there is no answer. What, then, was Miller's purpose in calling the policeman brother Victor (i.e., winner)?

I suppose that Miller's viewpoint was somewhat too oblique for his own good. And to quote his laugh-a-minute secondhand furniture man, "If you don't understand the viewpoint, you don't understand the price."

Tango Argentino

Tango Argentino first came to town in 1985. Like many similar non-English-language "special" attractions, it was booked for a single week at City Center. The response was good enough for the show to arrange a quick transfer to the empty Mark Hellinger Theatre for a four-week run. Business was phenomenal; apparently, there was an enormous South American audience in New York, just waiting for an attraction of this sort. So much so that *Tango Argentino* stayed on Broadway for an unprecedented six months.

As it happened, I was with a faltering show across the street at the Gershwin at the time. Walking past the Hellinger, which is now a church, we would marvel at the excited lines of patrons at the box office, and our not-very-busy treasurers would jealously fill us in on *Tango*'s daily ticket sales. It never occurred to me to actually see *Tango Argentino*; I suspected that it would be an endless succession of dancers tangoing around the stage in a circle. While the show was clearly a crowd pleaser, it was clearly aimed at a crowd that appreciated tango. Me, I figured I wouldn't last past fifteen minutes.

> It never occurred to me to actually see *Tango Argentino* back in 1985. I suspected that it would be an endless succession of dancers tangoing around the stage in a circle.

Tango Argentino parlayed its unexpected success into a lucrative "direct from Broadway" international tour. Creators Claudio Segovia and Hector Orezzoli followed up with three similar shows, including the 1989 hit *Black and Blue*, which ran two years and won three Tony Awards. Orezzoli died in 1991 at the age of thirty-eight, and the operation disbanded. In the fall of 1999, Segovia launched a new international tour of *Tango*

Argentino with an eight-week run at the Gershwin, so I figured I might as well give it a shot.

The curtain rose on a striking tableau: the band seated on a three-tiered bandstand, silhouetted against an inky blue cyclorama. It launched into the opening instrumental piece, which sounded strikingly unusual. The lights went up to reveal four accordion players on the lower level, playing something called "Quejas de Bandoneón." (A bandoneón, it turns out, is an accordion.) The thirteen-piece band consisted of four accordions (one of whom, rarely, pulled out a flute or a set of bongos), six violins, a cello, a bass, and a piano. Four accordions and six violins—this sounded truly strange, but striking.

The first number began, with six men tangoing in separate spotlights, a visually stunning and mysterious effect. Hmmm, I thought, maybe I was wrong about *Tango Argentino*. . . . Then six women came on, tangoing around the stage in a big circle.

Then came five people tangoing around the stage in a big circle to that familiar old tango, the one that goes dum, dum, dum, dum-dum. This was followed by another familiar old tango tune.

Then there was another orchestral number, but not so effective as the opening.

Then an old guy came out, looking like Tony Quinn but with white hair and bushy sideburns. He sang a song called "Mi Noche Triste," which probably means "My Sad Night." He was quite beside himself, actually.

Then came two youngsters doing a lively tango. They got a good hand. In this number, the second accordion player from the right was dancing too, with shiny black shoes.

Then came a middle-aged lady singing another dramatic song. During this number, I found myself thinking of a narrow corridor in the Boston Museum of Fine Arts that is lined with old master drawings; every once in a while you come to a wonderful little painting in a little frame, and I always wondered why the museum mixed these important paintings in with the miscellaneous sketches. What relevance this had, I can't tell you; I haven't spent all that much time at the Boston Museum of Fine Arts, and

I haven't been there since 1994. Nevertheless, this is precisely what I was thinking about, midway through the first act of *Tango Argentino*, so I figured I should share it with you. Perhaps it was because every number seemed so much alike—just couples dancing around in a big circle, with an occasional striking touch. But by this point, *Tango Argentino* had struck out.

The next number started with a young couple dancing. Was it the same young couple that got the nice hand? I can't tell you; the young ones all looked alike. After a couple of minutes of tangoing, the old distinguished guy

—not the one with the bushy hair, the other one—came on, and the girl left the young guy and started tangoing with the old guy.

Then a middle-aged lady came on carrying a gown, much fancier than

the one the girl was wearing. She went behind the dancing girl, the old guy stood in front and pulled her ribbons, and presto! The dancing girl was wearing the new dress. Was she naked in between? Hard to tell from where I was sitting. Then the middle-aged lady started tangoing with the young girl. The backdrop turned scarlet—quite effective—and twelve other women, in couples, started tangoing upstage. Now, the tango is supposed to be a very erotic dance, although the whole evening looked pretty sleepy to me. At any rate, the middle-aged lady and the young girl kept tangoing and then kissed. They tangoed some more, at which point the young girl seemed to spit in the old dame's eye. The girl then turned to her original partner—the young guy—and tangoed with him once more, until she kicked him and went back to the old guy. While they tangoed, the old dame came back downstage carrying a black shawl, crepe or something, and put it over the young girl's shoulders. She just kept doing the tango with the old guy, but meanwhile a guy in a hat and in a spotlight came on, approached them, pulled out a knife, and stabbed her just like Don José and Carmen outside the bullring. He dragged her into the wing—I can understand why she might be a wee bit tired after all this—and the music built to a finish. Blackout.

Tango Argentino **is no doubt a great, great, great crowd pleaser, if you like this sort of thing. Otherwise, a little tango goes a long, long, long, long way.**

Then came a pink number with a gal in a dress that looked like it was made of black baby Swiss cheese and a short guy who looked like he came from Las Vegas and seemed to be counting whenever the music got busy. Or maybe he was just sneezing rhythmically. Then came another singer, wearing a shiny silver dress and black vest; this one looked like Lea Delaria—who graced the Gershwin stage the previous season in *On the Town*—but she didn't sing like her. This song was called "Cautivo," which means "captive." By this point in the evening, it was me who felt "cautivo."

Then came yet another couple dancing; they ended their number by making rapid, abrupt steps, moving their legs like they were in a silent movie projected at too quick a speed. This must have been really hard to do; it got a big hand.

The act ended with an ensemble number with the guys wearing white jackets with their black pants. Each couple had its own solo section, and at the end of each cadence the women seemed to fly up in the air; not in a wide sweep, but in a very controlled fashion. Nice effect.

Then came the intermission, after which the dancers went on (and on and on) for another hour, but I need not (go on and on). *Tango Argentino* is no doubt a great, great, great crowd pleaser, if you like this sort of thing. Otherwise, a little tango goes a long, long, long, long way.

Kiss Me, Kate

Kiss Me, Kate, the 1948 musical comedy that remains one of the classics of Broadway's golden age, has for many years proven stubbornly nonrevivable. The main reasons: The show needs a charismatic, strong-voiced actor with a self-lampooning sense of humor and—hopefully—some ticket-selling ability; the libretto is weaker than you might expect for a classic musical comedy; and Bella Spewack, the surviving coauthor of the show, was overly protective of—and somewhat hypersensitive about—her biggest hit (and major source of income) until her death in 1990.

Fifty years after its premiere, Kate appeared in its first Broadway revival with generally splendid results. Director Michael Blakemore, choreographer Kathleen Marshall, and their designers, arrangers, and producers wisely chose to be always true to Kate, darling, in their fashion.

Brian Stokes Mitchell, as the uncontrollably hammy Fred Graham, and Marin Mazzie, as his estranged former wife, Lilli Vanessi, are both highly capable performers. Oddly, though, they were somewhat less effective together than apart. You never got the impression they'd been married and divorced in the back story; in fact, they seemed not to have even shared a pot of coffee before the first scene. The secondary couple, Amy Spanger and Michael Berrese, seemed strangers as well. Conversely, the two gangsters—Lee Wilkof and Michael Mulheren—appeared to have been old

Director Michael Blakemore, choreographer Kathleen Marshall, and their designers, arrangers, and producers wisely chose to be always true to Kate, darling, in their fashion.

buddies from reform school days. Is this why the two character men, in relatively minuscule roles, almost walked away with the proceedings?

Mitchell possesses a fine singing voice, a great command of the stage, and the comic sense humor necessary for the role. The great Alfred Drake, who originated the part, had an additional weapon in his arsenal: a lushly romantic baritone voice. So much so that Porter gave Drake a solo reprise of "So in Love," adding a moving moment to the second act. In Mitchell's hands, it was simply a reprise. Similarly, a high point of the original—Drake's rendition of the smolderingly seductive beguine "Were Thine That Special Face?"—came across like a stage wait in the overlong first act, despite Mitchell's ministrations. (This number was accompanied by a sexy pas de deux in 1948, which was not in evidence here; in fact, there was surprisingly little romance or sex in this production. It should be noted that on the cast album of this revival, Mitchell does infinitely better with this song than he did at the press performance I attended.)

This song aside, Mitchell gave a sturdy and ingratiating performance, doing especially well with the quick-rhyming patter songs "I've Come to Wive It Wealthily in Padua" and "Where Is the Life That Late I Led?"

Mazzie was also quite good, singing her three and a half songs with passion but never really catching fire. She was perhaps a bit more hoydenish than one might desire—her "I Hate Men" recalled *I Love Lucy*— but, like Mr. Mitchell, she got the job done with style and flair. Michael Berresse was fine as the athletic lead dancer and was especially sympathetic as Lucentio in the *Shrew* scenes. Amy Spanger appeared to lack the hunger to play Lois/Bianca, though, with her "Why Can't You Behave?" falling especially flat. Watching her other big solo, "Always True to You (In My Fashion)," I realized that she was victimized by the amplification system. Not by the

Hattie   Adriane Lenox
Paul   Stanley Wayne Mathis
Ralph (Stage Manager)   Eric Michael Gillett
Lois Lane   Amy Spanger
Bill Calhoun   Michael Berresse
Lilli Vanessi   Marin Mazzie
Fred Graham   Brian Stokes Mitchell

Harry Trevor   John Horton
Pops (Stage Doorman)   Robert Ousley
Cab Driver   Jerome Vivona
First Man   Lee Wilkof
Second Man   Michael Mulheren
Harrison Howell   Ron Holgate

"Taming of the Shrew" Players
Bianca (Lois Lane)   Amy Spanger
Baptista (Harry Trevor)   John Horton
Gremio (First Suitor)   Kevin Neil McCready
Hortensio (Second Suitor)   Darren Lee
Lucentio (Bill Calhoun)   Michael Berresse
Katharine (Lilli Vanessi)   Marin Mazzie
Petruchio (Fred Graham)   Brian Stokes Mitchell
Nathaniel   Jerome Vivona
Gregory   Vince Pesce
Philip   Blake Hammond
Haberdasher   Michael X. Martin
The Ensemble   Eric Michael Gillett, Patty Goble, Blake Hammond, JoAnn M. Hunter, Nancy Lemenager, Darren Lee, Michael X. Martin, Kevin Neil McCready, Carol Lee Meadows, Elizabeth Mills, Linda Mugleston, Robert Ousley, Vince Pesce, Cynthia Sophiea, Jerome Vivona

Setting: Ford's Theatre, Baltimore, June 1948

Original Broadway Revival Cast Album: DRG 12988

MARTIN BECK THEATRE
A JUJAMCYN THEATRE

JAMES H. BINGER
CHAIRMAN

ROCCO LANDESMAN
PRESIDENT

PAUL LIBIN
PRODUCING DIRECTOR

JACK VIERTEL
CREATIVE DIRECTOR

ROGER BERLIND   ROGER HORCHOW
PRESENT

BRIAN STOKES MITCHELL   MARIN MAZZIE
IN

KISS ME, KATE

MUSIC AND LYRICS BY
COLE PORTER

BOOK BY
SAM AND BELLA SPEWACK

STARRING
AMY SPANGER   MICHAEL BERRESSE

ALSO STARRING
MERWIN FOARD   JOHN HORTON   ADRIANE LENOX
STANLEY WAYNE MATHIS   MICHAEL MULHEREN   LEE WILKOF

AND
RON HOLGATE

WITH
PAULA LEGGETT CHASE   ERIC MICHAEL GILLETT   PATTY GOBLE   BLAKE HAMMOND   TRIPP HANSON   JOANN M. HUNTER
DARREN LEE   NANCY LEMENAGER   MICHAEL X. MARTIN   KEVIN NEIL MCCREADY   CAROL LEE MEADOWS   ELIZABETH MILLS
LINDA MUGLESTON   ROBERT OUSLEY   VINCE PESCE   T. OLIVER REID   CYNTHIA SOPHIEA   JEROME VIVONA

SCENIC DESIGN BY
ROBIN WAGNER

COSTUME DESIGN BY
MARTIN PAKLEDINAZ

LIGHTING DESIGN BY
PETER KACZOROWSKI

SOUND DESIGN BY
TONY MEOLA

ORCHESTRATIONS BY
DON SEBESKY

DANCE ARRANGEMENTS BY
DAVID CHASE

CASTING BY
JOHNSON-LIFF ASSOCIATES

FIGHT DIRECTION BY
B.H. BARRY

WIG DESIGN BY
PAUL HUNTLEY

PRODUCTION SUPERVISION BY
STEVEN ZWEIGBAUM

PRODUCTION MANAGER
ARTHUR SICCARDI

ASSOCIATE CHOREOGRAPHER
ROB ASHFORD

ASSOCIATE PRODUCERS
RICHARD GODWIN   EDWIN W. SCHLOSS

GENERAL MANAGEMENT
101 PRODUCTIONS, LTD.

PRESS REPRESENTATIVE
BONEAU/BRYAN-BROWN

MARKETING
TMG MARKETING & PUBLICITY

MUSICAL DIRECTION BY
PAUL GEMIGNANI

CHOREOGRAPHY BY
KATHLEEN MARSHALL

DIRECTED BY
MICHAEL BLAKEMORE

usual methods; rather, she seemed so comfortably confident singing into her microphone—sure that her words would be properly picked up and disbursed—that the rest of her performance wasn't projected. She sang the words right, did the steps right, but that's not enough; even in this age of digital enhancement, you've got to play to the audience. One need only watch someone like Bernadette Peters, in *Annie Get Your Gun*, to see what I'm talking about; she's wired for sound, certainly, but she concentrates every ounce of her talent on the people out front. Ms. Mazzie, too, for that matter, sang to the folks in the rear mezzanine despite her microphone. Ms. Spanger seemed to be having a private conversation with the sound operator.

The gangsters, though, were a breeze. These are foolproof roles, sure, a pair of Runyonesque thugs running around with their gats drawn two years before *Guys and Dolls* provided a stageful of them. Lee Wilkof and Michael Mulheren were worth their weight in gold to *Kate*. Wilkof has been a constant musical comedy character man over the last decade, always giving sturdy, if similar, performances. Here, as the "First Man" (how's that for a negligible-sounding role?), Wilkof was far funnier than ever before. There was a moment near the end of the first act when he stood snarling in his Italianate orange-and-yellow-striped tights, hands thrust deep in his pockets—tights with pockets??—looking like a delinquent Katzenjammer in the slammer. He didn't have lines in this scene, but he didn't need any. Wilkof and the more overtly thuggish Mulheren threatened to run off with the show altogether. Certainly, they got phenomenal mileage out of "Brush Up Your Shakespeare," complete with two encores. (The "encores" were written into the show back in 1948, but they are vociferously demanded—unlike the "Always True to You" encores, which, the night I saw the show, were performed despite being unearned.)

Part of the *Kiss Me, Kate* stumbling block has always been the not-so-well-written book,

> There was a moment near the end of the first act when Lee Wilkof stood snarling in his Italianate orange and yellow striped tights, hands thrust deep in his pockets—tights with pockets??—looking like a delinquent Katzenjammer in the slammer. He didn't have lines, but he didn't need any.

which is not quite up to the standards you'd expect from a "classic" show. For this production, playwright John Guare agreed to revise the book (without billing), and he did a very good and very unobtrusive job.

The new material and the new jokes are written, more or less, in the

Kiss Me, Kate

Opened: November 18, 2000

Still playing May 29, 2000

To date: 220 performances (and 28 previews)

Profit/Loss: To Be Determined

Kiss Me, Kate ($80 top) was scaled to a potential gross of $771,039 at the 1,422-seat Martin Beck. Weekly grosses averaged about $639,000, never attaining sellout status (rather puzzlingly) and only rarely breaking the $700,000 plateau. Total gross for the partial season was $19,811,140. Attendance was about 86 percent, with the box office grossing about 83 percent of potential dollar-capacity.

TONY AWARD NOMINATIONS

Best Revival of a Musical (WINNER)

Best Performance by a Leading Actor: Brian Stokes Mitchell (WINNER)

Best Performance by a Leading Actress: Marin Mazzie

Best Performance by a Featured Actor: Michael Berresse

Best Performance by a Featured Actor: Michael Mulheren

Best Performance by a Featured Actor: Lee Wilkof

Best Scenic Design: Robin Wagner

Best Costume Design: Martin Pakledinaz (WINNER)

Best Lighting Design: Peter Kaczorowski

Best Choreography: Kathleen Marshall

Best Direction of a Musical: Michael Blakemore (WINNER)

Best Orchestrations: Don Sebesky (WINNER)

DRAMA DESK AWARDS

Best Revival of a Musical (WINNER)

Best Performance by a Leading Actor: Brian Stokes Mitchell (WINNER)

Best Scenic Design of a Musical: Robin Wagner (WINNER)

Best Costume Design: Martin Pakledinaz

Best Director of a Musical: Michael Blakemore (WINNER)

Best Orchestrations: Don Sebesky (WINNER)

Critical Scorecard

Rave	6
Favorable	3
Mixed	0
Unfavorable	1
Pan	0

same style as the old. (Unlike the 1999 revival of *Annie Get Your Gun*, which exchanged creaky old material for creaky new material, making the whole show look even more passé.) A word should also be said for the music department—Paul Gemignani, Don Sebesky, and David Chase—which tastefully redid the show as necessary without changing the colors of the original. The only severe change had to do with transforming Lilli's high-powered fiancé—a bigwig in the then-current Truman administration—into an overbearing general à la Douglas MacArthur. (Cast in the role was Ron Holgate, who played similarly memorable egotists in *A Funny Thing Happened on the Way to the Forum* and *1776*.) This allowed for some truly silly jokes and a quick-paced interpolation of "From This Moment On," a 1950 Porter tune that was similarly inserted in the motion picture version of *Kate*. Porter provided this song with a truly dim-witted interlude—the lovers address each other as "ducky wucky, poopsy woopsy"—which fit the originally intended use but has heretofore made it unstageable. Blakemore had Wilkof react to these endearments with such a withering gimlet-eyed glance that the song cascaded merrily on. The scene now ends with a shot at the NRA, with Holgate fuming on like Charlton Heston. "Guns don't kill people," he chants. "We do," chime the gangsters.

All in all, capital entertainment.

Kiss Me, Kate settled down to very good business, though never quite attaining sellout status. (This might have been due, in part, to the advertising logo, which called the show "The Big Event" and seemed geared to prizefight enthusiasts. They switched midwinter to some generic script that at least looked musical.) As the Tony Award period got under way, it became apparent that *Kate* was favored by many voters. I had always guessed that I had seen a relatively poor performance of the show back in November—I understand that the cast had its own little flu epidemic—so I decided to go back to the Beck on Memorial Day weekend. Mitchell played with even greater authority than before; Spanger—who was noticeably excluded from the Tony nominations, unlike five of her coplayers—remained technically proficient but cold; and Wilkof and Mulheren were just as delectable as ever. There was a world of difference, though, in the performance of Ms. Mazzie.

Two things can happen when a legit singer type is thrown onstage, scene after scene, with a bunch of hams. She either goes crying to her dressing room every

Part of the stumbling block has always been the not-so-well-written book, which is not quite up to the standards you'd expect from a "classic" show. John Guare agreed to revise the book (without billing) and did a very good and very unobtrusive job.

night, appalled at the demeaning treatment she is forced to undergo; or she picks up on the game and flings it all right back at 'em. Mazzie had heretofore given sturdy performances, in noncomedic roles, in shows like *Passion* and *Ragtime*. After six months with Mitchell, Holgate, Wilkof, and Mulheren, Mazzie had become a clown, and watch your back, boys.

This picked up *Kate* immeasurably, giving the show the B$_{12}$ shot it needed. Mazzie's was a Tony-caliber performance, at least it was by May. How many voters saw the show earlier, when they were first invited by the producers to attend, and didn't bother to go back to judge her again? Enough, presumably, to prevent her from beating out Heather Headley for the Tony.

A side note: The original 1948 production featured two dark-skinned performers, Annabelle Hill playing the leading lady's maid (who led the ensemble in the first-act opening and had little else to do) and Lorenzo Fuller playing the leading man's valet (who led the ensemble in the second-act opening and had little else to do). It was rather unsettling to find that the only two dark-skinned performers in the 1999 production were once again relegated to playing the maid and valet. Yes, there was a third African-American performer in the cast, and he was the star; but Mr. Mitchell's casting surely had nothing to do with race. He was simply the best actor they could find for the role. His skin pigment is so neutral that I suppose many theatregoers didn't give his color a moment's thought, which is as it should be. (Mitchell was considerably lighter, I believe, than Alfred Drake appeared to be when he starred in *Kismet*.)

Color is and should be inconsequential, and I don't believe we should even need to talk about such a thing in this day and age. But the only two people onstage who looked African-American were playing the same old stereotyped roles. When I returned to *Kiss Me, Kate* six months later, Mr. Mathis was out. The only dark-skinned person onstage with Ms. Lenox, I was distressed to find, was Mr. Mathis's understudy. It is hard to believe, and sad to contemplate, that this casting was merely coincidental.

Putting It Together

"Welcome to this celebration of the music of Andrew Lloyd Webber." (Laugh . . . laugh . . . laugh.) "He can't be here tonight, because he's having his bangs trimmed." (Laugh . . . laugh . . . laugh.) "And if there's a God, a shampoo." (Laugh . . . laugh . . . laugh.)

The advertisements for *Putting It Together* indicated you were in for a sophisticated evening of entertainment by Broadway's most intellectually stimulating songwriter. Not exactly. Jokes about Regis Philbin and Katie Couric? (Laugh . . . laugh . . . laugh.)

"Art isn't easy," goes the title song, and the producers of Sondheim's last several musicals certainly learned that "art isn't easy" to sell commercially. *Putting It Together* attempted to be Sondheim's art made easy, complete with jokes that even a tourist could understand. But that's not what they ended up with. Sondheim fans and sophisticated theatregoers might well have walked away from *Putting It Together* puzzled by the trivialization of Sondheim's work. Tourists and unsophisticated theatregoers no doubt walked away liking Carol Burnett but wondering what on earth those people were carrying on about.

Experience teaches us to avoid shows with character names beginning with the word "the."

Despite the overly broad gaggery, the creators carefully informed us that *Putting It Together* was not simply a mindless revue. Rather, it was a review, as in a re-viewing of the material. This was because Stephen Sondheim, we were told at the start, wanted his audience to think. "If you're put off by thinking, go see *Cats*." (Laugh . . . laugh . . . laugh.)

The Wife   Carol Burnett
The Husband   George Hearn
The Younger Man   John Barrowman
The Younger Woman   Ruthie Henshall
The Observer   Bronson Pinchot
The Wife, *at certain performances*
  Kathie Lee Gifford

ETHEL BARRYMORE THEATRE
Ⓢ A Shubert Organization Theatre
Gerald Schoenfeld, *Chairman*   Philip J. Smith, *President*

Robert E. Wankel, *Executive Vice President*

CAMERON MACKINTOSH
in association with
MARK TAPER FORUM
Gordon Davidson, Artistic Director
presents

CAROL   GEORGE
BURNETT   HEARN
JOHN   RUTHIE   BRONSON
BARROWMAN   HENSHALL   PINCHOT
At certain performances
KATHIE LEE GIFFORD
performs the role of The Wife
in

PUTTING IT TOGETHER
a musical review

Music & Lyrics by
STEPHEN SONDHEIM

Designed by   Lighting Designed by
BOB CROWLEY   HOWARD HARRISON

Orchestrations by   Sound Designed by   Projections Designed by
JONATHAN   ANDREW BRUCE/   WENDALL K.
TUNICK   MARK MENARD   HARRINGTON

Musical Director   Miss Burnett's Costume Designed by
PAUL RAIMAN   BOB MACKIE

Associate Director/Choreographer   Casting by
JODI MOCCIA   JOHNSON-LIFF ASSOCIATES

General Manager   Executive Producers
ALAN WASSER   DAVID CADDICK and MARTIN McCALLUM

Musical Staging by
BOB AVIAN

Directed by
ERIC D. SCHAEFFER

Original 1992 production devised by Stephen Sondheim and Julia McKenzie
and produced by Cameron Mackintosh at the Old Fire Station, Oxford, England.
Original 1993 New York City production by Cameron Mackintosh and The Manhattan Theater Club.
Los Angeles premiere October 25, 1998 at the Mark Taper Forum.
Piano provided by Steinway & Sons.

Thinking in the theatre is all to the good, and I don't suppose any Broadway composer has given audiences more to think about than Sondheim. But what we were presented with in *Putting It Together* seemed to be geared for nonthinking audiences. That is to say, it was a string of three dozen Sondheim songs tied together by a skeletally skimpy plot. More a situation than a plot, really. A rich, jaded, middle-aged, unhappy married couple—called "The Wife" (Ms. Burnett) and "The Husband" (George Hearn)—throw a big, fancy cocktail party. The guests for this big, fancy cocktail party are a young, attractive, and apparently unmarried unhappy couple, called "The Younger Man" (John Barrowman) and "The Younger Woman" (Ruthie Henshall). A big, fancy cocktail party with only two guests doesn't make much sense, but I guess you're not supposed to think about it. The only other character in the evening's entertainment filled in as a Barrymore theatre usher, a caterer, a maid in a frilly skirt, and more of the same. He was called "The Observer" (Bronson Pinchot). Experience teaches us to avoid shows with character names beginning with the word "the." . . .

Over the course of the evening, the characters sing and sing and sing Sondheim songs (five solos for Burnett, two for each of the others). Now, there are arguably no better theatre songs of the last thirty years than those by Mr. Sondheim. One of the several reasons for this is their specificity. A song written for *Company*, set in New York City in the late 1960s, simply won't fit into *A Little Night Music*, set in turn-of-the-century Sweden and filled with entrancingly inventive waltzes. The musical style is drastically different, and Sondheim's lyrics—unlike those of many of his peers—are meticulously tailored to the time, the place, and the characters.

And that, in an eggshell, is why *Putting It Together* couldn't be put back together again. One character was asked to sing songs from as many as eight different scores, in as many styles. The format of this type of revue—review, that is—calls for nonspecific, generalized characters. Most Sondheim songs are highly descriptive; word-packed, to fit the characters they were written for.

This is difficult enough to handle musically—in one stretch they went from *Night Music* to *Follies* to *Assassins* to *Merrily We Roll Along* and back to *Follies*, like a five-disc CD player stuck in shuffle mode. For example, consider "Unworthy of Your Love," a plaintive folk-guitar-type song written for a pair of presidential assassins in love with Jodie Foster and Charles Manson. This sounded mighty strange, let me tell you, when sung by the snazzily sophisticated Younger Man (in evening clothes) and Younger Woman (in sexy black dress) at this elegant cocktail party. But I guess you're not supposed to think about it.

If the shifting musical styles are jarring, the lyrics are worse (because the lyrics are better). The Wife and The Husband are pretty clearly derived from Phyllis and Ben Stone, the rich, jaded, middle-aged, unhappy couple in *Follies*. (This is, no doubt, why the three *Follies* songs they sing come off so well; the words fit the characters.) Elsewhere, though, The Husband uses The

Wolf's seduction song from *Into the Woods*, in which he talks of devouring "Grandmother first, then Miss Plump. . . . Think of that scrumptious carnality twice in one day." The Wife complains that The Husband "talks softly of his wars, and his horses and his whores," and you wonder—what horses? Where does he keep them? Double-parked on Park Avenue?

Sometime later, the ultrasophisticated, weary-of-it-all Wife sings that neurotic breakdown-to-music, "Getting Married Today" from the 1970 musical *Company*. (Sondheim single-handedly revolutionized musical theatre writing, as far as I'm concerned, when he had his young bride sing, "I telephoned my analyst about it / and he said to see him Monday / but by Monday I'll be floating / in the Hudson with the other garbage.") One singer in a revue can effectively sing "The Ladies Who Lunch" and "Getting Married Today" and "Could I Leave You?" and "My Husband the Pig," and even "Everybody Ought to Have a Maid"; but how could these words all emanate from one *character*? Even a sketchily written character. To quote Ms. Burnett at about ten minutes to ten, "I don't know who we are anymore, and I'm starting not to care."

The Younger Woman—I suppose they called Ms. Burnett "The Wife," because they certainly couldn't call her "The Older Woman"—anyway, she flounces into this lavish cocktail party in this skimpy black dress and sings that she's lovely. "Oh, isn't it a shame," she sings, "I can neither sew, nor cook, nor read or write my name." Who would possibly go into an Upper East Side cocktail party in the Internet age, in the twenty-first century already, and sing that she can't write her name? This character obviously knows how to sign credit card slips, that's for sure. I suppose the creators felt that audiences wouldn't be so damn literal about it all. But they told us at the outset that Mr. Sondheim wanted us to think.

> One character was asked to sing songs from as many as eight different scores, in as many styles. In one stretch they went from *Night Music* to *Follies* to *Assassins* to *Merrily We Roll Along* and back to *Follies*, like a five-disc CD player stuck in shuffle mode.

After Ms. Henshall—who was very good, by the way—sang her refrain of "Lovely," Ms. Burnett chimed in with a goony chorus, aping Ms. Henshall and comporting herself like a homesick princess pining for the swamps of home. (For those of you who want to think, this is an allusion to Ms. Burnett's star-making role in *Once upon a Mattress*.) As "Lovely" ended, Burnett was clearly ready to tear the eyes out of the sockets of this pretty young thing who was trying to steal her husband; Henshall just as clearly was holding up a highly unflattering mirror to the (much) older woman. This interaction occurred twenty-three minutes into the evening, and I thought—well, why doesn't The Younger Woman just go home, or out to a cigar club? And why doesn't Carol just throw the youngsters out of the house, kick off her shoes, and open a pint of Starbuck's mocha almond fudge? Nobody else showed up for her cocktail party, anyway. What could possibly keep these two onstage for another hour and a half, other than a Run-of-the-Play contract?

> We were in for nothing less than *Who's Afraid of Virginia Woolf?* The bitter older couple playing their devastating interpersonal games; the pretty young couple used as pawns; even talk about the offspring they never had.

We knew it was a cocktail party, by the by, because at one point The Observer said, "Back to the cocktail party."

The characters stayed onstage, though, and stayed and stayed. Six songs later I realized that we were in for nothing less than *Who's Afraid of Virginia Woolf?* (Or, more properly, "Who's Afraid of Stephen Sondheim?") It was all there. The bitter older couple playing their devastating interpersonal games; the pretty young couple used as pawns; even talk about the offspring they never had. ("Ah," The Husband says when The Wife brings it up. "The child!")

This sort of sketchy revue format—pardon me, review format—calls for simplistic song words. Do it with songs by Irving Berlin or Jule Styne or Jimmy Van Heusen and Sammy Cahn or even Jerry Leiber and Mike Stoller, and you might be able to pull it off; the love songs, the happy songs, the sad songs are pretty much interchangeable. This type of song bag revue calls for songs with words no deeper than Hallmark-card messages. Sondheim's are lyrically dense, jam-packed with specific information the songwriter doesn't want us to ignore. Except that in *Putting It Together*, the creators seemed to assume that we *would* ignore all those suddenly extraneous character details. Some lyrics had clearly been altered to fit the new plot, implying that the unabridged versions were meant to stand on their own.

The pity is, the Messrs. Mackintosh and Sondheim assembled a fine cast. Some of the songs, and some of the performances, were especially nice to hear, among them "Every Day a Little Death," "Pretty Women," "Country House," "Could I Leave You?", and "Good Thing Going." But the magic faded as soon as you remembered the story it was all meant to support. They might have been better off borrowing the concept of the earlier revue *Side by Side by Sondheim* (which originated with Cameron Mackintosh in 1976, helping launch his career). That show featured three singers on barstools, with a narrator contributing reasonably snappy patter, and worked far better than this second Sondheim revue review.

Putting It Together, incidentally, was initially devised by Mr. Sondheim and director Julia McKenzie (an original cast member of *Side by Side*). Mr. Mackintosh mounted the equivalent of a regional theatre workshop production in Oxford (U.K.) in 1992, starring Diana Rigg. It didn't work. They then mounted a full-scale off-Broadway production at Manhattan Theatre Club in 1993, starring Julie Andrews. This didn't work either. The third *Putting It Together* opened at the Mark Taper Forum in Los Angeles in 1998, starring Ms. Burnett (with Barrowman and Pinchot but not Hearn or Henshall) and a new director, Eric D. Schaeffer. It *still* didn't work. Rather than finally scrapping the cocktail party format, everyone persevered and arrived on Broadway with the very same problem as before. The pieces of *Putting It Together* were very much changed from 1992 to 1999, except that they stuck with the underlying framework, and they were stuck with it.

The show had several stretches of jokes, not written—I truly hope—by Mr. Sondheim. (His program billing was for music and lyrics, with no one else credited for book or libretto or sketches or additional special material.) Jokes about the fact that Ms. Burnett was playing only seven shows a week, with a TV personality signed up for Tuesday nights. "Carol, where are you?" The Observer said into his cell phone. "One hundred-nineteenth and what? Don't take any more shortcut tips from Kathie Lee Gifford." (Laugh . . . laugh . . . laugh.) Jokes, as mentioned earlier, about Regis and Kathie and Andrew Lloyd Webber's dandruff. (Laugh . . . laugh . . . laugh.) After a burst of canned laughter, The Observer complained, "That is *so-oo* Nederlander." Yes, it got a laugh; but what, I wonder, did it mean?

There is also the joke that opened up this thinking person's show: "If you're put off by thinking, go see *Cats*." Many Broadway insiders readily confess to hating *Cats*; but *Putting It Together* bears the personal stamp of Cameron Mackintosh. The new review would never have reached Broadway without the stubborn determination of Mackintosh, who earned worldwide fame and fortune from this same *Cats*. Could it be that Mackintosh, too, thinks that *Cats* is so bad that it merits such a surefire laugh? Or are we thinking much too much here?

Putting It Together
Opened: November 21, 1999
Closed: February 20, 2000
101 performances (and 22 previews)
Profit/Loss: Loss
Putting It Together ($80 top) was scaled to a potential gross
of $557,560 at the 1,096-seat Ethel Barrymore. Weekly
grosses averaged about $349,000, dropping beneath
$400,000 three weeks after the opening and skidding as
low as $225,000. (These figures reflect the fact that the
show played many seven-performance weeks.) Total gross
for the run was $5,371,370. Attendance was about 69
percent, with the box office grossing about 63 percent of
potential dollar-capacity.

TONY AWARD NOMINATION
Best Performance by a Leading Actor: George Hearn

*Critical
Scorecard*

Rave 0
Favorable 2
Mixed 0
Unfavorable 3
Pan 5

Far be it from me to guess what Mr. Sondheim's thoughts and intentions might have been, but I can't imagine him standing in the back aisle of the Barrymore watching *Putting It Together* and saying, yes, that's it, that's precisely the way I want these songs to be remembered. Not to worry: Sondheim's songs have had, and will continue to have, a longer and more productive life than this *Putting It Together*, which expired unmourned and unlamented after thirteen weeks.

Marie Christine

Consider this: an unpalatable new musical—decidedly not musical comedy—from some of the theatre's top talents, with a provocative theme; a pessimistic outlook; unconventional music (at least by Broadway standards); strikingly modern staging and scenery; and a bunch of characters so unappetizingly drawn that you wouldn't especially want to go to dinner with them. A recipe for exciting, groundbreaking musical theatre that will shake up the form and convert the pagan nonbelievers? Or is it a recipe for disaster? The show I am describing, obviously, is Michael John LaChiusa and Graciela Daniele's *Marie Christine*. But no; I am speaking of Jason Robert Brown and Harold Prince's *Parade*. Well, actually not; I was referring to Stephen Sondheim and Prince's *Merrily We Roll Along*, or perhaps Sondheim and Prince's *Pacific Overtures*. Although if truth be told, I was really, truly, actually talking about Sondheim, Prince, and Michael Bennett's *Follies*.

The description fits all the above. All were controversial. Most received praise in some quarters, and a bunch of awards as well. All had small pockets of discerning fans who considered them brilliant, while many patrons couldn't wait to get out of the theatre into the fresh night air. And all have found—or in the case of the two newer shows, might find—legions of converts, thanks to the power of their cast albums. While I'm quite aware that artistic success and commercial success are all too often wildly divergent, all five of these costly shows closed in the face of audience apathy with severe financial losses.

The thing is, all were well worth seeing, all of them important, and all of them have helped—or might help—alter the course of musical theatre. Failures, yes, and no doubt discouraging for the creators. But I, for one, am certainly glad that Mr. Sondheim wrote *Follies*, and that Mr. Brown wrote *Parade*, and that I can put *Marie Christine* on the CD player whenever I feel like it and sink back and listen.

Marie Christine was conceived and written specifically for the talents of Audra McDonald. Now, Ms. McDonald is a one-of-a-kind talent in our musical theatre, as she can sing authoritatively in just about any style—classic or modern, opera or jazz. And she can act, too. If anybody could pull off *Marie Christine*, it would have to be her. Would any writer come up with such an idea—a Creole *Medea*—unless he had Ms. McDonald to sing it? (Imagine a producer walking in with this show and asking some hapless casting director to find an actress for it, and she has to be a ticket-selling star so they can raise the money.) Even with McDonald, *Marie Christine* was a tough sell, and I don't know that anyone other than Lincoln Center Theater would have gotten it on. The producing philosophy of Lincoln Center's André Bishop and Bernie Gersten seems to have always been that they will

do it if they believe in it, and hope for the best. They are dedicated to certain artists, including LaChiusa and Daniele, and their policy seems to be to provide artists with facilities and funding and turn them loose. Many a time you turn up something like *Marie Christine* or *Parade* or Billy Finn's *A New Brain*, none of which succeeded but all of which were admirable attempts. Once in a while, though, you wind up with something like Susan Stroman and John Weidman's *Contact*, which makes the whole development program worthwhile—and which has the financial potential to wipe out any deficits encountered along the way.

It is interesting to note that even before *Marie Christine* opened, Lincoln Center Theater had effectively posted its closing notice by announcing the transfer of *Contact* to the Vivian Beaumont. Which is to say, they seem to have known early on what they had in *Marie Christine*.

Cast (in order of appearance)

Prisoner No. 1 Jennifer Leigh Warren
Prisoner No. 2 Andrea Frierson-Toney
Prisoner No. 3 Mary Bond Davis
Marie Christine L'Adrese Audra McDonald
Marie *At Wednesday and Saturday matinees* Sherry Boone
Marie Christine's Mother Vivian Reed
Serpent Donna Dunmire
Dante Keyes Anthony Crivello
Celeste, a maid Lovette George
Ozelia, a maid Rosena M. Hill
Jean L'Adrese Keith Lee Grant
Paris L'Adrese Darius de Haas

Lisette, Marie Christine's maid Kimberly Jajuan
Joachim, a valet André Garner
Osmond, a valet Jim Weaver
Monsieur St. Vinson Jim Weaver
Monsieur Archambeau André Garner
Beatrice, Jean's fiancee Joy Lynn Matthews
Children Powers Pleasant, Zachary Thornton, Joshua Walter
Magdalena Mary Testa
Petal, Magdalena's "daughter" Janet Metz
Duchess, Magdalena's "daughter" Kim Huber
Gates Shawn Elliott
Bartender Peter Samuel
Bar Patron Michael Babin
Leary Michael McCormick
McMahon Mark Lotito
Esau Parker Peter Samuel
Olivia Parker Janet Metz
Grace Parker Kim Huber
Helena, Gates' daughter Donna Dunmire
Chaka (drums) David Pleasant
Ensemble: Franz C. Alderfer, Ana Maria Andricain, Michael Babin, Brent Black, Donna Dunmire, André Garner, Lovette George, Rosena M. Hill, Kim Huber, Mark Lotito, Joy Lynn Matthews, Michael McCormick, Janet Metz, Monique Midgette, Peter Samuel, Jim Weaver

Time moves from present to past, or to future.

Time: 1894–1899
Place: A prison, New Orleans and Chicago

Original Broadway Cast Album:
RCA Victor 09026-63593

LINCOLN CENTER THEATER AT THE VIVIAN BEAUMONT

under the direction of André Bishop and Bernard Gersten

presents

MARIE CHRISTINE
A NEW MUSICAL

words and music by
Michael John LaChiusa

with (in alphabetical order)

Franz C. Alderfer Ana Maria Andricain Michael Babin Brent Black
Sherry Boone Anthony Crivello Mary Bond Davis Darius de Haas
Donna Dunmire Shawn Elliott Andrea Frierson-Toney André Garner
Lovette George Keith Lee Grant Rosena M. Hill Kim Huber
Kimberly Jajuan Mark Lotito Joy Lynn Matthews Michael McCormick
Audra McDonald Janet Metz Monique Midgette Powers Pleasant
Vivian Reed Peter Samuel Mary Testa Zachary Thornton
Joshua Walter Jennifer Leigh Warren Jim Weaver

sets	costumes	lighting
Christopher Barreca	Toni-Leslie James	Jules Fisher & Peggy Eisenhauer

orchestrations	musical director	sound	casting
Jonathan Tunick	David Evans	Scott Stauffer	Alan Filderman

stage manager	associate choreographer	fight director	musical theater associate producer
Arturo E. Porazzi	Willie Rosario	Luis Perez	Ira Weitzman

general manager	production manager	director of marketing & special projects	director of development
Steven C. Callahan	Jeff Hamlin	Thomas Cott	Hattie K. Jutagir

directed and choreographed by
Graciela Daniele

Sponsored by AT&T: OnStage

MARIE CHRISTINE is supported by a generous grant from The Gilman and Gonzalez-Folla Theatre Foundation for new musical works at Lincoln Center Theater.

The Fan Fox and Leslie R. Samuels Foundation has provided a generous grant for MARIE CHRISTINE.

Thanks to the Jacob Burns Foundation for its support of MARIE CHRISTINE's costume design.

Lincoln Center Theater gratefully acknowledges extraordinary support from The Lila Acheson and DeWitt Wallace Fund for Lincoln Center, established by the founders of The Reader's Digest Association.

MARIE CHRISTINE is made possible with public funds from the National Endowment for the Arts, the New York State Council on the Arts, and the New York City Department of Cultural Affairs.

American Airlines is the official airline of Lincoln Center Theater.
Kendall-Jackson is the preferred winery of Lincoln Center Theater.

Lincoln Center Theater thanks the Theatre Development Fund for its support of this production.

A workshop of MARIE CHRISTINE was produced by Graciela Daniele and Jules Fisher.

Had it somehow turned into a hit, they would have found a way to accommodate both shows—even with a spring booking jam, one of the big
theatre owners would surely have made room for a preordained box office
bonanza like *Contact*. As it is, Lincoln Center left room for *Marie Christine* to extend—but for four weeks only. Ultimately, no extension was
warranted, and the show closed as originally scheduled.

Sitting onstage, as the audience filed in, was a dark, dank dungeon
taking up the center of the Beaumont's thrust stage, with the orchestra
hidden behind the sides of the proscenium. Where had we seen that before?? It was hard not to immediately think of *Man of La Mancha*, which
opened at the same theatre in
1965. Not the same theatre, exactly: at the ANTA Washington
Square, a similarly designed, tem-

**Would any writer come up with such an
idea—a Creole *Medea*—unless he had
Audra McDonald to sing it?**

porary theatre that housed the Repertory Theater of Lincoln Center company while its permanent home—now the Vivian Beaumont—was
being built.

La Mancha vacated the ANTA Washington Square when it was de-
molished, wandering through three other Broadway theatres during its
five-year run. A year after closing, the original stars reunited for a special
four-month summer run—at the Beaumont. Both *La Mancha* and *Marie
Christine*, as noted, started in a dank dungeon. The *Don Quixote*-
derived musical soared to the heights, leaving its audience enthralled
at the nobility of the human spirit. The *Medea*-derived musical remained leaden, leaving its audience desolate.

Marie Christine opened with some startlingly effective stage pictures,
thanks to lighting designers Jules Fisher and Peggy Eisenhauer, but
quickly settled into malaise. By my reckoning, there was but one lively
number early on, "Way Back to Paradise," which didn't exactly fit the
story. Following this, there was no excitement whatsoever until about
forty-five minutes into the first act. Suddenly, a drummer (David Pleasant) appeared in a cage high against the stage wall and sparked the show
into life with a number called "Bird Inside the House." *Marie Christine*
became suddenly alive—relatively, at least—with a series of fascinating songs. Next came "We're Gonna Go to Chicago," a fine, lazy-but-
dangerous duet that seemed somewhat derived from "There's a Boat Dat's
Leavin' Soon for New York." (Much of Michael John LaChiusa's work in
Marie Christine seemed inspired by George Gershwin and Marc Blitzstein.
Not that there's anything wrong with this; Blitzstein and Gershwin were

primary influences of Leonard Bernstein.) Then came the first-act finale, a wedding party/fratricide scene with all sorts of interesting writing going on. The second act was a parade of impressive writing, opening with a raggy "Cincinnati" and the well-conceived "You're Looking at the Man." There were more than a few further first-rate sequences, especially "Paradise Is Burning Down" and the menacing "Good Looking Woman." This last called to mind, more or less, both the "Taunting Scene" of *West Side Story*—when Anita goes to the drugstore to deliver Maria's message but is attacked by the boys—and "The Abduction" in *Man of La Mancha*, when Aldonza goes to the inn to deliver Quixote's message but is attacked by the boys. Marie then had a strong solo in the "And I Am Telling You I'm Not Going" vein, called "I Will Love You." While LaChiusa used recognizable song models, his writing was more than strong enough to speak for itself.

So what was the problem with *Marie Christine*, which I found one of the least enjoyable musicals in years? Knowing the perceptive integrity of Bishop, Gersten, and associate producer Ira Weitzman, I had to assume that there was some great worth hidden away within the piece, something all too transparent from my seat in the eighth row. Listening after the fact to the cast album, which wasn't released until mid-April, it became clear that the material prior to "Bird in the House" was in most cases artfully written. But it sure didn't appear so in the theatre. I suppose some of the trouble had to do with scale. *Marie Christine* had a large cast of about thirty, with plenty going on in the final hour; but most of the first act was taken up with the meeting, courtship, and romance of Marie and the Chicago-born ne'er-do-well Dante Keyes.

> The producing philosophy of Lincoln Center Theater seems to be that they will do it if they believe in it and hope for the best. Many a time you turn up something like *Marie Christine* or *Parade* or *A New Brain*; once in a while you wind up with *Contact*.

Therein lies the flaw of the piece, at least as presented at the Vivian Beaumont. The pair came across as the dullest, most uninteresting and disinterested couple imaginable; they displayed all the emotional intensity of a Park Avenue matron and the boy who delivers the dry cleaning, leaving it with the doorman. Whether this was the fault of the composer, the librettist, the director, the set designer (who placed the whole show in what seemed to be a dismal dungeon of darkness), the actors, or even the casting director, I can't tell you; but I could perceive no passion whatsoever radiating from Ms. McDonald and Anthony Crivello. There was also, early on, a terribly artsy and laughably off-putting interlude featuring a girl dressed as a ruby-sequined snake. By the time *Marie Christine* picked up with the "Bird" scene, most of the audience had been blunted into terminal drowsiness.

But LaChiusa also faced a graver problem, which might have been insurmountable: Medea herself. The old girl still does well in context, after 2,430 or so seasons; but she has a somewhat harsh personality by today's standards. Yes, I know that there have been modern-day murderous mothers—Susan Smith immediately comes to mind—but they were less regal and more trailer park. *Medea* proved difficult to translate into modern times. (For a play written in 431 B.C., 1899 is modern times.) Knowing that Marie was intended to be a modern Medea, it was impossible not to see LaChiusa moving the wheels of his plot. He was boxed in by the Greeks; where Medea got to be too much for Marie, he was nevertheless forced to go along in false directions he might not otherwise have chosen. The overall result, I'm afraid, was not what Euripides had in mind. The discovery of the murdered children was met with some guffaws the night I was there—not many, just two or three. But that was the only emotional reaction I noted, other than the horror-struck gasping of the actors.

The authors of *West Side Story* changed the end of *Romeo and Juliet,* to avoid overdoing it. (According to Jerry Robbins, Richard Rodgers convinced them not to kill off Maria, explaining "she's dead already, after this all happens to her.") Of course, it would have been more problematic to take the murder out of *Medea*.

There was a certain amount of conjecture in the press as to whether *Marie Christine* was theatre or opera. LaChiusa addressed this in a Sunday *Times* think piece: "When people ask: 'Is it an opera?' I'm inclined to say, 'Does it matter? Were you entertained?'" The answer, as it happened, was a resounding "no." *Marie Christine* was, perhaps, the least entertaining musical of the season. (Until the bloody-but-unbowed LaChiusa returned with his *Wild Party*, that is.) Certainly, it received the very worst reviews of any musical other than *Saturday Night Fever* and *Jesus Christ Superstar*, which—considering the artistic earnestness of *Marie Christine* and the generally kind treatment the show got from the press—is rather astounding to contemplate. Not so many years from now, no doubt, we will be hearing that *Marie Christine* was a brilliant musical, ahead of its time. Maybe so; but in its time is when it was produced, and it made for an excessively mirthless evening, one that even Ms. McDonald's presence couldn't enhance. To go back to Mr. LaChiusa: "A musical, or opera, or play does have the fundamental responsibility to entertain." And that, in the author's own words, might well serve as the epitaph for *Marie Christine*.

> **Marie and Dante came across as the dullest, most uninteresting and disinterested couple imaginable; they displayed all the emotional intensity of a Park Avenue matron and the boy who delivers the dry cleaning, leaving it with the doorman.**

Minnelli on Minnelli

The question in cases of this kind, I suppose, is does one encourage something that is not half bad? Or does one regret that it is only half good?

Liza Minnelli has had her ups and she's had her downs, and done so again and again to the point where I don't suppose anyone could say, at any given moment, in which direction she's heading. It's no wonder, perhaps. She was born with an exceptional singing voice, clearly related to but distinctive from that of her mother. Her mother, one of the most famous performers of her time, began a self-destructive slide when Minnelli was about three. Liza saw Judy go through broken marriages; numerous career crises; devastating addictions and binges; suicide attempts; and who knows what else. Mom finally died at the age of forty-seven, when Minnelli was twenty-three and still a few years shy of superstardom. Minnelli has mirrored her mother's life in such a way that it can be seen as a distinct victory that she has made it past her fifty-third birthday. "Gin and rum and destiny play funny tricks," family friend Ira Gershwin wrote back in 1941 about a fictional gal called Jenny, but that in some ways pretty much describes the fate of both Judy and Liza.

Minnelli on Minnelli was not about life with mother (although Liza is fated never to escape the ghost of Judy Garland), but rather life with father. A father who was divorced when Liza was five; who was highly successful until Hollywood passed him by when Liza was entering her teens; and who spent the remaining twenty-five years of his life underemployed and unproductive.

For her latest—and final?—comeback, Liza chose to fashion an entertainment around the songs from the movie musicals of her father. Vin-

Liza Minnelli

&

Jeffrey Broadhurst
Stephen Campanella
Billy Hartung
Sebastian LaCause
Jim Newman
Alec Timerman

Original Broadway Cast Album:
Angel 24905

≥N≤ **PALACE THEATRE**
OWNED AND OPERATED BY STEWART F. LANE
AND THE MESSRS. NEDERLANDER

RADIO CITY ENTERTAINMENT, LM CONCERTS, SCOTT NEDERLANDER
and STEWART F. LANE
present

Liza Minnelli

in

Minnelli
on Minnelli

Songs from
the movies of Vincente Minnelli

with
Jeffrey Broadhurst, Stephen Campanella, Billy Hartung,
Sebastian LaCause, Jim Newman, Alec Timerman

Scenery by **John Arnone**	*Costumes by* **Bob Mackie**	*Lighting by* **Howell Binkley**
Sound by **Peter J. Fitzgerald**	*Projections by* **Batwin+Robin**	*Film Sequence Prepared by* **Jack Haley Jr.**
Musical Arrangements and Supervision by **Billy Stritch and Marvin Hamlisch**		*Vocal Arranger* **Billy Stritch**
Dance Music Arrangements **David Krane and Peter Howard**		*Music Contractor* **Russ Kassoff**
Casting **Jay Binder**	*Production Stage Manager* **Karl Lengel**	*Technical Supervisor* **Neil Mazzella**
General Managment **101 Productions, Ltd.**		*Press Representative* **Barlow·Hartman public relations**
Executive Producers **Gary Labriola and Edward J. Micone Jr.**		*Musical Director* **Bill LaVorgna**

Choreographer
John DeLuca

Written and Directed by
Fred Ebb

---

cente Minnelli was not a songwriter, though, nor was he a man of music. He was, rather, a stage designer with such a remarkable gift for color and composition that he forged a successful career as a director of movie musicals, often with scores compiled from old song hits. Thus, the songs selected for *Minnelli on Minnelli* had little to do with Vincente Minnelli's talent. They were there because someone in the MGM music department once deemed that they be used.

The last time I saw Liza was in the spring of 1998, at a rehearsal hall run-through of a new musical. She was seated directly in front of me and was quite a spectacle. She didn't even look like herself. The makeup painted on her face gave it away, but the face itself was bloated almost past recognition. And she seemed unable to walk; all coordination was gone, and you were afraid she might keel over right there. (I learned, as I was writing this, that she had left her hospital bed that afternoon—at no small effort—to attend.)

Which puts the observer in something of a quandary. Do you cheer Liza on, simply for walking across the stage in a straight line without tumbling into the orchestra pit? Or do you judge her like you would an unknown housewife from Altoona, storming Broadway in a vanity production with money from some rich husband? Does she get extra points because she is a recovering alcoholic, addict, or whatever her combination of ills might have been? Or do you just judge her by her performance, as you would anyone else?

After a short musical introduction, the curtain parted to reveal a pair of scenic columns upstage center, which parted to reveal the new Liza. The distinctively oval face was now round; the body was round, too, and disconcertingly awkward. The eyes, though, were unmistakably Minnelli. They no longer glimmered like wide pools, no doubt due to the rounder shape of her face. I wondered and wondered where I had seen that oddly bloated face before, and then it finally hit me—in those frightening photographs from Judy Garland's "fat" periods.

Liza started with an old standard called "If I Had You." She sang it okay, although a severe lisp was in evidence and she looked like a stuffed Kewpie doll. She then went into a medley of songs from *Cabin in the Sky*, doing an adequate job although missing some notes and garbling a few words.

Then came some cheap comedy business, in which a muscle-bound fellow in an undershirt entered with a glass of water for the star. She looked at him thirstily and drank and drank. She tossed her handkerchief on the floor and ogled him as he bent over to pick it up. This not-so-subtle pantomime was repeated again in the second act. So much for taste, a Vincente Minnelli hallmark.

The star then sang a highly energetic rendition of "Love," a

Do you cheer Liza on, simply for walking across the stage in a straight line without tumbling into the orchestra pit? Or do you judge her like you would an unknown housewife from Altoona, storming Broadway in a vanity production with money from some rich husband?

nifty song Hugh Martin wrote for Lena Horne in the film version of *The Ziegfeld Follies*. Liza had been rather tentative in her opening numbers, but she really sang the hell out of this one. There was also quite a performance by the pit drummer, who was prominently placed in the conductor's normal spot. Turns out that he was the conductor as well, leading one to wonder who was leading the band when he was carried away with his bongos. I guess that's the way they do things in Las Vegas.

Liza then went to her dressing room, and the dancing boys—five of them, although the program listed six—came out dressed as fifties Hollywood beatniks. Black pants, dark gray shirts with darker black stripes, black shoes, and white socks. Very Gene Kelly. One of them wore a rak-ish black eyepatch, one carried a cigarette, another had a pocket watch he swung around on a chain like he was a hypnotist in a Salvador Dali–inspired nightmare ballet. They sang what turned out to be "Limehouse Blues," although I couldn't recognize the tune until halfway through. They danced like a bunch of Bob Fosse dancers who'd never actually worked with Fosse or met anyone who had.

Liza was soon back, singing "Under the Bamboo Tree," a 1902 "coon" song that was surely performed on the Palace stage in olden vaudeville days but seemed way out of place on Broadway in the twenty-first century. She then went into Hugh Martin's "The Boy Next Door," from *Meet Me in St. Louis,* in a so-so rendition that did not threaten memories of her mother. Liza went back to her dressing room, and on came the boys, and your heart sank. Whenever Liza needed a rest, these apparently talentless boys were going to dash out and give us something you might have seen on the old *Kraft Music Hall* TV show.

They tried to sing "That's Entertainment," doing their dangdest to ham it up but coming off cheesy. Very cheesy. (This is the song with Howard Dietz's lyric about "The clown with his pants falling down," each line acted out laboriously.) Liza came on to do "I Guess I'll Have to Change My Plan" with one of the boys, and she danced around with him in such a way that her top continually threatened to fall out of her top. She went back to her dressing room, and the rest of the boys came back to attempt "By Myself," in fedoras. They seemed to have each choreographed their own steps by remembering old Gene Kelly movies, working with each other in a rehearsal hall without mirrors.

> As the applause began and she cut off the final note, there was a wonderful moment: Liza flashed such a satisfied smile, as if to say "I made it, I actually made it," as if she'd just given confession and received absolution.

The nadir came with "Dancing in the Dark," Arthur Schwartz and Howard Dietz's stunningly evocative love song, performed by three boys with six flashlights. The act ended with "A Shine on Your Shoes," with Liza sitting in a chair on wheels and the boys rolling her around like a shopping cart full of watermelon. When late in the number she got up and went into her dance, you suddenly realized that maybe that shopping cart wasn't such a bad idea after all.

The intermission lasted an unprecedented twenty-two minutes, presumably to give the star a rest, although *Minnelli on Minnelli* surely had the longest men's room lines on Broadway since—well, since Judy Garland played the Palace in 1967.

The second act began with the boys singing a medley. Liza then reappeared, but not to sing. Rather, she presented us with a slide show of baby pictures. Next came a film clip of Gene Kelly and Leslie Caron doing the ballet from *An American in Paris*. Better they should have shown clips from *The Bandwagon*, instead of trying to sing the songs. Finally Liza sang again—a full *thirty-six* minutes since she'd last used the old pipes. The song was "I Got Rhythm," and it was Liza's first exciting moment of the evening. The uncredited orchestration was very good, by the way, with various Gershwin themes interwoven.

They worked their way around to *Gigi*, at which point Liza sang a parody lyric written by her special material man and director, Fred Ebb. "I'm Glad I'm Not Young Anymore" was the song, with Liza poking jabs at her former life. (Jokes about Studio 54; being fat; her friends in AA; and the

neatly turned couplet "I don't even flinch each time I see / Some seven-foot drag queen dressed like me.") As the applause began and she cut off the final note, there was a wonderful moment; the evening's only one, I'm afraid. Liza flashed such a satisfied smile, as if to say, "I made it, I actually made it," as if she'd just given confession and received absolution. So much so that it was hard not to admire her guts and determination. For the moment, anyway.

No sooner had Liza brightened the evening than the pall returned. The boys sang "Come Back to Me," each in their own little spotlight, and we were back at the *Bell Telephone Hour*. This number was notable for a little tushy-twist dance step the boys did, not once but three times.

Minnelli on Minnelli
Opened: December 8, 1999
Closed: January 1, 2000
20 performances (and 5 previews)
Profit/Loss: Loss
Minnelli on Minnelli ($125 top) was scaled to a potential
  gross of $782,622 at the 1,743-seat Palace for the
  scheduled five-performance week. Grosses for the first four
  weeks averaged $480,000, with a $630,000 gross on its
  final, holiday week when it played six performances (at a
  potential of $939,147). Total gross for the run was
  $2,549,836. Attendance was about 67 percent, with the
  box office grossing about 65 percent of potential dollar-
  capacity.

Critical
Scorecard

Rave 1
Favorable 1
Mixed 0
Unfavorable 3
Pan 3

At 10:14 Liza returned from her dressing room in a red sequined dress, looking like a pregnant hippy, and first said the word "Judy." She then went into "The Trolley Song" with her five boys, accompanied by Judy Garland—in full color, on no less than seven movie screens strung around the stage. The seven Judys, needless to say, were more riveting than the one Liza.

After a section of film clips from Vincente Minnelli films—some of which were so melodramatic and old-fashioned as to draw audible guffaws from the audience—Liza came out for her curtain call wearing what looked like a black velvet potato sack. Then came an encore, a new Fred Ebb and John Kander song honoring Vincente entitled "I Thank You." ("You gave me my strength / You gave me my hope / You gave me my smile / I thank you.") And then it was time to go home.

Audiences were there to see one thing, and one thing only: Liza Minnelli's hopefully triumphant return to the Palace, to hear Liza sing again. What they got was a 113-minute show (excluding the overlong intermission). This included 21 minutes' worth of film clips and slides. By my rough calculations, Liza sang a mere 49 minutes, which is pretty skimpy for what was basically meant to be a one-woman show. A strong opening act followed by an hour of Liza might be suitable for a concert; but we were not provided with a strong opening act. Rather, the show was interspersed with hapless chorus boys doing inane choreography. (It is my understanding that they were initially intended to simply back up Liza. As it became apparent in rehearsals that Liza's stamina was limited, the boys' chores were necessarily expanded—at the audience's expense.)

So this Minnelli lite lineup might not have been what the producers originally intended, but it is what they presented to audiences. And there's another issue to consider. *Minnelli on Minnelli* came in with an earthshaking $125 top; this for not only the orchestra section but also ten rows of the mezzanine. (Broadway's hottest ticket at the time, *The Lion King*, charged "only" $80.) Now, I'm sure that the producers could give us a lot of reasons for why they had to charge $125 a seat: It was a limited run, only five performances a week, all those sequins, and so on. But to charge $125 for what turned out to be 49 minutes of Minnelli, padded with painfully poor filler? You might just as well have stayed home and watched *Who Wants to Be a Millionaire?*

Is it fair to take all this into account when judging Liza's latest (last?) comeback? Should she be blamed for her lack of stamina, the high ticket price, and the low talent quotient? Maybe not. But Liza was her own producer here, under the name LM Concerts. What do you call a performer who professes to love and care for her fans but gives them a substandard show—at the performance I saw she acknowledged several times that she couldn't remember her lines or lyrics, although this was probably a scripted ploy for sympathy—and consciously gouges said fans for 125 bucks a seat?

> What do you call a performer who professes to love and care for her fans but gives them a substandard show— at the performance I saw she acknowledged that she couldn't remember her lines or lyrics—yet consciously (as producer) gouges said fans for 125 bucks a seat?

Under these circumstances, half a show that was only half good didn't seem enough except for the star's most loyal fans. *Minnelli on Minnelli* had big plans to transfer to the Gershwin Theatre for five weeks after the run at the Palace—one can only imagine what a $125 top would bring at Broadway's largest theatre—but the bad reviews and merely adequate business squelched it.

A ten-month road tour began March 9 in San Francisco. Six weeks later, Minnelli was back in the hospital and the whole thing scrubbed. As Ira Gershwin—best man at Judy and Vincente's wedding—wrote, "Gin and rum and destiny play funny tricks."

Swing!

A diminutive man with a ukulele, a small mustache, and a purple and blue pinstripe suit stepped downstage to the apron of the St. James, moving into a pool of light.

"What good is music?" he sang. "What good is melody, if it ain't got something sweet?" The lights came up on a bandstand lined with strips of chrome and neon, and a truly swinging band went into Duke Ellington's "It Don't Mean a Thing (If It Ain't Got That Swing)." Now, we have heard this song before on Broadway, in just about every anthology revue that has come along recently (except Sondheim's *Putting It Together*). It was hard, therefore, not to notice right off the bat that it sounded fresh and original and exciting. As the band continued, a dancing couple skittered on to do a short specialty; then another couple, then another. They were all dressed in whites and creams and beiges and coffees, all swinging their partners around the stage, and they all looked like they were enjoying themselves. Not stage smiles, the kind of thing the director gives notes about

The ensemble had all the energy and style that was missing from the dance revue across the street, *Fosse.*

every night during previews; they actually looked like they were having fun. After this extended opening number (which included four or five swing tunes), a tall, classy singer named Ann Hampton Callaway slipped out and sang "Bounce Me Brother (With a Solid Four)," a duet with the trumpet player. Fair enough.

Then the bandleader fellow from the opening number—whose name was Casey MacGill and who turned out to be as much a star of the evening as the three top-billed singers—was accosted by a frumpy-looking girl (a secretary, 1940s-style) in a frumpy blue dress. She explained her plight to him, in music, snapping her fingers on the beat; he responded that she's got to snap *off* the beat, on two and four (to a song written by the aforementioned Ms. Callaway). After MacGill rolled his eyes for a refrain or two, the frump caught on; in a flash, her dress flipped into a stylish gown—the first of two jaw-dropping onstage costume transformations from designer William Ivey Long—and the gal in blue turned out to be costar Laura Benanti, who prevailed upon us to "Hit Me with a Hot Note and Watch Me Bounce." As soon as Benanti went into high gear, I gave *Swing!* the benefit of the doubt and sat back and thoroughly enjoyed myself.

I quickly observed that the ensemble had all the energy and style that was missing from the dance revue across the street, *Fosse. Swing!* also brought to mind two other "dance" musicals, *Footloose* and *Saturday Night Fever.* The dances in the others all seemed forced and contrived, the participants trying to pretend that they were spontaneously igniting. No need to pretend at *Swing!*; that exclamation point said it all.

Then on came another new face, the third of the show's three stars, a tall, gangly, and totally unknown fellow named Everett Bradley, with three gold hoops in his ears. He launched into a production number called "Throw That Girl Around," in which he sang, danced, and played a variety of percussion instruments as if he were in *Stomp* (which is where he came from). He was also coauthor of the song. The number led into a pair of rather dazzling dance specialties, with two couples in mortal combat while Mr. Bradley beat out dat rhythm on de drum (to borrow a song title from Oscar Hammerstein). Bradley had no sooner finished this rather extended number than he launched into the next with Ms. Callaway, a nonsense song called "Bli-Blip," (also composed by Mr. Ellington,

Ann Hampton Callaway
Everett Bradley
Laura Benanti
Casey MacGill
Michael Gruber

&

Laureen Baldovi
Kristine Bendul
Carol Bentley
Caitlin Carter
Geralyn Del Corso
Desirée Duarte
Beverly Durand
Erin East
Scott Fowler
Ryan Francois
Kevin Michael Gaudin
Edgar Godineaux
Aldrin Gonzalez
Janine LaManna
Rod McCune
J. C. Montgomery
Arte Phillips
Robert Royston
Carlos Sierra-López
Jenny Thomas
Keith Lamelle Thomas
Maria Torres
& The Gotham City Gates

Original Broadway Cast Album:
Sony Classical SK 89122

ST. JAMES THEATRE

A JUJAMCYN THEATRE

JAMES H. BINGER
CHAIRMAN

ROCCO LANDESMAN
PRESIDENT

PAUL LIBIN
PRODUCING DIRECTOR

JACK VIERTEL
CREATIVE DIRECTOR

Marc Routh   Richard Frankel   Steven Baruch   Tom Viertel   Lorie Cowen Levy/Stanley Shopkorn
Jujamcyn Theaters in association with BB Promotion   Dede Harris/Jeslo Productions
Libby Adler Mages/Mari Glick   Douglas L. Meyer/James D. Stern and PACE Theatrical Group/SFX

present

Featuring

Ann Hampton Callaway   Everett Bradley   Laura Benanti

Laureen Baldovi   Kristine Bendul   Carol Bentley   Caitlin Carter
Geralyn Del Corso   Desirée Duarte   Beverly Durand   Erin East   Scott Fowler   Ryan Francois
Kevin Michael Gaudin   Edgar Godineaux   Aldrin Gonzalez   Janine LaManna
Rod McCune   J. C. Montgomery   Arte Phillips   Robert Royston   Carlos Sierra-López
Jenny Thomas   Keith Lamelle Thomas   Maria Torres

with

Casey MacGill and The Gotham City Gates

and

Michael Gruber

Scenic Design
Thomas Lynch

Costume Design
William Ivey Long

Lighting Design
Kenneth Posner

Sound Design
Peter Fitzgerald

Original Concept by
Paul Kelly

Aerial Flying
ANTIGRAVITY, Inc.

Casting
Carol Hanzel & Associates

Orchestrations
Harold Wheeler

Music Supervisor
Michael Rafter

Music Direction
Jonathan Smith

Music Coordinator
John Miller

Production Manager
Peter Fulbright

Production Stage Manager
Karen Armstrong

General Management
**Richard Frankel Productions
Joe Watson**

Press Representative
Helene Davis

Associate Producers
TV Asahi/Hankyu   MARS Theatrical Productions   Judith Marinoff

Associate Choreographer
Lindy Specialist
Ryan Francois

Associate Choreographers
**Scott Fowler
Rod McCune**

Production Supervised by
Jerry Zaks

Directed and Choreographed by
Lynne Taylor-Corbett

Piano courtesy of Steinway & Sons

Drums courtesy of GMS Drum Company

Music Arrangements by: Everett Bradley, Ann Hampton Callaway, Joe C. Cowherd, Yaron Gershovsky,
Ian Herman, Casey MacGill, Michael Rafter, Jonathan Smith and Jeanine Tesori
The Producers wish to express their appreciation to Theatre Development Fund for its support of this production.
The Producers and Theatre Management are members of The League of American Theatres and Producers, Inc
Cast Album available on Sony Records.

with additional lyrics by Ms. Callaway). This built into a courtship duet, a whole little one-act play. Delightful and funny. I glanced at my watch. Only twenty-five minutes had passed, and I was having a wonderful old time.

Next came a pajama party dance to a Hoagy Carmichael tune—Casey MacGill and his uke appeared in a purple nightcap, with garters holding up his socks. And then came "Harlem Nocturne." This was the seduction of a string bass (and its player, Conrad Korsch) by a girl in a bodysuit with *f*-shaped sound holes like those on the body of the instrument (Caitlin

Carter). She caressed the wood, wrapping herself around the sound board; she fingered, he bowed, giving new meaning to the word "pizzicato." At one point she formed her body to the curve of the bass. The number (and the costume) recalled, in some ways, Anita Morris's "Phone Call to the Vatican" from *Nine*, which was also costumed by Mr. Ivey Long. All in all, this was the best actor-musician duet on the Broadway stage since Teresa Stratas and a clarinetist did "Blame It on a Summer Night" in *Rags*, back in 1986.

The second act was even better than the first, with a knockout opening number; a fine Duke Ellington instrumental, featuring solos from the eight-piece Gotham City Gates; and more. Ms. Benanti came out to sing "Cry Me a River" with trombone player Steve Armour, routined in the form of an argument. She attacked the trombonist, yanking him across the stage by his slide. Later, his slide caressed her hips, she shimmered at the touch of his vibrato. All in all, this was the best actor-musician duet on the Broadway stage since Caitlin Carter and the string bass, back in the first act.

Midway through the second act the band started to play the unmistakable vamp of one of my favorite songs. Ms. Callaway—accompanying herself on the blue Steinway—had only to sing the first words of the refrain ("My mama done tol' me"), and I knew

Ann Hampton Callaway sang "Blues in the Night" plain and simple and exquisite. Composer Harold Arlen and lyricist Johnny Mercer, up in musical heaven—both remarkable vocalists themselves—no doubt would have dug it.

I was about to hear one of the best renditions of "Blues in the Night" ever. This is a song we've had to sit through in countless 1940s-themed revues, most recently the soporific *Dream*. Callaway sang plain and simple and exquisite, accompanied by a somewhat torrid pas de deux. Composer Harold Arlen and lyricist Johnny Mercer, up in musical heaven—both remarkable vocalists themselves—no doubt would have dug it.

And then, just when you thought you'd seen everything, along came "Bill's Bounce." While perusing the Playbill before the show, I had noticed the credit "Aerial Flying by Antigravity, Inc.," so I knew something was coming. It turned out to be two girls attached to bungee cordlike contraptions, being flipped about by two boys onstage; imagine your typical swing dancing, except that when the girls are flipped, they careen high into the flies. And whatever goes up, must come down.

Swing! was all the more delightful because it was totally unexpected.

Swing!
Opened: December 9, 1999
Closed: January 14, 2001
461 performances (and 43 previews)
Profit/Loss: Loss

Swing! ($75 top) was scaled to a potential gross of
$782,586 at the 1,710-seat St. James. Weekly grosses
averaged about $391,000, with business stubbornly
remaining below the $500,000 mark. Total gross for the
run was $24,623,691. Attendance was about 61 percent,
with the box office grossing about 50 percent of potential
dollar-capacity.

TONY AWARD NOMINATIONS
Best Musical
Best Performance by a Featured Actress: Laura Benanti
Best Performance by a Featured Actress: Ann Hampton
  Callaway
Best Choreography: Lynne Taylor-Corbett
Best Direction of a Musical: Lynne Taylor-Corbett
Best Orchestrations: Harold Wheeler

*Critical
Scorecard*

Rave 2
Favorable 5
Mixed 1
Unfavorable 1
Pan 1

The guiding force, director-choreographer Lynne Taylor-Corbett, was all
but unknown; this was her first Broadway show as a director, her third as
choreographer (following the not overly impressive *Titanic* and *Chess*).
Ann Hampton Callaway, a fairly well known cabaret singer and composer—and sister to Broadway's Liz Callaway—was making her Broadway debut, as was Everett Bradley; Ms. Benanti's first Broadway job was
replacing Rebecca Luker in the revival of *The Sound of Music*, playing opposite Richard Chamberlain. To make matters even less promising,
Swing! appeared in the shadow of Susan Stroman's dance musical *Contact*,
which was just then racking up a whopping advance sale for its upcoming
transfer from off-Broadway.

Most of the credit, presumably, must go to Ms. Taylor-Corbett. *Swing!*
was ninety-odd minutes of pure dance, which is quite a task; the trick is
to keep coming up with freshly different numbers, so that one builds off
another and we never sit through something we feel like we've seen before. Taylor-Corbett and her corps did just that, and did it well, with a little help from her friends. (Three cast members were billed as associate
choreographers; five cast members were credited for choreographing
themselves in specific numbers.) Taylor-Corbett also had Jerry Zaks on

hand as production supervisor; cast, band, sets, costumes, and lighting all melded impeccably, which I guess is what Zaks supervised. The show was buoyed from first to last by Casey MacGill and the impeccable Gotham City Gates, with Jonathan Smith conducting from the piano. I don't know when I've ever heard eight musicians sounding this good in a Broadway theatre. Orchestrator Harold Wheeler not only did an expert job; he also made these songs—some of which have been used again and again in recent Broadway revues—sound fresh and refreshing.

Watching the dancers go through the finale, you could actually identify most of them from their earlier specialties. Especially outstanding were Beverly Durand, in "Throw That Girl Around" and the aerial number; Caitlin Carter, in the string bass number and "Blues in the Night"; Scott Fowler and Carol Bentley, in "I'll Be Seeing You" and the aerial number; Ryan Francois and Jenny Thomas, lindy hop specialists; and an athletically pert Geralyn Del Corso in the finger-snapping "Dancers in Love." (This was yet another Duke Ellington tune, one of six in Swing! The year 1999 was the centennial of Ellington, who made a much better showing than the more celebrated Noël Coward.) But the stage was filled with exciting dancers, including two of the stars. Mr. Bradley did some dancing here and there—legs flailing out as if they were on springs, with rubber bands in his knees—somewhat reminiscent of Ray Bolger. Ms. Benanti also led a section of the finale, moving like she was in the middle of one of those Michael Bennett dance combinations in A Chorus Line. All three stars gave distinctive performances. The twenty-year-old Ms. Benanti especially, with her singing, acting, dancing, and looks, should have a big musical comedy career ahead of her.

Swing! was not universally praised; some of the critics were clearly annoyed that Smokey Joe's Cafe—from the same producers and Jerry Zaks—had a record-breaking run, and repeated their criticisms of the earlier show in their reviews of Swing! I quite disliked Smokey Joe myself, but Swing! more than made up for it. In fact, Swing! made up for all those boring musical revues we've had to sit through, year after year, since Ain't Misbehavin' opened in 1978. Swing! was unable to counteract its less than enthusiastic reception and was forced to vacate the premises after little more than a year. But me, I had a swell time.

The twenty-year-old Laura Benanti, with her singing, acting, dancing, and looks, should have a big musical comedy career ahead of her.

Amadeus

There is something disconcerting about sitting down in a Broadway theatre and watching a revival of something that you worked on in the first place. The words are the same, but the world of the play is, by necessity, different.

In the case of *Amadeus* the words were changed, too, some of them. Playwright Peter Shaffer was "a little uneasy about the turn the play took into melodrama," he told an interviewer, adding that "I loved the theatricality, but it seemed to lack some credibility." Salieri still subtitles the story he is about to tell in the play "The Death of Mozart; or, How Did I Do It," which sounds melodramatic enough to me. Shaffer, however, saw fit to make the villain of the piece somewhat less villainous. Salieri still maneuvers Mozart to his death, but now he says he's sorry.

Amadeus, of course, is Shaffer's fictionalized character study of the all-but-forgotten eighteenth-century composer Antonio Salieri. The leading court composer of his time, Salieri meets the newcomer Mozart and realizes—to his horror—that his work is nothing compared with that of the repugnant young Amadeus. And it drives him nuts, literally. In Mozart's music, Salieri hears the voice of God; "Amadeus," in Latin, means "voice of God." (Neat work, Mr. Shaffer.)

Salieri presides at the deathbed creation of Mozart's *Requiem*, which provides the climactic scene of the play (with Salieri realizing—with wonderment surmounting jealousy—that this music "will help the ages to mourn"). As the play ends in 1823, thirty-two years after Mozart's

> **Peter Shaffer saw fit to make the villain of the piece somewhat less villainous. Salieri still maneuvers Mozart to his death, but now he says he's sorry.**

premature death, it is Salieri's curse to find himself obsolete while Mozart's compositions have been recognized as "the most perfect things made by man in the eighteenth century."

The new *Amadeus* began quite effectively. David Suchet, the Salieri of the occasion, was totally unknown along Broadway when he hit the boards of the Music Box (except to viewers of public television, where he played Agatha Christie's Hercule Poirot). But, then, Ian McKellan wasn't known locally when he opened *Amadeus* here in 1980. F. Murray Abraham wasn't much of a name when he undertook the part in the 1984 motion picture, either, earning an Oscar in the process. Suchet got things off to a good start, as

the ancient Salieri on the eve of his death; a young actor named Michael Sheen breezed in like a whirlwind of a Mozart; and things seemed to be rolling along smoothly into the middle of the first act. From there on, though, *Amadeus* seemed to grow less and less effective by the moment.

The most critical change, perhaps, was not in the words but in the physical production. John Bury's original design had been dark and stark, dominated by a steeply raked deck with a dark blue, shiny surface—Plexiglas, if I remember correctly. The upstage wall had panels that opened on occasion; this was used to create a marvelous effect of a two-tiered set of opera-house boxes. But the general look was severe, and the sleek surface of the raked deck made it look somewhat nebulous in time, which made it perfect for Shaffer's tricky, time-shifting memory play. There was no touch of the eighteenth century in the set, although the dazzling costumes were very much in period. (Bury won Tony Awards for both scenery and costumes; Tonys also went to McKellan and Shaffer.) William Dudley's new set was far more literal, far more period, and at times rather good-looking: a harpsichord extending behind the downstage left portal, two room-heating ovens in the corners, and a roomy playing area behind

THE MUSIC BOX

THE ESTATE OF IRVING BERLIN AND THE SHUBERT ORGANIZATION, OWNERS

KIM POSTER   PW PRODUCTIONS   ADAM EPSTEIN
SFX THEATRICAL GROUP AND CENTER THEATRE GROUP/AHMANSON THEATRE
IN ASSOCIATION WITH OLD IVY PRODUCTIONS

PRESENT

DAVID SUCHET

MICHAEL SHEEN   CINDY KATZ

AMADEUS

BY
PETER SHAFFER

WITH
MICHAEL KEENAN   J.P. LINTON   DAVID McCALLUM   TERENCE RIGBY

AND
JEFFREY BEAN   GLYNIS BELL   GEOFFREY BLAISDELL   JAKE BRODER
CHARLES JANASZ   ROBERT MACHRAY   DAN MASON   KATE MILLER
KEVIN ORTON   JOHN RAINER   WILLIAM RYALL   ROCCO SISTO   JOHN TOWEY

DESIGNED BY   LIGHTING BY   SOUND BY
WILLIAM DUDLEY   PAULE CONSTABLE   MATT McKENZIE

U.K. CASTING   U.S. CASTING   U.K. MARKETING   U.S. MARKETING
GILLIAN DIAMOND   PAT McCORKLE, C.S.A.   A.K.A. LTD.   THE NANCY RICHARDS GROUP

PRODUCTION STAGE MANAGER   PRODUCTION MANAGER   ASSOCIATE LIGHTING DESIGNER
SUSIE CORDON   PETER FULBRIGHT   TONY SIMPSON

GENERAL MANAGEMENT   PRESS REPRESENTATIVE   ASSOCIATE PRODUCERS
101 PRODUCTIONS, LTD.   BONEAU/BRYAN-BROWN   BRADLEY R. BERNSTEIN AND MARC EPSTEIN

DIRECTED BY
PETER HALL

Antonio Salieri   David Suchet
Wolfgang Amadeus Mozart   Michael Sheen
Constanze Weber   Cindy Katz
Emperor Joseph II of Austria   David McCallum
Count Johann Kilian Von Strack   J. P. Linton
Count Orsini-Rosenberg   Terence Rigby
Baron Van Swieten   Michael Keenan
The "Venticelli"   Jake Broder, Charles Janasz
Major Domo   John Ranier
Salieri's Valet   William Ryall
Salieri's Cook   Robert Machray
Kapellmeister Bonno   John Towey
Teresa Salieri   Glynis Bell
Katherina Cavalieri   Kate Miller
Servants   Jeffrey Bean, Geoffrey Blaisdell, Dan Mason, Kevin Orton
Citizens of Vienna   Jeffrey Bean, Glynis Bell, Geoffrey Blaisdell, Robert Machray, Dan Mason, Kate Miller, Kevin Orton, John Rainer, William Ryall

Place: Vienna
Time: November 1823 and 1781 to 1791

"Official Companion CD":   Decca Broadway 289 466 975 (incidental music only)

---

the upstage wall of Salieri's digs that could be filled with people or light. Dudley's costumes for Salieri and Mozart were especially ravishing, with rich golds and scarlets against black.

Another change in the tone of the evening came from the supporting players. I barely remembered *Amadeus* as having a supporting cast. I recalled the actors, twenty or so, as I used to pay them every week; but as onstage presences, all I can really picture were Salieri, Mozart, and Constanze. *Amadeus* is basically Salieri's nightmare/dream. In the original production, it seemed as if you were watching McKellan—or John Wood,

Frank Langella, David Dukes, or one of the others who played the role here—in a dart of light at the end of a dark tunnel. You were always focused on Salieri, and Mr. and Mrs. Mozart when they played a scene with him. Everyone else was in the periphery, like hazy figures on the outskirts of consciousness.

The new *Amadeus* featured a more prominent supporting cast. (Not better, mind you; just more prominent.) It was hard not to notice Emperor Joseph II, as no audience member over thirty-five could possibly overlook someone who was the middle-aged spitting image of that dashing secret agent Ilya Kuryakin. Even my wife, who grew up in Argentina, took one look and recognized David McCallum from *The Man from U.N.C.L.E.*, or *El Agente de C.I.P.O.L.*, as she called it. (Consider the plight of the poor ex-TV star. Put him in a small role, and he can become a negative, distracting the audience from the play.)

The audience's attention was no longer telescoped on Salieri and his interactions with Mozart. I suppose this was part of the overall problem, and it was surely enhanced by the warm and scenic scenery. Everything was more realistic, which was surely the intention of Shaffer and his director, Peter Hall; but *Amadeus*, I think, doesn't *want* realism. "Its impact is now more tragic and humanistic," said Hall, explaining that "it has shifted from being a melodrama into something very moving that speaks to all of us." But it seems that the new version spoke more to Hall and Shaffer than to the rest of "all of us." Had some brilliant revisionist director come along and "fixed" *Amadeus*, he or she would no doubt have been chastised for ruining it. Since the tinkering in this case was done by the playwright himself and his original director, we can only surmise that they did what they thought best. "If it works, don't fix it," goes the saying, although this was more a case of "if it works spectacularly, why tinker?"

Watching Mozart fall to pieces and break down into a gibberish nursery rhyme, I was suddenly thunderstruck: *Amadeus* is *Equus* with music.

Amadeus was a major hit in London in 1979 (with Paul Scofield) and in New York in 1980 (with Ian McKellan, initially); the new, improved twentieth-anniversary production was a hit in neither. They loved it in Los Angeles prior to Broadway, though.

Watching Mozart fall to pieces and break down into a gibberish nursery rhyme, I was suddenly thunderstruck. Well, not thunderstruck, exactly, but at least roused from my lethargy. Here we had two characters: a strange, socially repugnant, badly behaved young man who virtually overflowed with emotion; and an older, well-behaved onlooker-turned-father figure he turns to for help. The main character was not the firebrand at the center of the plot but the less flashy fellow, with the play turning on his shattering realization that the youngster—despite grievous lapses in character—had more passion and life within him than he himself could ever hope to have. What I am describing, of course, is *Equus*, Peter Shaffer's 1973 hit play (which directly preceded *Amadeus*). The Amadeus of *Equus* was Alan Strang, a teenager who incomprehensibly blinded a stableful of horses; the Salieri character was the analyst who, in trying to understand the boy, discovered the emptiness of his own life. *Amadeus* is *Equus* with music. Why this suddenly occurred to me sitting in the Music Box, I don't know; but it is a bad sign when you start thinking of a play you saw during the Nixon administration in the middle of the second act on the eve of the millennium.

Waiting in the Wings

The Broadway debut of Noël Coward's forty-year-old *Waiting in the Wings* was based on two assumptions. First, that there was a large and clamorous audience breathlessly awaiting a centennial celebration of Sir Noël; and second, that any tattered old Coward script would do as long as it had room for an "all-star" cast.

Yes, folks, the accomplished British playwright and wit would have turned one hundred years old on opening night. That is indeed cause for celebrating, I guess, for Coward fans at least. A good reason to pop round to the Savoy for high tea, or at least hoist a pint at the Lamb and Flag. But a revival on Broadway? What, to paraphrase another accomplished British playwright, is he to America, or America to him?

Coward made quite a splash hereabouts in 1925, as playwright, actor, and enfant terrible in his scandalous 1924 play, *The Vortex*. His early successes in the West End caused his adoption by New York City's uppercrust, Anglophiliac carriage crowd. Coward's Broadway visits in *Private Lives* (opposite Gertrude Lawrence, with young Larry Olivier as the other man, in 1931), *Design for Living* (a ménage à trois with Alfred Lunt and Lynn Fontanne, in 1933), and *Tonight at 8:30* (with Lawrence, in 1936) were high points of the Depression years for the Smart Set. But Coward's Broadway popularity peaked with his ghostly comedy *Blithe Spirit*, which opened here in 1941—a month before Pearl Harbor—and ran an impressive 650 performances. Nothing else of Coward's ever even hit the 250-performance mark on Broadway; all his plays after *Blithe Spirit* failed here, up to and including *Noël Coward in Two Keys*, which lasted eighteen weeks in 1973 with Jessica Tandy and Hume Cronyn. (Coward's centen-

The Residents
May Davenport   Rosemary Harris
Cora Clarke   Rosemary Murphy
Bonita Belgrave   Elizabeth Wilson
Maudie Melrose   Patricia Conolly
Deirdre O'Malley   Helena Carroll
Almina Clare   Bette Henritze
Sarita Myrtle   Helen Stenborg
Lotta Bainbridge   Lauren Bacall
Topsy Baskerville   Victoria Boothby

Just Visiting
Osgood Meeker   Barnard Hughes
Dora, Lotta's dresser   Sybil Lines
Zelda Fenwick, a journalist   Crista
   Moore
Alan Banfield   Anthony Cummings

The Staff
Sylvia Archibald, the superintendent
   Dana Ivey
Perry Lascoe   Simon Jones
Doreen, the maid   Amelia Campbell
Ted, the help   Geddeth Smith
St. John's ambulance man   Collin
   Johnson

The play takes place in "The Wings," a
   residential home for retired
   actresses. The time is the early
   sixties.

WALTER KERR THEATRE
A JUJAMCYN THEATRE

JAMES H. BINGER
CHAIRMAN

ROCCO LANDESMAN
PRESIDENT

PAUL LIBIN
PRODUCING DIRECTOR

JACK VIERTEL
CREATIVE DIRECTOR

ALEXANDER H. COHEN   CHASE MISHKIN   MAX COOPER
LEONARD SOLOWAY   STEVEN M. LEVY

PRESENT

LAUREN BACALL · ROSEMARY HARRIS

NOËL COWARD'S
WAITING IN THE WINGS

As Revisited by
JEREMY SAMS

with (alphabetically)

VICTORIA BOOTHBY	AMELIA CAMPBELL	HELENA CARROLL	PATRICIA CONOLLY	ANTHONY CUMMINGS
BETTE HENRITZE	BARNARD HUGHES	DANA IVEY	SIMON JONES	SYBIL LINES
CRISTA MOORE	ROSEMARY MURPHY	HELEN STENBORG	ELIZABETH WILSON	

Scenery by
RAY KLAUSEN

Costumes by
ALVIN COLT

Lighting by
KEN BILLINGTON

Sound by
PETER FITZGERALD

Production Manager
BEVERLEY RANDOLPH

Production Supervisor
ARTHUR SICCARDI

Wigs & Hair by
MITCH ELY

Dialect Coach
ELIZABETH SMITH

Associate Producer
SKYLIGHT PRODUCTIONS

Casting
JOHNSON-LIFF ASSOCIATES

Press Representative
DAVID ROTHENBERG ASSOCIATES

General Management
SOLOWAY/ LEVY

Directed by
MICHAEL LANGHAM

---

nial was also celebrated with an off-Broadway revival of the latter, with
Hayley Mills, Judith Ivey, and Paxton Whitehead, which opened in April
2000 and quickly folded.)

Coward's mots and quips have enjoyed a celebrated presence in the
States through revival after revival of the same four plays: *Private Lives*,
Hay Fever, *Blithe Spirit*, and *Present Laughter*. While these have for the
most part had a healthy life in the regional theatres, the last commercially
successful Coward seems to have been Maggie Smith's 1974–1975 *Private
Lives*. The most recent Coward revivals have all been big money losers:
Private Lives with Elizabeth Taylor and Richard Burton (1984), and with
Joan Collins (1992); *Hay Fever* with Shirley Booth (1970), and with

Rosemary Harris (1985); *Blithe Spirit* with Geraldine Page and Richard Chamberlain (1987); and *Present Laughter* with Frank Langella (1996). Which takes us back to the assumption that there was a large audience simply clamoring for a centennial celebration of Sir Noël. Maybe on the West End, but on Broadway?

And why *Waiting in the Wings*? Here you had an undistinguished comedy that was pretty much shooed off the stage of the Duke of York's Theatre when it opened on September 7, 1960. (Coward referred to the reviews as "like being slashed repeatedly in the face.") The play quickly expired and was confined to the discard pile, and not without reason.

Of course, the choice for a centennial salute was somewhat restricted. Coward's overly familiar four are—well, overly familiar. And in order to make this an event that couldn't fail to sell tickets, in theory, the producers apparently wanted a play with a cast list they could theoretically fill with box office stars (or at least one box office star). *Waiting in the Wings*, with room for at least ten septuagenarian "names," won the lottery. So what if the play—written by "destiny's tot" turned sixty—wasn't any good? The producers—and when I say the producers, I mean the veteran Alexander H. Cohen, who came up with the idea—therefore disinterred a rickety, unsuccessful play for the sole purpose of celebrating an occasion of questionable public interest. And to make a pot of money from it, hopefully.

So how did they do?

The demand for all things Coward as the millennium approached was noticeably minimal, at least in America. *Sail Away*—the bland 1961 musical Coward wrote for Broadway, produced just after *Waiting in the Wings*—was performed in a concert version at Carnegie Hall's Weill Recital Hall in November, as previously discussed. But if Mr. Cohen expected long queues of Cowardophiles ringing up to fill the stalls—ads and ABC listings for *Waiting in the Wings* contained the legend "Sorry, no discount tickets available from any source

> Why *Waiting in the Wings*, an undistinguished comedy that was pretty much shooed off the stage when it opened in 1960? Coward referred to the reviews as "like being slashed repeatedly in the face."

during this engagement"—he was sorely disappointed. The nostalgically backward-looking disco musical *Saturday Night Fever* wracked up a large advance sale, but the similarly quaint *Waiting in the Wings* attracted a different audience. To a limited extent, that is.

And what of the play? It turned out to be as weak as one might have expected. Jeremy Sams—known here for his translations of Jean Cocteau's *Indiscretions*, produced on Broadway in 1995, and Jean Anouilh's *The Rehearsal*, produced at the Roundabout in 1996—was hired to "revisit" the play, as it says on the title page. Revisit it he did, apparently bringing

rather severe rewrites with him. How many of the weaknesses belong to Coward and how many of the quips belong to Sams is a matter of conjecture. There are quite a few witty exchanges characteristic of the master. "Excuse me, I'm sorry I spoke," says one. "So are we all," is the reply. "I used to stop the show," says a delicate mouse of an ex–dancing girl. "As far as I can recall," darts back another, "it was the reviews which stopped the show."

There is a running battle between the girls and an old Irish character lady (left over from the earlier Kerr tenant *Beauty Queen of Leenane?*), to whit: A: "The Irish could never resist cheap sentimentality." B: "The British could never resist foreign invasion"; and A: "Oh, was William Shakespeare Irish?" B: "No, but he would have been a much better writer if he had been." There's also a dotty old woman-round-the-bend who greets a stranger with "I don't know who you are, but you smell like horses." Some of the *mots* are less *bon*, like "All sensitive lads with mother fixations love *Peter Pan* and *The Wizard of Oz*. Anything with Judy Garland."

The play, at least in the version that reached Broadway, was more situation than comedy. A group of old actresses live in a group home for old actresses. A new resident, who has a long-standing grudge with a resident in residence, checks in. After an hour or so we learn that one of them stole the other's husband (or lover, it isn't clear). Once that is all sorted out, and in the last fifteen minutes of the play, the new resident's estranged son, whom she hasn't seen in thirty-seven years and we've barely heard of, suddenly arrives from Canada (sample joke: "Do you know Toronto? It's terribly Canadian") to rescue her from life on public charity.

Mr. Cohen sought to ensure the success of his venture by enlisting the great and glamorous Lauren Bacall to head his cast. Bacall has a certain flair, Bacall has a strong following, Bacall has an unmistakable aura. But Bacall was unmistakably wrong for *Waiting in the Wings*. This was a group of "washed-up old has-beens" from the British stage; Bacall looked like she was just back from a one-day sale at Marks & Spencer. While the cast was pretty well stocked with American actresses more or less comporting themselves like they were British, Bacall was pure Yankee. (While Bacall—even at seventy-five—had glamor, she was given a seriously unbecoming wardrobe, including a fancy black dress with what appeared to be her stomach sticking out.) Ms. Bacall was miscast and visibly uncomfortable as a "useless old has-been waiting to kick the bucket," resulting in a blatantly insincere performance filled with synthetic line readings. In the first act you felt she didn't mean a word if it, in the second act you felt that she felt the whole thing was a waste of time, and after the curtain you wondered whether Bacall would run out before her contract did. Lauren Bacall can indeed sell tickets, but not when she is bad and she knows it and the critics know it and her fans know it.

As costar, the producers wisely signed up Rosemary Harris. Ms. Harris is Broadway royalty, a member of that select group of actresses who are seemingly able to pull off almost anything (like Julie Harris, Uta Hagen, Zoe Caldwell, the late Jessica Tandy). Rosemary Harris did just that in *Waiting in the Wings*. Sitting on her sofa, stage left, draped in a velvet dress that appeared to be fashioned out of old dining room drapes, Ms. Harris dominated the proceedings even when she had little to do.

> **Lauren Bacall was miscast and visibly uncomfortable as a "useless old has-been waiting to kick the bucket." In the first act you felt she didn't mean a word if it, in the second act you felt that she felt the whole thing was a waste of time, and after the curtain you wondered whether Bacall would run out before her contract did.**

Which was most of the time. But a ticket-selling star Ms. Harris is not, and never has been. Her performance did garner a wildly enthusiastic rave from the reviewer for the *New York Times* ("There are few sights more warming on Broadway at the moment than that of Rosemary Harris being chilly," Ben Brantley began), without which *Waiting in the Wings* would no doubt have quickly stopped waiting.

As for all those other roles, the producers were unable to enlist any old-time stage or television stars to increase the box office lure of their Coward centennial salute. Instead, they were forced to turn to a roster of veteran character actresses—and hit the gold mine, relatively speaking. For the supporting cast of *Waiting in the Wings* proved to be the strongest part of the enterprise, entertaining audiences and enthusing almost every reviewer.

This was no stage full of warehoused retirees; in fact, the lot had more Tony Awards and nominations per dressing room than any cast you're ever again likely to see assembled on one payroll. Many of them regularly tackle larger, more important roles; here they poured their forty or more years of technique into parsimonious parts, with outsize results. Especially good were Elizabeth Wilson, who could get an enormous laugh from an innocuous phrase like "big exit"; Rosemary Murphy, seated in a turban and pouncing on her lines like a shortstop turning an unassisted double play; Helen Stenborg, as a senile old wraith who—at the performance I attended—received exit applause every time she flitted off the stage; Barnard Hughes, Stenborg's husband, who was entrusted with the plot's sentimental moments; and Patricia Conolly, Betty Henritze, and Helena Carroll as well. The "youngsters" in the cast included Dana Ivey (unrecognizably disguised as a brusque old dragon lady) and Crista Moore, with five Tony nominations between them; and Simon Jones, who himself deserved some sort of award for playing the Coward role opposite Joan Collins in the 1992 *Private Lives*.

After a surprisingly brisk start at the box office, *Waiting in the Wings* settled down at a moderate but respectable level of business. (In mid-January, Mr. Cohen's "Sorry, no discount tickets available from any source during this engagement" disappeared, and he began taking whatever business he could find.) As the pro-ducers booked the Walter Kerr on an interim basis, with Eugene O'Neill's *Moon for the Misbegot-ten* waiting in the wings, *Waiting in the Wings* packed up and trans-ferred to the Eugene O'Neill after only eleven weeks. The show was un-able to recover from the added costs of the move, and when grosses began to falter in May the producers—no longer including Cohen, who died in April—threw in the towel.

> In mid-January, Alex Cohen's "Sorry, no discount tickets available from any source during this engagement" disappeared and he began taking whatever business he could find.

Jackie Mason: Much Ado about Everything

One Sunday night back in October 1964, borscht belt comedian Jackie Mason was hoist on his own petard. His own finger, actually; the middle one, which he flashed at Ed Sullivan on prime-time, family-time TV. Mason was performing on Sullivan's top-rated variety show; the show was running late; Sullivan signaled Mason to cut his act short; and the short comedian sent a hand gesture that more or less put him in cold storage for the next twenty years. The outspoken Mason's entire career, thus, was dictated by one piece of pantomime.

Mason continued to work at casinos and clubs, but without further television exposure he was stuck in the small time. With little to lose (except $100,000), he braved Broadway in 1969 with his comedy *A Teaspoon Every Four Hours*. This was the *Moose Murders* of its day, which is to say a play so inane that it remains memorable through the years. At a time when a show typically played less than a week of previews, *Teaspoon* went on and on and on, presumably on the theory that once the critics saw it they would tell everyone how lousy it was, and it would close on opening night. *Teaspoon* played ninety-seven previews—twelve full weeks' worth—before the critics were allowed in. They told everyone how lousy it was, and it closed on opening night.

Just before *Teaspoon* began its endless preview period, another stand-

How many ethnic stand-up comedians of the early 1960s are starring on Broadway today? How many of them can you even remember? If nothing else, Ed Sullivan made Jackie Mason unforgettably famous.

up comic with a distinctive style opened in a new Broadway comedy. Woody Allen fared far better with *Play It Again, Sam*; but, then, he had a script by Woody Allen.

The Ed Sullivan finger kept Mason in show business limbo until 1986, when he returned to Broadway in a one-man show entitled *The World According to Me*. This time the critics loved him, the show was an unex-

pected hit with a healthy 367-performance run, and Mason has been back in the big time ever since. *The World According to Me* played a return engagement in 1988 and was followed by a string of similar shows: *Jackie Mason Brand New* (1990); *Jackie Mason: Politically Incorrect* (1994); and *Love Thy Neighbor* (1996).

Although the Sullivan fracas cut a deep hole into Mason's career, and he surely endured decades of hardship, that little episode—in retrospect—might well have made him. How many ethnic stand-up comedians of the early 1960s are starring on Broadway today? How many of them can you even remember? If nothing else, Ed Sullivan made Jackie Mason unforgettably famous.

Which brings us to *Much Ado about Everything*, which is not to be confused with Shakespeare's similarly titled comedy. Mason's has more jokes. Actually, Mason's has nothing but jokes, and he is a good joke writer with a high on-target percentage. His delivery is exceptional, too. Yet I found the whole thing rather unpalatable, for Jackie Mason is an insult comedian pretty much on a one-track course.

Mason stormed out to welcome us, informing one and all that "this is gonna be some fantastic show." After ten minutes of general humor, he said a couple of things in praise of Rudolph Giuliani—the mayor of New York City at the time—to minor applause, followed by a full five minutes targeted at Hillary Clinton. Some of this was extremely funny, some of it was perceptive. But a wise satirist quits while he's ahead; Mason really

GOLDEN THEATRE
Ⓢ A Shubert Organization Theatre
Gerald Schoenfeld, *Chairman*   Philip J. Smith, *President*

Robert E. Wankel, *Executive Vice President*

Jyll Rosenfeld and Fred Krohn
Present

Jackie Mason
in

MUCH ADO ABOUT EVERYTHING

Written and Directed by
Jackie Mason

Produced by
Raoul Lionel Felder, Esq. and Jon Stoll

Associate Producer
Howard Weiss and Henry Handler
JAM THEATRICALS

Legal Counsel
Raoul Lionel Felder, Esq., P.C.
Grubman Indursky & Schindler, P.C. by Donald Kaplan, Esq.

General Manager
Joseph Harris

Lighting Designer   Sound Designer
Stan Crocker   **Christopher Cronin**

Stage Manager   Company Manager
Don Myers   **Kathy Lowe**

General Press Representative
Larry Weinberg

seemed to hate the woman, and he kept on until his ranting became not funny but desperate. "She's a stupid shiksa" is not, in my view, effective social satire. Mason apparently had a not-so-hidden agenda here: his biographical material in the program told us that he was writing jokes for Rudy to use in his upcoming Senate campaign against Ms. Clinton —a campaign that never officially happened, as it happened. Mason was a cheerleading jester for Giuliani's first mayoral campaign, too—until he was furloughed because of racially inflammatory remarks about then-mayor David Dinkins.

Mason larded his Hillary attack—and all the other attacks throughout the evening—with phrases like "and I say this with the greatest respect," and "I hope it doesn't sound like I'm picking on her," as if to excuse the venom slobbering from his lips, but he did seem to enjoy it. "I should keep my mouth shut," he apologized again and again—but didn't. There was something unlikely about the marriage of Jackie Mason and Rudy Giuliani. The comedian stands upon his First Amendment right to insult anyone and everyone at will; he prides himself on being an equal opportunity annoyer. Giuliani, during his reign as mayor of New York City, had a penchant for attempting to restrict the speech of anyone and everyone he disagreed with, resulting in a string of court cases that he typically lost. Just before *Much Ado about Everything* opened, Giuliani waged a front-page battle with a local museum over an art exhibit he deemed offensive. Unable to force the museum board to cancel the exhibit, Giuliani threatened the museum's public funding—which the courts quickly ordered restored. Needless to say, Mason had nothing to say on this subject; in fact, while he blithely insulted people and races left and right—or should that be, left and left?—he didn't have a discouraging word to say about his pal Rudy. Good thing, too, or the Golden Theatre might have lost its license faster than you can say William Bratton.

For a funny man intent on skewering the high and mighty and anyone else who strikes his fancy, Mason displayed a highly defensive front. Early on, he picked out someone who wasn't laughing in the front row— "What, are you a homosexual?"—and returned to him whenever a joke fell flat: "Are the jokes too complicated for you?" "You understand this, mister?" "In case you don't know, I tell jokes here." "Am I a little too Jewish for you?" "You're looking at me like you're waiting for the comedian to show up." "You have to be a real schmuck to be offended." "I don't care if you like me, because I'm a hit." Yes, he admitted that some people don't like him; but that's because "Jews hate people who sound like Jews." I kind of think that religion has nothing to do with it, that Mr. Mason is likable or dislikable regardless of religion.

Other targets include haute cuisine, bottled water, hotel minibars, airline seats, sports cars, and more; not up-to-the-minute, exactly. He went on at length about how much he disliked Broadway musicals, an opinion apparently shared by many in his audience; but he then went off on a diatribe against the musical *Titanic*: "A shameful, disgusting, idiotic show." Now, I for one was not a fan of *Titanic*, which I found to be well-intentioned, worthy in places, but generally flawed. But

> A wise satirist quits while he's ahead; Mason really seemed to hate Hillary Clinton and kept on until his ranting became not funny but desperate. "She's a stupid shiksa," is not, in my view, effective social satire.

such outright hatred? And why, in 2000, pick on the long-shuttered *Titanic* with such prime targets as *Footloose*, *Saturday Night Fever*, and *Annie Get Your Gun* within a block of where you're standing?

But his biggest insults were for people he doesn't like. They're all stupid—a common punch line to his rhetorical questions is "because

they're stupid," or sometimes "stupid schmucks." People who disagree with
him are "sons of bitches." He went after African Americans. He went
after Italians. He went after people with AIDS. He really had it in for Indian cab drivers, "because they're stupid"; also because they smell "stinky."
And of course, he lambasted Bill Clinton. "The man is a f——ing liar,"
he said. Maybe so, Jackie; but is standing up on a soapbox in front of your
fans and calling people dirty names an effective way of proving your
point? Call me stupid, Mr. Mason, but I just don't see it.

The reaction from the house was, generally, roaring; but this was a specialized audience. Seated across the aisle from me was Phil Rizzuto, the
old Yankee shortstop. Two seats over from him was a twenty-something
man from New Jersey with curly hair who—so help me—pulled a pint of
Ben and Jerry's ice cream out of a plastic takeout bag and proceeded to eat
it with a plastic spoon. His girlfriend was mortified, and well she should
have been. (In the interests of reportorial accuracy, I tried and tried to
read the flavor from the carton but couldn't quite make it out.) Three
rows back were a couple of newlyweds, mobbed for autographs because
the groom was Jerry Seinfeld. Mason has his own special audience, that's
for sure, and there's nothing wrong with that. They seem to a great extent
to be left over from the Catskills; if this is the sort of humor you enjoy,
Mason is one of the few performers still offering it. While this audience
is limited, it is large enough to support a modest enterprise like Mason's
one-man shows for months on end.

Many of Mason's fans return over and over again with friends. Presumably, they don't mind hearing the same old jokes, which is a good thing because there appears to be quite an overlap from show to show. *Much Ado* headed its advertisements with the phrase "All New! All New! All New!"—the exclamation points are theirs—but I wonder just what they meant. Perhaps Mr. Mason's hair color is all new—an indescribable shade, close to rust?—but much of the material doesn't seem to be. Mason does impressions of Bing Crosby, Frank Sinatra, Ed Sullivan, Richard Nixon, and Henry Kissinger. And these are "All New!"? Here we are in the twenty-first century, and he's doing the Ink Spots—an impression that goes on and on and on and on, by the way—and you have to wonder how topical and fresh and "new" this material is. But again, Mason fans surely don't mind seeing the same old thing, and non–Mason fans were unlikely to attend his fifth one-man show anyway.

I expect that these shows have been highly profitable for Mason, as he has such low overhead. (Here Jackie Mason would unleash a string of jokes insulting short people, no doubt.) But what's so insulting about being short? One can't help but note

> For a funny man intent on skewering the high and mighty and anyone else who strikes his fancy, Mason displayed a highly defensive front whenever a joke fell flat: "Are the jokes too complicated for you?" "You have to be a real schmuck to be offended." "I don't care if you like me, because I'm a hit."

that the program photo of Mason and Giuliani showed the short Rudy towering over the shorter Mason. (A Broadway show with a publicity shot of a politician on the cast page???) But Mason has enough fans to continue his periodic returns to Broadway, as long as he is not too rich to work. (He told us again and again how rich he is.) Jackie has the format down pat and needs no help from others. Still, he might well have paid a visit to Dame Edna, three doors down from the Golden, for some lessons in deportment. Dame Edna would know how to handle Jackie Mason, all right.

As it turned out, Ms. Everage received a special Tony Award. Mr. Mason didn't. This allowed him to take one of the best Tony Award ads in memory: "92 TONY AWARD NOMINATIONS! (And we didn't get a single one.)"

James Joyce's The Dead

*J*ames Joyce's *The Dead* was inventive, evocative, artistic, and unquestionably admirable. I must confess, though, with due respect to the creators and cast and everyone involved, that I found it impossible to enjoy, or even much like.

A group of family and friends gather in Dublin's fair city for their annual Feast of the Epiphany get-together, a post-Christmas evening of supper and song. One after another, each of the actors—characters, I mean—gets up and sings a parlor song. One of the elderly spinster aunts hosting the party has just been turned out from her position in the local choir; another fellow, the son of a forbiddingly dour old character lady, finally—and after much general concern—tiptoes tipsily in and proceeds to do a fairly entertaining drunk act. Music students of the aunts sing; a visiting opera singer sings; a revolutionary firebrand of a lass sings; they all sing. Two-thirds of the way through the ninety-eight-minute piece, things finally start to happen. The favorite nephew of the aunts, who turns out to be the protagonist of the evening, discovers that his wife carries in her heart the memory of a long-lost suitor who died; her never-before-expressed memories of this boy overshadow anything she ever felt for her husband. Oh, and the old lady who was forced from the choir dies, as they sing "Snow will be falling, falling softly upon the living and the dead." All in all, a slice of life—or, rather, a slice of death.

The Dead went along pastorally—or, to some, lethargically—for what seemed like hours until the spinster aunts and their spinster niece sang a song called (naturally) "Naughty Girls." This built into a festive dance, with everyone forming the Irish version of a conga line, snaking through the drawing room and waking the not-insubstantial segment of the audience that was in need of waking. As the number came to an end, the cashiered old spinster suddenly fainted.

Now, in musical comedy terms, this can mean only one thing. When a woman faints just before the end of a production number, and the band withers to a stop, and everybody mills around to help—she is always preggers, usually illegitimately so. The old spinster aunt was *not* pregnant, as it turned out, merely about to die after one more big song, a duet with her ghostly self as a child. As she was carried offstage, the red-nosed ne'er-do-well led the company in a song called "Wake the Dead"—the tenth number of the evening, and only the first that appeared to refer to what was going on onstage.

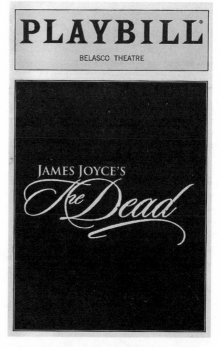

This was not an oversight on the part of the authors; their aim, I suppose, was to weave an atmospheric tapestry of music until the show shifted from public (the party) to private (the deaths of the aunt and the tale of the long-ago suitor). Admiring theatregoers familiar with James Joyce's original story (published in 1914), or the 1987 John Huston film version, commented that these seemingly generic parlor songs did, actually, fit the inner life of the characters who sang them. Maybe so, but that didn't help me any.

Leafing through the Playbill before the play, I noted—though not too carefully—a dense program note explaining the sources of the various songs. Sitting through the parade of noninvolving turn-of-the-century Irish parlor songs, I mused that the authors were somewhat hampered by their self-induced structure; while there are presumably hundreds of turn-of-the-century Irish parlor songs floating around, how many were relevant to the characters and plot of *The Dead*? This explained the sameness of the songs as they threatened to become numbingly somnolent—and also

BELASCO THEATRE

Ⓢ A Shubert Organization Theatre

Gerald Schoenfeld, *Chairman*   Philip J. Smith, *President*

Robert E. Wankel, *Executive Vice President*

Gregory Mosher & **Arielle Tepper**

present

the Playwrights Horizons production (**Tim Sanford,** Artistic Director)

JAMES JOYCE'S

The Dead

A NEW MUSICAL PLAY

Book by **Richard Nelson** Music by **Shaun Davey**

Lyrics conceived and adapted by **Richard Nelson** and **Shaun Davey**

featuring in alphabetical order

Blair Brown   Paddy Croft   Brian Davies

Daisy Eagan   Dashiell Eaves   Sally Ann Howes

John Kelly   Brooke Sunny Moriber   Marni Nixon

Alice Ripley   Emily Skinner   Stephen Spinella

Christopher Walken

Sets by **David Jenkins** Costumes by **Jane Greenwood**

Lighting by **Jennifer Tipton** Sound by **Scott Lehrer**

Orchestrations by **Shaun Davey** Musical Direction by **Charles Prince**

Wigs by **Paul Huntley** Technical Supervisor **Drew Siccardi**

Marketing **The Karpel Group** Press Representation **The Publicity Office**

Casting **James Calleri** (Playwrights Horizons) / **Mark Bennett** (Hopkins, Smith & Barden)

General Manager **Lynn Landis** Production Stage Manager **Matthew Silver**

Choreographed by **Seán Curran**

Directed by **Richard Nelson**

The Hostesses

Aunt Julia Morkan, a music teacher
Sally Ann Howes

Aunt Kate Morkan, her sister (also a music teacher)   Marni Nixon

Mary Jane Morkan, their niece (also a music teacher)   Emily Skinner

The Family

Gabriel Conroy, Julia and Kate's nephew   Christopher Walken

Gretta Conroy, Gabriel's wife   Blair Brown

The Guests

Mr. Browne, a friend of the aunts
Brian Davies

Freddy Malins   Stephen Spinella

Mrs. Mallins, Freddy's mother   Paddy Croft

Miss Molly Ivors   Alice Ripley

Bartell D'Arcy, an opera singer   John Kelly

The Help

Lily, the maid   Brooke Sunny Moriber

Michael, a music student of Mary Jane's   Dashiell Eaves

Rita, another student of Mary Jane's
Daisy Eagan

Cellist, a music student of Julia's
Daniel Barrett

Violinist, a music student of Kate's
Louise Owen

Ghost

Young Julia Morkan   Daisy Eagan

Setting: The Misses Morkans' annual Christmas-time party. Dublin. Near the turn of the century.

added to my surprise when "Wake the Dead" came along, as it sounded like it had actually been written to fill that specific moment in the piece.

When I finally got around to studying the Playbill, I discovered that these were not obsolete old turn-of-the-century songs after all. They were *new* turn-of-the-century songs intended to sound like the obsolete ones, and they did. (The program note on song sources was referring specifically to the lyrics, which were "adapted from or inspired by a number of 18th and 19th century Irish poems.") Which is to say, somebody—Shaun Davey is his name—actually sat down and wrote all those authentic-sounding outmoded old parlor songs on purpose.

When Stephen Sondheim wrote *Sweeney Todd*, he did not fill his score with authentic-sounding songs of the Victorian era. (There are two, "Sweet Polly Plunkett" and "The Tower of Bray," used for comic purpose.) *The King and I* doesn't use "real" Siamese music, nor does Mrs. Anna whistle a happy tune that you would have heard anywhere in the British Empire in 1861. *Man of La Mancha*, despite all its Spanish guitars, would sound as unworldly to Mr. Quixote as "We Kiss in a Shadow" would sound to the king of Siam; flamenco didn't come along until the early 1800s, two hundred years after the recalcitrant Don fought his last windmill. Mr. Davey (a respected Irish composer, with the sound track for *Waking Ned Devine* to his credit) and Mr. Nelson (a prominently successful playwright in London, with relatively little acclaim in his native America) chose to go for authenticity in *The Dead*. Their score was well received by many theatregoers, although not from where I was sitting.

Surprised by my lack of passion for a show that was so highly regarded by many, I did a highly informal *Dead* survey. The people I found who most enjoyed the musical already knew—and generally loved—the story and/or film; the characters assembled in the drawing room were old friends. The people who got little out of it, present company included, were unfamiliar with the piece; the characters assembled in the drawing room were

> **These were not obsolete old turn-of-the-century songs after all. They were new turn-of-the-century songs intended to sound like the obsolete ones, and they did.**

simply generic Irish types, only a few of whom stood out from the shadows. Reliance on the familiarity of your prospective audience with James Joyce is, perhaps, self-defeating. You have to figure that among the subset of the world population that attends Broadway musicals, the number of people who know their James Joyce will be slightly less numerous than those familiar with the underlying material of *Saturday Night Fever*, or even *Jesus Christ Superstar*. Ideally, familiarity should not be a requisite for enjoyment; with *The Dead*, to some extent it was.

Fans of *The Dead* seemed to find Christopher Walken, as the nephew, the weak link of the affair. I didn't mind him, myself; he seemed deeply pained by it all, which was right and proper under the circumstances. Just about everyone else was highly praised, and they were all pretty good. Sally Ann Howes, who replaced Julie Andrews in the Broadway *My Fair Lady*, was very good as the dying aunt, abetted by Marni Nixon—the singing voice of Eliza Doolittle on the screen—as her sister. Playing the wife with the secret was Blair Brown, who turned up in more places this season than even Kristen Chenoweth (having started as Fraulein Schneider in *Cabaret* and ended up in *Copenhagen*). Stephen Spinella, who gave a harrowingly unforgettable performance in *Angels in America*, was a great help as Freddy, the lost, drunken boy who sang "Wake the Dead" (and helped wake the audience). Also in the cast was Daisy Eagan, the girl from *The Secret Garden*; Alice Ripley and Emily Skinner, the twins from *Side Show*; and Brian Davies, the juvenile from both *The Sound of Music* and *A Funny Thing Happened on the Way to the Forum* (from the original productions, that is, now playing an aged Irish character man with a still-lovely voice).

> The people I found who most enjoyed the musical already knew—and generally loved—the story and/or film. Familiarity should not be a requisite for enjoyment; with *The Dead*, to some extent, it was.

The show received some very fine reviews when it originally opened in October 1999 at Playwrights Horizon, resulting in its quick transfer to the considerably larger Belasco. It got strong reviews again on Broadway, leading to the perception that it was a must-see hit. In both cases, it also received its share of negative reviews, leaving the average in middle ground. (Producers tend to ignore the nonfavorable comments when they take those full-page quote ads, which is fine by me. In the case of *The Dead*, though, the adverse criticisms were not inapt.) The originally announced ten-week run was extended with much fanfare, and converted to an open-end run when the Sondheim review *Putting It Together* closed. This allowed *The Real Thing*—for which *The Dead* would have had to vacate the Belasco due to a previous booking—to take the infinitely more desirable Barrymore. The foregoing notwithstanding, the show's stagnant box office grosses indicate that there wasn't all that much audience interest in *The Dead*, period. The show sold out at the 141-seat Playwrights but barely exceeded the 50 percent mark at the Belasco.

Maybe there was a problem with that title. The use of *The Dead* was apparently rejected as too depressing, or perhaps as indicative of an entertainment more in the nature of a horror movie (although producers Greg Mosher and Arielle Tepper called their previous effort *Freak*, with no adverse effect). Someone—James Joyce's agent??—came up with the bright idea of calling it *James Joyce's The Dead*, no doubt expecting the *Ulysses* man's moniker to make it sound less depressing. In truth, I'd suspect that little is more depressing to musical theatre fans than the name James Joyce. Maybe they should have tried something cheerier, in a friendly sort of way, like *Jerry Herman's The Dead*? Or, following the lead from the upcoming dueling musicalizations of Joseph Moncure March's epic poem, they might have simply entitled their musical *The Mild Party*.

At any rate, despite dedicated producers, strong fans, and some impressively glowing and well-thought-out critical reviews, *The Dead*—I mean, *James Joyce's The Dead*—never found an audience and was unable to make it through to awards season. Clearly, too few of the adventurous people who did attend the show went home and told their friends that you've got to go see this new show, like they did for *Dame Edna*.

But *The Dead* left me with a nagging feeling that I had missed something, so I went back a few days before it closed to try again. By this time, Faith Prince had replaced Brown—who had moved on to *Copenhagen*—and Stephen Bogardus was on as a vacation replacement for Walken.

Upon arrival at the theatre I was disgruntled to find understudies listed for not one or two but three of the most interesting performers. Stephen Spinella, who had been the best thing in the show, was out; so were the excellent aunts, Sally Ann Howes and Marni Nixon. (I needn't have worried; their understudies—Sean Cullen, Alice Cannon, and Patricia Kilgarriff, respectively—were quite good.)

> Someone came up with the bright idea of calling it *James Joyce's The Dead*. Maybe they should have tried something cheerier, like *Jerry Herman's The Dead*? Or perhaps *The Mild Party*.

I settled in my seat, somewhat annoyed, as the curtain rose. Bogardus came out beside the stage-left proscenium and welcomed us, telling us what we needed to know to enter Joyce's world. After a minute or so, I flashed back to the same narrative as performed by the dour and impersonal Walken. By this point with Walken, I had already turned off and

started looking around at the set, the other actors frozen onstage, and
even the cast list. Bogardus was much more involving from the very beginning, making warm what had been leaden. Walken's Gabriel was
alienated and alienating; Bogardus brought us into the parlor with the
characters, rather than keeping us outside observing them.

The trick to *The Dead* was to concentrate on the characters rather
than the songs. Several dramas were being played out throughout the
long first scene—but they were happening upstage of, or downstage of, or
to the side of the singers. Bogardus's delivery of the exposition, his heartfelt concern for each of the characters in his narrative, drew me into the
interpersonal relationships; Walken had driven me away. This made all
the difference.

The Dead still remained unconventional as a musical; the songs were
purposely incidental, an interesting idea that unfortunately didn't work.
But I could see the art in the piece with Bogardus, something that was totally elusive with his predecessor. *James Joyce's The Dead* closed four days
later.

Wrong Mountain

D avid Hirson's first play, the very strange *La Bête*, was a Molière-esque satirical comedy written entirely in rhymed couplets and—well, very strange. It opened on Broadway in January 1991, attracted howlingly negative reviews, and closed after twenty-four performances. The loss was $2 million, a record for a nonmusical in a day when you could comfortably produce a play for far less than half of that. (As I write this in the year 2000, a small play can still squeeze by on a million. *Wrong Mountain*, ultimately, dropped about $1,500,000.)

La Bête was strange, yes, but also startling, intriguing, and fascinating. So much so that many of the few people who saw it remember it vividly, which is more than you can say for most shows that shutter after three weeks. Even the people who didn't like it seemed to appreciate the unfulfilled promise of its premise. Nine years later, Hirson arrived with another play,

> **"The chief enemy of all writing is imprecision," we are told, advice that David Hirson might well have heeded. Nevertheless, this was a strange and wondrous, though not wonderful, play.**

similar in its specific attacks on theatrical creators and audiences but dissimilar in style. And strange, startling, intriguing, and fascinating.

Poet Henry Dennett has a problem; many problems, actually, but foremost among them is a ten-foot, forty-pound worm housed in his intestines. ("Don't eat too much corn," prescribes his musical comedy doctor, which is to say a real internist who tells bad jokes and even does a soft-shoe.) Other characters include Dennett's ex-wife, now engaged to "the most successful writer in Broadway history"; Dennett's daughter, who is

❚EUGENE O'NEILL THEATRE
A JUJAMCYN THEATRE

JAMES H. BINGER
CHAIRMAN

ROCCO LANDESMAN
PRESIDENT

PAUL LIBIN
PRODUCING DIRECTOR

JACK VIERTEL
CREATIVE DIRECTOR

Dodger Theatricals with
American Conservatory Theater, Lauren Mitchell
and The John F. Kennedy Center for the Performing Arts
present

RON RIFKIN   DANIEL DAVIS

in

WRONG MOUNTAIN

A new play by
David Hirson

with

Beth Dixon   Anne Dudek   Tom Riis Farrell
Reg Flowers   Jody Gelb   Daniel Jenkins
Ilana Levine   Bruce Norris   Mary Schmidtberger   Michael Winters

Scenery and Costumes Designed by
Giles Cadle

Lighting Designed by
Jennifer Tipton

Sound Designed by
John Gromada

Production Stage Manager
James Harker

Technical Supervision
Unitech II, Corp.
Brian Lynch, Ken Keneally

Casting
Jay Binder

Executive Producer
Dodger Management Group

Marketing Consultants
The Karpel Group

Press Representative
Boneau/Bryan-Brown

Directed by
Richard Jones

The producers wish to express their appreciation to Theatre Development Fund
for their support of this production.

Henry Dennett, a poet   Ron Rifkin
Claire, his ex-wife   Beth Dixon
Jessica, his daughter   Ilana Levine
Adam, his son   Bruce Norris
Peter, his son-in-law   Reg Flowers
Guy Halperin, Claire's fiancé   Michael Winters
Maurice Montesor, festival director   Daniel Davis

Festival Actors
Duncan Hyde-Berk   Tom Riis Farrell
Salome Blackwood   Beth Dixon
Jason Elmore   Reg Flowers
Miranda Cortland-Sparks   Jody Gelb
Ariel   Anne Dudek

Others
Winifred Hill, a playwright   Mary Schmidtberger
Clifford Pike, a playwright   Daniel Jenkins
Anne, a poet   Mary Schmidtberger
Leibowitz, Dennett's physician   Tom Riis Farrell
Stevens, a bookseller   Daniel Jenkins
Bookstore patrons   Anne Dudek, Daniel Jenkins

Place and Time: Here and Now

accompanied everywhere by her interracial husband and a stroller containing their infant daughter, Cheyenne, upon whom Dennett vomits in the middle of the first act; Dennett's chip-off-the-old-block son, who mimics his father's pronouncements and even dresses identically ("I have no opinion," he explains, "there is no me, I'm you"); and Guy Halperin, Dennett's ex-wife's fiancé, who is as successful as Dennett is not. "What do you mean by successful?" Dennett asks. "Wouldn't you like to know," says the ex-wife. Halperin bets Dennett $100,000 that he can't write a play and have it produced within three months. This propels Dennett to toss off a play—also called *Wrong Mountain*—and have it produced at a new-play festival in Midwestern corn country. He takes a train there, which in miniature traverses the stage and gets a round of applause. Here, Hirson moves into a somewhat different type of play altogether, peopled by small-time regional theatre types who are good for a whole barrage of corny laughs. "I'm Salome Blackwood," says one who swoops along looking like Marian Seldes. "I play the Sea Hag." Another fledgling writer arrives with her play about Eleanor Roosevelt and the opera singer Nellie Melba, entitled— what else?—*Ellie and Nellie.* ("Like being trapped inside a body bag for two hours," comments Dennett's son, who is as hypercritical as his dad.)

Standout among them all is the resident director, Maurice Montesor. This Montesor—presumably intended to be the corn that Dennett feeds upon—is a fellow of advanced age, with a luxuriant mane of indescribable color. (Is it the shade of corn oil?? *Wrong Mountain* was purposely overwhelmed by corn and kitsch, in dialogue, in staging, and even in set dressing.) Montesor constantly talks of the good old days when he worked with Kiki. (Laurence Olivier, to you and me.) Even now, he is off to rehearse *Romeo and Juliet*—starring himself as the lovelorn teen—which at seven hours and forty-one minutes is still too long. "We've got a bit of tightening to do before opening tonight," he admits. The role was played by an actor virtually unknown along Broadway named Daniel Davis, sharing full star billing with Ron Rifkin (as Dennett) and pretty much deserving it. Mr. Davis created quite a personage, a portrayal that might well have snatched a Tony Award in June had *Wrong Mountain* not washed out in February.

The show was chock-full of images and imagery, with Hirson abetted by the inventive British director Richard Jones (of *La Bête* and *Titanic*). Too many allusions, perhaps. "The chief enemy of all writing is imprecision," Dennett tells us, advice that Hirson might well have heeded. Nevertheless, this was a strange and wondrous, though not wonderful, play. As with *La Bête*, Hirson placed his philosophical arguments in the

context of theatricals. The main themes of *Wrong Mountain*: What happens when you realize that "you might have spent your whole life climbing
the wrong mountain?"; and "What does it mean if a man's greatest triumph
comes from having done something he viewed with absolute contempt?"

This last, in theatrical context, brings to mind a musical produced
when the theatre-conscious Hirson was twelve. The show underwent a
troubled rehearsal period, during which the director strong-armed change
after change upon the protesting authors. It opened and became a massive hit, with critics and audiences alike lavishing excessive (though mer-
ited) praise upon the directorial sleight of hand, at the expense of the
score and especially the book. ("Trite and uninteresting," said Clive
Barnes. "Trite" and "deflating," said Walter Kerr. "A book writer with no
story to tell and a point of view made of solid acne," said Martin Gottfried.) The songwriter and librettist, while happily collecting millions of
dollars in royalties, nevertheless blamed the universally praised and
award-bedecked director for ruining their work. Yes, the musical was *Pippin*, which opened in 1972 and ran 1,944 performances; and Hirson's
Henry Dennett might as well be describing Bob Fosse's work in that show
when he rails against Broadway as "a Biblia pauperum—a Bible in pictures for the benefit of the illiterate."

"What does it mean if a man's greatest triumph comes from having
done something he viewed with absolute contempt?" Dennett calmly ac-
cepts the wild success—artistic and financial—of the play he writes in
Wrong Mountain, subverting every argument he has made all evening.
This unleashes a stormy diatribe from his disbelieving son.

Now, I can't tell you that *Pippin*, in fact, has any bearing on *Wrong Mountain*. But the playwright readily admitted to some autobiographical aspects in the play. ("I don't think I'd create these characters if all these issues weren't warring inside my head," Hirson told Bruce Weber of the *New York Times* in an interview.) Certainly, Hirson's father's greatest (and only?) success was that selfsame, roundly trounced book for *Pippin*. Roger O. Hirson's other produced theatre work, as far as I can tell, consisted of two quickly forgotten off-Broadway plays—a three-week flop in 1963, a one-performance folderoo in 1969—and a rewrite job on the 1966 musical comedy failure *Walking Happy*. By coincidence, while *Wrong Mountain* was moving to Broadway from its tryout at San Francisco's ACT, the Papermill Playhouse (in suburban New Jersey) announced a new production of *Pippin*, with Hirson (Sr.) and songwriter Stephen Schwartz removing the improvements forced on them by Fosse. The Fosse-less *Pippin*, needless to say, didn't have the life of the original.

Anyway, one thing is clear: David Hirson has an impressive talent for writing stage dialogue that is rich, deep, and mellifluous. The two plays he has lavished his skill upon—and the ideas within the plays—were not strong enough vehicles, perhaps; what Hirson's characters say was far meatier than what he himself had to say. You can get away with this sort of unevenness in a musical, if the good stuff is good enough, but dramatic audiences are less forgiving. Especially nowadays, when Broadway is an inhospitable place for nonmusicals. *Wrong Mountain*, the first new Broadway play of the century, was only the second new play of the season; the lamentable *Voices in the Dark*, which closed in October, was the first. (I don't count the 1986 *Epic Proportions* or the 1960 *Waiting in the Wings* as new plays, although they were new to Broadway.) Hirson's language was reward enough for a certain portion of the audience. Myself included; I've spent plenty of wasted evenings in the Broadway theatre, but *La Bête* and *Wrong Mountain* were both fascinating enough to leave you thinking.

The quick demise of *Wrong Mountain* left poor Mr. Hirson with two consecutive, ignominious-yet-admirable failures. With all that talent, though, I trust he'll be back. With something to say.

> **I've spent plenty of wasted evenings in the Broadway theatre, but *La Bête* and *Wrong Mountain* were both fascinating enough to leave you thinking.**

On a Clear Day You Can See Forever

Lyricist-librettist Alan Jay Lerner and his composer-partner
Frederick Loewe were roundly hailed as successors to
Rodgers and Hammerstein upon the opening of *My Fair Lady* in 1956.
Their musicalization of Shaw's *Pygmalion* was instantaneously acclaimed
a classic—deservedly so—and its authors just as instantaneously lionized
as masters of musical theatre. (When *My Fair Lady* came to town,
Rodgers and Hammerstein's days of greatness had apparently passed. Both
were ailing, and they had written two consecutive failures.)

No one seemed to take into account, though, that Rodgers and Hammerstein's mantle was based on no fewer than six all-time classics, namely,
Show Boat, Pal Joey, Oklahoma!, Carousel, South Pacific, and *The King and
I*. Lerner and Loewe inherited the crown based on one show, *My Fair
Lady*. They had, indeed, written an excellent-but-underappreciated musical back in 1947; but *Brigadoon* was merely a hit, running less than a
year and a half. Lerner and Loewe's final show, *Camelot* in 1960, was successful despite clumsy crafting. It reappears frequently, a perfect vehicle
for overage male sex symbols who needn't sing but can still sell tickets, at
least on the road; but the material, with the exception of a few songs, is
not of the caliber of any of the above-mentioned shows. *Brigadoon*, which
does not have roles easily castable with stars, is far less visible. I suppose
and hope that someone will get around to doing a first-rate production of
it one of these days, and everybody will say, hey, this show is wonderful.

Anyway, in 1960, Hammerstein died and Loewe retired (after a near-
fatal heart attack). It did not take long for a marriage of Rodgers and

Lerner to be broached. The contracts were duly signed, and *I Picked a Daisy*—to be produced by the authors and directed by Gower Champion (before *Hello, Dolly!*)—was announced for the spring of 1963.

Rodgers soon discovered what Loewe learned on *Camelot*: Alan Jay Lerner had grown impossible to work with. (Moss Hart, the director and coproducer—with Lerner and Loewe—also had a *Camelot* heart attack and died a year later.) Among Lerner's problems was an addiction to the miracle injections—laced with speed—given by society doctor Max Jacobsen, popularly known as "Dr. Feelgood." Rodgers was a man who set strict schedules. When Lerner failed to turn up with long-promised material at a work session, and Rodgers learned that he had jetted off to Capri instead, the composer decided to sever the relationship. (Rodgers next tried to collaborate with Lionel Bart of *Oliver!*—who was even more unreliable than Lerner—before moving on to Stephen Sondheim for *Do I Hear a Waltz?*) Lerner's six post-Loewe musicals were all poorly written failures; in fact, over the course of Lerner's thirty-eight years on Broadway,

only *Brigadoon, My Fair Lady,* and *Camelot* can be considered commercial or artistic successes.

Lerner turned to Burton Lane, with whom he'd written the 1951 Fred Astaire movie *Royal Wedding.* Lane had one of Broadway's oddest careers. After writing the excellent score for *Finian's Rainbow* in 1947, he had written—nothing. He accepted (with misgivings) Lerner's call on *I Picked a Daisy,* which was reannounced for the spring of 1964 as a Feuer and Martin production, to be directed by Bob Fosse. But Lerner simply couldn't get around to writing it. *Daisy* was put off once again, with the pro-

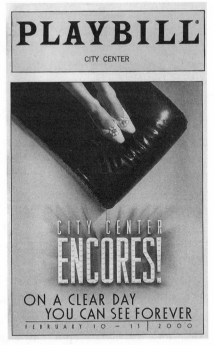

duction staff finally withdrawing. The underbaked show, ultimately produced by Lerner himself, finally arrived on Broadway as *On a Clear Day You Can See Forever* in the fall of 1965. Not surprisingly under the circumstances, it was not very good. The book started with a highly workable

Dr. Mark Bruckner Peter Friedman
Preston Brooks Ashmanskas
Mrs. Hatch Nancy Opel
Daisy Gamble Kristin Chenoweth
Muriel Darcie Roberts
Millard Jim Newman
Mr. Welles Dale Hensley
Mrs. Welles Beth McVey
Sir Hubert Insdale Ed Dixon
Edward Moncrief Brent Barrett
Warren Smith Roger Bart
Flora Rachel Coloff
Dr. Conrad Bruckner Gerry Bamman
Bolagard Bryan T. Donovan
Themistocles Kriakos Louis Zorich
Airline Official Timothy Breese
Singing Ensemble Anne Allgood, Timothy Breese, Rachel Coloff, Susan Derry, Bryan T. Donovan, Colm Fitzmaurice, Dale Hensley, Damon Kirsche, Ann Kittredge, Beth McVey, Joseph Webster, Laurie Williamson
Dancing Ensemble Stephen Campanella, Celina Carvajal, Kim Craven, Derric Harris, Tina Ou, Shonn Wiley

&

Melinda (Perhaps) Kristin Chenoweth

CITY CENTER

CITY CENTER
Judith E. Daykin, President & Executive Director

CITY CENTER
ENCORES!
ARTISTIC DIRECTOR
Kathleen Marshall
MUSICAL DIRECTOR
Rob Fisher

ON A CLEAR DAY YOU CAN SEE FOREVER
BOOK AND LYRICS BY   MUSIC BY
Alan Jay Lerner   Burton Lane
Produced for the Broadway stage by Alan Jay Lerner

STARRING
Kristin Chenoweth   Peter Friedman
Brent Barrett
Roger Bart
ALSO STARRING
Brooks Ashmanskas   Gerry Bamman   Ed Dixon
Jim Newman   Nancy Opel   Darcie Roberts
AND
Louis Zorich

Anne Allgood Timothy Breese Stephen Campanella Celina Carvajal Rachel Coloff
Kim Craven Susan Derry Bryan T. Donovan Colm Fitzmaurice Derric Harris
Dale Hensley Damon Kirsche Ann Kittredge Beth McVey Tina Ou
Joseph Webster Shonn Wiley Laurie Williamson

The Coffee Club Orchestra
Rob Fisher, CONDUCTOR
SCENIC CONSULTANT   COSTUME CONSULTANT   LIGHTING   SOUND
John Lee Beatty   Wallace G. Lane, Jr.   Donald Holder   Scott Lehrer
CONCERT ADAPTATION   PRODUCTION STAGE MANAGER   ORIGINAL ORCHESTRATION   MUSICAL COORDINATOR
David Ives   Gary Mickelson   Robert Russell Bennett   Seymour Red Press
CHOREOGRAPHER   CASTING
John Carrafa   Jay Binder
DIRECTED BY
Mark Brokaw

Major sponsorship for City Center Encores!℠ is provided by a grant from
Time Warner Inc.
The development of Encores! is assisted by seed support from The New York Times Company Foundation
ON A CLEAR DAY YOU CAN SEE FOREVER is presented by arrangement with Tams-Witmark Music Library, Inc.
560 Lexington Avenue, New York, New York 10022
City Center 55th Street Theater Foundation, Inc. gratefully acknowledges the significant support it receives from the
New York City Department of Cultural Affairs including support through the Cultural Challenge Program
Baldwin Piano, Official Piano of City Center

idea but kind of withered away into nothingness; the score was for the most part incredibly good but strangely spare, with only twelve songs (compared with the seventeen in shows like *My Fair Lady* or *Guys and Dolls*).

The mission of City Center Encores!, more or less, is to disinter non-producible but worthwhile musicals, so *Clear Day* made a fine choice for the first offering of their eighth season. The weaknesses of the show, however, shone through exceptionally clear; portions of the audience seemed somewhat surprised by how inept the book turned out to be. (The second act, by my count, lasted all of thirty-five minutes.) But the music sounded glorious, and isn't that the purpose of doing these staged readings with a full orchestra playing the original orchestrations? Expert ones in this case—which apparently hadn't been dusted off since the show closed in the spring of 1966—by Robert Russell Bennett, whose career went back to 1922 and included Kern's *Show Boat*, Gershwin's *Of Thee I Sing*, Rodgers's *Oklahoma!*, Porter's *Kiss Me, Kate*, and *My Fair Lady*.

Given the lack of clarity on the part of lyricist-librettist-producer Alan Lerner, it's remarkable that the *Clear Day* score is so very good. Two of the songs are minor standards, the title song—with its leisurely, long-lined main phrase—and "Come Back to Me," a list song built on a three-note stepwise progression that continually begs for resolution. There are a pair of remarkably good, moody ballads—"Melinda" and "She Wasn't You"—and a pair of absolutely perfect comedy character songs for the leading lady, "Hurry! It's Lovely Up Here!" and "What Did I Have That I Don't Have?" These two have notably delicious lyrics, probably Lerner's best post-Loewe work. Almost as impressive, somehow, are two throwaway comedy songs, "On the S.S. Bernard Cohn" and "Wait Till We're Sixty-Five." These are not in any way important, simply shoehorned into the show; but they both have irrepressible melodies, a jaunty, corny strain for the first and a syncopated waltz for the second. Burton Lane, who throughout his career seems to have gone out of his way to avoid writing, was just brimming over with melody. Eight wonderful songs in one show—that's something you rarely find, and absolutely unheard of in a flop. (It is curious to note that the attractive young leading lady finds love but has absolutely no ballad or love song to sing. Two not-so-good ones were written for the not-so-good 1970 Barbra Streisand film version of the show.)

The other songs are not very good, although with extenuating circumstances. Two of them fit the hazy eighteenth-century story-within-the-story, and they are hazy. Another was overly generic, written to order for a clumsily conceived character with one scene-and-song in the second act. The fellow was one of those Greek shipping magnates who were great figures of fun until Jackie Kennedy married one of them. (Lerner knew his way around Kennedys, having attended Choate with Jack—a fellow pa-

> Portions of the audience seemed somewhat surprised by how inept the book turned out to be; the second act lasted all of thirty-five minutes. But the music sounded glorious, and isn't that the purpose of doing these staged readings with a full orchestra playing the original orchestrations?

On a Clear Day You Can See Forever
Opened: February 10, 2000
Closed: February 13, 2000
Profit/Loss: Nonprofit
5 performances (and 0 previews)
On a Clear Day You Can See Forever ($65 top) played the
2,753-seat City Center. Box office figures not available.

Critical Scorecard

Rave 2
Favorable 3
Mixed 2
Unfavorable 0
Pan 0

tient of Dr. Max; "produced" the president's final birthday party, at the Waldorf; and undergone a lengthy affair, extending through the writing of *Clear Day*, with JFK's sister Jean Kennedy Smith.)

Kristen Chenoweth, just off *Epic Proportions* and en route (presumably) to Hollywood sitcom stardom, came in to play Daisy Gamble, the role that made Barbara Harris a star (until her career imploded, but that's another story). Chenoweth had only to launch into her opening number, "Hurry, It's Lovely Up Here!," for you to realize that she was going to be magical, strutting around her potted daisy as she implored it to grow and building to a finish that would make Judy Holliday or even Al Jolson proud. The crowd exploded, and no wonder. But there's something that makes *me* wonder. Chenoweth used a cutesy voice for Daisy; she's used a cutesy voice for every role I've seen her in so far. Now, she's very good at these funny voices, they work well for comedy, and she presumably gets extra laughs from them. But the cutesy voice is only a small part of her talent arsenal; I suppose she'd be just as good with a normal voice, and that much more vulnerable/lovable/real. (She does have a fine, normal singing voice; at least, she did at an Adam Guettel concert at Town Hall in 1999.) Chenoweth might want to take a look at the career of the similarly talented Carol Channing. A funny voice, grafted onto every single role that comes along, can grow stale and prove ultimately self-defeating.

> Eight wonderful songs in one show—that's something you rarely find, and absolutely unheard of in a flop. It is curious to note that the attractive young leading lady finds love but has absolutely no ballad or love song to sing.

Chenoweth was joined by Roger Bart, with whom she'd shared matching Tony Awards for the otherwise flat 1999 revival of *You're a Good Man, Charlie Brown*. I didn't quite buy Bart's performance as Snoopy; I voted for him, over the lack of competition, but found him too determinedly adorable (whereas Chenoweth's performance in that show was breathtakingly cyclonic). Here, as Warren—the role William Daniels originally played, before moving on to 1776—Bart was delightfully cartoonish, performing his "Wait Till We're Sixty-Five" number with such relish that I thought he was going to gnaw on one of the microphones standing along the apron of the stage.

The hole in the cast was in the leading role of Dr. Bruckner, here played by Peter Friedman (recently the immigrant Tateh in *Ragtime*). When *Clear Day* was struggling in Boston back in 1966, Lane insisted that top-billed Louis Jourdan (from Lerner's film *Gigi*) be fired and replaced by John Cullum. If the show was going to fail anyway, he reasoned, at least the songs should sound good. Had Lane been in the City Center rehearsal hall, he might well have said the same thing. (The composer—who no doubt would have been thrilled by Rob Fisher's fine treatment of his music—died in 1991, at the age of eighty-five.) Casting is especially treacherous on these short-term concert readings; with only five or six days before you go onstage, by the time you discover a problem there's no time to fix it. In this case, though, they had the solution right there in the room: Brent Barrett, who was playing hooky from *Chicago* to fill the relatively small role of Chenoweth's rakish husband. Barrett stopped the show cold with his one solo, "She Wasn't You," receiving an explosive ovation (infinitely stronger than anything accorded Chenoweth at the performance I attended). He could have easily played Bruckner, and with that voice surely would have landed the three "big" songs in a way that Friedman—more actor than singer—couldn't. It wouldn't have solved the show's problems, but as Burton Lane might have said, at least the songs would sound good. And it is also usually inadvisable to cast the romantic lead in a musical comedy with an actor who's bald, unless you have Yul Brynner.

Unlike other Encores! offerings, there wasn't much for the director or choreographer to contribute—how do you make sense of material that doesn't make sense? The best staging of the night came during the "Entr'acte" from the percussionist, dashing from the tympanis to the xylophone to the vibraphone and back to the tymps, with the respective mallets tucked beneath his arms and chin.

All in all, we were left with a problematic show, enhanced by an expertly enjoyable star performance and some truly soaring music. But in the context of Encores!, that adds up to success.

Saturday Night

The vast majority of plays and musicals written for Broadway, it goes without saying, never make it from page to stage. Although this has surely resulted in shattered hopes and blasted careers for numerous talented people, it is nevertheless safe to generalize that most of these scripts are—at the least—nonstageable. So are some of the shows that actually make it to Broadway, but that's another discussion.

Very few of these scripts have any chance whatsoever. A vast minority make it into a producer's office; a fraction of these are actually read; and a mere fraction of a fraction attract attention. An infinitesimal number are officially optioned, which is to say that the authors grant a producer the exclusive production rights in exchange for a few bucks. And then the producers have to raise the money, which more often than not ends in futile frustration.

Front Porch in Flatbush, a comedy by screenwriters Julius J. Epstein and Philip G. Epstein, made its way to the desk of Lemuel Ayers. Ayers was a well-regarded set designer, with the original *Oklahoma!* among his credits. He turned producer in 1948, with Cole Porter's big hit *Kiss Me, Kate*; this was followed in 1950 with Cole Porter's big flop *Out of This World*. (This

After the success of *West Side Story* and *Gypsy*, *Saturday Night* was announced for production in December 1959. But Sondheim decided the show would be "a step backward" and called it off.

last, I am told, had some of the most lavish and beautiful scenery seen on Broadway till that time, which is what happens when one of the producers is a designer coming off a hit with a big budget.) After splitting with

2econd StageTheatre 307 W43 St / 8 Ave NYC

Carole Rothman *Artistic Director*

Carol Fishman *Managing Director*   Alexander Fraser *Executive Director*

presents

A MUSICAL COMEDY

SATURDAY NIGHT

BOOK JULIUS J. EPSTEIN

STEPHEN SONDHEIM MUSIC & LYRICS

Based on the play *Front Porch in Flatbush* by Julius J. Epstein & Philip G. Epstein

WITH **Andrea Burns, David Campbell, Donald Corren,
Natascia A. Diaz, Christopher Fitzgerald, Kirk McDonald, Michael Pemberton,
Joey Sorge, Clarke Thorell, Rachel Ulanet, Frank Vlastnik,
Lauren Ward, Michael Benjamin Washington, David A. White, Greg Zola**

ORCHESTRATIONS **Jonathan Tunick**

MUSICAL DIRECTION **Rob Fisher**

SETS **Derek McLane**   COSTUMES **Catherine Zuber**   LIGHTS **Donald Holder**

SOUND **Scott Lehrer**   PRESS **Richard Kornberg & Associates**

CASTING **Johnson-Liff Associates, Tara Rubin**   MUSIC COORDINATOR **Seymour Red Press**

PRODUCTION STAGE MANAGER **Karen Moore**   ASSOCIATE DIRECTOR **Rob Ashford**

STAGE MANAGER **Karen Evanouskas**   MUSICAL CONTINUITY **Sean Patrick Flahaven**

DIRECTED & CHOREOGRAPHED BY **KATHLEEN MARSHALL**

Christopher Burney *Assoc. Artistic Director*   C. Barrack Evans *General Manager*   Peter J. Davis *Production Manager*

Second Stage Theatre dedicates this production to the memory of Flora Roberts.

Saturday Night is made possible, in part, by the generous support of
The Hale Matthews Foundation, The Blanche and Irving Laurie Foundation
and the **City of New York Department of Cultural Affairs Cultural Challenge Program**.
Additional support provided by **United States Trust Company of New York**.

Baldwin Piano is the official piano of Second Stage Theatre.

Ted   Michael Benjamin Washington
Artie   Kirk McDonald
Ray   Greg Zola
Dino   Joey Sorge
Bobby   Christopher Fitzgerald
Celeste   Andrea Burns
Hank   Clarke Thorell
Gene   David Campbell
Pinhead   Frank Vlastnek
Mildred   Rachel Ulanet
Vocalist   Donald Corren
Plaza Attendant   Michael Pemberton
Helen   Lauren Ward
Mr. Fletcher   Donald Corren
Mr. Fisher   David A. White
Florence   Natascia A. Diaz
Clune   Michael Pemberton
Dakota Doran   Natascia A. Diaz
Waiter   David A. White
Lieutenant   David A. White

Time: Spring, 1929
Place: Flatbush (Brooklyn) and
   Manhattan

Original Off-Broadway Cast Album:
   Nonesuch 79609

producing partner Saint Subber, Ayers optioned the comedy by the Epstein twins. (These Brooklyn brothers were best known for *Casablanca*, but Howard Koch—who shares screenplay credit—apparently made wholesale changes to their work.) Determining that *Front Porch* needed songs, Ayers commissioned a score from twenty-four-year-old novice Sondheim. *Saturday Night*, as the musical was named, was midway through the money-raising stage when Ayers died of leukemia in the summer of 1955, and that was the end of that. It goes without saying that no other producer bothered to pick it up. Not the most successful musical show producer of the day, Oscar Hammerstein, who was Sondheim's mentor; not Sondheim's producer-pal Hal Prince, who had just produced two Tony Award–winning musical hits in fourteen months.

Sondheim rebounded, writing lyrics—to music by established composers—for *West Side Story* (1957) and *Gypsy* (1959). *Saturday Night* was announced for production in December 1959, with *Gypsy* composer Jule Styne producing and Bob Fosse directing. But Sondheim decided the show would be "a step backward" and called it off. His composing career didn't begin until 1962, with *A Funny Thing Happened on the Way to the Forum*, and by 1973 or so he was crowned king of the modern Broadway musical.

Which meant that people continued to ask about *Saturday Night*. Half of the songs found their way into the Sondheim fan's consciousness over the years, via charity benefits and recordings. This only kept the mysterious "lost" musical tantalizingly out of view. Sondheim finally allowed a concert reading of the show in London in 1995, which resulted in a fully staged version at an off-off-Broadway-type theatre in London in 1997, which led to a semiprofessional production in Chicago in 1999 and—finally—this top-of-the-line off-Broadway production by the nonprofit Second Stage Theatre.

Which is, presumably, as far as *Saturday Night* will, or should, go. It turned out to be a charming, good-natured piece. It seems likely to have a healthy stock and amateur life ahead of it, as it is relatively funny, relatively melodic, relatively clever, relatively clean, and filled with funny lyrics. But at the same time, it appeared way too mild for Broadway in 2000—and I suppose it was way too mild for Broadway in 1955 as well.

> **Saturday Night seems likely to have a healthy stock and amateur life ahead of it, as it is relatively funny, relatively melodic, relatively clever, relatively clean, and filled with funny lyrics. But it appeared to be way too mild for Broadway.**

It is, perhaps, inappropriate to fully judge *Saturday Night*'s 1955 potential. A show of this sort, back then, would have undergone numerous changes along the way. The authors would have started with a "finished" prerehearsal script. A director, once hired, would demand changes, rewrites, and new songs. Once in rehearsal, the show would be further refined and rewritten as weak spots became apparent. Then the show would face the out-of-town critics—all musicals underwent a tryout in those days—and the show would be torn apart and stitched together once again. (Mind you, even *The King and I*—from the mighty Rodgers and Hammerstein—tossed out songs, characters, and actors in New Haven.)

The most "finished" version of *Saturday Night*, apparently, was a prerehearsal script of the unstaged show. Sections that might well have been

Saturday Night
Opened: February 17, 2000
Closed: March 26, 2000
48 performances (and 28 previews)
Profit/Loss: Nonprofit
Saturday Night ($61 top) played at the 296-seat Second
    Stage. Box office figures not available.

DRAMA DESK AWARD
Best Lyrics: Stephen Sondheim (WINNER)

*Critical
Scorecard*

Rave   0
Favorable   6
Mixed   1
Unfavorable   2
Pan   0

thrown out in rehearsal or fixed during the tryout remain baldly visible. While Sondheim added a new number for the new production, he apparently left the rest alone—understandably so, given the circumstances. (The new song, "Montana Chem," was a dandily crafted concerted number that accomplished its purpose—following stock market quotes of the neighborhood gang's investment, over a week's worth of time—with style. It's not anything, though, that I imagine Sondheim would have come up with forty-five years earlier.)

Sondheim's first score shows promise, as they say. The opening number is a wonderful song and—yes—pretty novel for its time. It's a quartet for a bunch of boys fated to spend Saturday night alone, together, on a front porch in Flatbush; inventive and wonderfully alive, and filled with bright lyrics. ("Here's a revival of Ben Hur / Goes on at 9:15 at the Cushman," suggests one of the guys. "So when I got my mind on sex / Who gives a damn for Francis X. Bushman?" responds another.) The show's main ballad, "So Many People," also came across very nicely, far better than on its several previous recordings. "All for You" was also pleasing, while "What More Do I Need?" has a nice Rodgers and Hart–style bounce to it.

But more than a couple of the songs seem extraneous and way out of place. There is an extended number ("In the Movies") satirizing films of the twenties, comparing the actions of Theda Bara to a typical girl in Brooklyn. ("You can start with a bagel and end up with Conrad Nagel," Sondheim rhymes, bless him.) This song is shoehorned in, solely because the boys happen to take the girls to a double feature. The boys' section of the song does suit the action, and neatly so; they are busy divvying up the cost of the shared date. But the Hollywood daydreams of the girls, while amusing, have little to do with *Saturday Night*. A song called "Exhibit A," in which a pretend Lothario demonstrates his supposed seduction skills, was wonderfully entertaining as performed by a fellow named Christopher Fitzgerald (who brought to mind a combination of Danny Kaye and Red Skelton). But it was merely a stopping point in the action for entertainment's sake; the character was never called upon to *use* his Lothario skills, or in fact to do anything much the rest of the evening. There was another spot in the second act, where everyone stood on the porch of a police station, wondering where the leading man—who had gotten himself into a heap of trouble—could be. So what did they do? They sang "That Kind of a Neighborhood," about how wonderful Brooklyn and its denizens are. (This was pretty much the "Gee, Officer Krupke" spot, by the way.) Again, it appeared to be intended as an entertaining stopping-off point, but it really had nothing to do with the problem at hand. The same can be said for an earlier song, the first-act finale, "One Wonderful Day" (which has the same, extended opening note and some of the feel of the title song from *Oklahoma!*).

Not bad, overall, for a beginner. But not bad, probably, would not have been nearly good enough. Not in 1955 and not in 2000. Would anyone, anywhere, have unearthed *Saturday Night* without a famous composer's name attached?

Sondheim wasn't the only first-time Broadway composer hitting the backers' audition circuit at the time. Richard Adler (with his collaborator Jerry Ross) wrote a similarly unpromising musical—about striking garment workers—which managed to get off the ground in 1954 and achieved a then-impressive run of 1,063 performances. *The Pajama Game*, coproduced by Hal Prince, included such songs as "Hey There," "Hernando's Hideaway," and "Steam Heat," which stack up pretty well against *Saturday Night*. Another novice, Albert Hague, wrote the music for the 1955 Pennsylvania Dutch–themed musical *Plain and Fancy*. While not in a class with *Pajama Game*, the score was exceedingly pleasant and included two lovely ballads, "Young and Foolish" and "It Wonders Me." If it took Sondheim longer to get his career under way, neither Adler nor Hague has found success on Broadway since Eisenhower left office. And not for lack of trying.

Despite some weaknesses, the Second Stage production of *Saturday Night* was so good-natured that it was impossible to dislike. Credit director-choreographer Kathleen Marshall, who kept things bright and glossy enough to avoid the hazards in the material; Sondheim's longtime orchestrator, Jonathan Tunick, who scored the piece for ten players with a light hand and plenty of charm; and the uniformly pleasant cast. David

Would anyone, anywhere, have unearthed *Saturday Night* without a famous composer's name attached?

Campbell managed to keep the not-so-admirable hero in a pleasant light; he's an admittedly phony social climber, who swindles his pals and loses his cousin's Pierce Arrow to loan sharks. Singing honors went to Lauren Ward, as the girl from Albemarle Avenue, a mile up from Flatbush, who was especially good on "So Many People" and "All for You." The aforementioned Mr. Fitzgerald provided a cheerful presence, and Andrea Burns—as the only mature member of the group—helped keep the second act from wobbling apart. They were all good, in fact, including the boy's quartet; and someone—Sondheim? Marshall? musical director Rob Fisher?—provided an excellent piece of recurring comic business during the oft-repeated title number for a red-haired boy (Kirk McDonald) with a wayward ukulele.

So chalk it up as an entertaining divertissement, if not the best musical of 2000 or even 1955.

Squonk

How do you get to Broadway with an unconventional, indecipherable, non-star-driven piece of modernistically esoteric theatre? Assuming you don't have a rich uncle who owns a theatre chain, or who has a corporation that owns a theatre chain. One way is to mount said esoterica in some off-off-Broadway matchbox and hope that somebody bothers to attend, loves the show, and turns out to be the first-string critic of the *Times*. This is what is commonly referred to as a long shot; yet it happens once in a very long while along the fabled street of dreams. And thus it was that *Squonk* journeyed to Forty-fourth Street, courtesy of and just west of the *New York Times*.

The eyes of the creators of *Squonk* were not set on Broadway, as it happens. Their limited engagement in August 1999, at P.S. 122 on lower First Avenue—an experimental performance space, not a public school—garnered great acclaim and producers eager to transfer it; but they were looking for an off-Broadway venue. *Blue Man Group, Stomp,* and *De La Guarda* have demonstrated that there is a definite audience for these nonverbal, nonlinear pieces of nontraditional theatrical nonsense down around the fringes of Union Square and Astor Place. A suitable 299-seat off-Broadway

At one point, a creature with three crocodile heads wobbled its way down the aisle to the stage, almost colliding with three one-headed patrons scurrying up the aisle to the exit.

address wasn't in sight, so when the 579-seat Helen Hayes was suddenly vacated by the not-so-epic *Epic Proportions, Squonk* snapped it up.

(A year earlier, Margaret Edson's *Wit* was unable to book the Helen Hayes—on the landlord's belief that there was no audience for a serious play

Keyboard & Accordion Jackie Dempsey
Electronic & Acoustic Percussion, Sound Textures Kevin Kornicki
Flutes, Electronic Winds, Many-Belled Trumpet Steve O'Hearn
Double Bass T. Weldon Anderson
Vocals Jana Losey

Original Broadway Cast Album:
Angel 26523

THE HELEN HAYES THEATRE
MARTIN MARKINSON   DONALD TICK

WILLIAM   MICHAEL   LAUREN   COOKIE   CHRIS
REPICCI   MINICHIELLO   DOLL   CENTRACCO   GROENEWOLD

in association with RARE GEM PRODUCTIONS and MICHAEL STOLLER

Present

squonk

BigSmörgåsbørdWünderWerk

Created by
STEVE O'HEARN AND JACKIE DEMPSEY
in collaboration with the original NY Squonk Ensemble
CASI PACILIO KEVIN KORNICKI JANA LOSEY T. WELDON ANDERSON

Music by   Image Book   Lyrics by
JACKIE DEMPSEY with SQUONK   STEVE O'HEARN   JANA LOSEY with JACKIE DEMPSEY

Performers
T. WELDON ANDERSON   JACKIE DEMPSEY   KEVIN KORNICKI
JANA LOSEY   STEVE O'HEARN

Sets, Puppets and Costumes   Lighting   Sound
STEVE O'HEARN   TIM SATERNOW   BERNARD FOX

Projections   Musical Direction   Choreography and Movement
STEVE O'HEARN   JACKIE DEMPSEY   PETER KOPE and
with CASI PACILIO   MICHELE DE LA REZA
and NICK FOX-GEIG

Additional Casting   Assistant Musical Direction   Technical Consultant   Technical Supervisor
STEPHANIE KLAPPER, CSA   KEVIN KORNICKI   GENE O'DONOVAN   BOB ZIMMERMAN

Production Stage Manager   General Manager   Press Agent   Associate Producers
CASI PACILIO   WILLIAM REPICCI   JEFFREY RICHARDS   MASTANTUONO/PALUMBO
                        ASSOCIATES   ASSOCIATES   ERIC FALKENSTEIN

Direction
TOM DIAMOND

about cancer. While other theatre owners have made larger and far more costly blunders of late, the Hayes proprietors turned up their noses at the 1999 Pulitzer Prize winner in favor of the quickly forgotten *Band in Berlin*. Thus, while *Wit* ran successfully at the Union Square Theatre for sixty-eight weeks, the Hayes sat unbooked and empty half that time—and nearly empty the rest, with *Band in Berlin*, *Night Must Fall*, *Epic Proportions*, and *Squonk*.)

Squonk was, simply put, a *BigSmörgåsbørdWünderWerk*. That was their word for it, anyway, seemingly incomprehensible but easily broken down to a big smorgasbord of wonder work. Of course, one person's *wünderwerk* is another's snooze. The show itself proved far less comprehensible than the word *BigSmörgåsbørdWünderWerk*. True, it was a smorgasbord of sorts; eggs played a large part in the dramaturgy of the piece. At one point—one of the more lucid of the evening—two of the actors were clearly eating lunch. The leading man was apparently eating raw hot dogs, off a devil's pitchfork; the drummer was gnawing on a severed hand he pulled from his lunch box. There was also a severed head, on a platter, that sang. Actually, it wasn't really a severed head, as it popped out of the prop table wearing a straitjacket with arms the width of the stage. The head didn't really sing, either; I mean, it sang, but was it singing? The person attached to the head chanted her way through the evening, in an otherworldly manner. Sometime later, during what appeared to be a filmed section projected on a clear plastic tarp, she became an underwater woman in a white dress, apparently struggling to make her way to the surface. I don't think she made it, though. Long before then, I confess, I was all squonked out.

As is the case with much environmental theatre, the "action" began well before curtain time. A woman with an accordion—composer/cocreator Jackie Dempsey—roamed the aisles, playing for tips. We knew she was playing for tips because there was a sign attached to the back of her costume saying "Tips," with two dollar bills adhesived in place to give you the idea. She would play a song, stop by an aisle-sitter, leer at them with dancing eyebrows, and then point to the tip can. A fellow sitting a couple of rows up actually did, sheepishly, place a dollar bill in the bucket. This, in retrospect, was probably a great idea; certainly, Ms. Dempsey would not have gotten any tips if she'd waited till after the show to solicit them.

There was audience participation, too. The Squonkers pulled an unwilling fellow out of the audience, a device that has become all too commonplace of late. Usually, the selected chump makes a pretense of unwillingness, but this guy they literally had to drag out of his seat. He was suitably dressed for the occasion, wearing a black leather jacket, black jeans, and beige Hush Puppies. (Oh, what Dame Edna would have done with him!!) They placed him behind a makeshift screen and —in short order—pulled a clarinet with a lightbulb out of his stomach. It seems to me that Penn and Teller did a similar shadow box effect in their first Broadway show, but they were experts at making their volunteers squirm. The way *Squonk* did it, their guinea pig had no idea of what they were doing to

him; he was therefore unable to be apprehensive about what was going to happen, so he just stood there kind of grinning. The whole thing was over before he knew it; I suppose that after he got back to his seat he needed to ask his companion what happened. Of course, most members of the audience, most of the time, were asking their companions what happened until their collective eyes glazed over.

At one point, a creature with three crocodile heads wobbled its way down the aisle to the stage, almost colliding with three one-headed patrons scurrying up the aisle to the exit. Once onstage, the creature was joined by two others in a synchronized kick-step, looking like Floridian cheerleaders after a game-losing fumble in overtime in the playoffs. At another point, the sound of an unseen vacuum cleaner came from the stage right wing. Being clearer than anything else all evening, it got a big laugh. The logo—of a feathered headpiece-helmet sitting atop an egg, with goggles—made about as much sense as the show. Not only did I have to pay the baby-sitter for staying at home with the kids, I felt compelled to pay my wife, too, for sitting through it.

The East Village *Squonk* was—in the words of Ben Brantley of the *Times*—"a hallucinatory game." When it was performed in a tiny space, the audience was right in the middle of it; when theatregoers were moved to the safety of the far side of a proscenium, the piece apparently lost its effect. At least, that was the opinion of those critics who had seen the earlier incarnation. Whatever it was that they'd enjoyed in August was certainly missing in February. Mr. Brantley doesn't necessarily cover openings of shows that transfer; he didn't run opening night reviews of the Broadway versions of *The Dead* or *Contact*.

The producers of *Squonk* no doubt hoped that their off-off-Broadway review would stand; they helpfully provided it to the critics arriving at the

Hayes, as if it were a certificate of theatrical authenticity. Brantley—no doubt fielding puzzled looks in the hallways of the *Times* during the *Squonk* previews—changed course and rereviewed the show, explaining what was then and what was now. This didn't prevent the producers from continuing to run quotes from Brantley's original *Times* review—they didn't have anything much else to run—but the whole enterprise soon slithered back to Pittsburgh, from whence it hailed. The grand finale had eggs (marshmallows?) exploding into the audience. No gladiolas, though (ref. *Dame Edna*). While *Squonk* was officially eighty minutes long, I clocked it at sixty-five minutes. Sixty-five minutes, sixty-five dollars.

Not only did I have to pay the baby sitter for staying at home with the kids, I felt compelled to pay my wife, too, for sitting through it.

BigSmörgåsbørdWünderWerk.

Porgy and Bess

George Gershwin's folk opera *Porgy and Bess* is surely the finest twentieth-century work of its kind; it is also, perhaps, the only work of its kind. The majority of people walking into a modern-day opera house production of *Porgy*, I would guess, have a vague familiarity with—and ingrown fondness for—the piece. They don't know it backward and forward, as theatre aficionados and Gershwin fans might; but they can be sure of a familiar story in a familiar language, and they are sure to at least recognize some of the tunes.

For such an audience, any reasonably professional production of *Porgy* is a treat. As was this one. Due to the large complement of singers and musicians necessary, full-scale mountings are few and far between. Judged on the question of general worth, City Opera's *Porgy* merits appreciative praise. One could find considerable fault with it as a piece of theatre, which—given the nature of this book—I am bound to do. But keep in mind that this production was certainly acceptable and most welcome, and I was glad to see it.

Porgy premiered on Broadway in 1935, closing after a mere 124 performances. Yes, it was a failure, but commentators and musicologists seldom take into account that this was an inordinately expensive and decidedly noncommercial venture, especially in the depths of the Depression. George Gershwin died of a brain tumor less than two years later, at the age of thirty-eight. (At the time of his death, the residuary value of *Porgy and Bess* was appraised at $250, or less than the cost of three orchestra seats to this production.) His collaborator DuBose Heyward, who also wrote the novel upon which *Porgy* was based, died in 1940. Only Ira Gershwin—who shared the lyric chore with Heyward—lived long enough to see *Porgy* become a worldwide classic. Ira contributed the more intricate material, including Sportin' Life's "It Ain't Necessarily So" and "There's a Boat dat's Leavin' Soon for New York"; "I Got Plenty o' Nuttin'"; and the two big love duets.

Porgy first found success when it was remounted on Broadway in 1942, with most of the original principals recreating their roles for 286 performances (plus brief return engagements in 1943 and 1944). A highly successful international touring company visited Broadway in 1953, for 312 performances. As a result of that engagement, Leontyne Price—that production's first-string Bess—quickly springboarded to opera house stardom. Producer Sherwin Goldman and the Houston Grand Opera mounted a new and expanded production in 1976, which played Broadway's Uris Theatre (now the Gershwin) for 122 performances and continued on an extended U.S. tour. Goldman's production was remounted for an international tour in 1978 and retooled for a visit to the oversize Radio City Music Hall in 1982. The Metropolitan Opera did it in 1985, and Goldman—as executive producer of the New York City Opera—reassembled the pieces of his various *Porgy*s for the 2000 production under discussion. The 1976 version, though, was the piece's last Broadway stand. Economics being what they are, it is questionable whether *Porgy* will ever get back on the Broadway stage, where it belongs.

And *Porgy* does belong, ideally, in the theatre. It was written specifically for Broadway. (Gershwin had, in fact, received a commission from the Metropolitan Opera in 1929 for an earlier project that ultimately went unwritten. He specifically rejected the Met's offer to produce *Porgy*, opting to have it performed on Broadway.) There are any number of differences between theatre and opera, but two are especially apt. One is the size of the house, and the distance between actor and audience. It's not only

At the time of Gershwin's death, the residuary value of *Porgy and Bess* was appraised at $250, or less than the cost of three orchestra seats to this production.

a question of visibility, but also of the performer's ability to reach out and "touch," emotionally, the people in the seats. The original *Porgy and Bess* played at the very same theatre as the Gershwins' musical comedy hits *Funny Face* and *Girl Crazy*, the 1,334-seat Alvin (now the Neil Simon), with an orchestra section and one mezzanine/balcony. Compare this with the cavernous New York State Theatre, with a thousand-seat orchestra section plus five "rings," topped by a nosebleed gallery.

Cast (in order of appearance)

Jasbo Brown Gerald Steichen
Clara Anita Johnson
Mingo Robert Mack
Jake Kenneth Floyd
Sportin' Life Dwayne Clark
Robbins Michael Austin
Serena Angela Simpson or Monique
McDonald
Jim Edward Pleasant
Peter Bert Lindsey
Lily Shirley Russ
Maria Sabrina Elayne Carten
Scipio Nkosane Jackson

Porgy Alvy Powell or Richard Hobson
Crown Timothy Robert Blevins or
Lester Lynch
Bess Marquita Lister or Kishna Davis
Detective Wynn Harmon
Policemen Michael Hajek, Charles
Mandracchia
Undertaker Bryan Jackson
Annie Jeanette Blakeney
Frazier Marvin Lowe
Strawberry Woman Adina Aaron
Crab Man Duane Martin Foster
Nelson E. Mani Cadet
Coroner John Henry Thomas
Ensemble: Adina Aaron, Jeanette
Blakeney, Bert Boone, Elaugh Butler,
E. Mani Cadet, Aixa Cruz-Falú, David
Aron Damane, Jean Derricotte-
Murphy, Devonne Douglas, Mia
Douglas, Rochelle Ellis, Duane Martin
Foster, Anne Fridal, Chinyelu Ingram,
Clinton Ingram, Bryan Jackson,
Nicola James, Quanda Johnson,
Naomi Elizabeth Jones, Pamela E.
Jones, Jason Phillip Knight, Bert
Lindsey, Lisa Lockhart, Marvin Lowe,
Robert Mack, Edward Pleasant,
Dorian Gray Ross, Elizabeth Lyra
Ross, Leonard Rowe, Shirley Russ,
Martin Solá, Marcos Solá, Lucy
Salome Sträuli, Marcelin Summers,
Everett Suttle, Kellie Turner
Children: Khatif Diouf, Ayanna Francis,
Leilani Irvin, Nkosane Jackson, Kayla
Leacock, Grace Price, Afrika Rhames,
Khadijha Stewart, Lacey Thomas,
Jamal Russ, Verne Watley

Place: Charleston, South Carolina
Time: mid-1930s

The Gershwins®

Porgy and Bess™

By George Gershwin, DuBose and Dorothy Heyward, and Ira Gershwin

Conductor	John DeMain
Director	Tazewell Thompson
Choreographer	Julie Arenal
Set Designer	Douglas W. Schmidt
Costume Designer	Nancy Potts
Lighting Designer	Robert Wierzel
Hair and Makeup Designer	Everett Suttle
Supertitles	Cori Ellison
Fight Director	Roddy Kinter

Cast
(in order of appearance)

Jasbo Brown	Gerald Steichen
Clara	Anita Johnson
Mingo	Robert Mack
Jake	Kenneth Floyd
Sportin' Life	Dwayne Clark
Robbins	Michael Austin
Serena	Monique McDonald
Jim	Edward Pleasant
Peter	Bert Lindsey
Lily	Shirley Russ
Maria	Sabrina Elayne Carten
Scipio	Nkosane Jackson
Porgy	Richard Hobson
Crown	Lester Lynch
Bess	Kishna Davis*
Detective	Wynn Harmon
Policemen	Michael Hajek, Charles Mandracchia
Undertaker	Bryan Jackson
Annie	Jeanette Blakeney
Frazier	Marvin Lowe
Strawberry Woman	Adina Aaron
Crab Man	Duane Martin Foster
Nelson	E. Mani Cadet
Coroner	John Henry Thomas

Ensemble:
Adina Aaron, Jeanette Blakeney, Bert Boone, Elaugh Butler, E. Mani Cadet,
Aixa Cruz-Falú, David Aron Damane, Jean Derricotte-Murphy, Devonne Douglas,
Mia Douglas, Rochelle Ellis, Duane Martin Foster, Anne Fridal, Chinyelu Ingram,
Clinton Ingram, Bryan Jackson, Nicola James, Quanda Johnson, Naomi Elizabeth Jones,
Pamela E. Jones, Jason Phillip Knight, Bert Lindsey, Lisa Lockhart, Marvin Lowe,
Robert Mack, Edward Pleasant, Dorian Gray Ross, Elizabeth Lyra Ross,
Leonard Rowe, Shirley Russ, Martín Solá, Marcos Solá, Lucy Salome Sträuli,
Marcelin Summers, Everett Suttle, Kellie Turner

Children:
Khalif Diouf, Ayanna Francis, Leilani Irvin, Nkosane Jackson, Kayla Leacock,
Grace Price, Afrika Rhames, Khadijha Stewart, Lacey Thomas, Jamal Russ, Verne Watley

A more crucial difference has to do with the quality of performance. Put fifty singers together in a rehearsal room for six weeks, learning their roles together; put them onstage for rehearsals, previews, and—as in the case of the 1935, 1942, 1953, and 1976 *Porgy*s—a tryout tour. What you will get, especially if you have a brilliant director like *Porgy*'s visionary Rouben Mamoulian, is a stage full of performers who *live* the material. The conditions and the realities of the world of opera simply don't allow this. With a run of only fourteen performances—and alternating casts in the leading roles—rehearsal time is understandably minimal. Goldman's 1976 *Porgy* was directed by Jack O'Brien, a full-fledged theatre man. The 2000 *Porgy* appears not to have been directed at all; rather, it was staged by Tazewell Thompson (or, from the looks of it, restaged). It is one thing to instruct the singers what to do and when to do it; it is another thing to let them discover who their characters are, and why they behave as they do. An opera house production might get you good singers, but an effective *Porgy and Bess* demands that they act as well.

Of course, in the opera house the conductor is unquestionably the star. For beginners, he—it's almost always a man, isn't it?—is listed in the ads even before the singers. (Conductor John DeMain—who by this point probably knows the *Porgy* score as well as anyone—is the only holdover from the 1976 staff.) In the theatre, it is the director who calls the shots, from casting on down the line; a Broadway conductor is always consulted on casting but occasionally is overruled. Look at the program for any revival of *West Side Story*, say, and you'll see the name of the original director prominently displayed. Most anyone reading this book doesn't even have to look it up to know that *West Side* was Jerry Robbins's show; many can also easily identify Hal Prince as one of the producers, and possibly the designers Oliver Smith and Irene Sharaff. Some will even rattle off the names of the orchestrators, but I defy more than a handful of readers to tell me the name of the musical director. The same goes for *Porgy*; while Mamoulian is remembered in at least some circles as the director of three landmark musicals (*Porgy and Bess, Oklahoma!* and *Carousel*), Alexander Smallens—the man behind the podium—was there to serve the director, not the other way around.

The City Opera production was moderately well sung, except that the Porgy (Richard Hobson) had a bum microphone and was therefore inaudible throughout the evening. You have misbehaving microphones on Broadway, too, but they are usually replaced as soon as the actor momentarily steps into the wings. Bess (Kishna Davis) was okay, if not excep-

Porgy and Bess
Opened: March 7, 2000
Closed: March 25, 2000
10 performances (and 4 previews)
Profit/Loss: Nonprofit
Porgy and Bess ($95 top) played at the 2,779-seat New York
  State Theatre Box office figures not available.

*Critical
Scorecard*

Rave 1
Favorable 1
Mixed 2
Unfavorable 0
Pan 1

tional; she sang the notes but didn't look all that comfortable. The only person onstage who gave a performance I would care to see again was Dwayne Clark, as Sportin' Life. My press tickets were for the second night, so I saw a different set of principals than some of the other reviewers; if Wednesday night's leads were inferior to Tuesday's, so be it. If you wish to offer audiences alternating actors of differing qualities at the same ticket price, be prepared to be judged by the worst. I'd also like to point out, as I've done in the past, that the original stars Todd Duncan and Anne Wiggins Brown sang eight performances a week for five months in 1935 and nine months when *Porgy* was revived in 1942, without mechanical amplification and without any noticeable adverse affect. (Duncan, who also starred in musicals by Vernon Duke and Kurt Weill, died in 1998 at the age of ninety-five; Brown, who tired of racial prejudice and moved to Norway, is at this writing alive and well and feisty at eighty-five.)

Here's the way this *Porgy* began: During the instrumental prelude, the curtain rose to reveal a scrim painted with a watercolor-like view of Catfish Row, the Charlestown courtyard where the piece takes place. As the music moved into the jazzy "Jasbo Brown" section, lights behind the scrim revealed eight dancers and Sportin' Life doing sinuous choreography. As that section ended, the lights dimmed as the orchestra segued into the opening song. If you looked carefully, you could find the singer in a small pool of light behind the scrim, high above the stage. (We eventually learned that she was not, indeed, floating in midair; she was standing on a fire escape–like platform above the arched-gate entrance to Catfish Row. You couldn't follow her voice, as the sound was emanating from the speaker system.) All through the song, the lyric—with misspellings of some of the colloquialisms—was emblazoned above the darkened proscenium by the supertitle system. After the soprano stopped, the dancers came back on—still behind the scrim—to do more sinuous choreography. The singers followed, taking their places for the crap game. As Jake started to sing, the scrim finally flew out—nine minutes into the show— and you could finally see, for real, the live actors.

Mind you, the song that the nearly invisible, disembodied soprano was singing was not some throwaway opening number placed in that spot to hold the stage while latecomers parked their cars, checked their coats, and climbed over the nonlatecomers. It was "Summertime," Gershwin's powerfully evocative lullaby, which he specifically placed as the opera's opening song. What we saw at City Opera was a full-stage-sized, lazy-lined watercolor in shades of brown; a floating head in a balloon of light; and a starkly legible banner of black letters on a white screen spelling out the lyric. In other words, "Summertime" was presented as if it were a comic strip. Clara and her baby and the sweltering atmosphere of the slum were absent; what we got was the literal words, telling us that down in Catfish Row "the livin' is easy"—which it sure ain't—and that the baby is safe with "Daddy and Mammy standin' by." They were both washed away by a hurricane before intermission.

And a word about that hurricane. We all know, thanks to CNN, exactly how devastating these hurricanes along the Blackfish banks can be. In *Porgy*, though, you had an uneducated, unprotected, superstitious mass of near indigents without the Weather Channel or automobiles to take them inland or bottled water or even L. L. Bean waterproof slickers. At City Opera, they huddled in a cramped interior during the storm scene— forty of them—as the wind blew and the music raged and God's

It is one thing to instruct the singers what to do and when to do it; it is another thing to let them discover who their characters are. An opera house production might get you good singers, but an effective *Porgy and Bess* demands that they act as well.

retribution took the form of pounding noises battering the walls. After much consternation—to a spiritual called "Oh, There's Somebody Knockin' at the Door"—the door fairly burst open. At this tense, death-threatening moment, I couldn't help but notice that only three of the forty people on stage looked *scared*. The rest were just singing.

This opera house version lacked any spark, any fire, any emotion between the principals. Theatre was what was missing; no sense of theatricality whatsoever. But professional productions of *Porgy and Bess*, as aforesaid, are few and far between. If theatricality must be sacrificed in exchange for a full cast and a full orchestra and all the trappings, it is still a treat to get to visit Gershwin's denizens of Catfish Row.

As an afterthought, I consulted my friend William W. Appleton, a retired Columbia University professor who has been attending Gershwin musicals since the brothers fashioned *Lady, Be Good!* for Adele and Fred Astaire back in 1924. Todd Duncan, he tells me, was the finest and most memorable Porgy he has seen. Anne Brown was excellent, but Leontyne Price was even better. Price and William Warfield—who performed opposite her on the tour that preceded the 1953 Broadway engagement—made the most electrifying

What we saw was a full-stage-sized, lazy-lined watercolor scrim in shades of brown; a floating head in a balloon of light; and a starkly legible banner of black letters on a white screen spelling out the lyric. In other words, "Summertime" was presented as if it were a comic strip.

pair of leads. The best mounting he's seen since then has been the Glyndebourne Festival production in 1989. But nothing compares to the excitement of 1935, in part, he said, because you sat there having never heard any of the songs before. From "Summertime" onward, you were overwhelmed with a cascade of simply remarkable music, which even a die-hard Gershwin fan simply could not have possibly anticipated.

True West

R eaders of the major overnight reviews on the morning of
March 10 were greeted with the unexpected sight of six
outright raves for Sam Shepard's *True West*. Not simply good reviews; ecstatic, all in all. While a couple of less overwhelming opinions eventually
surfaced, the reception of the revival of Shepard's 1980 comedy was staggeringly enthusiastic, and easily the best reviews for a Broadway play
since the revival of Arthur Miller's *The Price* opened four months earlier.

True West got off to a quick start, as opposed to the Miller play. This is
easily explainable, perhaps, by comparing the action-packed, laugh-filled
Shepard play to Miller's static, laugh-filled talkfest. Although they were
first produced only a decade apart, Shepard wrote with the voice of a
thirty-six-year-old rebel. (Miller, at the time of *The Price*, was a fifty-
seven-year-old rebel with a differ-
ent cause.) In 1999–2000, Shepard is understandably the more
relevant playwright. Except that
Miller's truly ancient play *Death
of a Salesman*, from way back in
1949, was the artistic and commercial hit of the 1998–1999

**This sort of rotating cast schedule can
only work under three conditions. First,
the two roles must be equal; second,
the two stars must be anonymously
interchangeable; and third, both actors
must be pretty damn good.**

dramatic season. Shepard, on the other hand, has virtually no Broadway
record; first produced in New York in 1963, he didn't even breach Broadway until 1996. The revival of his 1979 Pulitzer Prize winner *Buried Child*
received a stormy reception, with some vehement partisans, but met audience apathy and quickly folded. So perhaps a Broadway *True West*
wasn't such a sure thing, after all.

Austin/Lee*   Philip Seymour Hoffman
Austin Lee*   John C. Reilly
Saul Kimmer   Robert LuPone
Mom   Celia Weston

*Mr. Hoffman and Mr. Reilly alternate
 in each role.

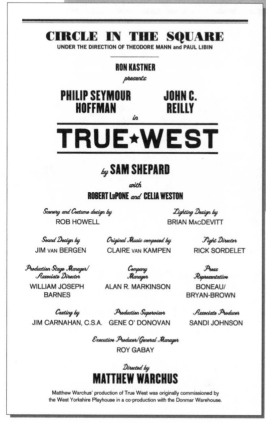

CIRCLE IN THE SQUARE
UNDER THE DIRECTION OF THEODORE MANN and PAUL LIBIN

RON KASTNER
presents

PHILIP SEYMOUR HOFFMAN   JOHN C. REILLY
in

TRUE★WEST

by SAM SHEPARD

with
ROBERT LuPONE *and* **CELIA WESTON**

Scenery and Costume design by		*Lighting Design by*
ROB HOWELL		BRIAN MacDEVITT

Sound Design by	*Original Music composed by*	*Fight Director*
JIM van BERGEN	CLAIRE van KAMPEN	RICK SORDELET

Production Stage Manager/ Associate Director	*Company Manager*	*Press Representative*
WILLIAM JOSEPH BARNES	ALAN R. MARKINSON	BONEAU/ BRYAN-BROWN

Casting by	*Production Supervisor*	*Associate Producer*
JIM CARNAHAN, C.S.A.	GENE O' DONOVAN	SANDI JOHNSON

Executive Producer/General Manager
ROY GABAY

Directed by
MATTHEW WARCHUS

Matthew Warchus' production of True West was originally commissioned by
the West Yorkshire Playhouse in a co-production with the Donmar Warehouse.

Complicating matters was the matter of casting. The producers of *True West* informed us that the two leads, Philip Seymour Hoffman and John C. Reilly, were going to be switching roles every three performances. (Hoffman and Reilly came to Broadway as stars who weren't stars; they had a strong following from joint featured roles in quirky, much-discussed—but not necessarily seen—films like *Boogie Nights* and *Magnolia*.) Not "alternating" as in taking the night off, like Carol Burnett in *Putting It Together* or Audra McDonald in *Marie Christine*, but actually putting on the other fellow's pair of jeans. Broadway audiences had a chance to see Laurence Olivier playing both Becket and Henry II in Jean Anouilh's 1960 historical drama *Becket*; but this was a permanent switch to accommodate a change in costars, from Anthony Quinn's Henry to Arthur Kennedy's Becket. Otherwise, I think you'd have to go back to Edwin Booth moving from Othello to Iago and back—and I, for one, have neither the time nor the inclination to research the point.

This sort of rotating schedule is virtually impossible to accommodate on Broadway. Rather than simply wanting to go see the show, audiences are inclined to first figure out which casting alternative is supposed to be better. *True West* wasn't even advertising who was playing when, although the information was available over the Internet. This scheme can only work under three conditions. First, the two roles must be equal; in length, in prominence, and in flash. Second, the two stars must be anonymously interchangeable; someone like Kevin Kline or Al Pacino, picked at random, might tend to overpower another actor. As it is, I suspect that many audience members recognized Hoffman and Reilly's familiar faces but didn't know precisely who was who until glancing at the Playbill photos after the play, by which point, the riveting performances made the two actors once and forever separable. The third, and most important, criterion for making this gimmick work is this: both actors must be pretty damn good. Which, as it turned out, they were, making it all appear a stroke of genius.

One can imagine director Matthew Warchus sitting in a folding chair in an overheated rehearsal hall watching Hoffman and Reilly, then suddenly smiting his forehead in a Eureka pose—with a lightbulb appearing above his head—as he experienced a veritable brainstorm. Not so, as it happens; Warchus originated the alternating star scheme when he directed *True West* at the Donmar Warehouse in 1994, with Mark Rylance and Mark Rudko. This was back before Warchus hit the big time with *Art*; did his masterful handling of the two actors in *True West* get him the three-actor *Art* assignment? The role switch made a certain amount of sense, in the context of the play. While Mr. Shepard drew Lee and Austin like southern Californian counterparts of Mr. Simon's Oscar and Felix, they are brothers under the skin. In the course of the play, the controlled, educated Austin and the unkempt, uncontrollable Lee basically switch characteristics, ultimately crawling under each other's skin—almost literally so, as they pummel each other to near death. (Their mother, making her first en-

trance near the end of the play, simply said, "You're not killing him, are you?") So if Hoffman (or Reilly) starts out as Austin (or Lee) one night and Lee (or Austin) the next, it is not as big a jump as one might expect.

The play itself was greeted in some quarters as an all-time classic, a view to which I can't quite adhere. I found much of it engrossing, with an air of doom pervading the atmosphere from the moment the overactive crickets invaded the sound system. Certainly, most of the audience was riveted by the dialogue and even the pauses between the speeches, expectantly awaiting the next salvo as if they were watching a championship tennis match. But there was always the feeling that this was one of those plays where the author would eventually run out of words and resort to trashing the scenery. And that he did, in a frenzy of smashing cutlery and flying Wonder Bread. I shall no doubt always retain the image of the steely-eyed Mr. Hoffman golf-clubbing to death a manual Olivetti (which is right out of James Thurber, I believe), body-slamming a telephone receiver, and grinding his heels into buttered toast like a deranged José Greco. (Here's a logistical question: How many kitchens, circa 1980 or even 2000, are equipped with enough power—let alone electrical outlets —to operate twelve toasters simultaneously without blowing a fuse? Or maybe this is a California thing.)

Not inconsequential to the success of *True West*, perhaps, was the makeup of the audience. Broadway has been preparing, since forever, for an invasion of young people to the drama. The truth is, the nonmusical Broadway theatre wasn't simply lacking a young audience; the *entire* nonmusical audience has all but disappeared. The nonmusical lineup on the day *True West* arrived consisted of revivals of two British plays—Peter Schaffer's *Amadeus* and Noël Coward's *Waiting in the Wings*—and Jackie Mason's solo show. The latter two, especially, catered to what we might call a "mature" audience (i.e., mature in years, not in maturity).

The faces in *True West*'s seats were noticeably younger than at any play in a generation, perhaps since Peter Schaffer's *Equus* opened here in 1974. While it is impossible to call one show a turning point, *True West* certainly marked a new direction. And this cannot be ascribed merely to the presence of Sam Shepard; *Buried Child* decidedly did not draw young audiences (or old audiences, for that matter). The last push in this direction, it will be instructive to recall, was in this very same theatre: Pam Gems's *Stanley*, the play that finally and irretrievably forced the Circle in the Square organization into bankruptcy in 1997. Gregory Mosher, the former director of both the Goodman Theatre and Lincoln Center Theater (and producer of this season's *The Dead*), was brought in in a last-ditch attempt to save the foundering Circle. He came up with a plan under which memberships were offered for $37.50, with tickets to the attractions—the first and only one of which turned out to be *Stanley*—costing $10 each. The official price for nonmembers was $45. (I seem to recall some controversy when it was

> *True West* demonstrated that you didn't need to give under thirties—or over thirties, for that matter—a special discount to get them to buy a ticket to a Broadway play. All you have to do is give them something they want to see.

discovered that in order to inflate the subscription base they were distributing free memberships, thus allowing some theatregoers to see *Stanley* for a mere ten bucks.) Whatever the merits of the plan, the problem turned out to be that *Stanley*—a controversial hit in England—was pretty much a snooze at any price. *True West* demonstrated that you didn't need to give under thirties—or over thirties, for that matter—a special discount to get them to buy a ticket to a Broadway play. All you have to do is give them something they want to see.

And this one they wanted to see. *True West* rode in with a set of overwhelmingly ecstatic reviews and was easily able to fill Broadway's second-tiniest theatre. (Average 600 patrons a night in a 631-seat theatre and you're a hot ticket, with scattered singles; fill 600 a night in a 1,078-seat theatre like the Royale—home of *The Price*—and you might as well book a nonexchangeable, nonrefundable bargain fare to London next month to see the new plays.)

True West was a phenomenal hit, at least until Reilly and Hoffman left on June 17. Josh Brolin came in as Austin, opposite Elias Koteas as Lee. The plan was for them to begin switching roles on July 26, but box office grosses plunged from $300,000 to $62,000. (Apparently Reilly and Hoffman were the attraction after all, not Shepard.) The show limped along until Ben Brantley of the *Times* ran a review of the new *True West* on July 18, saying that the effect of the new cast "can most kindly be described as flattening." The closing notice went up that night.

Riverdance on Broadway

You had only to look around you at the goings-on before the curtain rose on *Riverdance on Broadway* to realize that there was no question in anybody's mind—this was a hit, and a big one.

The lobby was littered with souvenir stands. You could tell that they were souvenir stands because there were large, typeset signs that said "Official *Riverdance* Merchandise." (No unofficial *Riverdance* merchandise was in sight.) The two rotundas of the Gershwin Theatre—engraved with the names of the members of the so-called Broadway Hall of Fame—contained display cases containing the "Rd by design" collection of innovative jewelry. The literature explained that these "limited edition pieces capture the essence of Irish creativity from its ancient roots to modern times." The five pieces on sale—"hand-crafted by skilled crafts people in Ireland"—were based on the actual jewelry worn in the show, although I have a sneaking suspicion that the actual jewelry worn in the show was based on the stuff sold in the lobby. Elsewhere, there were multimedia, multiscreen exhibits like "Ireland—The Land, The People, The Music"; "Irish Music—Its Roots, from 500 BC to Riverdance"; and "Instruments at the Heart of Irish Traditional Music." Inside the theatre proper, peddlers of programs and posters roamed the aisle like beer barkers at Yankee Stadium. Not only that; people were eagerly buying their

> Peddlers of programs and posters roamed the aisle like beer-barkers at Yankee Stadium. People were eagerly buying their wares, packed in plastic bags printed with the *Riverdance* artwork. All of this made Disney's merchandisers look like a couple of kids with a sidewalk lemonade stand with Dixie cups.

Cast

Pat Roddy
Eileen Martin
Maria Pagés
Tsidii Le Loka
Brian Kennedy

The Riverdance Irish Dance Troupe
Dearbhail Bates, Natalie Biggs, Lorna
Bradley, Martin Brennan, Zeph
Caissie, Suzanne Cleary, Andrea
Curley, Marty Dowds, Lindsay Doyle,
Shannon Doyle, Susan Ginnety, Paula
Goulding, Conor Hayes, Gary Healy,
Matt Martin, Tokiko Masuda, Sinéad
McCafferty, Holly McGlinchy,
Jonathan McMorrow, Joe Moriarty,
Niall Mulligan, Catherine O'Brien,
David O'Hanlon, Debbie O'Keeffe,
Ursula Quigley, Kathleen Ryan,
Anthony Savage, Rosemarie Schade,
Ryan Sheridan, Claire Usher, Leanda
Ward, Margaret Williams

The Riverdance Singers
Soloist . . . Sara Clancy
Patrick Connolly, Brian Dunphy, Joanna
Higgins, Darren Holden, Michael
Londra, Tara O'Beirne, Sherry Steele,
Ben Stubbs, Yvonne Woods

Moscow Folk Ballet Company
Denis Boroditski, Andrei Kisselev, Yulia
Koryagina, Olena Krutsenko, Svetiana
Malinina, Ilia Streltsov, Vitaly
Verterich, Yana Volkova

The Riverdance Tappers
Walter "Sundance" Freeman, Charming
Cook Holmes, Karen Callaway
Williams

The Amanzi Singers
Ntombikhona Dlamini, Fana Kekana,
Ntombifuthi Pamella Mhlongo,
Francina Moliehi Mokubetsi, Keneilwe
Margaret Motsage, Isaac Mthethwa,
Andile Selby Ndebele, Mbuso Dick
Shange

"Music from the Broadway Show":
Decca Broadway 012 157 824
(featuring two cast members)

wares, packed in plastic bags printed not with "I♥NY" but with the *Riverdance* artwork. The Playbill included a handsome four-page, full-color insert welcoming the audience—"Céad Míle Fáilte," it exclaimed—and then outlining the stuff you could buy (this part was written in English) and touting the *Riverdance* Web site. All of this reeked of assured success and made Disney's merchandisers look like a couple of kids with a sidewalk lemonade stand with Dixie cups.

Riverdance on Broadway—which was the official title of this show— started with the now-ubiquitous speech about cameras and cellular phones. This one was a little different than what you'd hear at *Kiss Me, Kate* or *Saturday Night Fever*, in that the greeting started in Irish. They moved to English for the flash camera and beeper section, then back to Irish for a brief good-bye, something like "enjoy the show," I suspect. For whatever reason, they didn't feel the need to warn the audience in Irish not to use cameras.

After a sharp clang of music came a sonorous voice—so sonorous that it turned out to be a disembodied Liam Neeson on tape—saying (in English), "Out of the dark we came, out of the sea . . ." I suspect that Mr. Neeson got a potload of gold for contributing his name and voice, so I don't begrudge him. The likes of Laurence Olivier, Gregory Peck, and Walter Cronkite have lent (or, rather, rented) their voices to lowly musical shows, so why not Neeson? Anyway, they were soon off into the first of (alas!) innumerable step-dancing displays.

Now, step dancing isn't as bad as it might sound to the uninitiated (which included me when I took my seat). Yes, they dust off their boots with a lot of noise, and they line up in long rows like Rockettes. But when the choreographers break the corps up into small groups and weave the groups among each other in different patterns, it can be visually pleasing. The lead dancer of the evening, a fellow named Pat Roddy, was quite exceptional. In his solo numbers,

> Pat Roddy skittered back and forth across the vast Gershwin stage—a stage almost as vast as his ever-present smile—never seeming to touch the ground, until I was convinced that he was Road Runner reincarnated.

he skittered back and forth across the vast Gershwin stage—a stage almost as vast as his ever-present smile—never seeming to touch the ground, until I was convinced that he was Road Runner reincarnated. (I'm not up on past-life theory, but can a cartoon character be reincarnated?) Mr. Roddy seemed to be wearing something that looked like a boxing champion's belt, although it was embroidered rather than weighted down with medallions. Roddy's opposite, Eileen Martin, was okay; but nobody should be forced to partner with Roddy. He had a special flair that made him, at any given moment, stand out from the sixty-odd dancers and singers with whom he shared the stage.

The impressive *Riverdance* Web site tells us what the show is about: "At the root of all native cultures is the primal quest to come to terms with spiritual and elemental forces. Just as they harnessed fire, water, wood and stone, our ancestors also learned to harness their creativity. They quickly learned also how to express and celebrate their own lives and spirits, their own human relationships and their bond with the place they called home." Frankly, I can't say that I got this from watching the first act, but hey, I didn't think to bring my laptop to my seat.

The second act, strangely enough, featured Tsidii Le Loka, the tribal chant specialist from *The Lion King*, and the Amanzi Singers from South Africa (who were wonderful); the Moscow Folk Ballet Company, many of whom were veterans of the Moiseyev; and the "*Riverdance* Tappers," two guys and a gal apparently from the streets of Harlem. There was also a flamenco dancer, Maria Pagés, who shared star billing with Roddy and Martin. The Web site explains this international contingent as well: "To leave the homeplace because of war, famine or slavery has been the fate of many native peoples. Such a dislocation is the central theme of act two." There was some dislocation by audience members from their seats, but surprisingly little. The thing is that, although much of the evening was repetitive and indecipherable and—where it was decipherable—somewhat pretentious ("Out of the dark we came, out of the sea . . ."), *Riverdance* did deliver a fair share of entertainment.

You wouldn't know this from the reviews it received. Most of the critics seemed to go in with an "I know it's going to sell out no matter how bad it is" attitude—an attitude that was pretty much borne out in fact. (Less than a week after opening to mixed-to-negative reviews, *Riverdance* announced that its three-month run was being extended an additional ten weeks. And just after winning no Tony Awards, they converted to an open-ended run.) The show's weekly grosses were regularly among Broadway's highest. Yes, *Riverdance* played in Broadway's largest theatre; but previous Gershwin tenants like *Tango Argentino*, *1776*, and *Candide* never came anywhere near selling the seats. The only favorable major review was courtesy of the one major New York critic who happens to be Irish, who also happens to be a pretty good writer, who also happens to have written a laudatory essay (apparently for hire) posted on the *Riverdance* Web site. He liked it. The music was played by an energetic eleven-person band seated along the sides of the Gershwin auditorium (which is the only time I've seen that unwieldy space well used). Most of the musicians had onstage solos in the spotlight; one of them, fiddler Athena Tergis, looked like she could hold her own with the thirty-eight members of the "*Riverdance* Irish

Dance Troupe." She danced and fiddled—or fiddled and danced—with abandon in her blue felt dress and was quite impressive. This was the first time I'd seen a violin with its own body mic.

What is this *Riverdance*, anyway, and how did it grow? It seems that the television producer of the Eurovision Song Contest in April 1994 commissioned a seven-minute Irish dance piece to be used during a break between contestants. Watching the reaction to this, the producer—a Donegal native named Moya Doherty—decided to enlarge the seven minutes into a stage show, which opened in February 1995 in Dublin. *Riverdance* moved to London in June, then back to Dublin, then back to

London, releasing a top-selling video version in the meantime. After a one-week engagement at Radio City Music Hall in March 1996 (for St. Patrick's Day), the show moved to Belfast, then back to London once more. In the meantime, it released a top-selling CD, which earned songwriter Bill Whelan a Grammy Award. The second *Riverdance* company opened in October 1996—with a return engagement at Radio City—followed by a third company in Edinburgh in February 1997 and another in Sydney in March.

The *Riverdance* story goes on and on. I could go on and on, too, but what's the point?

Lead dancer Michael Flatley left the show in 1995, after fifteen weeks, to create his own competing show, *Lord of the Dance*; that seems to be the only loss *Riverdance* ever faced. (The extensive choreographer list in the program credits Flatley as the "Original Principal Irish Dance Choreographer.") According to the producers, *Riverdance* —in less than five years—has sold ten million tickets and six million videos, and who knows how many official souvenirs (not to mention trinkets from the "Rd by design" collection). Anyway you look at it, that's a lot of step dancing.

The only favorable major review was courtesy of the one major New York critic who happens to be Irish, who also happens to be a pretty good writer, who also happens to have written a laudatory essay (apparently for hire) posted on the Riverdance website. He liked it.

For the record, let me add that this was the first time in my vast experience in the Broadway theatre that I ever heard a teenager yell across the lobby at intermission, "Hey, Moira."

A Moon for the Misbegotten

Cherry Jones is a name you're not likely to forget. I first came across her—her name, anyway—in the summer of 1989, a good eighteen months before she arrived on Broadway.

I was doing a new play that was transferring from the American Repertory Theatre in Cambridge, Massachusetts. There is a union rule which provides that should such a production have a future life under another (and more remunerative) Actors' Equity contract, all Equity members must be offered the job. Otherwise, they are entitled to a buyout equivalent to four weeks of Broadway scale.

Several of the cast members were not invited to Broadway. One of the chosen, though, chose not to take the part; ART, it seems, had scheduled *The Caucasian Chalk Circle* for her. Not having seen the play in Cambridge, I didn't mind her absence, especially since a pal of mine got the role. But what sort of beginning actor turns down a chance at Broadway, especially in a major role in a masterful play by a celebrated multiple-Tony-and-Oscar-winning playwright who is one of America's greatest satirists? What sort of actor, I wondered, is this Cherry Jones?

Having rejected the job, she was not entitled to a buyout. We paid her off anyway, as the playwright—who was also the controlling producer—was a man who positively reeks of decency. Ms. Jones resurfaced in April 1991, when she came to the Nederlander Theatre in a low-budget Broadway Alliance production of a curious play called *Our Country's Good*. This was a drama about eighteenth-century Australian prison colonization—not a hot topic at the time—that struggled on listlessly for six weeks. It wasn't exactly easy

Variety called the original production "a psychopathic *Tobacco Road.*"

Josie Hogan Cherry Jones
Mike Hogan Paul Hewitt
Phil Hogan Roy Dotrice
James Tyrone Jr. Gabriel Byrne
T. Stedman Harder Tuck Milligan

Scene of the play: The play takes place in Connecticut at the home of tenant farmer Phil Hogan, between the hours of noon on a day in early September 1923 and sunrise of the following day.

to identify Ms. Jones. The women in the cast first appeared as English naval officers, so it was impossible to tell at a glance who was who, and the lighting was way too dark to unravel the secrets of the Playbill during the performance. What was perfectly clear, though, was that there were two strikingly good young actresses in the play, namely, Ms. Jones and J. Smith Cameron. Jones was nominated for a Tony Award for her troubles, as were Smith Cameron and a third actress in the play. All were alphabetically billed below the title of the play, but Jones ended up in the leading actress category while her castmates were nominated for the featured award. Jones had little chance against Julie Harris, Stockard Channing, and Mercedes Ruehl (who took the prize for *Lost in Yonkers*), but it was quite a feat for an unknown actress in a confusing and poorly received play to even come up with a nomination.

Jones returned to Broadway in 1994 in *Angels in America*, replacing Ellen McLaughlin as the Angel. Most serious theatregoers, I suspect, attended the play before she entered the cast. Looking through the record books, I find that Jones actually made her Broadway debut in January

1987, in a small role in *Steppin' Out*. This was a negligible British play directed by Tommy Tune at the Golden, with a cast headed by Carole Shelley. I vaguely remember Jones as an uncomfortable-looking character with tall legs in a striped leotard.

In 1995, Lincoln Center Theater announced Jones as the title character in its revival of *The Heiress*, a decent, if not terribly exciting, play. Based on memories of *Our Country's Good*, I wondered if André Bishop and Bernie Gersten might not have a surprise for us—and they did! It took but one evening for Jones to spring atop the list of brilliant actresses of our generation. Julie Harris, Maureen Stapleton, Colleen Dewhurst, and Gerry Page first made their mark on Broadway in the 1950s. While other fine stage actresses have come along since, Jones— who was born in 1956—is arguably the only one who belongs in the company of the others. She easily took the Best Actress Tony for *The Heiress*, and quite possibly would have taken another for *Pride's Crossing* had it moved from Lincoln Center's Mitzi Newhouse to the Tony-eligible Beaumont upstairs (like *Six Degrees of Separation* before and *Contact* after). Such is Ms. Jones's reputation that her casting in this *Moon for the Misbegotten* actually helped sell

tickets—this based on a Broadway career consisting, mainly, of one performance in a revival of a minor play.

The Heiress and *Moon for the Misbegotten* are not without parallels, the first being that both were initially tryout casualties, opening (and closing) within a month of each other. *The Heiress* premiered in New Haven in January 1947 (under the title *Washington Square*) and closed a week later in Boston. Jed Harris—the provocative boy wonder of the late 1920s, with George Abbott's *Broadway*, Hecht and MacArthur's *The Front Page*, Kaufman and Ferber's *The Royal Family*, and Thornton Wilder's *Our*

Town to his credit—took over the play, recast it, and turned it into an unlikely hit the following season. British actress Wendy Hiller played the role re-created, so many years later, by Cherry Jones.

Moon for the Misbegotten was O'Neill's final completed play, finished in 1943. It opened in Columbus in February 1947, closing five weeks later in St. Louis. (*Variety* called it "a psychopathic *Tobacco Road*.") It wasn't until May 1957, four years after O'Neill's death, that the play finally reached Broadway. Wendy Hiller played the role re-created, so many years later, by Cherry Jones. The 1957 *Moon* was also unsuccessful, closing after eight weeks. (Brooks Atkinson called it "a descent into squalor.") The play returned to the dusty old shelf until O'Neill champions José Quintero, Jason Robards, and Ms. Dewhurst gave it a try in 1973. Everyone decided it was a brilliant play all along, and the production remains one of those legendary evenings in the theatre people never tire of talking about.

Which brings us to another question: Should revivals automatically be judged against their earlier incarnations, especially when said incarnations are of legendary status?

The answer, rationally, is probably not. I am a firm believer that a revival is only a revival if you saw the show the last time. On your first visit in 1947, 1957, 1973, or 2000, *A Moon for the Misbegotten* was as valid a "new play" experience as was your first *Hamlet*, unless you happened to see *Hamlet* with the original cast. So let's not compare these productions, okay? Rationally, that is. But the fact remains that many who saw the 1973 production—including most of the reviewers, apparently—were unable to forget the magic woven by Robards and Dewhurst.

Josie Hogan, the pig farmer's daughter, is described by the playwright as being 180 pounds, five feet eleven, "with large, firm breasts, her waist wide but slender by contrast with her hips and thighs," and "more powerful than any but an exceptionally strong man." That is hardly a description of Ms. Jones, who appeared to have bulked up for the role but not *that* much. Although if you factored in her acting, she certainly appeared more powerful than anyone else on the stage.

If she was not quite so stolid as Dewhurst, it really did not matter. As in her other performances, Jones dominated the stage the moment she met the lights. There was something about her, simply standing there craning her neck. Even without speaking, she looked, she listened, she simply inhabited the character and the stage and the play and the theatre. As the evening progressed, there were times when you almost wanted her on freeze frame; there was so much going on—with her voice, with her body, but mostly deep within her character's mind—that you felt that you could only process half of what she was sending out. O'Neill's Josie is busy spinning her own set of untruths throughout the play, but in unguarded moments—when Gabriel Byrne's Jim Tyrone wasn't looking at her—you caught Jones staring at him, transfixed. Transcendent, when she took his head to her breast; stunned, after the big kiss. There was a moment when she looked at him so intensely that her hand grasped the porch step for life, as if to keep from toppling over. At the end of the play, she wrapped him in a hug, as if she was an all-powerful and all-protecting mother earth (or perhaps Michelangelo's *Pietà*). Jones's face was lit up, like an angel. I suspect that lighting designer Pat Collins helped out here, but she needn't have. As far as I'm concerned, Cherry Jones acted that halo.

Irish actor Gabriel Byrne made a highly accomplished Broadway debut as Tyrone, described by Josie as "a dead man walking slow behind his own coffin." Best known here for his film career, Byrne has sturdy acting credits in Dublin—where he was a member of the Alley Theatre—and London. And he is an arresting stage actor, although I think the edge has to go to Robards (who had, like O'Neill and Quintero and Jim Tyrone, struggled through many periods of self-induced torture).

Jason's Tyrone was a man sunk in a pool of molasses-like quicksand, halfheartedly flailing his arms from time to time as his subconscious fought for survival. Tyrone is on his last legs, literally; the character is about to die. Byrne's performance had the same desperation as Robards's, but from his first entrance Byrne seemed to have given up even thinking about a struggle for survival. Byrne effectively expressed his character's precarious state with a shaking hand, while

Should revivals automatically be judged against their earlier incarnations, especially when said incarnations are of legendary status? A revival is only a revival if you saw the show the last time.

Robards seemed to be walking blindfolded on a tightrope through the long night's journey into day.

Jim Tyrone, of course, was held over from O'Neill's previous play, *Long Day's Journey into Night*. This was finished in 1941 but not produced in America until November 1956, with Robards making his Broadway debut as the young Jim Tyrone. For a brief spell, theatregoers could see both *Long Day* and *Misbegotten* on the same Wednesday or Saturday; both shows closed on June 29, 1957. While Tyrone/O'Neill's mother and father

—already deceased by the September 1923 night on which *Moon* takes place—figure prominently in the discussion, younger brother Edmund (O'Neill's portrait of himself) goes unmentioned in *Moon*.

While comparisons are futile, the late Ben Edwards's 1973 set—a big front porch fronting a skeletal farmhouse, against a cyclorama big as the sky—seemed to help the play in a way that Eugene Lee's more realistic 2000 set did not. (I don't suppose anyone alive can tell us about the 1947 set, which was the final work of O'Neill's longtime collaborator, Robert Edmond Jones. The great, innovative stage designer—who virtually created the concept of modern stage scenery—died a year less a day after the playwright.) Edwards—who, like Jones, served as his own lighting designer—had full control of the background; the effect, as I remember it, was of an inky blue night sky that could engulf the actors at director Quintero's will. (Those who have stood in a dark New England field on a late summer night, illuminated solely by a far-removed moon, might recognize the feeling of being enveloped by darkness.) This was not possible on Lee's stage full of rocks. No reason that it should have been, of course; but in 1973 the characters' mood enveloped the audience in a way that it didn't in 2000. Lee's set was piled high with boulders; the only boulder in 1973, if you will, was the massive presence radiated by Ms. Dewhurst.

The 2000 production was announced as a re-pairing of Ms. Jones and her *Heiress* director Gerald Gutierrez. His name disappeared from the project in September, three months before rehearsals for the tryout at Chicago's Goodman Theatre, when he was replaced by Daniel Sullivan. Sullivan did a good job on O'Neill's long and difficult script, and the limited engagement quickly sold most of its tickets. The show had less of an impact than the 1973 production, at least for theatregoers who had been mesmerized by Robards and Dewhurst. Which brings up another element in the comparative-revival argument. In 1973, people of my generation knew Jason Robards and Colleen

Even without speaking, Cherry Jones looked, she listened, she simply inhabited the character and the stage and the play and the theatre. There were times when you almost wanted her on freeze frame; there was so much going on—with her voice, with her body, but mostly deep within her character's mind.

Dewhurst as great stars for as long as we could remember, and . . . well, they were *old*. Old enough to be our parents. The characters, too, were much older than we ever expected to be, with old people's problems. In

A Moon for the Misbegotten

Opened: March 19, 2000

Closed: July 2, 2000

120 performances (and 15 previews)

Profit/Loss: Profit

A Moon for the Misbegotten ($70 top) was scaled to a
potential gross of $444,168 at the 936-seat Walter Kerr.
Weekly grosses averaged about $317,000, with a high
gross of $364,000 in late April. Total gross for the run
was $5,354,179. Attendance was about 81 percent, with
the box office grossing about 71 percent of potential
dollar-capacity.

TONY AWARD

Best Revival of a Play

Best Performance by a Leading Actor: Gabriel Byrne

Best Performance by a Leading Actress: Cherry Jones

Best Performance by a Featured Actor: Roy Dotrice (WINNER)

DRAMA DESK AWARD

Best Performance by a Featured Actor: Roy Dotrice (WINNER)

Critical
Scorecard

Rave	2
Favorable	5
Mixed	1
Unfavorable	2
Pan	0

2000, with actors our age discussing the type of problems that have been faced by friends of ours, *Moon for the Misbegotten* was clearly a different experience. Part of the magical haze of the Quintero-Robards-Dewhurst production, then, has to do not just with the experience of the performance but also with the experience of the viewer. But that doesn't take into account the especial magic of Cherry Jones—a performance that the talent-nurturing Dewhurst, who died in 1991, would presumably have cheered.

Aida

How bad does a musical have to be for the producers to take their names off it? I'm not talking about selling away one's share of the potential profits—and responsibility for future losses— like most of the original *Scarlet Pimpernel* producers did. Rather, simply putting a cloak of anonymity around your good name while nevertheless peddling the merchandise.

I can recall a case when David Merrick so disliked a play, its author, its director, and its drug-addicted legendary ex–movie star that he ordered his propman, Leo Herbert, to go out front at the Forrest Theatre in Philadelphia and cover up the words "David Merrick Presents" with red adhesive tape. But Merrick had already decided to close the show at the end of the week, thereby refunding the advance sale money to the customers. He didn't merely replace his name with a pseudonym and keep the Broadway booking, which is what Hyperion Theatricals (aka Disney) did three weeks before starting previews at the Palace. Disney has several film-releasing units, for different types of movies; but they don't generally switch from the family-oriented Disney to the controversial Miramax after the film has opened in a couple of cities.

There's something ingenuous about deciding that your show, something you conceived and commissioned and staffed and revised and supervised every step of the way, isn't good enough for your customers—but going ahead with it nevertheless. Especially when you have already used your mighty marketing machine to sell millions and millions of dollars' worth of tickets to the show to your customers, when it still said "Disney presents." Did they think, maybe, that these very same customers forgot the name that was very definitely above the title? As it turned out, within months Disney was running co-op ads for their "three hit Broadway musicals" and featuring *Aida* at disneyonbroadway.com.

The thing is, *Aida* wasn't all that bad. Not that it was a good musical, mind you; but there were a few elements that made it worth a visit, and that's something I can't say about *Saturday Night Fever* or *Footloose*; or, for that matter, *Beauty and the Beast* (official title: *Disney's Beauty and the Beast*).

Heather Headley gave one of those exciting performances that makes a young performer a star, at least for the moment. Her rendition of "The Gods Love Nubia" was *Aida's* one truly exciting moment; it certainly would have stopped the show had it not been the first-act finale. I suppose that Ms. Headley will perform this song for the rest of her career on awards shows and "Best of Broadway" benefits and public television fund-raisers. For some performers, this sort of immense personal success is impossible to top; they remain forever known principally for that one moment in their career, like Jennifer Holliday in *Dreamgirls* or Andrea McArdle's "Tomorrow." Others move on to greater triumphs, like Mary Martin or Gwen Verdon or Bernadette Peters. I'd wager that Headley belongs in company with the latter. She has a sturdily strong voice, an intensely attractive stage presence, and a fine sense of comedy that was not called upon in the present instance. Headley gave the impression of giving every ounce of her talent and skill to her *Aida*, while never failing to maintain her poise (and posture). This was a truly regal performance, despite the material she had to work with.

Aida was also exceptional for its physical production. Bob Crowley provided a fine assortment of creative and highly pleasing stage pictures, most of them with an Egyptian motif. There was an especially stunning flying piece representing the Nile Delta, with the illusion of a mirrored

Amneris Sherie René Scott
Radames Adam Pascal
Aida Heather Headley
Mereb Damian Perkins
Zoser John Hickok
Pharaoh Daniel Oreskes
Nehebka Schele Williams
Amonasro Tyrees Allen
Ensemble Robert M. Armitage, Troy
   Allan Burgess, Franne Calma, Bob
   Gaynor, Kisha Howard, Tim Hunter,
   Youn Kim, Kyra Little, Kenya Unique
   Massey, Corinne McFadden, Phineas
   Newborn III, Jody Ripplinger,
   Raymond Rodriguez, Eric Sciotto,
   Samuel N. Thiam, Jerald Vincent,
   Schele Williams, Natalia Zisa

Original Broadway Cast Album:
Buena Vista 60671-7

≥N≤ **PALACE THEATRE**
OWNED AND OPERATED BY STEWART F. LANE
AND THE MESSRS. NEDERLANDER

HYPERION THEATRICALS
under the direction of
Peter Schneider and Thomas Schumacher
presents

A I D A

Music by | Lyrics by
ELTON JOHN | TIM RICE

Book by
LINDA WOOLVERTON
and
ROBERT FALLS & DAVID HENRY HWANG

SUGGESTED BY THE OPERA

Starring
HEATHER HEADLEY   ADAM PASCAL   SHERIE RENÉ SCOTT
JOHN HICKOK   DAMIAN PERKINS
TYREES ALLEN   DANIEL ORESKES

ROBERT M. ARMITAGE   TROY ALLAN BURGESS   FRANNE CALMA
CHRIS PAYNE DUPRÉ   THURSDAY FARRAR   KELLI FOURNIER   BOB GAYNOR
KISHA HOWARD   TIM HUNTER   YOUN KIM   KYRA LITTLE   KENYA UNIQUE MASSEY
CORINNE McFADDEN   PHINEAS NEWBORN III   JODY RIPPLINGER   RAYMOND RODRIGUEZ
ERIC SCIOTTO   TIMOTHY EDWARD SMITH   ENDALYN TAYLOR-SHELLMAN
SAMUEL N. THIAM   JERALD VINCENT   SCHELE WILLIAMS   NATALIA ZISA

Scenic & Costume Design | Lighting Design
BOB CROWLEY | NATASHA KATZ

Sound Design | Hair Design | Makeup Design
STEVE C. KENNEDY | DAVID BRIAN BROWN | NAOMI DONNE

Music Produced and | Music Arrangements | Orchestrations
Musical Direction by | GUY BABYLON | STEVE MARGOSHES
PAUL BOGAEV | PAUL BOGAEV | GUY BABYLON
 | | PAUL BOGAEV

Music Coordinator | Dance Arrangements | Technical Supervision
MICHAEL KELLER | BOB GUSTAFSON | THEATERSMITH, INC
 | JIM ABBOTT
 | GARY SELIGSON

Development Casting | Casting | Fight Direction
JAY BINDER | BERNARD TELSEY | RICK SORDELET
 | CASTING

Associate Producer | Press Representative | Production Stage Manager
MARSHALL B. PURDY | BONEAU/BRYAN-BROWN | CLIFFORD SCHWARTZ

Choreography by
WAYNE CILENTO

Directed by
ROBERT FALLS

Originally developed at the Alliance Theatre Company in Atlanta, Georgia

reflection (marred, unfortunately, by a small but noticeable hole near the top of the backdrop). There was also an especially stunning swimming pool, with bathers kick-stroking their way up into the flies. More Olympic than Egyptian, perhaps, but hey—it worked. (This set was reminiscent of Crowley's skewed tenement courtyard scene in Paul Simon's *The Capeman*, which is as unforgettable as the show itself wasn't.) Crowley's costumes were wonderful in places, although elsewhere—like in the underwear fashion show—they seemed to have sprung from a different sensibility. I wouldn't blame this on Crowley, though, as he was clearly creating what the director (and songwriters) desired.

Just about every pleasing moment of the show was enhanced by the lighting of Natasha Katz, who more or less sculpted her way through the piece. There was a song early on called "Another Pyramid," for example, that was fascinating only for the shards of light and darkness through which the villain and his henchman traversed. (John Hickok, as the villain Zoser, seemed to have studied acting not at the HB Studio under Uta Hagen but at City Hall with Rudolph Giuliani.) Ms. Katz also came up with a wonderful effect of encasing her star in a veritable crown of light, not unlike the artwork logo for the original Broadway production of *Evita*. Imagine seven or eight beams from different overhead angles converging directly behind Ms. Headley's head, in a kind of inverted peacock effect.

But one star performance and a striking physical production don't add up to too much excitement, at least in this case. *Aida* was worlds above *Disney's Beauty and the Beast*, and I suppose it would have been more favorably received but for one thing: *Disney's The Lion King*. That extravaganza was stocked with a similarly ineffective score and libretto, and it hadn't anything approaching Headley's star performance (although Headley was featured in the earlier musical, and was pretty good, too). *Lion King* had magic, though, in director Julie Taymor's vision. *Aida's* director Robert Falls seemed to have had vision, too, and an effective way of moving bodies and scenery; but that, in itself, wasn't enough. *Lion King* had, first and foremost, an opening sequence that was visually breathtaking, even for staid Broadway types. Nothing in *Aida* was quite enough to impel you toward the Palace—Amneris's or the Nederlanders'—but it was still far more accomplished than some of the other musicals in town.

Perhaps *Aida* was tainted by Disney's experience on *Beauty and the Beast*, which proved that the quality of the merchandise was less important than the quality of the merchandising. *Aida* was Disney's fourth stage musical; the third, *Der Glöckner von Notre Dame*, opened in Berlin in June 1999 to a lukewarm reception. Its prospects at present seem tied to the fate of the Paris hit *Hunchback de Notre-Dame*, which had a head start on the Disney version and by May 2000 had already visited Toronto, Las Vegas, and London.

There's something ingenuous about deciding that your show, something you conceived and commissioned and staffed and revised and supervised every step of the way, isn't good enough for your customers—but going ahead with it nevertheless.

While the other Disney musicals were adaptations of hit Disney animated features, *Aida* was written from scratch (as they say). The songs were by Elton John and Tim Rice, who provided the core of the *Lion King* score (although I counted eleven collaborating songwriters credited in small print in the Playbill). The rest of the *Aida* creators came from *Beauty and the Beast*, which was a curious choice given that show's overall lack of distinction.

Aida began its life, under the title *Elaborate Lives: the Story of Aida*, in a high-profile tryout at the Alliance Theatre in Atlanta in October 1998. Linda Woolverton, author of the especially weak *Beauty and the Beast* libretto, provided the book; Robert Jess Roth and Matt West, veterans of Disney theme parks who had hit the big time with their pedestrian direction and choreography (respectively) of *Beauty and the Beast*, repeated their assignments. They were joined by that show's design team, Stanley A. Meyer (scenery), Natasha Katz (lighting), and Ann Hould-Ward (costumes). The savage reception of *Elaborate Lives* resulted in an almost total overhaul for the second go-round, which opened a pre-Broadway tryout in November 1999 at the Cadillac Palace in Chicago (under the simplified title *Aida*, with the "Disney presents" banner). John, Rice, Woolverton, and Katz were the only creators retained. Highly praised costars Heather Headley and Sherie René Scott kept their roles, while leading man Hank Stratton and the rest of the cast were dismissed.

New hires included director Robert Falls, an unlikely choice for a musical, who had leaped to prominence with his Tony Award–winning staging of the 1998–1999 revival of Arthur Miller's *Death of a Salesman*; choreographer Wayne Cilento, an original *Chorus Line* dancer—the short fellow who saw his sister tapping and said "I can do that"—and choreographer of the Broadway musical version of *Tommy*; and designer Crowley.

Also, listed initially under the nebulous credit "Creative Consultant" was playwright David Henry Hwang, author of the 1988 dramatic hit M. *Butterfly*. By the time *Aida* reached Broadway, the book was credited to Linda Woolverton (on one line, by herself) and Robert Falls and David Henry Hwang (on the next line, together). This can mean just about anything, but experienced readers of the hieroglyphic scrolls called Broadway billing boxes will tell you that this layout indicates that the first book writer was fired but retained billing due to contractual obligations. For example, the landmark Frank Loesser–Abe Burrows musical *Guys and Dolls* has a book credited to Jo Swerling and Burrows, although it's no secret that they threw out Swerling's version when Abe was brought in. The same thing occurred on the Loesser-Burrows hit *How to Succeed in Business Without Really Trying.* Jack Weinstock and Willie Gilbert retained billing and royalties, but when the Pulitzer Prize arrived, the only names listed were Burrows and Loesser. When assessing the contestants for the 2000 award, the Pulitzer committee had no cause to delve into the actual authorship of *Aida.*

Reviews in Chicago were not quite as bad as in Atlanta, showing minor improvements. (Richard Christiansen in the *Chicago Tribune* called it "very mixed—the good, the bad and the what were they thinking?")

Rewrites and revisions continued in Chicago, during which time the Disney moniker mysteriously vanished in place of Hyperion Theatricals. (This, we were told, was "to guide our audiences to projects we think may be right for

Nothing in *Aida* was quite enough to impel you towards the Palace—Amneris's or the Nederlanders'—but it was still far more accomplished than some of the other musicals in town.

them.") Hyperion was the father of Helios, the sun god, in Greek mythology. Perhaps the omens would have augured better had they used an Egyptian deity?

It is too early, at this writing, to determine the ultimate fate of *Aida.* It will surely do substantial business for a good while; one suspects that it needs to do substantial business now and forever to pay off the production costs. Because Disney is Disney—I mean, because Hyperion is Disney, I doubt we'll ever know how much those production costs were. The figure touted was $15 million, but that presumably doesn't take into account the losses in Atlanta and the revisions in Chicago.

Speaking of names absent from the credits, there were complaints here and there about the short shrift afforded poor Guiseppe Verdi. The Playbill boasts that *Aida* is "suggested by the opera," in type smaller than that used for the "developmental casting by" person. (Developmental casting means, in Broadway lingo, that this person was fired or quit along the way. Since Headley and Scott were presumably cast by this developmental person—Jay Binder, one of Broadway's most accomplished casting directors—maybe his billing should be circled in red and put in a box with flashing electric lights.) Verdi's name did not appear in the program, but I guess it is of little matter. I don't suppose a tiny smidgen of the audience for

Perhaps *Aida* was tainted by Disney's experience on *Beauty and the Beast*, which proved that the quality of the merchandise was less important than the quality of the merchandising.

Aida—Hyperion/Disney's, that is—had heard of Verdi, or would care to hear his 1872 version. Verdi's *Aïda* is pretty good, by the by, although the Met could make it a hell of a lot livelier next time if they added the underwear song.

Tenderloin

In a program note, City Center Encores! artistic director Kathleen Marshall termed the 2000 presentation of the 1960 musical *Tenderloin* a happy reunion. *Fiorello!*—the Pulitzer Prize–winning 1959 musical by the same quartet of authors—was the inaugural production of Encores!, back in 1994. *Tenderloin* also reunited former Encores! artistic director Walter Bobbie, who was swept away to fame and fortune by *Chicago*, and John Weidman, who once again adapted a script coauthored by his father.

The original *Tenderloin* was, too, a reunion of *Fiorello!* folk. Not only songwriters Jerry Bock and Sheldon Harnick and librettists George Abbott and Jerome Weidman, but also producers Bobby Griffith and Hal Prince, director Abbott, and orchestrator Irwin Kostal. *Tenderloin* went into rehearsal barely nine months after the opening of *Fiorello!* In interviews over the years, various participants agreed that reuniting the team was in itself a major problem. As Prince wrote, "We had such a good time doing *Fiorello!* that we could not bear splitting up after it opened. . . . We made the first mistake in choosing to adapt *Tenderloin* as a musical. And then we just went on making mistakes. We had reconvened the creative team so we could be together." *Tenderloin* was Griffith and

> At the late night post-mortem after *Tenderloin*'s original New Haven opening, Abbott said, "I had a concept for this show, and it doesn't work. Any suggestions?" What happens in such cases is that you end up with an assortment of moments that seem to work better, individually, than what you tried the night before.

Tommy Patrick Wilson
Reverend Brock David Ogden Stiers
Gertie Yvette Cason
Nita Debbie Gravitte
Margie Jessica Stone
Liz Sara Gettelfinger
Purdy Guy Paul
Joe Tom Alan Robbins
Martin Stanley Bojarski
Jessica Melissa Rain Anderson
Laura Sarah Uriarte Berry
Frye Bruce MacVittie
Lt. Schmidt Kevin Conway
The Women Julie Connors, Mindy Cooper, Margaret Ann Gates, Sara Gettelfinger, Ann Kittredge, Shannon Lewis, Tina Ou, Angie L. Schworer
The Men David Eggers, Angelo Fraboni, Gregg W. Goodbrod, Sean Grant, Derric Harris, Dale Hensley, Denis Jones, Mark Price, Gregory Emanuel Rahming, Timothy Shew

Original Revival Cast Recording:
DRG 94770

CITY CENTER
Judith E. Daykin, President & Executive Director

CITY CENTER
ENCORES!

ARTISTIC DIRECTOR
Kathleen Marshall
MUSICAL DIRECTOR
Rob Fisher

TENDERLOIN
based on the novel by Samuel Hopkins Adams

BOOK BY MUSIC BY LYRICS BY
George Abbott AND Jerome Weidman Jerry Bock Sheldon Harnick

Original production presented by Robert R. Griffith and Harold S. Prince

STARRING
David Ogden Stiers Patrick Wilson
Debbie Gravitte
Tom Alan Robbins Sarah Uriarte Berry

ALSO STARRING
Yvette Cason Jessica Stone Guy Paul
Bruce MacVittie Stanley Bojarski Melissa Rain Anderson
AND
Kevin Conway

Julie Connors Mindy Cooper David Eggers Angelo Fraboni Margaret Ann Gates
Sara Gettelfinger Gregg W. Goodbrod Sean Grant Derric Harris
Dale Hensley Denis Jones Ann Kittredge Shannon Lewis Tina Ou
Mark Price Gregory Emanuel Rahming Angie L. Schworer Timothy Shew

The Coffee Club Orchestra
Rob Fisher, MUSICAL DIRECTOR

SCENIC CONSULTANT COSTUME CONSULTANT LIGHTING SOUND
John Lee Beatty Jonathan Bixby Mike Baldassari Scott Lehrer

CONCERT ADAPTATION PRODUCTION STAGE MANAGER ORIGINAL ORCHESTRATION MUSICAL COORDINATOR
John Weidman & Maximo Torres Irwin Kostal Seymour Red Press
Walter Bobbie

CHOREOGRAPHER CASTING
Rob Ashford Jay Binder

DIRECTED BY
Walter Bobbie

Major sponsorship for City Center Encores!™ is provided by a grant from
Time Warner Inc.

The development of Encores! is assisted by seed support from The New York Times Company Foundation

TENDERLOIN is presented through special arrangement with and all authorized performance materials
are supplied by Music Theatre International, 421 West 54th Street, New York, NY 10019

City Center 55th Street Theater Foundation, Inc. gratefully acknowledges the significant support it receives from the
New York City Department of Cultural Affairs including support through the Cultural Challenge Program

Baldwin Piano, Official Piano of City Center

Prince's first musical failure, after five hits in five years (four of them directed and coauthored by Abbott).

A similar fate befell the creators of the first Pulitzer Prize–winning musical. George and Ira Gershwin, George S. Kaufman, and Morrie Ryskind followed *Of Thee I Sing* (1931) with the sequel *Let 'Em Eat Cake* (1933), finding themselves in the same trap as the *Tenderloin* group. Midway through the writing they realized that they had unsolvable troubles, but the acclaim of the first musical made it impossible to withdraw from the second.

At the late-night postmortem after *Tenderloin*'s New Haven opening, the refreshingly matter-of-fact Abbott said: "I had a concept for this show, and it doesn't work. Any suggestions?" Work they did for the next five weeks, grasping at any ideas that came along. (In addition to the official librettists, James and William Goldman helped doctor the book.) But as there was no purpose in doing *Tenderloin* in the first place, it remained purposeless.

What happens in such cases, though, is that you don't necessarily end up with the "best" version of the show. Rather, you end up with an assortment of moments that seem to work better, individually, than what you tried the night before. Which made *Tenderloin* a questionable choice for Encores! Part of the value of the series is that it gives us the opportunity to experience worthy failures. This is invaluable in the case of ill-fated shows with lofty though unattainable aims, like the fascinating *St. Louis Woman* that capped the 1998 season. It is even instructive with problematic properties like *On a Clear Day You Can See Forever*, with the exceptionally good sections providing grand entertainment in spite of the nonmaskable weaknesses. *Tenderloin*, though, merely served as an illustration of a bad show by good writers. (It also, happily, resulted in a first-rate cast recording of the Encores! production.)

Not that *Tenderloin* is without its high points; any show mounted on Broadway by top-of-the-line professionals is sure to be, at least, professional, especially with people like Bock, Harnick, and Abbott. Here was a story about an upright minister on a crusade to clean up New York's red light district, circa 1893. "Why can't this damn do-gooder keep his hands off little old New York," goes the opening number, and that's the problem right there. Who wants to spend time with a "damn do-gooder"? Who wants to "march with the army of the just" when they can slum with the good-time gals and guys? Who wants to sit through a production number full of "good clean fun" when they know that the other kind of fun—with friskier choreography —is readily available in the next scene? Who wants to watch well-dressed churchgoers play spoons, living statues, and wiggle-waggle when they can watch undressed nonchurchgoers grease the all-too-willing cops as the double

eagles change hands? (A double eagle, which was not identified in the adaptation, was a twenty-dollar gold piece.)

There are many ways to tackle the adaptation of a novel, but the creators stumbled when they determined to make *Tenderloin* a struggle between the goodly reverend and the forces of evil. Someone hit upon the idea of casting Maurice Evans as the Reverend Dr. Brock, and they might as well have just quit then and there. The now-forgotten Evans was a major star of Shakespeare and Shaw from the time he arrived on our shores as Romeo in 1935 until—well, until *Tenderloin*. He also successfully produced his own shows, including notable productions of *Hamlet* and *Richard II*, as well as more popular fare like the comedy hits *No Time for Sergeants* and the Pulitzer Prize–winning *Teahouse of the August Moon*. (Evans, who died in 1989, is best remembered today—ignominiously so—as the warlock father of heroine Samantha Stevens on the midsixties TV series *Bewitched*.) Evans's presence promised *Tenderloin* an air of class, strengthened the advance sale, and totally threw the show off focus. He was clearly the star, necessarily in the spotlight; the other major roles—a tabloid reporter who plays both sides of the fence and a madam with a heart of (guess what?) gold—were filled with featured players from *Fiorello!* Keeping the racy characters offstage in favor of Maurice Evans in a one-piece bathing costume is a fine way to lose your audience.

This very same problem, in reverse, sabotaged an earlier Abbott musical, *A Tree Grows in Brooklyn* (1951). In that case, the main story veered into tragedy; they therefore cast what should have been the third lead with a comedy star, who proceeded to steal the audience's heart and the show in general. But at least Shirley Booth provided *Brooklyn* with hundred-proof entertainment; Evans, and his Dr. Brock, was the opposite of entertaining. (*Brooklyn*, incidentally, is one of the few failed Broadway musicals that could—with care and proper respect—find a new and more successful life.)

The elements that make shows like *St. Louis Woman* and *A Tree Grows in Brooklyn* cry out for new life are, pretty much, lacking in *Tenderloin*. All that is good in the show is the score, which is presented to better effect on the cast album. Half of the score, that is; Bock and Harnick couldn't get much life into the stodgy church music, and no wonder. (The character of the "good" girl, who tries to reform the reporter, is so insipidly drawn by librettists and songwriters that she becomes the opposite of appealing.) A few songs worked extremely well at City Center, but a few songs do not make an evening. My favorite *Tenderloin* song is a stunning waltz ballad called "My Gentle Young Johnny." I have been recommending it to people for years; a while back, in fact, I found myself explaining to Jerry Bock that this was one of his best songs and he should be proud even if he never made a nickel off it. So I was highly pleased, and vindicated, to see that the song—in the accomplished hands of Debbie Gravitte—stopped the show cold.

The most instructive part of the evening, perhaps, was the "Entr'acte." After a couple of refrains of "Artificial Flowers"—done as an audience sing-a-long—the band went into a breezy rendition of the ballad "Tommy, Tommy." But as the bridge hit, the salvationist trumpets came in with two bars of the "Army of the Just." "Tommy" ended juxtaposed with Dr. Brock's moralistic "Good Clean Fun," with the music sweeping into two refrains at once: the crisply righteous "Good Clean Fun" against a drunkenly reedy rendition of the bordello song "The Picture of Happiness," with a little "My Miss Mary"—in the strings—thrown in for good measure. The intention behind *Tenderloin* was suddenly clear. Good and evil, morality and immorality overlapping, with the hero-in-fact—the young writer—smack in the narrow space in between. Now *that* has the makings of a show. Except the two sides overlapped only in the "Entr'acte" (with or-

Thirty years later, you can polish it up and whittle it down and put the girls in starkly sexy underwear. But you can't wash garbage.

chestrator Kostal outdoing himself). The rest of the time they simply alternated, from church to den of vice and back again.

Tenderloin, as the creators clearly realized, was a show without a chance. To make matters worse, a competing musical about prostitution, morality, desire, and corruption opened two weeks before *Tenderloin* came to town. And the authors—three Englishmen who'd never been on

Broadway and a French lady composer, no less—made it look light-hearted, ingratiating, and stylish. *Irma La Douce* was everything that the follow-up to *Fiorello!* wasn't, including a hit. *Tenderloin* lasted until the sizable advance sale ran out after six months and 216 performances, while *Fiorello!* continued merrily on.

William Goldman, one of the book doctors, wrote an invaluable book about Broadway called *The Season* (1969). He told an anecdote about Sheldon Harnick standing in the back of the theatre, listening to the twelfth rewrite of a hopelessly lousy book scene. The librettist—unidentified, but pretty obviously Goldman himself during *Tenderloin*—admitted, "It still isn't any good, is it?" Harnick's reply, which really ought to be one of the golden maxims of the Broadway musical: "The trouble with washing garbage is that when you're done, it's still garbage."

Thirty years later, you can polish it up and whittle it down and put the girls in starkly sexy underwear. But you can't wash garbage.

Contact: "A Dance Play in Three Short Stories"

A s the decade ended, Lincoln Center Theater gambled its
resources on two innovative, uncompromising musical
tragedies. *Parade*, in December 1998, dealt with a true-life lynching;
Marie Christine, in December 1999, dealt with matricide out of *Medea*.
Both, surprisingly enough, were exceedingly glum; both marked the
Broadway debut of modernistic young composer-lyricists; both were
rooted in the American South, with race-rooted overtones of the Civil
War; and both were pretty much inaccessible to most audiences. Despite
some vociferous fans, *Parade* and *Marie Christine* met walls of resistance
from critics and audiences, and quickly failed. (Cast albums of the two
shows demonstrated that they were, indeed, important—if difficult—
musical theatre works.)

The financial losses were huge, markedly so in an era when inordinate
costs have significantly choked off the production of new musicals—built
from scratch—on Broadway. While both experiments were to some extent underwritten by outside sponsors, ticket sales play a large part in Lincoln Center Theater's health—specifically, the "single-ticket," nonsubscriber sales. Lincoln Center subscribers pay an annual $35 fee, which
goes toward overall costs, plus $30 for tickets to each show they choose to
attend. The nonsubscriber price for orchestra seats is presently $80. (Un-
fortunately for nonmembers who do the math, there has been a longtime
moratorium on new subscriptions.) Thus, there's big money to be made
once the membership has been accommodated, and long-running Lincoln Center Theater hits like *Anything Goes* and *Six Degrees of Separation*

Cast

Part 1: Swinging

A forest glade, 1767

A Servant, an Aristocrat, a Girl on a Swing

Girl on the Swing Stephanie Michels

Frenchmen Sean Martin Hingston, Scott Taylor

Part 2: Did You Move?

An Italian restaurant, Queens, 1954

A Wife, a Husband, a Headwaiter

Wife Karen Ziemba

Husband Jason Antoon

Headwaiter David MacGillivray

Rocker Verastique

Robert Wersinger

Tomé Cousin

Peter Gregus

Nina Goldman

Dana Stackpole

Scott Taylor

Sean Martin Hingston

Pascale Faye

Shannon Hammons

Part 3: Contact

New York City, 1999

An Advertising Executive, a Bartender, a Girl in a Yellow Dress

Michael Wiley Boyd Gaines

Girl in the Yellow Dress Deborah Yates

Bartender Jason Antoon

Jack Hayes

Robert Wersinger

Nina Goldman

Scott Taylor

Shannon Hammons

Stephanie Michels

Sean Martin Hingston

Rocker Verastique

Pascale Faye

Mayumi Miguel

Tomé Cousin

Dana Stackpole

Peter Gregus

Cast Album: RCA Victor 09026-63764 (prerecorded compilation)

LINCOLN CENTER THEATER AT THE VIVIAN BEAUMONT

under the direction of
André Bishop and Bernard Gersten
presents

contact

by Susan Stroman and John Weidman

written by
John Weidman

directed & choreographed by
Susan Stroman

with (in alphabetical order)

Jason Antoon	Peter Gregus	Stephanie Michels
John Bolton	Shannon Hammons	Mayumi Miguel
Tomé Cousin	Jack Hayes	Dana Stackpole
Holly Cruikshank	Seán Martin Hingston	Scott Taylor
Pascale Faye	Stacey Todd Holt	Rocker Verastique
Boyd Gaines	Angelique Ilo	Robert Wersinger
Steve Geary	David MacGillivray	Deborah Yates
Nina Goldman	Joanne Manning	Karen Ziemba

sets	costumes	lighting
Thomas Lynch	William Ivey Long	Peter Kaczorowski

sound	associate choreographer	production stage manager
Scott Stauffer	Chris Peterson	Thom Widmann

casting		associate producer, musical theater
Johnson-Liff Associates, Tara Rubin Daniel Swee		Ira Weitzman

general manager	production manager	director of marketing & special projects	director of development
Steven C. Callahan	Jeff Hamlin	Thomas Cott	Hattie K. Jutagir

Leadership support for the Newhouse production of CONTACT was generously provided by The Blanche and Irving Laurie Foundation.

Special thanks to The Harold and Mimi Steinberg Charitable Trust for supporting new American plays at LCT.

Thanks to Prudential Securities for its support of CONTACT's Beaumont production design.

CONTACT is also made possible with public funds from the National Endowment for the Arts.

American Airlines is the official airline of Lincoln Center Theater.
Kendall-Jackson is the preferred winery of Lincoln Center Theater.

were veritable gold mines. Which *Parade* and *Marie Christine* most decidedly were not.

Meanwhile, though, something else was brewing in the rehearsal studio downstairs. Lincoln Center Theater has a history of inviting important musical theatre artists to investigate new material. In the spring of 1998, just as *Parade* was gearing up for production, artistic director André Bishop called choreographer Susan Stroman. Would she like the time and the place and the funding to develop whatever it was she might wish to develop?

Stroman called on John Weidman, librettist for her 1996 musical *Big* and coadapter of Lincoln Center's *Anything Goes*. While the pair searched for an idea, Stroman mentioned a recent experience. Research for a film project had taken her to a Soho pool parlor that transformed itself, after hours, into a dance club. Sitting there one midnight, Stroman watched as a mysterious girl in a yellow dress entered, electrifying the entire room as she dared and stared down prospective dance partners. This memory served as point of departure for what would become *Contact*. ("Contact" is also the official title of the third piece in *Contact*, which for sake of clarity I'll refer to as "The Girl in the Yellow Dress.") Stroman and Weidman hung the piece on a frame grafted from "An Occurrence at Owl Creek Bridge" (1891), a short story by Ambrose Bierce. As a Civil War spy is about to be executed, he slips the noose, escapes, and journeys back home. At the final moment, we discover that his adventure—which had been described in detail—took place entirely in his mind, in the moment between the drop of the noose and his death. For Stroman and Weidman's purposes, the hero—who imagines the trip to the Soho dance club—manages to escape death in the end, and find the girl in the yellow dress in yellow pajamas. Hey, it's musical comedy.

The unusual-for-theatre format of the piece was not preordained; as Stroman and Weidman worked, they discovered that the dance-driven material did not call for singing characters, original music, or much in the way of dialogue. Lincoln Center set a workshop of the material for February 1999, just after Stroman finished her choreography for the Royal National Theatre/Trevor Nunn *Oklahoma!* (Weidman, meanwhile, was trying to finish his

> As the meek Mafia wife in blue taffeta, Karen Ziemba seemed to fade into the golden curtains. Hit her with a red spot and strike up the ballet music, and she turned into a prima comic danseuse, seeming to combine the essence of Angela Lansbury and Lucille Ball.

long-in-gestation Sondheim collaboration, *Wise Guys*.) The *Contact* workshop indicated that this unconventional piece had legs, as they say, and
Lincoln Center agreed to produce it at its smaller, off-Broadway-sized
house in the fall. The sixty-minute one-act had to be expanded, so Stroman and Weidman undertook to create two additional dance pieces.
(Lest anyone care about such matters, *Contact* was not the first of its kind.

Was *Contact* a Broadway musical? It was in a Broadway theatre, with Broadway people, and could not be done without music. That seems sufficient to me.

Ballet Ballads was a program of
three dance plays, set to music by
Jerome Moross and lyrics by John
Latouche. It was developed by
the Experimental Theatre, a wing
of ANTA, and transferred to
Broadway. *Ballet Ballads* opened on May 18, 1948, at the Music Box, to
strong reviews and weak business. Choreographer Hanya Holm's acclaim
resulted in an immediate Broadway offer, though, on the hit *Kiss Me,
Kate*. Moross and Latouche later collaborated on another fascinating musical theatre piece, *The Golden Apple* in 1954.)

All three of *Contact*'s "short stories" dealt with contact—personal
contact, or the lack thereof. The protagonist in "The Girl in the Yellow
Dress" was dying, literally, for lack of contact. His trip to the dance club,
his struggle to communicate with the Girl, his climactic moment of dancing with her—all was imaginary. Except for the final moment, when he
met his neighbor—in yellow pajamas—and finally connected.

"Swinging," the curtain raiser, was a ten-minute tease lifted—quite
literally—from Jean-Honoré Fragonard's painting *The Swing* (1768).
Conveniently, the painting was reproduced in the Playbill. It's one of
Fragonard's many such views, with a gowned gentlewoman on a swing in
the sun, legs akimbo, with a shoe flying off. A servant stands behind her,
pushing the swing, while a swain lies on the ground—well, is he gazing
right up her dress? It seems so, and Stroman and Weidman followed this
line of thinking.

"Swinging" was the one piece where the contact is literal. The heroine
made love, as they would say in the eighteenth century, with the well-
mannered swain. Once she sent him off, she made love, as they would say
in the twentieth century, with the frisky servant. The contact was real;
the context, though, was imaginary. It turned out that the acrobatic servant on the swing was really the master. The supposed swain was the servant, paid off with a bag of coins. At any event, "Swinging" brought new
meaning to the phrase "swing shift."

"Did You Move?" was a longer and meatier piece. A Mafia wife in blue taffeta sits in an Italian buffet restaurant in Queens, circa 1954. While her overbearing husband goes off to load his plate with cannelloni, she dreams—via dance—of a quite different existence. In the first dream, she dances through the restaurant and around the other characters; in the second she dances with the other characters, making love to the headwaiter; finally, she makes contact with her husband. By shooting him.

"Did You Move?" took place in real time, with a real couple in a real restaurant with real waiters and real rolls. (The roll business—with about five enormous laughs and another dozen or so peppered through the piece—was inspired.) The wife, though, was totally isolated; her only contact came in her daydreams. It was all in a "real" setting, but the contact—including the shooting—was imaginary.

Contact opened October 7, 1999, at the Mitzi Newhouse Theater to some ecstatic reviews—including one from Ben Brantley in the *Times*, who called it "a sustained endorphin rush of an evening" that is "throbbing with wit, sex appeal and a perfectionist's polish." *Contact* quickly became the hit of the season, with a five-week extension and the inevitable transfer upstairs to Lincoln Center's Tony-eligible Vivian Beaumont.

Contact was aided by four marvelous performers. "Did You Move?" appears to have been molded around Karen Ziemba, in her sixth Stroman show since 1991. As the meek Mafia wife in blue taffeta, she seemed to fade into the golden curtains. Hit her with a red spot and strike up the ballet music, and she turned into a prima comic danseuse. She did all the steps perfectly, at the same time marveling that she could do all the steps; comedy-

wise, she seemed to combine the essence of Angela Lansbury (at her broadest) and Lucille Ball (at her zaniest). But the performance was

Contact
Opened: March 30, 2000
Still playing May 31, 2000
To date: 69 performances (and 31 previews)
Profit/Loss: Nonprofit [Profit]
Contact ($80 top) was scaled to a potential gross of
$656,080 at the 1,067-seat Vivian Beaumont (following a
four-month run at the off-Broadway Mitzi Newhouse).
Weekly grosses averaged about $548,000. Total gross for
the partial season (at the Beaumont) was $6,852,584.
(These figures are not indicative, as the potential was
calculated at the top ticket price, but subscribers paid
less.) Attendance was about 96 percent, with the box
office grossing about 84 percent of potential dollar-
capacity.

TONY AWARD NOMINATIONS
Best Musical (WINNER)
Best Performance by a Featured Actor: Boyd Gaines
   (WINNER)
Best Performance by a Featured Actress: Deborah Yates
Best Performance by a Featured Actress: Karen Ziemba,
   (WINNER)
Best Choreography: Susan Stroman (WINNER)
Best Direction of a Musical: Susan Stroman

DRAMA DESK AWARDS
Best Musical (WINNER)
Best Performance by a Featured Actress: Karen Ziemba
   (WINNER)
Best Lighting Design: Peter Kaczorowski (WINNER)
Best Choreography: Susan Stroman (WINNER)

Critical
Scorecard

Rave	5
Favorable	3
Mixed	1
Unfavorable	1
Pan	0

strongest at its saddest; here was a woman who was suffocating, and Ziemba almost overwhelmed us with her pathos. And it was all acting, without words.

Boyd Gaines, who played a charming *She Loves Me* back in 1993, brought his charm to the less sympathetic role of Michael Wiley, the suicidal hero of "The Girl in the Yellow Dress." A nondancer in a company of nothing-but-dancers, Gaines stood out awkwardly. His character, of course, was supposed to stand out awkwardly. Gaines didn't dance; he kind of clumped around on the ball of his foot. ("I guess the word I'd use is athletic," as Dolly Gallegher Levi used to say.) During most of the piece the dancers swirled around him, but he managed to pull off his "real" dance—opposite the Girl in the Yellow Dress—with victorious assurance.

The Girl herself, Deborah Yates, was a stunningly hypnotic presence. Happily, we got to see her without the yellow dress in the final scene. (She wore yellow pajamas.) She even said some lines, which she did very nicely for an ex-Rockette. A hidden asset was a fellow named Jason Antoon. In "Did You Move?" he was the menacing husband about to explode. "No fahken' rolls," he snarled over and over, until he more or less did explode—with "fahken'" rolls. In "The Girl in the Yellow Dress," he was the supportive bartender-psychiatrist. Speaking with his eyebrows, he seemed a composite of every film noir bartender you've ever seen; every line, every gesture, every raised eyebrow was fraught with meaning. Antoon displayed all the versatility of Richard Libertini, that treasurable eccentric character comedian. And he got to deliver most of Weidman's jokes.

There was a good deal of controversy about *Contact* come Tony season, borne, I suppose, out of a lack of anything else to discuss. Should *Contact*— without an original score, without a live orchestra, without any singing —be eligible as Best Musical?

Was *Contact* a Broadway musical? It was in a Broadway theatre, with Broadway people, and it could not be done without music. That seems sufficient to me. No, there was no original music written for *Contact*; but you could say the same for Best Musical winners *Fosse, Jerome Robbins' Broadway, 42nd Street, Dancin'*, and *Ain't Misbehavin'*. No live music? "The Girl in the Yellow Dress" needed "pop" songs, a sound track emanating from the hero's mind. Michael Bennett's 1978 musical *Ballroom* tried to create a not dissimilar "dance hall" atmosphere, but it used new songs and live singers. An unfortunate result was that instead of concentrating on the dancers and the action, we were listening to what sounded like the same songs over and over again, sung by the same two anonymous singers—a result not unknown to Bernard Gersten, who coproduced both *Ballroom* and *Contact*.

The Best Musical argument was specious, anyway. Consider *Marie Christine, James Joyce's The Dead*, and *The Wild Party*, three musicals that few people enjoyed, two of which were long gone by Tony Sunday. Which of these, pray tell, was Best Musical if not *Contact*?

John Weidman's nomination for Best Book was similarly disparaged because *Contact* didn't have a book. At least, that's what people were saying. In fact, it had a strong book. "Did You Move?" and "The Girl in the Yellow Dress" were both carefully plotted. The former was a marvel, in the amount of information that Stroman and Weidman managed to get across *without* words. The wife and the Mob husband were clearly drawn; but the other characters, nonspeaking dancers all, were similarly complete. (For instance, we saw the husband at the downstage table sending his very pregnant wife to the rest room, so he could flirt with the cigarette girl.)

Contact was not simply the work of a choreographer with a tape recorder who e-mailed some hack to fax over a few lines of dialogue. Weidman, with Stroman, devised a scenario—three scenarios, actually—informing the choreographer What Happened Next. He also managed to fill it with gags, some verbal and some sight, which made *Contact* the funniest new musical of the season. (This against an especially morose crop, including *Marie Christine*, *The Wild Party*, *Aida*, *Saturday Night Fever*, and *Putting It Together*.)

The Tony voters overlooked Weidman in favor of Richard Nelson's book for *James Joyce's The Dead*, settling on a literary libretto over a dramatic one. Weidman was robbed; I suppose he'll have to be content with his *Contact* royalties, which should make him set for life. (In addition to coadapting Lincoln Center's *Anything Goes*, Weidman's work includes *Pacific Overtures*, *Assassins*, and *Big*—none of which paid much in the way of royalties.) That and the satisfaction of having helped create what was clearly the season's best musical.

Contact, in and by itself, vindicated Lincoln Center Theater's musical program. It will be remembered long after *Parade* and *Marie Christine* are forgiven and forgotten.

Contact, in and by itself, vindicated Lincoln Center Theater's musical program. It will be remembered long after *Parade* and *Marie Christine* are forgiven and forgotten. Bishop gave Stroman the same opportunity he had offered Jason Robert Brown and Michael John LaChiusa; you can't expect a winner every time. If the idea of turning a choreographer—rather than a writer—loose in a rehearsal room with music and dancers but no specific project sounds slightly familiar, there is a precedent. The time was 1975, the choreographer was Michael Bennett, the show was *A Chorus Line*. While this is not the place to go into personalities and contributions and creative support, there is a common denominator between *Chorus Line* and *Contact*—and *Hair*, for that matter—and his name is Bernie Gersten. Although Gersten does not handle the artistic side of producing, he has always been highly supportive of his artists and has gone out of his way to make things possible. Which can lead, with luck, to a *Chorus Line* or a *Contact*, or both.

The Ride Down Mt. Morgan

The acclaim accorded recent revivals of A *View from the Bridge*, *Death of a Salesman*, and *The Price* led, apparently, to the decision to bring the 1998 New York Shakespeare Festival production of *The Ride Down Mt. Morgan* to the Ambassador. Or maybe it was simply that Patrick Stewart, the *Star Trek* star, wanted to do it. At any rate, Arthur Miller was back on Broadway in 2000, fifty-five years after his long-forgotten *The Man Who Had All the Luck* opened across the street at the Forrest Theatre (now the Eugene O'Neill).

Not a new play, exactly. *The Ride Down Mt. Morgan* was first produced in London in 1991, at a time when Miller's stock on Broadway was at a forty-five-year low. (The director, oddly enough, was this season's golden boy, Michael Blakemore.) The original production of *The Price*, back in 1968, had been modestly successful. Miller's next play, the Genesis-derived *Creation of the World*, was given a first-class, top-notch production in 1972, with Zoe Caldwell, Bob Dishy, and George Grizzard as Eve, Adam, and Lucifer. The play nevertheless fizzled in less than three weeks, and that was pretty much the end of Miller on Broadway. (Except for revivals, that is.) *The Arch-bishop's Ceiling*, a drama about an American writer visiting friends behind the Iron Curtain, starring **There is a problem with being Arthur Miller, of course, which is that everybody expects you to be Arthur Miller.** John Cullum, Bibi Andersson, and Tony Musante, closed during its tryout at the Kennedy Center in 1977. *The American Clock*, about people coping with Depression-era hardships, made it to Broadway for twelve hard performances in 1980. *Broken Glass*, about a woman who becomes paralyzed

Lyman Patrick Stewart
Nurse Logan Oni Faida Lampley
Theo Frances Conroy
Bessie Shannon Burkett
Leah Katy Selverstone
Tom John C. Vennema
Pianist Glen Pearson
Hospital Staff/Dream Figures Portia Johnson, Terry Layman, Jennifer Piech, Sherry Skinker

Time: The Present
Place: Clearhaven Memorial Hospital, Elmira, New York

AMBASSADOR THEATRE
Ⓢ A Shubert Organization Theatre
Gerald Schoenfeld, *Chairman*   Philip J. Smith, *President*

THE SHUBERT ORGANIZATION SCOTT RUDIN ROGER BERLIND
SPRING SIRKIN ABC INC.

in association with

THE PUBLIC THEATER/NEW YORK SHAKESPEARE FESTIVAL,
GEORGE C. WOLFE, PRODUCER

present

PATRICK STEWART
in

THE RIDE DOWN MT. MORGAN
by

ARTHUR MILLER

also starring
FRANCES CONROY

with
SHANNON BURKETT   ONI FAIDA LAMPLEY
KATY SELVERSTONE   JOHN C. VENNEMA

Scenic Design by   Costume Design by   Lighting Design by
JOHN ARNONE   ELIZABETH HOPE CLANCY   BRIAN MacDEVITT

Original Music & Sound by   Casting by   Production Stage Manager
DAN MOSES SCHREIER   PAT McCORKLE, CSA   ERICA SCHWARTZ
JORDAN THALER/
HEIDI GRIFFITHS

General Management   Press Representative   Production Supervisor
NIKO ASSOCIATES, INC./   BARLOW•HARTMAN   FRED GALLO, JR.
MARVIN A.   PUBLIC RELATIONS
KRAUSS ASSOCIATES, INC.
CARL PASBJERG

Directed by
DAVID ESBJORNSON

The world premiere of The Ride Down Mt. Morgan was presented by Robert Fox Ltd. at Wyndham's Theatre, London, England in 1991. The American premiere of The Ride Down Mt. Morgan was produced by Williamstown Theatre Festival, Michael Ritchie, Producer.

---

upon reports of Kristallnacht, made it to the Booth for nine weeks in 1994.

None of Miller's other post-*Price* works has made it even that far. These include several one-acts and *Up in Paradise*, a 1974 musical version of *Creation of the World*. *The Last Yankee*, which takes place in a mental hospital, played eight weeks on the Manhattan Theatre Club's smaller stage in 1993. Miller's most recent play, *Mr. Peters' Connections*, was produced off-Broadway at the Signature Theatre in 1998 for a limited run. Like *Mt. Morgan*, it is about a man on his last legs, with his life drifting through his mind; like *Mt. Morgan*, it had a major star in the lead. I assume we've heard the last of *Mr. Peters*, unless Peter Falk decides that he wants to do it again on Broadway. (It briefly surfaced in London in the summer of 2000 with John Cullum in the lead.)

Miller has been somewhat more appreciated in England of late; hence, *Mt. Morgan*'s London debut. It was finally presented in America in 1996 at the Williamstown Theatre Festival, with F. Murray Abraham in the lead and Michael Learned as the elder Mrs. Felt, under the direction of Scott Ellis. A new and rewritten version—with Patrick Stewart as Felt, supported by Frances Conroy—made it to the New York Shakespeare Festival in 1998 for a limited one-month run. The Broadway *Mt. Morgan* was a close transfer, with minor rewrites, of the 1998 version, using the same director, designers, and cast (with the exception of the actresses playing Leah and Bessie).

Mind you, I would gladly go see Mr. Stewart in anything, if only based on his performance in George C. Wolfe's 1995 production of *The Tempest.* Stewart's reputation, alas, was not quite enough to carry *Mt. Morgan* past underappreciative reviews to a successful run. No, the play wasn't great; no, it wasn't another *Death of a Salesman.* But it was intelligent, imaginative, and often funny.

Miller was in a provocative mood. Lyman Felt is an egoistic hedonist; Miller wrote this play in response to the excesses of the Reagan years of the 1980s. "I may be a bastard, but I'm not a hypocrite," he boasts. "A man can be faithful to himself or to other people—but not to both. The first law of life is betrayal."

What about the jokes scattered across the evening about Leah's panties? Miller surely means something, but what? What about that dream sequence where the two wives are 1950s suburban-style Dresden dolls cooking glazed ham and gefilte fish (from the husband of Marilyn Monroe)?

When a character cries "the truth is terrible because it's embarrassing," Lyman responds, "The truth is embarrassing because it's the truth." He compares man to a fourteen-room house. "In the bedroom he's asleep with his intelligent wife, in his living room he's rolling around with some bare-assed girl, in the library he's paying his taxes, in the yard he's raising tomatoes, and in the cellar he's making a bomb to blow it all up."

There is a problem with being Arthur Miller, of course, which is that everybody expects you to be Arthur Miller. (The same held true for Tennessee Williams, and holds true for Edward Albee.) What is he writing about in this play? What is it supposed to mean? How does this play reflect and/or affect me and/or my life? These questions place an undue burden on any playwright, let alone an octogenarian ex-husband of Marilyn Monroe, and the answers in this case were fuzzy. I mention Ms. Monroe only because Mr. Miller's Mr. Felt expresses some truly eccentric ideas about women and wives—and when Miller talks, we listen.

This was a play with holes as well. Lyman Felt, an immensely successful insurance man, crashes while "skiing down Mt. Morgan in a Porsche."

His two wives converge on his hospital bed, only to find that their husband is a bigamist. But not a bigamist with separate identities; he lives in two cities at once, with two wives and two children, under the same identity. He even opens a branch office of his business in the second city, with his second wife working across the desk from him. In life, some secretary or bookkeeper at headquarters would surely stumble across the second Mrs. Felt soon enough; or one wife would try to track her hubby down at the other office, if only to tell him to mark down a dinner engagement or bar mitzvah in his calendar. For that matter, Miller's Lyman Felt is so obnoxiously despicable that some business enemy would surely have uncovered the deception and smeared it across the front page of some friendly tabloid.

There was also a surprising lack of clarity. Miller is such a precise writer that we have grown to expect everything to have a meaning. Like the character name Lyman Felt—is that a man who lies in order to feel? Miller implies that Felt's ride down Mt. Morgan was possibly suicidal; the road was closed due to icy conditions. But late in the game Felt tells us that he was trying to call his wife Leah. Getting hours' worth of busy signals—don't these people have call waiting?—he remembered her words when accepting his marriage proposal: "I might lie to you." (Does this make her Ly-woman Felt?) Is it jealousy that impelled him to rush home across the ice, because he was afraid she was talking to another man? When Lyman first met Leah, she had a different man each night, which Miller seems to explain by the fact that she's a Jewess. Is Lyman implying that the whole situation—his accident, and the discovery of his deception—is Leah's fault? Hard to say. Instead of giving us half the picture and letting us decide, Miller gives us a quarter of the picture.

And why Elmira, a city of thirty-three thousand in Middle-of-

The Ride Down Mt. Morgan
Opened: April 9, 2000
Closed: July 23, 2000
120 performances (and 23 previews)
Profit/Loss: Loss
The Ride Down Mt. Morgan ($65 top) was scaled to a
  potential gross of $506,971 at the 1,109-seat
  Ambassador. Weekly grosses averaged about $219,000,
  with the show building to a high of almost $320,000
  when Stewart made his infamous curtain speech. Within
  three weeks grosses were down around the $200,000
  mark, falling as low as $128,000. Total gross for the run
  was $3,948,515. Attendance was about 62 percent, with
  the box office grossing about 43 percent of potential
  dollar-capacity.

TONY AWARD NOMINATIONS
Best Play: Arthur Miller
Best Performance by a Featured Actress: Frances Conroy

Critical
Scorecard

Rave	0
Favorable	4
Mixed	1
Unfavorable	3
Pan	1

Nowhere, New York? Not exactly the place you'd open a branch office of a major insurance company. And what about the four jokes scattered across the evening about Leah's panties? Miller surely means something, but what? And what about that dream sequence where the two wives are 1950s suburban-style Dresden dolls cooking glazed ham and gefilte fish (from the husband of Marilyn Monroe)? Or how about the section where the crows come in and disembowel Felt by pulling yards of red nylon rope out of his stomach?

Nevertheless, Miller's language was a joy to listen to, and David Esbjornson's imaginative production—with Felt springing from his hospital bed into his dreams, and an airborne piano player floating across the stage playing "You Made Me Love You"—made for a fanciful evening. Mr. Stewart was a treat to watch, and he was especially well supported by Frances Conroy, John C. Vennema, and Katy Selverstone. (Conroy, incidentally, played Miller wives in both *The Last Yankee* and *Broken Glass*.) If *Mt. Morgan* wasn't nearly so good as *Death of a Salesman*, well—how many plays are?

The Ride Down Mt. Morgan started out fairly strongly, doing far better than the revivals of *View from the Bridge* and *The Price* (which both received more favorable reviews). *Mt. Morgan* seemed to be healthy enough until the afternoon of April 29, when Stewart made an extraordinary curtain speech after the matinee excoriating his producers. It seems that he didn't feel they were buying enough newspaper ads. "Arthur Miller and I no longer have confidence in our producers' commitment to this production, especially the Shubert Organization, or their willingness to promote and publicize it. Arthur and I feel frustrated and helpless."

This brought *The Ride Down Mt. Morgan* and Stewart plenty of publicity. It also trumpeted that business was bad and that the producers had given up on the show due to poor reviews. This was not the case, in fact; but it sure was not the best way to encourage people to pass by *Copenhagen* or *The Real Thing* or *Dirty Blonde* for a ride with Mr. Stewart down Mr. Miller's mountain.

> *Mt. Morgan* seemed to be healthy enough until Patrick Stewart made an extraordinary curtain speech excoriating his producers. This brought *The Ride Down Mt. Morgan* plenty of publicity. It also trumpeted that business was bad.

When the Tony Award nominations were announced the following week, Stewart was conspicuously absent. The Shuberts filed charges with Actors' Equity against Stewart for unprofessional conduct, and the affair fizzled away. But so did *The Ride Down Mt. Morgan*, after its initially scheduled eighteen-week run.

Copenhagen

The Broadway season of nonmusicals began inauspiciously in August with the thrill-less thriller *Voices in the Dark*; moved on to the farceless farce *Epic Proportions* in September; and hit an early peak in October with the hybrid play-revue with songs, *Dame Edna: The Royal Tour*. We then proceeded through a series of revivals, with two March entries of more than passing interest (namely, the twenty-year-old *True West* and the sixty-year-old *Moon for the Misbegotten*). It wasn't until April that there was finally, happily, a totally satisfying new play; something where you could leave the theatre thinking, by gosh, that you'd just been to the theatre. As we will see, a second dazzling evening of pure theatre came along a mere six nights and four shows later.

The party of the first part, if you will, was Michael Frayn's *Copenhagen*. This British import had a figurative question mark next to its name as the opening approached. Yes, the word was that it was superb. But would this very European play—with its Danish and German characters—work with American actors? And would American audiences sit still through a necessarily dense evening of theoretical science and historical theory?

The fact that it sprang from the mind of Michael Frayn was in its favor. Frayn is best known here as the author of *Noises Off*, which enjoyed a 553-performance Broadway run in 1983. I won't say that *Noises Off* is the best farce of the last sixty years, as I have not seen every farce of the last sixty years. It is the best new farce I've ever seen, though. It is a far distance from farce to physics, perhaps; but if Frayn, in his sixteenth play, saw fit to address fission and fusion and philosophical fuss, I would at least give him the benefit of the doubt. Frayn also made it to Broadway with his comedy *Benefactors*, which had a six-month run in 1985. The play was

ROYALE THEATRE
242 West 45th Street
Ⓢ A Shubert Organization Theatre
Gerald Schoenfeld, *Chairman*   Philip J. Smith, *President*
Robert E. Wankel, *Executive Vice President*

BY ARRANGEMENT WITH
MICHAEL CODRON, LEE DEAN AND THE ROYAL NATIONAL THEATRE

JAMES M. NEDERLANDER   ROGER BERLIND   SCOTT RUDIN

ELIZABETH IRELAND McCANN

RAY LARSEN   JON B. PLATT   BYRON GOLDMAN   SCOTT NEDERLANDER

PRESENT

PHILIP BOSCO   BLAIR BROWN   MICHAEL CUMPSTY

IN

COPENHAGEN

BY
MICHAEL FRAYN

DESIGNED BY
PETER J. DAVISON

LIGHTING DESIGNED BY
MARK HENDERSON AND MICHAEL LINCOLN

COSTUME SUPERVISOR
CHARLOTTE BIRD

SOUND BY
TONY MEOLA

CASTING
JIM CARNAHAN, C.S.A.

GENERAL MANAGER
JOEY PARNES

PRODUCTION STAGE MANAGER
R. WADE JACKSON

PRESS REPRESENTATIVE
BONEAU/BRYAN-BROWN

DIRECTED BY
MICHAEL BLAKEMORE

NT
THE ROYAL NATIONAL THEATRE PRODUCTION IS
PRESENTED IN LONDON BY MICHAEL CODRON AND LEE DEAN

THE PRODUCERS WISH TO EXPRESS THEIR APPRECIATION TO THEATRE DEVELOPMENT FUND FOR ITS SUPPORT OF THIS PRODUCTION

entertaining enough, especially as enhanced by Sam Waterston, Glenn Close, and Mary Beth Hurt.

Copenhagen was something else again. I was quite amazed by Frayn's ability to draw me into the subject. Physics is not my strong suit, exactly; I managed to maneuver through college without taking a single science course. But I'll be damned if I didn't walk out of the Royale with a vague but clear understanding of nuclear fission and the history that led from Bohr's discovery of quantum theory in 1913 to the explosion of the atomic bomb in 1945.

But Frayn's aim wasn't to instruct; the science played background to the human puzzle at the center of the story. Niels Bohr and Werner Heisenberg were both Nobel Prize–winning physicists (in 1922 and 1932, respectively). History relates that Heisenberg—who headed the German research on the possible military applications of fission—visited the half-Jewish Bohr in *Copenhagen* in 1941, shortly before Bohr escaped to America (where he joined the Manhattan Project and helped produce the atomic bomb). Was Heisenberg there as a friend or as a colleague? As a conspirator, an informer, or a spy? Did Heisenberg want information from Bohr, about the progress of the scientists allied to the Allies? Or did he want to pass word on, through Bohr, for humanitarian reasons? Did he propose to Bohr that they both unequivocally state the impossibility of creating a neutron bomb, hopefully convincing their leaders not to investigate further? Or did he want to trick Bohr into believing that he himself was going to do so? Frayn suggests that Heisenberg recognized the madness of supplying Hitler with the bomb; even if it meant that he—a brilliant scientist and a loyal German—more or less sabotaged the German effort and, by so doing, guaranteed the loss of the war. ("Supply a homicidal maniac with a means of mass murder. . . . That is an interesting idea.") For whatever reason, Heisenberg—in 1942—advised Hitler's munitions man, Albert Speer, against continued funding of the nuclear project.

Of course, Frayn admits that his suppositions—and, thus, the lines that the actors say—are merely suppositions. Nobody knows what Heisenberg and Bohr spoke about on that September afternoon; even Heisenberg and Bohr, in later years, couldn't seem to agree. But that is the point of the play.

Central to the plot and the plotting was Heisenberg's uncertainty principle, which states more or less that the very act of observing one aspect of an object necessarily changes its relationship to other aspects. Frayn continually hones in on the thoughts and motivations of his two Nobel Prize–winning physicists. As he gets close to the "real" meaning of one, though, the other always seems to slip away.

The playwright was helped, every step of the way, by director Michael Blakemore (in his eighth collaboration with Frayn). Besides *Noises Off*, Blakemore has some creditable Broadway credits, including *City of Angels*, *Lettice and Lovage*, and this season's revival of *Kiss Me, Kate*. (*Kate* and *Copehagen* won him twin Tonys, the only time one person has won both directing awards in the same season.) His work on *Copenhagen*, though, was far subtler than one might have expected. Blakemore was constrained by the simplest of setups: three actors and three chairs, playing on a circular surface of inlaid wood. This seemingly represented a flattened globe, with a narrow wedge splitting down from the North Pole. Upstage of the playing space was a curved amphitheatre—also of wood—incorporating two rows of bleacher seats, on sale to the public. (This ticket-buyer-as-on-

It wasn't until April that there was finally a totally satisfying new play; something where you could leave the theatre thinking, by gosh, that you'd just been to the theatre.

stage-jury scheme had also been used effectively in the 1974 Broadway production of *Equus*.) How do you sustain the audience's interest, with no props or scenery or additional actors, for over two hours of nothing but talk?

By weaving a spell, which is what Blakemore did. He deployed his actors in meticulous, almost dancelike patterns. The circular globe was used like the face of a compass, with the actors attracted to or repelled by each other. At other times it was a gyroscope, or moons orbiting a planet. This might seem contrived, described in mere words, but Blakemore's staging enhanced the text throughout the evening.

For example, let us suppose that Heisenberg and Bohr are facing off against each other, the uninvited guest at what would be the 9:00 position on a clock, Bohr planted at 3. Bohr's wife Margrethe observes, silently, from 1. As Heisenberg makes telling points, Margrethe seemingly

floats around the top rim of the clock until she reaches 8. Bohr suddenly notices her by Heisenberg's side, at precisely the instant that Frayn has Bohr run out of words. There is an embarrassed beat, after which Heisenberg and Margrethe burst apart; he spins to 5, she goes to 12, and Bohr cuts diagonally across from 3 to a chair placed midway between 9 and dead center. Margrethe picks up the conversation, crossing supportively to Bohr's chair.

I made up the preceding staging, as I was too engrossed by the play to sit there making diagrams of the blocking. But it gives you an idea of what Blakemore did throughout—and how staging can add an extra layer of subtext to the text. The trick in all this is to cloak the mechanics from the audience; you don't want them to observe the geometric patterns as they pass, you merely want to stress certain words, thoughts, and actions. (The three chairs were used in different positions at different times—very effectively so in a case where Bohr and

Heisenberg were facing the audience but Margrethe, seated between them, was facing upstage. But I can't recall noticing the actors ever actually moving the chairs.) Frayn's words and Blakemore's staging melded together, becoming one and the same. This is just as it should be, with the movement—and the actors—enhancing the text every step of the way.

Philip Bosco made his Broadway debut in 1960, picking up a Tony nomination for a nine-performance flop called *Rape of the Belt*. A regional theatre stalwart, he has developed a Broadway presence only in the last decade. He is best known for the farces *Lend Me a Tenor* (1989) and *Moon over Buffalo* (1995), neither of which struck me as especially funny, and both of which failed despite Bosco's sturdy presence. I must confess, though, to a long-standing bias against the actor. Back when I was twelve, I was lassoed into seeing a production of Shakespeare's *Coriolanus*, which was a bad idea all around. All I can remember is that this Coriolanus fellow talked and talked and talked and talked; they had to stab him to stop him, but that wasn't until late in the fifth act. I long ago wiped out the memory of the production and everything about it; unfortunately for poor Mr. Bosco, he shared his surname with what was at the time my favorite chocolate syrup. The whole experience surely would have dimmed in my memory had Bosco's name been something like John Cunningham or Rex Everhart—both of whom, the record books tell me, were also in the production. (Cunningham, long before *Company* or *Zorbá* or *Six Degrees of Separation*, killed Bosco's Coriolanus. About three hours too late for my taste.) But ever since that midsummer day's matinee in 1965, poor Philip Bosco has been fighting an uphill battle for my appreciation. This is immature, perhaps, but hey—I was only twelve.

> How do you sustain the audience's interest, with no props or scenery or additional actors, for over two hours of nothing but talk? By weaving a spell, which is what Michael Blakemore did.

The point of this digression is that Bosco gave a wonderful performance in *Copenhagen*, finally and for all time winning me over. Niels Bohr is described in the program notes as being a "master of consistency, caution, and physical insight"; he is quoted as saying, "We shall never understand anything until we have found some contradictions" and "Never express yourself more clearly than you think." This is how Mr. Frayn wrote the character, and this is precisely how Bosco played it. Thus we were watching a man who knew everything but knew nothing, and Bosco communicated this. While he was in the midst of conversation, you could almost see his mind absorbing and processing information, then formulating a response and putting it into words. Forty years of standing around onstage has turned this man into quite a marvelous actor.

He was equally matched by Michael Cumpsty, a relative youngster who has been impressively good in Tom Stoppard's *Artist Descending a Staircase* (1989), the fabled *La Bête* (1991), and especially David Hare's *Racing Demon* (1995). His was a driving, unpredictable Heisenberg; Frayn wrote a character who intensely bored into Bohr, if you will, without exactly knowing where he was going. The character couldn't know his aims, as the central event of the play played back again and again, with different words and different motivations. Cumpsty's performance was riveting. Blair Brown, as Margrethe, served as sounding board for them both. Whenever the science talk became too technical, Bohr would stop and say that they must explain it so Margrethe could understand it. ("We don't do science for ourselves," Bohr said, "we do it to explain to others.") Ms. Brown was in the midst of a notably busy season, moving from a replacement chore in the Lotte Lenya role in *Cabaret* to *James Joyce's The Dead* to Frayn's *Copenhagen*. This activity managed to win her a Tony Award (for *Copenhagen*). Neither of her worthy costars was even nominated, although both gave what I consider to be more important and memorable performances.

So Broadway had a smashingly sophisticated new play in *Copenhagen*, complete with strong reviews (including a deserved rave from the *Times*). But was that enough to sell tickets to an audience not known, generally speaking, for seeking intellectual stimulation? A great deal of the house at the final preview I attended was hanging on to every word of the play, as was I. Yet I readily admit that I went to *Copenhagen* prepared for a night of concentration. What would I have made of it all had I been tired, or worn out, or en route from a wine tasting?

While Philip Bosco was in the midst of conversation, you could almost see his mind absorbing and processing information, then formulating a response and putting it into words. Forty years of standing around onstage has turned this man into quite a marvelous actor.

I couldn't help but observe the reaction of the people sitting onstage. As mentioned earlier, the set featured two rows of benches built into the upstage "wall" above the circular playing area, with forty people looking down upon the actors (at thirty bucks each). Whether

Copenhagen
Opened: April 11, 2000
Closed: January 21, 2001
326 performances (and 21 previews)
Profit/Loss: Profit
Copenhagen ($65 top) was scaled to a potential gross of
$462,320 at the 1,076-seat Royale. Weekly grosses
averaged about $267,000, breaking $350,000 after the
Tony Awards but tapering off below $250,000. Total gross
for the run was $11,570,839. Attendance was about 71
percent, with the box office grossing about 58 percent of
potential dollar-capacity.

TONY AWARD NOMINATIONS
Best Play: Michael Frayn (WINNER)
Best Direction of a Play: Michael Blakemore (WINNER)
Best Performance by a Featured Actress: Blair Brown
  (WINNER)

NEW YORK DRAMA CRITICS CIRCLE AWARDS
Best Foreign Play: Michael Frayn (WINNER)

DRAMA DESK AWARDS
Best Play: Michael Frayn (WINNER)
Best Direction of a Play: Michael Blakemore (WINNER)

*Critical
Scorecard*

Rave	2
Favorable	4
Mixed	2
Unfavorable	1
Pan	0

these seats were comfortable or not, I don't know. As the first act progressed, I couldn't help but notice a couple in their twenties, presumably
student tourists. As the first act progressed, the girl's head grew closer and
closer to the boy's shoulder, until by 8:45 it more or less rested there.
When the second act began, six of the formerly occupied places were
empty. (Maybe the people moved to unused orchestra seats they had
scouted out during the first act?) This was not a good sign, and unfortunately a highly visible one from where I sat (directly behind Kirk Douglas,
by the way).

My general recommendation to friends was that they should definitely
go to *Copenhagen*, they would love it—but "make sure you're in the mood
to concentrate."

Rose

M artin Sherman's *Rose* was born in a shtetl in the Ukraine, where she lived through a pogrom; moved to Warsaw, where she lived through the establishment and destruction of the ghetto; watched as a clean-shaven young soldier, for no reason, shot and killed her three-year-old daughter; fled to the sewers, where she spent two years ("You *do things* to stay alive," she intones); journeyed to Palestine on the dilapidated hulk of a boat called the *Exodus*; avoided a displaced person camp by marrying an American deckhand; ran a beach-chair concession in Atlantic City during the Miss America pageant (which was maybe more frightening than some of her other experiences); became a Miami Beach hotelier, under the name Rose Rose (don't ask); escaped to a Connecticut commune with a long-haired guitar player half her age, where she smoked pot and was known as "Cool Mama"; watched her son leave Miami to fight in the Six-Day War; visited her son and his wife—a converted shiksa from Kansas named Kim —on the kibbutz; journeyed to see Kim —now divorced—who had become a radical settler in the occupied territory; and watched on television as her right-wing grandson, for no reason, shot and killed a young Palestinian girl. As you can see, playwright Sherman touched more bases than Sammy Sosa at a twinight doubleheader—and mind you, our heroine was only eighty. Should *Rose* be revised and revived in 2015, I imagine she'll get a brain transplant and take the first time-share on Mars.

> Rose admits that it is all jumbled in her mind. How much of her memory, she wonders, comes from the movies? And there lay the problem. All of Sherman's memories came from the movies. Or books, or old photographs, or newspapers.

They raised a banner on the boat with the name *Exodus*, she tells us. But how could she see it? Was she standing under it? Maybe she remembers it, she says, or maybe she remembers it from the movie with Paul Newman. Rose tells us of that pogrom when she was a teen-ager, and of the smooth, clean faces of the Cossacks. Or is she thinking of the Cossacks in the movie *Fiddler on the Roof*, chorus boys on horseback? Rose admits that it is all jumbled in her mind. What is real? What is remembered? (Her favorite saying, other than "on the other hand," is "I can't remember.") How much of her memory, she wonders, comes from the movies?

And there, perhaps, lay the main problem. While many of Rose's memories were real within the context of the play, all of Sherman's memories came from the movies. Or books, or old photographs, or newspapers. *Rose* was a litany of events of the twentieth century, kind of a Forrest Gumpowski view of the Diaspora. (*Zelig* would be a more apt analogy, but I suppose *Zelig* has faded from general memory.) Rose must be real for us to care about *Rose*, but she's not so we didn't. Sherman's stacking of the decks proved his undoing, resulting in a marked backlash from viewers who went into the theatre expecting an engrossing experience.

Sherman is an American playwright who has been living in London for twenty years, ever since his play *Bent* opened on Broadway (December 2, 1979, for 241 performances). *Bent* had its champions, among whom I was not. However, it can be handily compared to *Rose*. Both deal with the Holocaust; but *Rose* speaks in generalities, while *Bent* is highly specific. *Rose* seemed to be compiled by Sherman from a histori-cal time line; the ideas and events in *Bent*—while presumably well re-searched—seemed to come from Sherman himself. Say what you will about *Bent*, I don't suppose anyone would describe it as cliché piled upon cliché.

Rose   Olympia Dukakis

Rose was first produced in June 1999 at the Cottesloe, the intimate off-Broadway-sized house in London's Royal National Theatre complex. It was a surprise hit, playing to virtual capacity during its forty-performance run (four performances a week, in rep). Given the strong overseas reception, Sherman and Dukakis must have seemed like a surefire bet for Broadway, and in September it was announced by producers Robert Fox, Scott Rudin, and the Shubert Organization. They eventually withdrew, and *Rose* was picked up by Lincoln Center Theater, whose 1999–2000 season had been especially lean. (In 1998–1999, LCT offered *Twelfth Night*, *A New Brain*, *Parade*, *Via Dolorosa*, *The Far East*, and *Ring Round the Moon*. The 1999–2000 lineup— not including two-performance-a-week staged readings—consisted of *Contact*, *Marie Christine*, and a revival of Arthur Laurent's *Time of the Cuckoo*.)

The character of Rose was presumably something of a novelty to British audiences. To the audience that patronizes nonmusical Broadway plays, though, Rose was not such a rare bird. Several of the major reviewers pointed out, in a negative context, that they had Rose-like characters in their own experience. ("You may react to her as a child to a relative who has overtaken one too many family gatherings," said Bruce Weber in the *Times*. "Yes, Grandma. Now can we go out and play?")

Advance word on *Rose* was pretty good, until previews began. Many of the critics were surprisingly severe; rather than just writing politely unfavorable notices, they laced their reviews with disparaging remarks that seemed slightly out of proportion. (The seven pans in the scorecard below appeared so out of line that I went back and retabulated them. While they are not as violent as your typical pan, they very clearly express critical annoyance—the dividing line between negatives and pans.) Part of this, no doubt, can be ascribed to disappointed expectations raised by the advance word. For whatever reason, *Rose* certainly struck a nerve.

Compare it to 1998–1999's Lincoln Center Theater, London-born, Jewish-themed, one-person show *Via Dolorosa*; well, there's no comparison. David Hare's piece about the Israeli-Palestinian situation was heartfelt and urgent. One had the distinct impression that the playwright was impelled to stand up on stage himself, visibly discomfited, in order to bring us a message he felt passionate about. *Rose*, though, was just another play, with Ms. Dukakis presenting a well-crafted but unimpassioned performance. An impressive and controlled performance, mind you, with the fifty-eight-year-old Greek-American actress doing well enough as the eighty-year-old Ukrainian-Jewish heroine. But there was no spark in evidence, which I will ascribe to the material rather than the actor. Perhaps it was the steady stream of Henny Youngman–style jokes Mr. Sherman laced through the narrative. (Judaism is "a culture of sore behinds and complainers.") Perhaps it was the languorous mood of the evening. Sherman's Rose made continual swipes at poor old Molly Picon, **Rose must be real for us to care about *Rose*, but she's not so we didn't.** who danced across the screen with a twinkle in her eye in the Yiddish-language movie *Yiddle and His Fiddle*; Ms. Dukakis herself sat motionless on a bench for two hours, without a twinkle in her eye. She didn't move from her seat until the curtain call, although more than a couple of ticket holders did.

This is not to say that Mr. Sherman didn't have some provocative things to say. Rose was horrified by the Mount Hebron massacre, and she

Rose
Opened: April 12, 2000
Closed: May 21, 2000
42 performances (and 13 previews)
Profit/Loss: Nonprofit [Profit]
Rose ($60 top) was scaled to a potential gross of $329,980
at the 924-seat Lyceum. Weekly grosses for the seven-
performance week averaged about $157,000, steadily
building from $140,000 to $175,000. Total gross for the
run was $1,230,595. (These figures are not indicative, as
the potential was calculated at the top ticket price, but
subscribers paid less.) Attendance was about 80 percent,
with the box office grossing about 48 percent of potential
dollar-capacity.

Critical Scorecard

Rave 0
Favorable 1
Mixed 0
Unfavorable 1
Pan 7

didn't hesitate to say so. The violent militancy of the religious right seemed to Sherman decidedly un-Jewish, an opinion that many might find on the mark. But Sherman's Rose had already expressed too many opinions about too many topics, overloading the listener's incoming message box.

Two Wild Parties

There's no domain like public domain.

Let's say someone—Lerner and Loewe, for example—wanted to write a musical version of George Bernard Shaw's 1914 play, *Pygmalion*. First they had to make a deal with the estate of Gabriel Pascal, the colorful Hungarian film producer to whom Shaw had assigned the performance rights. Pascal's estate was contentiously split between his ex-wife and his nonwife, with artistic decisions ultimately empowered to a banker. Once the authors in question came to terms with the Pascal estate, they had to go—hat in hand—to the Shaw estate for approval. Shaw left his estate to a tangle of British charities, which meant even more dickering. Finally, all conditions were met, and the estates demanded a princely sum for their valuable property.

On the other hand, let's say someone—Bernstein, Sondheim, and Laurents, for example—wanted to write a modern version of *Romeo and Juliet*. *Romeo* was written in 1602; Shakespeare died in 1616; and his estate's solicitors haven't been heard from since the Great Fire of London. Want to set it amid the gang wars waged on the racial battlefields of Manhattan playgrounds? Sure, why not, no bankers or lawyers need approve. And as for rights payments, the new authors were able to keep all the royalties to themselves. The Bard's tragedy of Verona and all his other works are sitting there for the taking, do with them what you will.

Which is to say, there's no domain like public domain. Except, that is, if somebody else happens to come along at the same time with the same idea.

Not very likely, true. Consider the odds of two novice Broadway song-

MANHATTAN THEATRE CLUB

CITY CENTER STAGE I

artistic director
LYNNE MEADOW

executive producer
BARRY GROVE

presents

THE WILD PARTY

book, music and lyrics by

ANDREW LIPPA

based on the poem by JOSEPH MONCURE MARCH

with

TAYE DIGGS   BRIAN d'ARCY JAMES   IDINA MENZEL   JULIA MURNEY

and

TODD ANDERSON   JAMES DELISCO BEEKS   KEVIN CAHOON
JENNIFER CODY   CHARLES DILLON   KENA TANGI DORSEY
FELICIA FINLEY   PETER KAPETAN   LAWRENCE KEIGWIN
ALIX KOREY   KRISTIN McDONALD   RAYMOND JARAMILLO McLEOD
MEGAN SIKORA   RON J. TODOROWSKI   AMANDA WATKINS

set design
DAVID GALLO

costume design
MARTIN PAKLEDINAZ

lighting design
KENNETH POSNER

sound design
BRIAN RONAN

orchestrations
MICHAEL GIBSON

music director
STEPHEN OREMUS

music coordinator
MICHAEL KELLER

wig design
PAUL HUNTLEY

fight director
RICK SORDELET

production stage manager
ED FITZGERALD

choreography
MARK DENDY

directed by
GABRIEL BARRE

casting
BERNARD TELSEY CASTING

press representative
BONEAU/BRYAN-BROWN

director of musical theatre program
CLIFFORD LEE JOHNSON III

production manager
MICHAEL R. MOODY

associate artistic director
MICHAEL BUSH

general manager
VICTORIA BAILEY

The Wild Party was partially developed and received readings at the O'Neill Theatre Center during the 1997 National Music Theatre Conference with the support of the Lila Wallace-Reader's Digest Fund.
Manhattan Theatre Club productions are made possible in part with public funds from the New York City Department of Cultural Affairs and the New York State Council on the Arts, a State Agency.

The Wild Party (Lippa)

Queenie	Julia Murney
Burrs	Brian d'Arcy James
Reno	Todd Anderson
Kegs	Ron J. Todorowski
Madelaine True	Alix Korey
Eddie	Raymond Jaramillo McLeod
Peggy	Megan Sikora
Max	James Delisco Beeks
Rose Himmelsteen	Felicia Finley
Sam Himmelsteen	Peter Kapetan
Ellie	Amanda Watkins
Jackie	Lawrence Keigwin
Oscar d'Armano	Charles Dillon
Phil d'Armano	Kevin Cahoon
Dolores	Kena Tangi Dorsey
Mae	Jennifer Cody
Nadine	Kristin McDonald
Kate	Idina Menzel
Black	Taye Diggs
The Neighbor	Charlie Marcus
The Cop	Steven Pasquale

Time: 1929
Place: An Apartment

Original Off-Broadway Cast Album:
RCA Victor 09026-63695

writers individually coming upon an obsolete, seventy-year-old poem; musicalizing the thing; finding a major, first-class theatre company wishing to produce it and capable of financing it; and having them both open in New York in the West Fifties within six weeks.

Not very likely; but strange things happen along the side streets of Broadway and Seventh Avenue.

This strange thing began with an unsuccessful poet named Joseph Moncure March. A student of Robert Frost—literally, at Amherst—March got himself wrapped up in the scandal-ridden, Prohibition-driven world of Manhattan in the Roaring Twenties. He came from a wealthy, upper-crust family; his uncle was army chief of staff in World War I, no less. But March was the black sheep in the fold; he seems to have been the prototype for *The Wild Party*'s "ambi-sextrous" character Jackie, who

The Wild Party (LaChiusa)
Queenie Toni Collette
Burrs Mandy Patinkin
Jackie Marc Kudisch
Miss Madelaine True Jane Summerhays
Sally Sally Murphy
Eddie Mackrel Norm Lewis
Mae Leah Hocking
Nadine Brooke Sunny Moriber
Phil D'Armano Nathan Lee Graham
Oscar D'Armano Michael McElroy
Dolores Eartha Kitt
Gold Adam Grupper
Goldberg Stuart Zagnit
Black Yancey Arias
Kate Tonya Pinkins

Setting: New York, NY 1928

Original Broadway Cast Album:
Decca Broadway 012 159 003

goes slumming through life. March was, briefly, the first managing editor of the *New Yorker* in 1925. (He came peddling cartoons, but he had edited an in-house magazine for New York Telephone. *New Yorker* editor Harold Ross was desperate for help.) In 1926, March sat down and wrote his singularly unusual poem of the deviant, decadent world of the Jazz Age.

Publishers understandably shied away from the prurient and potentially censorable material, so it wasn't until 1928 that *The Wild Party* was published in a small edition by an obscure press. The work became something of a cult favorite but never achieved widespread circulation. It was pretty much forgotten over the years, although in 1974 it was adapted into a not very good Merchant-Ivory film of the same title starring Jimmy Coco and Raquel Welch.

And then one fateful day, illustrator Art Spiegelman, of *Maus* fame, decided to prepare a new 1994 edition of *The Wild Party*—a decision that would unwittingly result in millions of dollars of losses for two of New

York's major nonprofit theatres. March's long-forgotten poem was suddenly back in circulation, and it circulated to both Michael John LaChiusa and Andrew Lippa. The alcoholic, narcotic, and sexual excesses of the characters—which were truly shocking to many readers back in the late 1920s—were mild by modern-day standards and certainly not unsuitable as subject matter for a post-Fosse Broadway musical.

> **Consider the odds of two novice Broadway songwriters individually coming upon an obsolete, seventy-year-old poem; musicalizing the thing; and having them both open in New York in the West Fifties within six weeks. Not very likely; but strange things happen along the side streets of Broadway and Seventh Avenue.**

How and why *The Wild Party* lapsed into the public domain, I can't tell you. Most works initially published in 1928 are still under copyright; March, apparently, did not bother to file an extension when his poem came up for renewal in 1956. For whatever reason, *The Wild Party* was unencumbered and sitting there for the taking. Which Mr. Lippa did, and Mr. LaChiusa (and his coauthor, George C. Wolfe) did. You yourself could write your own version of *The Wild Party* too, if you wish, although I can't say that I would recommend it.

Back in the summer of 1998, the New York Shakespeare Festival announced LaChiusa's *Wild Party* for an off-Broadway run at the Public Theatre, with a February 4, 1999, preview date. Due to unforeseen circumstances—that is, the collapse of Wolfe's troubled Broadway revival of *On the Town*—*The Wild Party* was postponed in early December. The Shakespeare Festival went ahead with a February workshop of the piece instead. Two months later, the Manhattan Theatre Club mounted a workshop of Lippa's *Wild Party*, and in July it announced a full production for February 2000. In August, the Shakespeare Festival announced that LaChiusa's *Wild Party* would be produced—on Broadway, due to the growing size of the production—in the spring. (LaChiusa was already booked for the fall of 1999, with Lincoln Center Theater's production of *Marie Christine*.) Thus, LaChiusa's *Wild Party*—which was to have been first, back in the 1998–1999 season—ended up following both *Marie Christine* and *Wild Party* in quick succession. All three, as it happened, failed in quick succession.

Lippa's *Wild Party* worked the best of the three, so far as I am concerned, and seemed to have the best word of mouth. I did a very much off-the-cuff survey of everyone I could find who had seen both *Wild Partys*. Half of them preferred Lippa's. The other half liked neither.

Over the last several years, just about every article on the future hopes of the Broadway musical has centered on four important "new" composers: Adam Guettel, Jason Robert Brown, Ricky Ian Gordon, and Mr. LaChiusa. This despite the fact that until recently only Brown had reached Broadway, with his unsuccessful *Parade*. Andrew Lippa was very noticeably never mentioned in the same breath as the others, which led unknowing observers to assume that he was not in their league. He was known, if at all, for the underwhelming 1995 off-Broadway musical, *john and jen* (without capital letters). While preparing *The Wild Party*, Lippa reached Broadway as musical director for the 1999 revival of *You're a Good Man, Charlie Brown*. He also interpolated a couple of his own songs, one of which—"My New Philosophy"—was a knockout showstopper for Kristen Chenoweth. So it was clear that Lippa could at least write an effective comedy song; but why would anyone think he could write a searing, modernist concept musical?

But he could. Lippa's *Wild Party* was crammed with songs in constantly varying styles; the best were quite good, as good as anything new heard on Broadway in 1999–2000. The show was not artistically successful in many respects, for sure; but then neither were such influential musicals as *Cabaret* or *Chicago*. Lippa's *Wild Party* was spotty in places, and it ran down seriously in the second act. But it possessed an electric excitement—like *Cabaret* and *Chicago*. At one point it occurred to me that *The Wild Party* pretty much *was Cabaret*, without the banal book scenes.

Choreographer Mark Dendy made an impressive musical theatre debut. His ensemble was everywhere, magically appearing and moving through the show like a multiarmed machine. Yes, there were vestiges of Bob Fosse; but Dendy used them to create something marvelously new. Scenic designer David Gallo built a moat around his set, framed by dangerously skewed walls. Late in the first act, when the characters were heading into breakdown mode, the deck (stage floor) suddenly split apart into fragmented pieces—a stunning effect, giving new meaning to the word "deconstruct." Gallo's work was well matched, every step of the way, by lighting designer Kenneth Posner. Shafts of light cut through the open

space like structural columns. There was one section—with the ensemble parading around the moat of the stage in fragmented light—where the work of Dendy, Gallo, and Posner was miraculously aligned. Director Gabriel Barre deserves credit for the overall look of the show, although his direction (and his show) suffered from an overall lack of clarity.

Lippa's *Wild Party* also had several especially good performances. Julia Murney was quite a find as the blonde-haired Queenie, in what was apparently her first New York appearance (other than in readings). Brian D'Arcy James—who offered impressive vocal strength to the otherwise waterlogged *Titanic*—took on the role of the brutal Burrs. He managed to display far greater dramatic depth than one would have expected from his boyish appearance, especially with a red clown's nose pasted to his face. D'Arcy James looked something like Peter Gallagher, without the too-good-to-be-true looks; his performance indicated a promising future. Taye Diggs was the strongest of the principals, despite the most underwritten role. He displayed great presence, a strong voice, and an air of mystery. Idina Menzel, who like Diggs hailed from the original cast of *Rent*, was the other member of the central quartet. She was far too shrill for my taste. Lippa gave his best song to singer-comedienne Alix Korey; her knockout lament, "An Old-Fashioned Love Story," stopped the show dead. Somewhat extraneous, as many of the specialty songs for the supporting characters tended to be; but this was one helluva comedy number.

The show opened on February 24, but it died, effectively, a week earlier. This was when Jeffrey Sellers and Kevin McCollum—who produced the tremendously successful transfer of *Rent*—announced that they were planning to move Lippa's *Wild Party* to the Richard Rodgers Theatre, just in time for the May 1 Tony Award eligibility deadline. The intention, no doubt, was to build on the highly favorable word of mouth the show was receiving, quickly sell out the remaining seats for the Manhattan Theatre Club run, and get a head start on what was necessarily going to be a quick transfer. Announcement of the pending transfer, though, appeared to have put some critics on edge.

You yourself could write your own version of *The Wild Party* too, if you wish, although I can't say that I would recommend it.

The reviews were evenly mixed, from raves to pans. Those who loved *The Wild Party* loved it despite the announcement; but those who didn't like it appeared to heighten their vitriol. Reviews saying "This show should move to Broadway!" are more helpful than reviews saying "This show should move to Broadway??"

LaChiusa's *Wild Party* was something else again, with an accent on "wild" and a damper on "party." The show started out promisingly, with a "backstage vaudeville" stage picture reminiscent of the artwork for the original production of *Gypsy*. The introductory number was effective, but then on came Mandy Patinkin.

Now, Mr. Patinkin has always been what you might call an eccentric performer. Some folks tend to admire his performances, some don't, but he is certainly distinctive. In LaChiusa's *Wild Party*, he came barreling on in blackface—a truly startling sight. This was no doubt intended to shock the audience, but I'm afraid it was more appalling than shocking. He then launched into an all-but-unintelligible number while cavorting about the stage.

I suppose they were trying to draw Burrs as a Jolson-like entertainer. What came across was not Jolson, though. Jolson possessed a problematic personality, it's true; but Jolson, onstage, could charm the audience into anything. A Jolson performance was a love fest, even if no one in the audience loved Jolson quite as much as the guy onstage. Patinkin seemed less like Jolson and more like Frank Fay, the wiseguy comedian and abusive first husband of vaudeville dancer Ruby Stevens (who later changed

The Wild Party (Lippa)
Opened: February 24, 2000
Closed: April 9, 2000
54 performances (and 34 previews)
Profit/Loss: Nonprofit [Loss]
The Wild Party ($60 top) played the 299-seat Manhattan
   Theatre Club's Stage One. Box office figures not available.

DRAMA DESK AWARD
Best Music: Andrew Lippa (WINNER)

Critical Scorecard

Rave 2
Favorable 2
Mixed 3
Unfavorable 0
Pan 3

her name to Barbara Stanwyck). Patinkin was the opposite of charming, as hateful as could be—both his character and his performance. One could only marvel at Patinkin's willingness to appear in such an unfavorable light. Marvel, yes; admire, no.

As the evening progressed, Burrs and/or Patinkin continually approached the audience, demanding applause. This only served to antagonize the theatregoers even more. The show ended with him, finally, getting shot. For my money, they should have shot him at the beginning.

While there were several other major performances on hand, Patinkin permeated the atmosphere. This was too bad, as the leading women were pretty good. Toni Collette made a strong bow as Queenie. Like Murney in Lippa's version, she was new to Broadway. However, Collette came to town bearing a Best Actress Oscar nomination, which she matched with a nomination from the Tony committee; she won neither, as it turned out. Her Queenie was conceived as an anachronistic Marilyn Monroe. (Marilyn Monroe as a small-time vaudeville dancer? Questionable, but not Collette's fault.) Tonya Pinkins played Kate as if she were Josephine Baker, and she was first-rate. Pinkins received acclaim and a Tony for her performance in *Jelly's Last Jam* (1992), another antagonistic George C. Wolfe modernistic musical at the very same Virginia Theatre. Pinkins was just as good, though overlooked, in *Play On!* (1997). Here, she helped add some much-needed life to the latter half of the piece.

More or less stealing the show, for whatever that was worth, was Eartha Kitt in a custom-built role designed to more or less steal the show. Kitt is quite a personage—a self-invented personage, as it happens—and she displayed total command of every move she made. Whether it fit the proceedings, technically, is immaterial; it didn't matter in the least. She delivered her big number, "When It Ends"—a cousin to Sondheim's "I'm

Still Here"—totally oblivious of the material or the show or anything. She was onstage, she had the spotlight, and she had the audience—that was that, and nothing else mattered. Although by that point, almost two hours into the show, I myself was wondering "when it ends" as well.

The show was dotted with other fine performances, although one had to feel sorry for Jane Summerhays as Madelaine True. She was competing with Alix Korey in the Lippa version, but Korey had a solo as effective as Kitt's; Summerhays didn't. Also standing out were Marc Kudisch, as the slumming Jackie; and the mismatched Adam Grupper and Stuart Zagnit as Gold and Goldberg, who had their hands (and other appendages) full with Ms. Kitt.

LaChiusa's *Wild Party* had a major advantage over the earlier work: It was well organized. The characters were distinctive, and the story moved in a clear progression, rather than in the meandering fashion of the other. Credit this to director-colibrettist George C. Wolfe. Unlike most of the people who make their living trying to direct musicals nowadays, the man knows something about structure. But the show was unvaryingly ugly, presumably at Wolfe's behest. I couldn't help comparing things, again, to *Cabaret* and *Chicago*. Those two Kander and Ebb musicals had harsh things to say; but each musical number—no matter how dark or crass—was, in itself, designed to entertain. LaChiusa's *Wild Party* was the opposite of entertainment; the creators seemed to challenge us to enjoy anything they put on the stage, and so we didn't. It all made for a rather grim two hours, without intermission. I left Lippa's *Wild Party* intent on recommending it to friends interested in adventurous musical theatre. I left LaChiusa's *Wild Party* intent on recommending it to absolutely no one (although I highly recommend the score on compact disc).

I left Lippa's *Wild Party* intent on recommending it to friends interested in adventurous musical theatre. I left LaChiusa's *Wild Party* intent on recommending it to absolutely no one.

Would Lippa's have been a hit had the critics seen it after LaChiusa's? Quite possibly. A later opening, though, would have made it impossible to transfer in time for the Tony Awards. Not only for the possible awards themselves, but for a shot at the national television audience on the ceremonies. As it was, the first *Wild Party* closed April 9, four days before the brutal opening of the second. Too late, too late.

Jesus Christ Superstar

Jesus Christ Superstar was the first of the big British pop music spectacles that overtook Broadway in the last three decades of the twentieth century. An invasion which, as I write this, seems to have ended. *Cats*, by far the most successful of the shows, finally packed up its litter and departed after nearly eighteen years; and by the time this book appears in print, *Miss Saigon*—the 1991 musical that was the weakest of the big four—will have dismantled its helicopter and evacuated the Broadway. *Les Misérables* and *Phantom of the Opera* still have legs, but all the rest of the Andrew Lloyd Webber and/or Cameron Mackintosh London blockbusters have met failure stateside: *Starlight Express*, *Aspects of Love*, *Five Guys Named Moe*, *Sunset Boulevard*, *Putting It Together*, and—closing during pre-Broadway tryouts—*Whistle Down the Wind* and *Martin Guerre*.

Superstar began the parade, although one wonders if it should even be considered a British musical. Yes, it was written by two Englishmen (Tim Rice and Andrew Lloyd Webber) and presented by a third (Robert Stigwood); but it was initially produced, to great success, in America, with an American director, American designers, an American musical director, and American actors. The concept of how to effectively translate the piece from a two-disc record album to the stage came from director Tom O'Horgan; the changes in the show implemented for the stage version—principally, the addition of "Everything's Alright," one of the best songs in the piece—were made at O'Horgan's

> The 1970 concept album was wildly successful. Every person under the age of twenty in the English-speaking world apparently bought a copy, except me.

FORD CENTER FOR THE PERFORMING ARTS
UNDER THE DIRECTION OF SFX THEATRICAL GROUP

The Really Useful Superstar Company Inc and Nederlander Producing Company of America Inc
in association with Terry Allen Kramer
PRESENT

JESUS CHRIST SUPERSTAR

LYRICS BY	MUSIC BY
Tim Rice	Andrew Lloyd Webber

Glenn Carter   Tony Vincent   Maya Days
Kevin Gray   Paul Kandel
Frederick B. Owens   Ray Walker
Michael K. Lee   Rodney Hicks
Christian Borle   Lisa Brescia   Hank Campbell   Merle Dandridge   D'Monroe
Bernard Dotson   Manoel Felciano   Deidre Goodwin   Lana Gordon   Somer Lee Graham
J. Todd Howell   Daniel C. Levine   Anthony Manough   Joseph Melendez
Eric Millegan   Keenah Reid   Devin Richards   Michael Seelbach
Alexander Selma   Adam Simmons   David St. Louis   Shayna Steele
Max von Essen   Timothy Warmen   Joe Wilson, Jr.   Andrew Wright

SCENIC DESIGN	COSTUME DESIGN	LIGHTING DESIGN
Peter J. Davison	Roger Kirk	Mark McCullough

MUSICAL SUPERVISOR		SOUND DESIGN
Simon Lee		Richard Ryan

ASSOCIATE MUSICAL SUPERVISOR	MUSICAL DIRECTOR	MUSICAL COORDINATOR
Kristen Allen Blodgette	Patrick Vaccariello	David Lai

CASTING BY	ASSISTANT CHOREOGRAPHER
Johnson-Liff Associates	Denny Berry
Tara Rubin	

PRODUCTION SUPERVISOR	PRODUCTION STAGE MANAGER
Arthur Siccardi	Bonnie Panson

PRESS REPRESENTATIVE	MARKETING	GENERAL MANAGEMENT
Boneau/Bryan-Brown	The Karpel Group	The Charlotte Wilcox Company

ORCHESTRATIONS BY
Andrew Lloyd Webber

CHOREOGRAPHED BY
Anthony Van Laast

DIRECTED BY
Gale Edwards

Jesus of Nazareth   Glenn Carter
Judas Iscariot   Tony Vincent
Mary Magdalene   Maya Days
Pontius Pilate   Kevin Gray
King Herod   Paul Kandel
Caiaphas   Frederick B. Owens
Annas   Ray Walker
Simon Zealotes   Michael K. Lee
Peter   Rodney Hicks
Apostles/Disciples   Christian Borle, Lisa Brescia, D'Monroe, Manoel Felciano, Somer Lee Graham, J. Todd Howell, Daniel C. Levine, Anthony Manough, Joseph Melendez, Eric Millegan, Michael Seelbach, Alexander Selma, David St. Louis, Shayna Steele, Max Von Essen, Joe Wilson Jr., Andrew Wright
Soul Girls/Disciples   Merle Dandridge, Deidre Goodwin, Lana Gordon
Priests/Guards   Hank Campbell, Devin Richards, Timothy Warmen
Swings   Bernard Dotson, Keenah Reid, Adam Simmons

"Definitive" London Cast Album:
Really Useful 314 533 735 (featuring one Broadway cast member)

express request. Kern, Gershwin, Rodgers, Porter, Styne, Strouse, Arthur and Stephen Schwartz, and even Galt MacDermot wrote scores for London shows, none of which have ever been considered American musicals. So why should *Superstar* be labeled British?

Be that as it may, *Superstar* was certainly the beginning of a non-American revolution. It started, as aforesaid, as a 1970 concept album that was wildly successful. Every person under the age of twenty in the English-speaking world apparently bought a copy, except me. Unauthorized concert performances of *Superstar* began springing up across America, so Robert Stigwood—the entrepreneur who unleashed Lloyd Webber and Rice on the world and made millions upon millions off their talents—closed down the pirates and produced a series of "official" *Superstar* concerts across the United States. These were so successful that a full-scale stage musical version was soon under way. Was New York chosen over London simply because Broadway success would garner world-class publicity and notoriety? Perhaps so.

Tom O'Horgan occupied a rare position in the commercial theatre at the time; he was the first, and only, director to demonstrate an ability to sell theatre tickets to the vast under-thirty crowd who theretofore would not be caught anywhere near the vicinity of a Broadway or West End theatre. *Hair* was O'Horgan's meal ticket, an incredible box office bonanza with what today might be called crossover appeal. (O'Horgan was clearly responsible, in large part, for *Hair*'s success; two earlier productions, with another director, failed to catch fire.) O'Horgan followed *Hair* with Julian Barry's play *Lenny*, which was enhanced by an absurdly fanciful production. It was at this point that Stigwood fired his original *Superstar* director and turned to O'Horgan. Stigwood was just then raking in profits as producer of the London *Hair*, which opened in September 1968 (five months after Broadway) and lasted an impressive two thousand performances.

The 1971 *Superstar* was highly successful, although certainly not another *Hair*. The reviews were mixed, with several predictably poor notices offset by some unexpected raves. *Superstar* was clearly acknowledged, though, as a pop culture phenomenon destined for success. The show has made two return visits—in non-O'Horgan versions—over the years. A clunky production played the Longacre for three months in 1977, and a clunkier one visited Madison Square Garden's Paramount Theatre for two weeks in 1995.

As one of the relatively few people who went to the original *Superstar* with no knowledge of the piece, I found it simplistic in its loose formatting and certainly the noisiest show (till then) on Broadway. Some of the music was notably sweet, namely "I Don't Know How to Love Him" and the added number, "Everything's Alright." (The former was not intended for *Superstar*; it was written by Lloyd Webber and Rice years earlier, under the title "Kansas Morning.") The show had two memorable elements. One was the performance of Ben Vereen, a *Hair* replacement whom O'Horgan insisted on casting as Judas. (The authors and producer wanted Carl Anderson, who had played the role in the pre-Broadway

Lloyd Webber spoke of "the artistic failure" of O'Horgan's "wayward" production—the reviews of which, as it happens, were far more appreciative than the withering pans with which Lloyd Webber's 2000 production was greeted.

concerts. The other stars of the concert version, Jeff Fenholt and Yvonne Elliman, re-created their roles of Jesus and Mary on Broadway.) Vereen played the role with a fiery, unrestrained energy that was highly unusual at the time; within the year he had been stolen away by Bob Fosse, who created a leading role for him in the 1972 musical *Pippin*.

The other element worthy of note was a startling scenic device. Robin Wagner had already begun to make a name for himself, with *Hair* and *Lenny*. Wagner was to create a new kind of stage movement in which scenery "danced," especially in his work with director-choreographer Michael Bennett (which began between *Hair* and *Superstar*, with *Promises! Promises!* in 1968). *Superstar's* stage deck (floor) was divided into three massive pieces—left, center, and right—that were hinged along the apron (front) of the stage. At the end of the first act, Judas—who had just accepted blood money for the betrayal of Jesus—found himself "damned for all time." As he sang of his turmoil at cutting himself off from Jesus and the apostles, the upstage sections of the deck began to rise hy-

draulically; Judas was, indeed, cut off from the rest. The machinery worked gradually, allowing Judas to run upstage, into the building incline; fall, rolling back down to the apron; and try again as if attempting to jump the gap between a drawbridge and the castle entrance. As the number ended, the deck had turned into a wall, shutting the athletic Vereen (and the audience) off from the rest of the stage. Stage machinery was relatively primitive in those days, so let me tell you—this effect was startling.

In order to lure O'Horgan and his then-golden touch into the project, Stigwood promised total control over the production—which culminated in Lloyd Webber, Rice, and Stigwood himself being barred from rehearsals. It is no wonder, then, that Lloyd Webber has publicly professed antipathy to O'Horgan's

Superstar. Sir Andrew eagerly awaited the day when Stigwood's long-term rights lapsed, allowing him to finally mount his own production of his first hit. In an interview in the *Times,* Lloyd Webber spoke of "the artistic failure" of O'Horgan's "wayward" production—the reviews of which, as it happens, were far more appreciative than the withering pans with which Lloyd Webber's 2000 production was greeted. Talk about "artistic failure." . . .

Stigwood countered Lloyd Webber's revival with his competing production of *Saturday Night Fever.* Both shows catered to the same audience; both received equal critical lambastings; and both favored the same dance step, the one in which everybody moved upstage and formed a line just before the finish, so they could do a big finale step where they all rushed down to the footlights.

Although I have listened to the score a few times in the last three decades, my impression of *Superstar* was fixed on that evening late in 1971 when I sat watching it at the Mark Hellinger Theatre, which is now a church. So I was surprised when the curtain rose at the Ford Center to reveal an invasion of actors seemingly dressed for a punk rock version of *West Side Story,* spraying graffiti on what looked to be a secluded stretch of the Berlin Wall. They carried machine guns, AK-47s, or maybe just menacing-looking super-squirter water pistols. We were clearly a long way from Jerusalem. The sound was blastingly loud, compared with which the original production was merely a bit noisy. The sound this time was so loud, in fact, that I literally couldn't hear whether the audience was applauding. Jesus entered, wearing a white toga, white linen trousers, and open-toed sandals (amid the others, in heavy combat boots). Is it any wonder he stood out from the crowd? He also appeared to have his own hairdresser, down in the star dressing room.

> **The only arresting idea in Gale Edwards's new production was the use of video cameras to show live closeups of Jesus as the spikes were driven through his palms. If you enjoy that sort of thing.**

The show continued on this basis, with the drab Berlin Wall unit in evidence much of the evening. The temple of the moneylenders was strictly Las Vegas, with slot machines, stock market tickers, a jumble of video monitors, and a big cage of surplus rockets for sale (labeled U.S. Army). The costumes remained stark, with the punk look balanced by the villains (wearing black spaceman outfits). Judas wore leather and sported saffron-colored hair in a porcupine cut, while Jesus continued to roam around in his light white shift as if he were two climate zones away from the rest. One does not walk into a revival expecting to see the old staging or the old scenery, of course. But what the point was I can't tell you, except that it was different. The only arresting idea in Gale Edwards's new production was the use of video cameras to show live closeups of Jesus as the spikes were driven through his palms. If you enjoy that sort of thing.

Ms. Edwards did bring up a provocative question I've never seen addressed elsewhere, namely: If the apostles had kept their machine guns handy for the Last Supper scene, Caiaphas's men might never have taken Jesus, and he'd still be alive today.

The Real Thing

One Indian summer afternoon I was sitting in the Chinese restaurant around the corner when my attention was engaged by a conversation from the next table. Facing me was an elderly, British colonel type, although he was dressed more like a college professor on recess. The woman I could not see, except for the back of some highly dignified white hair.

The woman was speaking in quiet but commanding tones, so I could hear only certain phrases. She was talking about some party to which she had been obliged to attend, despite clearly disliking such affairs. The colonel presumably knew as much, as he was clearly an old acquaintance. I heard something about "the cast"—which piqued my attention—and how "Jerry" was there and she spoke to "André." This was obviously Lincoln Center Theater's André Bishop and, presumably, director Gerry Gutierrez. Although I couldn't hear enough to make much sense of the conversation—to which the colonel, incidentally, contributed not a word—I decided that I must figure out who the woman eating chicken with broccoli might be, so I put down my six-month-old copy of the *New Yorker* (I'm perennially way behind) and listened.

The white-haired woman next started talking about some show,

The phrase "not as good as the original" has become a constant refrain from critics and theatregoers who saw the earlier productions (and some who didn't). This *Real Thing*, was clearly not "as good as" the American premiere, it was considerably better.

and how good it was; and then about Jennifer, and how exciting it was for Jennifer; and how there were hopes of bringing it to Broadway. It could be

Max   Nigel Lindsay
Charlotte   Sarah Woodward
Henry   Stephen Dillane
Annie   Jennifer Ehle
Debbie   Charlotte Parry
Billy   Oscar Pearce
Brodie   Joshua Henderson

Two years elapse between Acts I
and II.

ETHEL BARRYMORE THEATRE

243 West 47th Street
Ⓢ A Shubert Organization Theatre

Gerald Schoenfeld, *Chairman*   Philip J. Smith, *President*

Robert E. Wankel, *Executive Vice President*

ANITA WAXMAN   ELIZABETH WILLIAMS   RON KASTNER
AND
MIRAMAX FILMS

PRESENT

THE DONMAR WAREHOUSE PRODUCTION OF

THE REAL THING

BY **TOM STOPPARD**

WITH

| STEPHEN DILLANE | JENNIFER EHLE | NIGEL LINDSAY | SARAH WOODWARD |

JOSHUA HENDERSON   CHARLOTTE PARRY   OSCAR PEARCE

| TINA BENKO | MATTHEW GREER | TINA JONES | RAY VIRTA |

| SETS AND COSTUMES BY | LIGHTING BY | SOUND BY |
| VICKI MORTIMER | MARK HENDERSON & DAVID WEINER | JOHN A. LEONARD for Aura Sound Design Ltd. |

| PRODUCTION STAGE MANAGER | ASSOCIATE SET DESIGNER | ASSOCIATE COSTUME DESIGNER |
| BONNIE L. BECKER | NANCY THUN | IRENE BOHAN |

| TECHNICAL SUPERVISOR | U.K. CASTING BY | PROMOTIONS |
| PETER FULBRIGHT | ANNE McNULTY | PRO-MARKETING |

| PRESS REPRESENTATIVE | GENERAL MANAGEMENT | ASSOCIATE PRODUCERS |
| BONEAU/BRYAN-BROWN | 101 PRODUCTIONS, LTD. | ACT PRODUCTIONS RANDALL L. WREGHITT |

DIRECTED BY
DAVID LEVEAUX

The Producers wish to express their appreciation to Theatre Development Fund for their support of this production.

assumed from the conversation —more of a monologue, really— that Jennifer was an actress, and a good one, and that the colonel knew this. As the white-haired woman started talking about how Jennifer said this and she told her that, it became apparent that the speaker was Jennifer's mother. It was similarly apparent that the classy white-haired lady was not a stage mother like Ethel Merman in *Gypsy*.

A fine dramatic actress named Jennifer? Who could that be, I wondered, becoming concerned that the couple would finish their lunch and exit without my getting a good look. Fortunately, she next started talking about somebody—a playwright, perhaps—and said that he had "once sent something to Ellis." Ellis Raab, certainly, the late director—and the former husband of Rosemary Harris. Mystery solved. Ms. Harris was just then rehearsing *Waiting in the Wings*; she must have lived nearby, as over the next several months I saw her frequently through the window of the sidewalk terrace of the Chinese restaurant. Always with the colonel, whom I eventually learned was not a colonel at all but novelist John Ehle, husband of Rosemary and father of Jennifer. Not long thereafter, the Broadway transfer of the Donmar Warehouse production of Tom Stoppard's *The Real Thing* was announced, with Jennifer Ehle in the Glenn Close role.

Now, the casual reader of these pages will observe that Broadway is presently overrun by revivals; even some of this season's offerings that were officially labeled new plays by the Tony Awards administration committee were, in actuality, revivals. The phrase "not as good as the original" has become a constant refrain, from critics and theatregoers who saw the earlier productions (and some who didn't). In the case of *The Real Thing*, though, I must report that in my opinion David Leveaux's production was clearly not "as good as" the American premiere of the play. This new *Real Thing* was considerably better.

Mike Nichols's production was impeccably assembled, with Tom Stoppard's intricate word puzzle of a play gleaming like a diamond in a white gold setting. And the leading actors, Jeremy Irons and Glenn Close, both gave well-considered performances. But the play had little emotional effect, at least for me. The words dazzled, the tricks of plotting pleased, and I left the Plymouth Theatre satisfied but not otherwise engaged. The first Broadway *Real Thing* opened January 5, 1984, and ran for 566 performances. Although it won five Tony Awards (for Stoppard, Nichols, Irons, Close, and supporting actress Christine Baranski as Charlotte), I myself found Michael Frayn's *Noises Off*—which opened four weeks earlier, for 553 performances—considerably more enjoyable and far more memorable. The original London production of *The Real Thing*, which I did not see, opened in 1982 under the direction of Peter Wood, with Roger Rees and Felicity Kendall. Certain changes were made for the Nichols production, which seem not to have been retained for the Leveaux production.

The Real Thing is a densely worded play about adultery in the theatre, in which the main character—a famous playwright who writes a densely worded play about adultery in the theatre—commits adultery with his leading lady. The play was written by Tom Stoppard, a famous playwright who writes densely worded plays and—during the course of it all—divorced his wife for his leading lady. Felicity Kendall, that is. *The Real Thing*, thus, is incredibly layered; when are we watching the play, and when is it the real thing? The opening scene, in which a man (Max) captures his wife (Charlotte) in a web of lies and finds himself cuckolded, turns out to be a scene from the play within the play. We soon learn that Max, in reality—within the *Real Thing*—is indeed being cuckolded by his "real" wife Annie, with the man in the case being Charlotte's "real" husband Henry, the playwright of the play within the play (and Stoppard's stand-in).

Henry ultimately marries Annie and, in a fascinating replay of the opening scene, learns that she herself is cuckolding him with her leading man (in a new play Henry has written for her).

All of this works on an intellectual level, as it did in the Mike Nichols production. But Irons (as Henry) and Close (as Annie) were cool as ice. Stephen Dillane's Henry was just as irascible but with a warm core, like an infuriating child who manages to get out of scrapes by flashing a smile that can melt your heart (a quality shared by Alan Bates or Alan Cumming but not Jeremy Irons or Roger Rees). And Jennifer Ehle—to get back to where we started—was a revelation as Annie. And yes, she is a wonderful actress, possessing the same stage presence—and the ability to dominate the stage while simply sitting silently still—as her mother, the white-haired woman in the Chinese restaurant. Ehle's Annie was not merely Henry's pawn; she drove the action. From her first entrance—when she dares Henry to make love to her while her husband and his wife are in the kitchen making pineapple dip— she controls the playwright who is supposedly in control. She informs Max of the adultery; she cements the breakup and her resulting marriage to Henry; she browbeats Henry into writing the new play for her, a propaganda piece for a cause he belittles; and she then forces Henry not only to relive the cuckold scene from his play within the play but also to swallow his pride and agree to accept it. What choice does he have, with Ms. Ehle delivering the lines. (I have no memory of any of this coming through from Glenn Close's performance.)

The new elements in David Leveaux's production were passion and sex. Jennifer Ehle poured them in, with Stephen Dillane proving a receptive if perplexed receptor; and that was the real thing which made this *Real Thing* the real thing.

The new elements in Leveaux's production of *The Real Thing*, simply put, were passion and sex; not elements readily apparent in the work of Stoppard but clearly supportable by the text. Ms. Ehle poured them in, with Mr. Dillane proving a receptive if perplexed receptor; and that was the real thing that made this *Real Thing* the real thing.

With rave reviews, good word of mouth, and an overall level of excellence, one would expect *The Real Thing* to have quickly sold out its limited engagement and—perhaps—extend with a replacement cast of American movie stars. (Miramax, from Hollywood, was one of the producers.) Ticket sales were surprisingly sluggish, however. To blame, perhaps, was the presence of two equally excellent, recently opened plays, *True West* and *Copenhagen*. At Tony time, *The Real Thing* was rightfully victorious, taking three top awards—including one to Jennifer Ehle, competing against her mother in a Tony Awards first. (Ehle gave the charmingest acceptance speech, thanking her parents "for teaching me to talk and walk and read.") But even with the Tonys in hand, *The Real Thing*'s business remained at a moderate level, and an extension was uncalled for.

The Green Bird

There is something admirable about the notion of riffling through hundreds of years of stagecraft to come up with a new form of entertainment. Or is it more properly called an old form of entertainment? Maybe a modern entertainment in olden guise, or an olden entertainment for today.

Call it what you will; the ads simply called *The Green Bird* "a wicked comedy." One thing's for certain: Confront audiences with something unconventional, and the standard for acceptance is automatically raised high. It better be pretty good, or else you're in the soup. Julie Taymor's "wicked comedy" was merely intermittently entertaining.

Long a denizen of avant-garde theatre, Taymor wandered onto Broadway's radar screen in March 1996. An early version of *The Green Bird* was presented for four weeks at the New Victory Theatre, one of the first restored houses on old Forty-second Street. It received some ecstatic notices, generating momentary talk of transfer to Broadway.

Taymor did indeed reach Broadway in November of that year. *Juan Darién: A Carnival Mass* was one of the oddest ever main-stage offerings from Lincoln Center Theater. The puppet-and-people piece—I wouldn't term it a play or musical, exactly—was somewhat unfathomable. Unquestionably, though, it displayed some remarkable images. It was not the sort of thing likely to please LCT's subscribers, that's for sure, and it quickly disappeared. (*Juan Darién* is best remembered for garnering five 1996–1997

Confront audiences with something unconventional, and the standard for acceptance is automatically raised high. It better be pretty good, or else you're in the soup.

Brighella   Reg E. Cathey
Pantalone   Andrew Weems
Smeraldina   Didi Conn
Truffaldino   Ned Eisenberg
Barbarina   Katie MacNichol
Renzo   Sebastian Roché
The Green Bird   Bruce Turk
Ninetta   Kristine Nielsen
Voice of Calmon   Andrew Weems
Tartaglia   Derek Smith
Tartagliona   Edward Hibbert
Beauticians   Andrew Weems
Pompea   Lee Lewis
Pierrot   Andrew Weems
Voice of Serpentina   Lee Lewis
Singing Apples   Sophia Salguero (soloist), Meredith Patterson, Sarah Jane Nelson
Dancing Waters   Erico Villanueva (soloist), Ramon Flowers
Servants/Marching Band/Puppeteers   Ken Barnett, Ramon Flowers, Sarah Jane Nelson, Meredith Patterson, Sophia Salguero, Erico Villanueva

The play is set in the imaginary city of Monterotondo, Serpentina's garden, the Ogre's mountain lair and other suitably fabulous places.

Original Broadway Cast Album: DRG 12989

CORT THEATRE
138 West 48th Street
Ⓢ A Shubert Organization Theatre
Gerald Schoenfeld, *Chairman*   Philip J. Smith, *President*

Robert E. Wankel, *Executive Vice President*

O S T A R
ENTERPRISES

presents with
Theatre for a New Audience
Jeffrey Horowitz, Artistic Director
and
Nina Lannan

THE GREEN BIRD
by **Carlo Gozzi**
Translated by **Albert Bermel and Ted Emery**
Original Music Composed and Orchestrated by **Elliot Goldenthal**

Starring
Ken Barnett   Reg E. Cathey   Bill Cohen   Didi Conn   Ned Eisenberg   Ramon Flowers
Jan Leslie Harding   Edward Hibbert   Lee Lewis   Katie MacNichol   Reggie Montgomery
Sarah Jane Nelson   Kristine Nielsen   Tricia Paoluccio   Meredith Patterson   Sebastian Roché
Sophia Salguero   Derek Smith   Bruce Turk   Erico Villanueva   Andrew Weems

Scenic Design	Costume Design	Lighting Design	Mask and Puppet Design
Christine Jones	**Constance Hoffman**	**Donald Holder**	**Julie Taymor**

Sound Design
Jon Weston

Wig/Make-up Design
Steven W. Bryant

Casting	Press Representative	Marketing
Deborah Brown	**The Publicity Office**	**The Walton Group**

Production Manager	General Management	Production Stage Manager
Arthur Siccardi	**Nina Lannan Associates**	**Kristen Harris**

Music Director	Vocal Director	Assistant Director
Rick Martinez	**Joe Church**	**Kamyar Atabai**

Musical Staging by
Daniel Ezralow

Additional Text by
Eric Overmyer

Directed by
Julie Taymor

"The Green Bird" was originally produced by Theatre for a New Audience, Jeffrey Horowitz, Artistic Director,
in March, 1996, at The New Victory Theatre in New York City, and was subsequently presented at
The La Jolla Playhouse in La Jolla, California, Michael Greif, Artistic Director, Terrence Dwyer, Managing Director.

Theatre for a New Audience is a participant in the National Theatre Artists Residency Program,
administered by Theatre Communications Group, the National
Organization for the American Theatre, and funded by the Pew Charitable Trusts.

Tony nominations four months after it closed, knocking *Jekyll & Hyde* out of the Best Musical, Best Score, and Best Director categories.)

Like other avant-garde directors before her, Ms. Taymor might simply have disappeared into her cloister after *Juan Darién*, never to return to the commercial world. Except that at precisely this time, Disney Theatricals was trying to come up with a way to adapt their animated hit *The Lion King* to the Broadway stage. They entered the field in 1994 with the theatrically primitive *Beauty and the Beast*, which sold lots of tickets but garnered no respect. Casting their eye on Taymor's New Victory *Green Bird*, Disney made a truly radical gamble: They turned over Simba and his friends and millions of dollars' worth of resources to the highly artistic but just as highly noncommercial Taymor. The gamble paid off handsomely for Disney and made Taymor supremely "bankable." For the moment, anyway. *The Lion King* opened in November 1997, filled with spectacular stagecraft—culled from various theatrical disciplines—which gave Broadway audiences a breathtaking experience unlike anything they'd ever seen. (Remove Taymor's work from *The Lion King*, and I suppose it would have fared even worse, critically, than *Beauty and the Beast*.)

Taymor's success with Disney opened new doors to her, including the opportunity to direct a 1999 film version of *Titus Andronicus*, starring Anthony Hopkins and Jessica Lange. Not unexpectedly, *Titus* was—well, strange. Taymor returned to Broadway with a second *Green Bird*, this one mounted with real money and expanded to full length. Or maybe overexpanded; the Cort production, at two hours and ten minutes (plus a twenty-minute intermission), apparently was a good half hour longer than what played the New Victory. Or maybe a bad half hour.

Augellin Belverde, to begin with, was a fantasy fable in commedia dell'arte style written in 1765 by a Venetian aristocrat named Count Carlo Gozzi. Albert Bermel and Ted Emery translated some of Gozzi's plays back in 1989, which apparently brought *The Green Bird* to the attention of Taymor and her composer-companion, Elliot Goldenthal. Bermel and Emery are credited with the translation. Some uncredited somebody, obviously, adapted the material; it is chock-full of jokes and ideas that couldn't have been in the eighteenth-century original. The dungeon—in which the Queen languishes in exile—was transformed into a fetid underground ladies room; the wizard became a jiving Rastafarian, who services the Queen Mother beneath her Victorian bustle; and so-called jokes were added, like the one about underwear from "Vittoria's

Only one of the actors truly mastered his mask. Derek Smith seemed to move from his shoulders; the left one would point up and seem to rise above his ear, then he would swoop across the stage in the opposite direction as if propelled by "action" lines inked in by a cartoonist.

da Secret." Hidden among the six lines of dense staff credits on the title page was someone named Eric Overmyer, who provided "additional text." That usually connotes a last-minute book doctor who adds jokes. Most of the adaptation work was surely done, by someone, long before *The Green Bird* entered its troubled preview period. Or maybe Count Gozzi was just futuristically prescient?

This was not the first *Green Bird* to reach the modern-day stage; there was a musical comedy version, too. *Royal Flush*, it was called; they apparently converted the dungeon into a toilet as well. It opened in New Haven on December 30, 1964, and closed three weeks later in Philadelphia. Book and score were by Jay Thompson, one of the *Once upon a Mattress* authors. Jack Cole directed and choreographed. (Actually, he was replaced as director by Savoyard Martyn Green, who was replaced by June Havoc; Ralph Beaumont came in as choreographer.) Kaye Ballard played five roles, including the wicked Queen Mother (here named Sadie); Jane Connell played the Queen in the toilet; Kenneth Nelson and Jill O'Hara played the young orphans. Top-billed comedian Eddie Foy knew enough to walk out of this stinker during rehearsals.

Taymor's *Green Bird* had a couple of immense obstacles in its path, one of which, I believe, was the masks themselves. While the use of exaggerated masks goes back to the ancient Greeks, it seems to present a problem

in modern-day theatre. Today's audiences want to see, and hear, the actors. Maybe it's a result of all those years of watching the big screen and especially the small screen, with its close-ups and remote control volume control. Having gone to the trouble of attending the so-called live theatre, they want live, breathing actors. This might not apply to mass-market musicals, where much of the material is sung, or tiny shows in tiny theatres; but two hours of talking actors in masks can quickly turn nontheatrical.

This was made clear to me when I worked on a 1982 production of *Alice in Wonderland*, with sets and costumes patterned closely on the familiar John Tenniel illustrations. Like *The Green Bird*, the show had incidental songs and lots of musical underscoring (with Jonathan Tunick at the helm). Like *The Green Bird*, the show was filled with "magical" images—Alice going through the looking glass and all that—and myriad puppets of diverse types.

Alice in Wonderland had numerous charms, not the least of which were the performance of Katie Burton in the title role, John Lee Beatty's sets, and Pat Zipprodt's costumes. But very little charm traveled across the orchestra pit. Many of the actors were encased in cagelike masks, the better to match the facial characteristics of the famous Alice illustrations; the rest were smothered in makeup. The very

Who was it for? Not for children, certainly, as the subject matter was overtly sexual and the language racy. It was not for adults either, as the pace was plodding and the dialogue often puerile.

concept of live theatre was thereby defeated. It was hard to care about, or sympathize with, or even enjoy an actor covered with latex or papier-mâché. At the same time, we suffered audibility problems, resulting in unrealistic electronic amplification. Thus, many of the performers neither looked nor sounded remotely real.

Ms. Taymor's view on the matter is clearly different, as expressed in a *New York Times* interview: "People always make a mistake in assuming that masks limit an actor's expression. It's quite the opposite. In fact, it liberates an actor to use his entire body to express himself, to find inner places that his outer body, his own exterior, would not allow him to go. All of the expression and all of the character traits become more fleshed out and heightened."

Maybe so, Ms. Taymor, but not in *The Green Bird* at the Cort. Only one of the actors, a fellow named Derek Smith, truly mastered his mask. He was playing the misfortunate King Tartaglia—"just another melancholy monarch"—and he had to work under a wide-eared mask of a suffering face that looked like a balloon-headed cross between Prince Charles and the late David Merrick. Smith inhabited his mask; he made it live. He managed to impart an impression of a bored, spoiled-but-nice child mixed up with a sympathetic Elmer Fudd—all without the use of his facial muscles. He seemed to move from his shoulders; the left one would point up and seem to rise above his ear, then he would swoop across the stage in the opposite direction as if propelled by "action" lines inked in by a cartoonist. Watching him simply slump into his overstuffed easy chair of a throne was quite a treat. Smith was absolutely marvelous, despite lines like "it's as easy to make a friend as to wipe your ass on a

The Green Bird
Opened: April 18, 2000
Closed: June 4, 2000
56 performances (and 15 previews)
Profit/Loss: Loss
The Green Bird ($75 top) was scaled to a potential gross of
$496,717 at the 1,027-seat Cort. Weekly grosses averaged
about $202,000, breaking $260,000 the week after the
opening but soon dwindling to starvation level. Total
gross for the run was $1,787,997. Attendance was about
50 percent, with the box office grossing about 41 percent
of potential dollar-capacity.

TONY AWARD NOMINATIONS
Best Performance by a Featured Actor: Derek Smith
Best Costume Design: Constance Hoffman

*Critical
Scorecard*

Rave 2
Favorable 2
Mixed 0
Unfavorable 3
Pan 2

rose." After which he turned front and said, "I didn't write it." Smith's supple performance—which won him an Obie Award in the 1996 production of *The Green Bird*—earned him a deserved Tony nomination here, although I suppose he is the only faceless nominee in history.

A few paces behind him was Edward Hibbert, playing Smith's evil mother, Tartagliona. Hibbert made capital use of his voice, rather than his body (which was encased in an ungainly bustle that ultimately transformed itself into a turtle shell). Hibbert—who gave a memorable performance in Paul Rudnick's *Jeffrey*, as the title character's acid-tongued pal—has a wonderful Anglo-American acting voice. Trained in London at the Royal Academy of Dramatic Art, he is American by birth; he was born in New York while his British father was playing the dirty old man in the Broadway company of *The Boy Friend*. As it happens, Hibbert also appeared under a mask, as the Gryphon, in the 1982 *Alice*. The cast was headed by Eva Le Gallienne, who wrote and directed it and insisted on being "flown by Foy" even though she was eighty-three. (It was quite an experience to sit backstage with someone who made her Broadway debut in 1915, chatting about her pals Eleonora Duse and Ethel Barrymore; she was just as amazed to find someone under thirty who knew what she was talking about.) Also in the company were the comedienne Mary Louise Wilson, who was in those days severely underappreciated; sixteen-year-old Mary Stuart Masterson, as the White Rabbit; and Nicholas Martin—a former Ellis Rabb protégé—as the Dormouse. Nicky helped with the casting and served as kind of a dramaturge; we'd all have been better off, no doubt, if he'd been directing it himself. Codirecting the production was the scion of a famous theatre family, except that he himself had apparently never been inside a Broadway theatre. Why he was hired I don't know, except that he was married to the producer (who also had apparently never been inside a Broadway theatre). Pity the plight of poor professional actors, who struggle and struggle to get a job—any job—and then have to put their careers in the hands of amateurs and bumblers. And hope the surefire flop lasts enough workweeks to qualify for unemployment. And medical coverage.

The Green Bird didn't. The most puzzling aspect of the show, I suppose, was the unanswered question: Who was it for?

Not for children, certainly, as the subject matter was overtly sexual and the language racy. (So was traditional commedia dell'arte, but traditional commedia dell'arte was not children's theatre.) *The Green Bird* was not for adults either, as the pace was plodding and the dialogue often puerile. As best as I can guess, Taymor and her producers were presumably aiming for anyone who enjoyed *The Lion King*. But the theatrical effects of *The Green Bird* weren't as dazzling or as clever as those in the Disney musical. I suppose that most of *The Green Bird* audience was made up of *Lion King* fans; I also suppose that many of them walked out of the Cort after the show, or during the show, not on an ecstatic high but on a deadly low. Or perhaps they were merely angry, especially if they brought children—at seventy-five bucks a ticket, higher than the prevailing rate for a non-musical on Broadway. One thing's for sure: They didn't go back to the office or the beauty salon or the country club and tell their friends, "Oh, you've got to see it." During previews, I overheard some twenty-something civilians—that is, non–theatre people—at the birthday party of a one-year-old. "Don't waste your time with *The Green Bird*," they told the assembled parents. "It's awful—and we got free tickets."

Awful it wasn't; simply unnecessary and misguided and misdirected. Not misdirected as in poorly directed; it was simply aimed at a hypothetical audience that didn't show up at the box office because they didn't exist. Thus, this *Green Bird* simply didn't fly.

Taller Than a Dwarf

One of the beneficial side effects of Broadway's present-day drought of nonmusicals is that we get far fewer really awful plays. *Voices in the Dark* was exceedingly clumsy; *Epic Proportions*, which was in fact fifteen or so years old, was exceedingly inept; *Wrong Mountain* was exceedingly—well, wrong; and *Squonk* was unfathomable. But nothing prepared us, other than a devastating pre-Broadway review in *Variety*, for *Taller Than a Dwarf*.

Elaine May's farce was aggressively stupid. ("It's just too stupid," said the leading lady, fifteen minutes into the evening.) The play was about a market researcher named Howard Miller, living in lower-middle-class near poverty in Queens. Howard wants, above everything, to be well liked. Unable to cope with mounting bills, a broken shower faucet, and a ticket for littering, he quits his job and simply plants himself in bed doing jigsaw puzzles. His wife, Selma, his parents, his mother-in-law, and his boss try to snap him out of his depression, to no avail. He is finally roused from his lethargy by a physical free-for-all with his bully of a superintendent.

This was the sort of play that typically closes during its pre-Broadway tour. Certainly, it would have saved Ms. May, director Alan Arkin, stars Matthew Broderick and Parker Posey, and the producers plenty of embarrassment had they just shuttered in Boston. One was, most of all, appalled by the presence of Arkin and Broderick. Arkin has—or, at least, had—a fine comic mind, which was nowhere in evidence throughout the evening. All that was in evidence was several of the actors comporting themselves like Alan Arkin, running, jumping, stumbling, and climbing around the set. This stuff was always funny when Arkin did it—take a look at the comic gem of a film called *The In-Laws*—but it fell repeatedly and resoundingly flat here. As for Broderick, his presence was truly puzzling. A talented and highly capable comic actor, he presumably could have improvised his way past such intolerable material. Instead, he simply said the stupid lines and did the stupid things they told him, with amateurish results. Broderick certainly wasn't doing it for the money; any fool (or any fool of an agent) could have told him that he'd wind up with less than three months' salary, plus no percentage of no profits.

The presence of Elaine May promised higher quality material than was in evidence, but that might have been a faulty expectation. The team of Mike Nichols and Elaine May has achieved near-legendary status. Contrary to popular assumption, though, the partnership was short-lived; they hit the big time in 1958—springing to sudden stardom over a wild two-month period—and parted in 1962, after the disastrous tryout of a play May wrote for Nichols. Nichols continued on to greater fame and fortune, but May's post-Nichols career has been checkered. *Adaptation-Next* (1969), an off-Broadway pairing of two one-acts, was a considerable hit; but it was the latter part of the bill—Terrence McNally's riotously funny *Next*, starring James Coco as an unlikely army recruit—that carried the evening. (May directed both one-acts.) In Hollywood, she directed and wrote *A New Leaf* (1971), directed *The Heartbreak Kid* (1972), and—after a forty-year hiatus, reteamed with Nichols to write the screenplays for *The Birdcage* (1995) and *Primary Colors* (1998). May's other credits are not so creditable, with her hitting bottom in 1987 as director-screenwriter of the Warren Beatty–Dustin Hoffman dud *Ishtar*.

Howard Miller   Matthew Broderick
Selma Miller   Parker Posey
Mrs. Miller   Joyce Van Patten
Mr. Miller   Jerry Adler
Mrs. Shawl   Marcia Jean Kurtz
Milton (at certain performances)
   Marc John Jefferies, Dajon Matthews
Mrs. Enright   Cynthia Darlow
Policeman   Greg Stuhr
Mr. Enright   Micheal McShane
Mr. Dupar   Sam Groom
Fireman   Greg Stuhr

Stagewise, May contributed one-acts to two off-Broadway offerings, *Death Defying Acts* (1994) and *Power Plays* (1998), the latter in tandem with Arkin.

Taller Than a Dwarf, the publicity told us, was May's first Broadway play. Well, not exactly. This didn't sound quite right to me; I seemed to remember something she did with Jerome Robbins, which closed during previews at Henry Miller's Theatre (now reconfigured as the Kit Kat Klub). Checking the record books, I found May and Robbins doing *The Office*, which played ten previews in 1966. May didn't write it, though; she headed the cast, along with Jack Weston and Ruth White.

But my research also turned up something called *A Matter of Position*, which opened at the Walnut Street in Philadelphia on September 29, 1962. This long-forgotten farce was about a statistician named Howard Miller, living in lower-middle-class near poverty in the Bronx. Howard wants, above everything, to be well liked. Unable to cope with mounting bills, a broken shower faucet, and a ticket for littering, he quits his job and simply plants himself in bed doing jigsaw puzzles. His wife, Selma, his parents, his mother-in-law, and his boss try to snap him out of his depression, to no avail. He is finally roused from his lethargy by a physical free-for-all with his bully of a superintendent.

Wait a minute! Can it possibly be that Ms. May pulled A *Matter of Position*—written at the height of her fame—out of mothballs, added some radio voice-over lines about dot-com millionaires, and passed it off as new? Seems so. *Taller Than a Dwarf* had an advantage, in that it arrived on Broadway at eighty-eight minutes, while the crumbly old Philadelphia reviews tell us that A *Matter of Position* clocked in at three hours and a quarter (!), which is longer than Eugene O'Neill. A *Matter of Position* had an advantage over *Taller Than a Dwarf*, though, in that it wisely canceled its October 25, 1962, booking at the Booth and quietly folded in Philly. Unfathomably, it was disentombed thirty-seven years later, for no earthly reason. Except, presumably, that the playwright and the producers thought they'd make some money. Most of the critics complained that *Taller Than a Dwarf* seemed like it was written forty years ago. The reason for this, it turns out, is quite obvious: It was.

May wrote A *Matter of Position* as a vehicle for Nichols. Familiar names in the cast included Beatrice Arthur as his mother, John McMartin as his boss, Mark Dawson as his superintendent, and Rex Everhart as the Policeman. (Ms. May did not, I suppose, include an Amadou Diallo joke in the original version.) The play's failure ended both Nichols's acting career and the Nichols and May partnership. The character of Howard Miller was somewhat patterned around Nichols, who suffered severe depressions that would drive him to simply plant himself in his bed. (Both Nichols and May apparently had mothers like the ones written into the play.)

A *Matter of Position* was produced and directed by Fred Coe, directly following his *Two for the Seesaw* (1958), *The Miracle Worker* (1959), *Gideon* (1961), and A *Thousand Clowns* (1962). A *Matter of Position*, somehow, doesn't seem to belong on this list. While producing May's play, Coe also had under option a musical called *Tevye and His Daughters*; May's husband at the time, Sheldon Harnick, was the lyricist. Unable to raise the money, Coe eventually took on Hal Prince as coproducer. By the time the show reached Broadway, retitled *Fiddler on the Roof*, Coe's name had disappeared from the credits.

Most of the critics complained that *Taller Than a Dwarf* seemed like it was written forty years ago. The reason for this, it turns out, is quite obvious: It was.

Nichols quickly rebounded by becoming a director, breaking onto Broadway with Neil Simon's 1963 smash hit *Barefoot in the Park*. Which shares numerous similarities with both *A Matter of Position* and *Taller Than a Dwarf*, except that it's funny. So much for Mike Nichols and *A Matter of Position*, which was quickly forgotten—but not forgotten enough, as it turned out. As a footnote, I'm told that Mike Nichols stepped in to try to fix *Dwarf*. The patient, though, needed more than a doctor.

Taller Than a Dwarf left you feeling, mostly, embarrassed for the cast. It is tough being a stage actor nowadays; unless you have an ongoing movie career like Broderick, you can't afford to turn down a Broadway gig no matter how bad the script. There was only one memorable moment, in the big fight scene wherein most of the cast ganged up against the hulking super. In the middle of it all, someone handed Joyce Van Patten (playing Broderick's mother) a kitchen cleaver. She kind of swung it over her shoulder like a tomahawk, then watched in stunned fascination as the cleaver seemed to swing toward the super's scalp with a will of its own. She was suddenly a psychotic in a horror film; she seemed to be trying to hold the cleaver back, giving the audience a wide-eyed stare as if to say, "I can't control this thing." She didn't scalp him, as it turns out; he was pushed through a hole in the bathroom floor into the flooded apartment below instead. (Don't ask.)

Van Patten was very much at home in *Taller Than a Dwarf*. She has had some good roles in good plays, most notably as Broderick's aunt in Neil Simon's *Brighton Beach Memoirs* (1983); but she has been featured in countless unfunny comedies. (Anyone remember *Murder at the Howard Johnson's?*) Van Patten has been on Broadway longer than just about anyone, I'll warrant; while she was too young to fit in with this season's *Waiting in the Wings* gals, *Taller Than a Dwarf* marked the *sixtieth* anniversary of her Broadway debut. Her older brother, then known as Dickie Van Patten, was a popular child actor in the late thirties, so it seemed natural for Joyce to take to the stage of the Plymouth at the age of six (in May 1940, in William Saroyan's *Love's Old Sweet Song*). In 1943, the nine-year-old Joyce garnered raves in *Tomorrow the World*. ("One of the finest child performances you will ever see," said Howard Barnes in the *Herald Tribune*.")

What are the odds of being in the worst Broadway play of 1998–1999 and the worst play of 1999–2000? Joyce Van Patten did it, but it's a living.

Her stint in *Tomorrow the World* came about under interesting circumstances. The anti-Nazi drama—which is pretty good, by the way—was directed by Elliott Nugent. (Nugent was one of those rare theatre people who were successful on Broadway as an actor, producer, director, and playwright. He is best remembered as star and co-author—with James Thurber—of the nifty 1939 comedy *The Male Animal*.) It is unpleasant, though not uncommon, for a director to have to fire a child performer during a tryout. This happened just recently, when Martin Charnin fired the kid playing the title role in the 1997 revival of *Annie*. (Come to think of it, Charnin also fired the original Annie back in 1977.) But you know how it is; you've got to do what's best for the show, no matter how difficult. In the case of *Tomorrow the World*, the child whom Van Patten was rushed in to replace was Nancy Nugent—the director's own ten-year-old daughter. Which presumably made for some interesting discussion around the Nugents' dinner table for years to come.

Van Patten has worked steadily since before Pearl Harbor, consistently giving sturdy performances, sometimes against all odds. What are the odds of being in the worst Broadway play of 1998–1999 *and* the worst play of 1999–2000? Van Patten did it, with *More to Love* ("A Big Fat Comedy") and *Taller Than a Dwarf*. But it's a living.

The Music Man

"**B**ut he doesn't know the territory," complains the bad guy in *The Music Man*. That's pretty much what they said on Broadway back in 1957, not only about Professor Harold Hill (the hero) but also about second-rank Hollywood lead Robert Preston (the star) and composer-lyricist-librettist Meredith Willson as well. As it turned out, they knew the territory well enough. Harold got the girl; "Press" got a Tony and a new Broadway career; and Willson got two Tonys—beating out Leonard Bernstein, Stephen Sondheim, and Arthur Laurents for their work on *West Side Story*—and an Oscar as well.

Willson was a decidedly small-town music man from Mason City, Iowa. At the age of nineteen he joined John Philip Sousa's band as a flutist, later moving on to the New York Philharmonic. (He changed his name from Robert Meredith Reiniger along the way, borrowing "Willson" from his first wife.) He spent the 1930s working as music director for a series of West Coast radio stations, ending up with a network job at NBC. Willson's one theatrical foray had been writing incidental music and a hymn for the original 1939 production of Lillian Hellman's *The Little Foxes* starring Tallulah Bankhead; he also, somehow or other, got the assignment as music director for Charles Chaplin's 1940 film, *The Great Dictator*. Willson came to *The Music Man* with some minor pop songs to his credit, including the Korean War–era inspirational hit "May the Good Lord Bless and Keep You" (the theme song for Tallulah's radio program, *The Big Show*); "Till I Met You," a 1950 tune that—with minor lyric alterations—became the ballad hit of *The Music Man*; and "It's Beginning to Look a Lot Like Christmas," which was similarly recycled into the 1963 musical *Here's Love*.

If Willson didn't know the territory—the Rodgers and Hammerstein/ Lerner and Loewe territory, that is—he had a perfect guide in Frank Loesser. One of Loesser's song pluggers, a young fellow named Stuart Ostrow, heard *The Silver Triangle*—as it was called at the time—and urged his entrepreneur-of-a-boss to get behind this unconventional musical. Loesser brought the show to Kermit Bloomgarden, coproducer of Loesser's then-running hit *The Most Happy Fella*. Frank signed on as associate producer of the new show, nabbing what would prove to be highly lucrative publishing and licensing rights. Loesser also sent over his *Most Happy Fella* music men, orchestrator Don Walker and music director– vocal arranger Herbert Greene, to guide Willson through the shoals of Broadway. (While new arrangements and orchestrations were clearly necessary to accommodate Susan Stroman's directorial and choreographic vision of the revival, swaths of Walker and especially Greene remained in the show. Typically, neither received any credit whatsoever for their work.)

Willson did not simply come up with a good collection of tunes, though. His score is a canny and careful assemblage of crowd-pleasing melody, laced with musical games and tricks. These songs are overly familiar to quite a few of us by now, but it was an enlightening experience to sit in the theatre and watch Willson's wares ensnare new listeners, one song after another. Willson starts with "Rock Island," a rhythmic chant performed a cappella. (In this production, the notion and buttonhook drummers were accompanied by the drummer in the pit.) Several critics compared this rhythmic speaking to rap music; it goes back fifty years, to a device Willson perfected during his radio days as Tallulah's musical director. Next up is a more standard opening number, "Iowa Stubborn," marked by a straight-faced rendition of a caustically clever lyric. (The guest in town is welcomed to the Fourth of July picnic, where

Conductor   Andre Garner
Charlie Cowell   Ralph Byers
Traveling Salesmen   Liam Burke, Kevin Bogue, E. Clayton Cornelious, Michael Duran, Blake Hammond, Michael McGurk, Dan Sharkey, John Sloman
Harold Hill   Craig Bierko

Olin Britt   Michael-Leon Wooley
Amaryllis   Jordan Puryear
Maud Dunlop   Martha Hawley
Ewart Dunlop   Jack Doyle
Mayor Shinn   Paul Benedict
Alma Hix   Leslie Hendrix
Ethel Toffelmier   Tracy Nicole Chapman
Oliver Hix   John Sloman
Jacey Squires   Blake Hammond
Marcellus Washburn   Max Casella
Tommy Djilas   Clyde Alves
Marian Paroo   Rebecca Luker
Mrs. Paroo   Katherine McGrath
Winthrop Paroo   Michael Phelan
Eulalie Mackecknie Shinn   Ruth Williamson
Zaneeta Shinn   Kate Levering
Gracie Shinn   Ann Whitlow Brown
Mrs. Squires   Ann Brown
Constable Locke   Kevin Bogue
Residents of River City   Cameron Adams, Kevin Bogue, Sara Brenner, Chase Brock, Liam Burke, E. Clayton Cornelious, Michael Duran, Andre Garner, Ellen Harvey, Mary Illes, Joy Lynn Matthews, Michael McGurk, Robbie Nicholson, Ipsita Paul, Pamela Remler, Dan Sharkey, Lauren Ullrich, Travis Wall

Time: July, 1912
Place: River City, Iowa

Original Broadway Revival Cast Album: Q Records 92915

NEIL SIMON THEATRE

Dodger Theatricals
The John F. Kennedy Center for the Performing Arts,
Elizabeth Williams/Anita Waxman, Kardana-Swinsky Productions, Lorie Cowen Levy/Dede Harris
present

Craig Bierko   Rebecca Luker

in

MEREDITH WILLSON'S
THE
MUSiC MAN

Book, Music & Lyrics by
Meredith Willson

Story by
Meredith Willson and Franklin Lacey

and starring
Max Casella   Paul Benedict   Ruth Williamson
Katherine McGrath   Ralph Byers

Clyde Alves   Kate Levering   Michael Phelan

Ann Brown   Tracy Nicole Chapman   Martha Hawley   Leslie Hendrix   Jordan Puryear

and The Hawkeye Four
Jack Doyle   Blake Hammond   John Sloman   Michael-Leon Wooley

with
Cameron Adams   Kevin Bogue   Sara Brenner   Chase Brock   Ann Whitlow Brown   Liam Burke
E. Clayton Cornelious   Michael Duran   Jennie Ford   Andre Garner   Ellen Harvey   Cynthia Leigh Heim
Mary Illes   Joy Lynn Matthews   Michael McGurk   Robbie Nicholson   Ipsita Paul   Pamela Remler
Dan Sharkey   Jason Snow   Lauren Ullrich   Travis Wall   Jeff Williams

Scenery Designed by   Costumes Designed by   Lighting Designed by
Thomas Lynch   William Ivey Long   Peter Kaczorowski

Sound Designed by   Production Supervisor   Casting   Wigs & Hair Designed by
Jonathan Deans   Steven Zweigbaum   Jay Binder   Paul Huntley

Musical Supervision &   Dance & Incidental Music   Associate
Direction by   Orchestrations by   Arrangements by   Music Coordinator   Producers
David Chase   Doug Besterman   David Krane   John Miller   Jack Cullen
                                                                                    Chase Mishkin

Executive Producer   Technical Supervisor   Marketing Consultant   Press Representative
Dodger Management Group   David Bradford   Margery Singer   Boneau/Bryan-Brown

Direction and Choreography by
Susan Stroman

"you can have your fill of all the food you bring yourself.") This was followed by as rapid-fire a patter song as Gilbert and Sullivan never dreamed of, in which the spellbinding Harold Hill convinces the townspeople of the caliber of disaster indicated by the presence of a pool hall in their community and forecasting the "Trouble" that will ensue.

The musical pace quickly changes, as a ten-year-old girl in pigtails named Amaryllis practices her piano exercises. No sooner do you sit back in your seat than Marian-the-Librarian's mother starts baiting her about impending spinsterhood—sung to the pitch of little Amaryllis's thirds. "Don't get faster, dear," the piano-teaching Marian tells the girl. (In one of the numerous delightful touches of this production, the exasperated Marian and her mother speed up their singing, causing poor Amaryllis to visibly race through her paces.) Amaryllis's next exercise, her "cross-hand piece," serves as the setting for the lilting waltz ballad "Goodnight, My Someone." As soon as the show recovers from Marian's showstopping applause, Harold goes into a second spellbinding plaint about wayward youth, which serves as the extended introduction into the rousing march "Seventy-six Trombones." (For a second-act surprise, Willson demonstrates that "Goodnight, My Someone" and "Seventy-six Trombones" are intrinsically linked countermelodies.) As soon as the audience regains their collective breath after all those trombones, Willson has Harold combine four bickering townsmen into a glorious barbershop quartet (on the words "ice cream").

I needn't go any further. The point is, Willson didn't merely provide *The Music Man* with a bunch of pleasant show tunes. He grabbed the audience from the start and popped his songs out at them like cannon shots, consistently shifting his emphasis but always landing his punches pow right on the kisser. Just like a "rip-roarin', ever-time-a-bull's-eye salesman."

> Meredith Willson grabbed the audience from the start and popped his songs out at them like cannon shots, consistently shifting his emphasis but always landing his punches, pow, right on the kisser.

It's easy to say that *The Music Man* is a surefire charmer and there ain't no way to ruin it. That's not true, though; the last major *Music Man* had everything going for it, including the star presence of Dick Van Dyke and the staging expertise of Michael Kidd. The 1980 production was mounted for a full-scale national tour, but it fizzled after playing a very limited three weeks in New York. (Mr. Van Dyke was on the wagon, or maybe off the wagon, and I don't meant the one from Wells Fargo.) I dreaded attending that revival, as the nine-year-old kid of a close friend was playing young Winthrop Paroo. Fortunately for me, he was pretty good; I mean, what do you say to a nine-year-old—who knows you and trusts you—if he gives a lousy performance? Christian Slater held his own against losing odds, displaying more charisma and stage maturity than anyone else onstage except Meg Bussert (who played Marian). Michael Phelan, this revival's Winthrop, did a fine job as well. He was hampered, though, by the decision to let Harold sing "Gary, Indiana" in the first act (as he does in the film version). This made Winthrop's big moment a mere reprise, robbing him of the surprise of the moment.

The point is, pulling off *The Music Man* is by no means simple. Stroman —forced by circumstance to forge ahead without a star—did it, and did it well. The circumstance being, they couldn't find a suitable star to play the role. Rather than settle on an unsuitable star (like Dick Van Dyke), they came up with the risky idea of going with a total unknown. Craig Bierko made the most of his great opportunity of filling Preston's shoes. His performance was in some respects similar to Preston's; quite naturally, given the spoke-song nature of much of his role. But Bierko displayed an un-Preston-like charm of his own. Something about Bierko seemed uncannily familiar; I finally realized that it was a combination of the eyes (as round as Eddie Cantor's) and the smiling teeth (as wide as Tommy Steele's). Rebecca Luker, who has been generally excellent in her stage roles (except for the puzzling 1998 version of *The Sound of Music*), here found a perfect role for herself. Delicious. This Marian seemed somewhat more central to the proceedings than the excellent Barbara Cook's was back in 1957. Ms. Cook was merely a featured player supporting a movie star, while Ms. Luker was more of a star than her Harold.

It's easy to say that *The Music Man* is a surefire charmer and there ain't no way to ruin it. That's not true, though; the last major *Music Man* had everything going for it, including the star presence of Dick Van Dyke and the staging expertise of Michael Kidd.

Ms. Stroman kept her cast moving, as both choreographer and director. The highlight of her work, perhaps, was the library ballet "Marian the Librarian." In this number Harold— with the assistance of the kids —manages to get under Marian's skin, even trapping her into dancing with him. This was done with great skill and humor; and Stroman's dancing kids didn't even look like dancers—they just looked like kids. (Well, maybe three of them looked like dancers.) The climactic chase scene was wonderfully—and humorously—staged, too. She staged the show so that nobody walked—they all sprang from place to place, as if operated from the flies with elastic strings. And not only when they were front and forward; Stroman kept townspeople operating in the background, like extras in a restaurant scene on a soap opera. But her extras sprang to life. There was one crossover with an Iowan mother seemingly clawing her way through a windstorm, with a little boy hanging on to the wake of her dress and a little girl hanging on to the boy's jacket; the three of them looked like a horizontal kite. Stroman also made delectable use of a treadmill placed centrally along the apron of the

Something about Craig Bierko seemed uncannily familiar; I finally realized that it was a combination of the eyes (as round as Eddie Cantor's) and the smiling teeth (as wide as Tommy Steele's).

stage. The music director, David Chase, kept everyone—principals and chorus—punching out Willson's musical accents; choreographer Stroman took those punches and had them land visibly onstage.

Costume designer William Ivey Long outdid himself in River City, with a blaze of bright, ice-cream parlor colors. Especially fetching was his work on the resident character ladies. In the "Pick-a-Little" gossip scene, they wore outfits that transformed them into veritable hens—bringing an instant comparison to the cumbersome masks forced on the actors the previous week in *The Green Bird*. Long gave one of the old ladies—an overweight gray-haired matron called Maud (Martha Hawley)—a brown handbag, which she clutched closely throughout the evening. She carried it even when dressed in a filmy white thing while going through a display of eurythmic dance. For the curtain call, with the entire company outfitted in red and white marching band costumes, Mr. Long gave her a bright and shiny matching red handbag! This is the sort of designer's touch that only a small slice of the audience is likely to notice; but it will be rewarded by a small roar and everlasting memory. Long also dressed Eulalie McKechnie Shinn, the mayor's wife and head biddy, in a dazzling white outfit complete with parasol. She looked just like a Gibson girl, drawn early one morning when Charles Dana Gibson was sporting an absinthe hangover. This role was played by Ruth Williamson, who was similarly prominent in the September comedy *Epic Proportions* and the 1998–1999 revival of *Little Me*. I found Ms. Williamson overplaying for laughs in the earlier shows, although both clearly needed all the laughs they could get. Here she remained in the confines of her character—an overblown cartoon to begin with—and did an especially fine job. She also proved an adept glockenspiel player, in Stroman's knockout curtain call. Everybody came out with a band instrument—twenty-four trombones for the chorus, four saxes for the quartet, and so on. Charlie Cow-

The Music Man
Opened: April 27, 2000
Still playing May 29, 2000
To date: 37 performances (and 22 previews)
Profit/Loss: To Be Determined
The Music Man ($70 top) was scaled to a potential gross of
    $732,133 at the 1,333-seat Neil Simon. Weekly grosses
    averaged about $448,000, steadily building from
    $400,000 to $550,000 in the four weeks after the
    opening. Total gross for the partial season was
    $3,301,392. Attendance was about 73 percent, with the
    box office grossing about 61 percent of potential dollar-
    capacity.

TONY AWARD NOMINATIONS
Best Revival of a Musical
Best Performance by a Leading Actor: Craig Bierko
Best Performance by a Leading Actress: Rebecca Luker
Best Scenic Design: Thomas Lynch
Best Costume Design: William Ivey Long
Best Choreography: Susan Stroman
Best Direction of a Musical: Susan Stroman
Best Orchestrations: Doug Besterman

Critical
Scorecard

Rave 5
Favorable 4
Mixed 0
Unfavorable 1
Pan 0

ell, the nasty anvil salesman, was stuck playing—what else—an anvil. And they were all really playing; an hour of band practice was built into the daily rehearsal schedule from day one.

All in all, there wasn't a false note in the evening, except maybe the fireflies lighting up the summer night, which looked more like cue lights clipped to the scrim. The opportunity presented itself for me to attend not only a critics' preview but also the opening night performance forty-eight hours later. Observations: I liked the show just as much the second time. The performance, and the performers, were every bit as refreshing. The light and unexpected touches of Ms. Stroman's staging wore perfectly well, and both audiences expressed pretty much equal enjoyment. The only difference was in the loudness of the opening night audience, which gave out no fewer than four ecstatic bursts—and that was before we even got to River City. For the record: (1) when the show started, with a baton flying up out of the orchestra pit; (2) when the train curtain rose, revealing a portion of the orchestra seated on the train in band costume, playing the brief overture; (3) when the train curtain rose once more, revealing the male singers lurching in their seats as the train "braked to a stop"; and (4) when Charlie Cowell, the anvil salesman, ended the "Rock Island" number shouting—rhythmically—"but he doesn't know the territory!" At this point, I stopped counting ovations. I didn't mind them, anyway; they were the genuine, heartfelt type. And besides, I was enjoying the show again as much as anyone, and only two days later.

Uncle Vanya

P art of the mission of most nonprofit theatres, for better or worse, is to provide modern-day audiences with the occasional classic. I speak not of modern classics, like *Death of a Salesman*, or modern nonclassics, like *The Rainmaker*; but of real, old, "classical" classics, those that more or less predate the twentieth century.

These fall into two main categories. First, there are English-language plays. The vast majority of those still frequently produced were written by Mr. Shakespeare, along with others by Oscar Wilde and George Bernard Shaw (who straddles the line between modern and classical). Other classical classics come from the world theatre, which is to say anyplace that doesn't speak English. The Greeks left us a handful of still-viable titles, which turn up from time to time; but by and large, the most popular pre-twentieth-century playwrights are the French Molière, the Norwegian Henrik Ibsen, and the Russian Anton Chekhov. Chekhov is a great favorite nowadays, with *The Seagull*, *The Cherry Orchard*, *The Three Sisters*, and *Uncle Vanya* on his hit list.

> "I'm sure I'm at least as miserable as you are," says Yelena, speaking to the audience. "I'm going to face it, and suffer it, and keep going on until the end." But the end was a long time coming.

While Shakespeare and Shaw are seldom rewritten (though sometimes cut), it has become commonplace to tinker with Chekhov and Ibsen. There is a fairly good reason for this. *Uncle Vanya* was for many years known in the Constance Garnett translation. This was first produced in 1926, in London. Ms. Garnett's work was serviceable; but you were getting the words and thoughts of a post–World War I Englishwoman, not those of Mr. Chekhov (whose play first hit Moscow in 1899, with Stanislavski himself as Astrov). An American version by Rose Caylor—wife of Ben Hecht—was directed and produced by Jed Harris on Broadway in 1930. Osgood Perkins, star of Hecht and Harris's recent *Front Page* and father of Tony, played Astrov to the Yelena of Lillian Gish.

There was and is no reason that later audiences should view the play through Garnett's prism, so there have been a whole slew of other *Vanyas*, including versions by playwrights as diverse as Brian Friel, Harold Clurman, Pam Gems, Michael Frayn, and even David Mamet. Major American playwrights have also tackled Ibsen, namely, Thornton Wilder, who adapted *A Doll's House* for Ruth Gordon and Jed Harris in 1937; and Arthur Miller, who followed his *Death of a Salesman* with *An Enemy of the People* in 1950. An all-star 1973 *Uncle Vanya* used an adaptation by Albert Todd and Mike Nichols. Directed by the latter, it was a sold-out sensation at the Circle in the Square Uptown. (It was pretty good, too, with George C. Scott as Astrov; Nicol Williamson as Vanya; Barnard Hughes as Serebryakov; Julie Christie as Yelena; and the seventy-six-year-old Lillian Gish as Marina.) Broadway's most recent *Vanya* was also at the Circle in the Square, a 1995 Jean-Claude van Itallie adaptation that starred Tom Courtenay in the title role and met the same harsh critical reception as the Roundabout production.

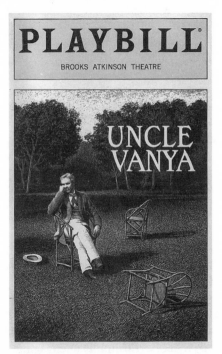

The advantage of doing new adaptations of these plays is that they can hit the audience in a new and unexpected way, like recent productions of *Electra* and *A Doll's House*, as opposed to just giving them their umpteenth helping of the same old thing. The pitfall is to come up with an adaptation that doesn't enhance the play, which is what the Roundabout did. Mike Poulton's script was first performed—with Derek Jacobi in the title role—at the Chichester Festival in 1996. What happened between Chichester and Forty-seventh Street I cannot tell, but it certainly was quite a chore to sit through it at the Brooks Atkinson. In fact, I can imagine a first-time *Vanya* attendee saying, "What was *that* about?" and wondering what makes a classic, anyway.

This *Vanya*, according to the press release, was "a comedy of unfulfilled dreams and unrequited love that has an almost visionary resonance for audiences at the beginning of this new Millennium." This *Vanya*, according to me, was painfully unengaging. Yes, we are meant to learn about the meaning of life by watching the characters' unrelenting boredom and monotony; but that's supposed to affect the characters, not the ticket-buying customers. "I'm sure I'm at least as miserable as you are," says Yelena, speaking to the audience. "I'm going to face it, and suffer it, and keep going on until the end." But the end was a long time coming.

I suppose the lion's share of the blame must go to director Michael Mayer. He has done some interesting things in the past, notably the Roundabout's *Side Man* and the off-Broadway *Stupid Kids*; but here he seems to have come up with a mix-and-match cast. Derek Jacobi was the biggest surprise of the evening, in that this usually brilliant actor was only passable. One supposes that his U.K. *Vanya* must have been more satisfactory, or else why would he sign on to do it again? Roger Rees was the best of the group. His Astrov was thoughtfully conceived and pretty well rounded, if in a vacuum as far as the rest of the cast was concerned. If we were watching scenes from *Vanya* in an acting class, Rees would have won hands down.

Brian Murray, whose first major Broadway role was as Rosencrantz in Tom Stoppard's *Rosencrantz and Guildenstern Are Dead* in 1967, has grown somewhat too familiar in recent seasons. He always seems to give sturdy performances, but rarely does he startle us as he did with his memorable turn in David Hare's *Racing Demon*. His Serebryakov was sturdy but unremarkable. If the three men seemed to be creatures from different countries, Laura Linney as Yelena seemed to come from a different hemisphere. She did, in fact, being a native New Yorker; Jacobi and Rees are British, and Murray hails from Johannesburg. But Linney was far too contemporary, Murray far too British. They're supposed to be Russian.

Anne Pitoniak was fine as the ancient Nanny Marina; but I couldn't help but remember Ms. Gish, who in her silent pauses evoked more of the boredom and decay of Chekhov's play—originally subtitled *Scenes from Country Life*—than the whole Roundabout group. Amy Ryan had a hard time of it as Sonya, forced to deliver such double-edged lines as "there's really no excuse for being bored." And then there was the Telegin (Waffles) of David Patrick Kelly, toting his guitar around pretty much as he had in Nicholas Hytner's 1998 *Twelfth Night* at Lincoln Center. Brian Murray was in that one, too.

I confess to a soft spot for Mr. Kelly, as I had to fire him from his first (and only) Broadway leading role. We were doing a musical revival in which nothing was working. One of the authors decided that it was the fault of

Yes, we are meant to learn about the meaning of life by watching the characters' unrelenting boredom and monotony; but that's supposed to affect the characters, not the ticket-buying customers.

the two leading men and insisted that they be replaced. (The other actor was Doug Katsaros, now a composer and recently the musical director of *Footloose*.) The decision was wrong, as Kelly and Katsaros were both fine in their roles. Their replacements were not as good, nor was Kelly's replacement's replacement. ("Fire him," said the author.)

We were at the Biltmore, right across the street from *Uncle Vanya*. I remember standing out by the stage door, one September Saturday between shows. A bomb threat had been phoned into the box office, and we were waiting for the bomb squad to appear. (The show was secretly bankrolled by the sister of the Shah of Iran; not secretly enough, it appeared. If I remember correctly, she survived an assassination attempt on the French Riviera shortly thereafter.)

Anyway, there we were, waiting for the police. A squad car came along, passing by the stage door alley. As the car waited at the Eighth Avenue traffic light, I asked the officer, "Aren't you responding to our call?"

"Huh?" he said. "No, they'll be right here, they're sending the bomb squad over." Pause, as the light remained red. Then he turned to me and said, knowingly, "I *heard* you had a bomb at this theatre."

Everyone's a critic.

Dirty Blonde

The 1993 off-Broadway hit *Blown Sideways Through Life* was an autobiographical play about a hard-to-classify performer—Claudia Shear—who drifted about until she crafted a suitable format to express her distinctive talents. *Dirty Blonde* was a biographical play about a hard-to-classify performer—Mae West—who drifted about until she crafted a suitable format to express *her* distinctive talents. Or was *Dirty Blonde* about Claudia Shear? It's hard to say. Ms. Shear played Jo, yet another out-of-place performer searching for her place. She also played Mae West—or, at least, Mae West as seen by Claudia/Jo.

Dirty Blonde initially opened in January 2000 at the off-off-Broadway New York Theatre Workshop. (The play was "developed," the credits tell us, at the Vineyard Theatre on Martha's Vineyard.) With the dearth of available theatres on Broadway, the well-received *Blonde* sat on the sidelines waiting. At the last minute, the producers grabbed the Helen Hayes when *Squonk* squonked out, squeaking in just before the Tony nomination deadline. Ben Brantley of the *New York Times* lobbed a valentine of a money review, calling *Dirty Blonde* "hands down the best new American play of the season." It was, too, especially if you define "new" as something written less than ten years ago; the competition ranged from *Voices in the Dark* to *Wrong Mountain*. A week later, *Dirty Blonde* was holding Tony nominations for Best Play, Best Director, and one for each of the three cast members.

> It can be treacherous to tackle a personage as distinctive as Mae West. Groucho, Chaplin, and Fields were so unique in their talents, and are nowadays so accessible on video, that stage incarnations are doomed to fall flat.

Frank Wallace, Ed Hearn, and others
Bob Stillman
Jo, Mae   Claudia Shear
Charlie and others   Kevin Chamberlin

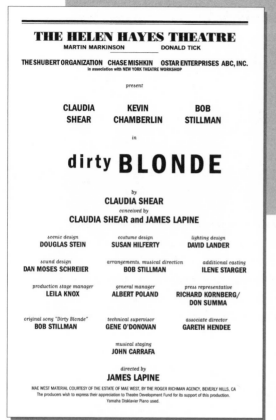

THE HELEN HAYES THEATRE
MARTIN MARKINSON   DONALD TICK

THE SHUBERT ORGANIZATION   CHASE MISHKIN   OSTAR ENTERPRISES   ABC, INC.
in association with NEW YORK THEATRE WORKSHOP

present

CLAUDIA   KEVIN   BOB
SHEAR   CHAMBERLIN   STILLMAN

in

dirty BLONDE

by
CLAUDIA SHEAR
conceived by
CLAUDIA SHEAR and JAMES LAPINE

scenic design   costume design   lighting design
DOUGLAS STEIN   SUSAN HILFERTY   DAVID LANDER

sound design   arrangements, musical direction   additional casting
DAN MOSES SCHREIER   BOB STILLMAN   ILENE STARGER

production stage manager   general manager   press representative
LEILA KNOX   ALBERT POLAND   RICHARD KORNBERG/
DON SUMMA

original song "Dirty Blonde"   technical supervisor   associate director
BOB STILLMAN   GENE O'DONOVAN   GARETH HENDEE

musical staging
JOHN CARRAFA

directed by
JAMES LAPINE

MAE WEST MATERIAL COURTESY OF THE ESTATE OF MAE WEST, BY THE ROGER RICHMAN AGENCY, BEVERLY HILLS, CA
The producers wish to express their appreciation to Theatre Development Fund for its support of this production.
Yamaha Disklavier Piano used.

Even with all this, the show was not exactly a hot ticket. It did far better than the season's other "new" American plays, which wasn't difficult. But it didn't come near attracting the hordes that crowded *True West*. When Tony Award Sunday arrived, *Dirty Blonde* was blanked. Four close races, I'd guess, but "close" doesn't get you the kind of box office boost that the victorious *Copenhagen* got. With its specialized subject matter and without any awards, *Dirty Blonde* faced an uphill battle. (*Torch Song Trilogy* transferred from off-Broadway to the same theatre in 1982 and became a major hit, but it was validated by Best Play and Best Actor Tonys.) *Dirty Blonde* also had a second cause for concern, one the producers knew about going in: Kevin Chamberlin, the heart of the play (as far as I'm concerned), had to leave nine weeks after the opening for rehearsals of the fall musical *Seussical*. Chamberlin created the incredibly difficult role of Charlie, a scared-of-his-own-shadow film librarian with one of Mae West's beaded Travis Banton gowns in his closet. Chamberlin's sensitive and sympathetic performance made all the difference to *Dirty Blonde*, especially since Ms. Shear's Mae was understandably overblown in spots. This is a play that probably can't work unless the audience wholeheartedly buys the scenes between the teenaged Charlie and the ancient Mae. Chamberlin—a mature, bald, two-hundred-sixty-pounder—had you believing every moment. That's acting, folks. Nobody is irreplaceable, true; but what producer or director or author would choose to lose such a key performance just when the show is trying to build its way into the hit column?

It can be treacherous to tackle a personage as distinctive as Mae West. Groucho, Chaplin, Bill Fields (who is briefly sketched into *Dirty Blonde*), and later idols like Marilyn, Judy, or Marlene: all of them were so unique in their talents, and are nowadays so accessible on video, that stage incarnations are doomed to fall flat. It is to Shear's credit that she didn't attempt to simply re-create West's performing style. Rather, she gave us—mostly—the offstage West.

Smart move. Few current-day theatregoers ever saw the offstage West, so accuracy wasn't an issue as long as Shear remained consistent. Which she did. Shear's sketching of the dodderingly ancient but sharp-as-a-tack West, in fact, was one of the evening's highlights. When the octogenarian Mae embarked on a visit to her favorite Chinese restaurant, Chamberlin and Bob Stillman—the play's man-of-all-work—had to cantilever her into an (imaginary) Bentley. Shear sat there rigidly, like a stuffed porcelain doll. Once in the restaurant, the seventeen-year-old Charlie exclaimed, "Wow, look, oh gosh, it's Natalie Wood!" Mae reacted stonily. "What d'ya care about her, you're here with Mae West, ain't cha?" was her icy response.

Another highlight was a tour de force, two-sided scene. Throughout the play, Shear showed Mae assembling her persona from bits of vaudeville, "colored" dancing, prissy 1920s-style camping, and plenty of sex. Then it was time for the dress. Ed Hearn, a 1920s-era female impersonator and friend, came in from stage right to help transform Mae into the icon we know. Charlie, Jo's present-day friend, came in from stage left to transform *her* into Mae for a Halloween masquerade. Ms. Shear played both roles simultaneously, two characters standing behind an onstage screen climbing into one dress. As the familiar image was constructed before us, a giddy excitement grew in the six eyes of the four characters—and the excitement extended to the audience. Perfectly planned and staged.

James Lapine directed *Dirty Blonde* and shares a "conceived by Claudia Shear and James Lapine" credit. The project began when Lapine called Shear with the suggestion that she investigate Mae West—a suggestion that, as it turned out, was pretty intuitive. Lapine is a playwright himself, although he gets no writing credit here. He is also an acclaimed director, with a strong visual sense born of his pretheatre experience as a graphic designer.

André Bishop brought Lapine to Playwrights Horizons, where he wrote and directed *Table Settings* (1980) and directed William Finn's groundbreaking *March of the Falsettos* (1981). Broadway came calling, resulting in a collaboration between the off-off-Broadway director and the great Stephen Sondheim. They have collaborated on three musicals to date, *Sunday in the Park with George* (1984), *Into the Woods* (1987), and

Passion (1994). Just before *Passion* came the Broadway production of *Falsettos* (1992), a combination of Lapine's two off-Broadway William Finn musicals. This has been Lapine's only Broadway hit, though, and as far as I can tell the only one of his stage works to show a profit.

Lapine's recent efforts have been oddly uninvolving. For Bishop at Lincoln Center Theater, he directed a revised version of his 1981 play *Twelve Dreams* (1995), which was all in all pretty puzzling. He also coauthored, but did not direct, Finn's *A New Brain* (1998). His last Broadway outings were directing jobs, on the unsatisfying 1997 revisal of *The Diary of Anne Frank*—which seemed pretty pointless to me—and on the visually fascinating but difficult *Golden Child* (1998). This play was far better than its reception indicated, but the subject matter—a multigenerational story about the Chinese custom of foot-binding—made it what you might call a "hard sell."

If Lapine's recent work has been disappointing, so be it; *Dirty Blonde*

ranks with his best. The fact that *Dirty Blonde* exists at all is due to Lapine, who brokered the wedding of Ms. Shear and Ms. West. But Lapine
deserves further credit; a script like *Dirty Blonde* is pretty nearly unstageable, and I don't know who else could have done it. Of course, it wasn't a
matter of staging a complex script; it was a matter of constructing the
script to suit the staging concept. Lapine was ably abetted by his designers. Douglas Stein provided a warmly pink, all-purpose cube of a box set;
Susan Hilferty balanced the set's imagined locales with realistic costumes;
and David Lander added another level with his area-specific lights.

How much of *Dirty Blonde* was true to West? How much was drawn
from Shear, who was playing both West and—as Jo—herself? It doesn't
matter; it worked dramatically. I, for one, enjoyed *Dirty Blonde* more than
I enjoy Mae West herself. Of course, the only Mae West performances I've
seen have been her movies, the earliest of which was filmed when she was
already in her forties.

Shear happily avoided stoking her play with selections from the wit
and wisdom of the great lady. Until late in the game, anyway, when she
slipped in all of them. The whole enterprise seemed to run out of steam in
the final third of the hundred-minute play. Bring on the double en-
tendres. Bring on anecdotes about boxers-turned-movie-actors offering
four-letter malapropisms. Bring on musical numbers for the arthritic star,
supported—in more ways than one—by choreographically challenged

musclemen. Bring on an actor pretending to be the codgerish W. C. Fields, which fell as flat as this sort of thing usually does. This questionable material tempered my earlier enthusiasm, but there was too much lovely work elsewhere to turn me against *Dirty Blonde*.

Dirty Blonde also helped set a modern-day record when it started previewing on Friday, April 14. For the first time in memory, each and every Broadway theatre—thirty-seven, at present—had a show on the boards. (This hasn't happened in at least thirty-five years. In fact, the propensity of negligible plays to shutter in less than a week makes it possible that this hasn't occurred since the boom days of World War II—if ever.) This remarkable occurrence lasted all of three days, until the Belasco gave up the ghost of *The Dead* on April 16. Remember it well; it's unlikely to occur again.

> **Dirty Blonde helped set a modern-day record when it started previewing. For the first time in memory, each and every Broadway theatre had a show on the boards. This remarkable occurrence lasted all of three days.**

Wonderful Town

Encores! ended their seventh season with one of their very happiest offerings. This was one of those occasions when everything simply seemed to come together. The score, the book, the staging, and the casting all melded to make for a pretty wonderful *Wonderful Town*.

Wonderful Town was easily the best Encores! offering since *The Boys from Syracuse* in 1997, three years and eight shows earlier. Not coincidentally, both were originally directed by George Abbott. *Call Me Madam*, in 1995, was also an Abbott show; in those days, directors helped carpenter shows into shape, a talent that seems to have been lost. Along with *Wonderful Town*, *Syracuse*, and *Madam*, my personal list of the best of Encores! includes *Chicago*, *Babes in Arms*, and perhaps *One Touch of Venus*. Each of which, oddly enough, was a commercial and artistic success in its original run. Flawed shows given the Encores! treatment—like *Allegro*, *St. Louis Woman*, *Do-Re-Mi*, and this season's *On a Clear Day* and *Tenderloin*—remained flawed in concert. Interesting the way it works, isn't it?

The surprise of the evening, perhaps, was the performance of Donna Murphy in the role written to order for Rosalind Russell. Russell was the unlikeliest of musical comedy stars, in that she could neither sing nor dance. Act she could do, and clown, and—fortunately—

The score, the book, the staging, and the casting all melded to make for a pretty wonderful *Wonderful Town*.

croon somewhat rhythmically. The authors were extra careful to write around her talents, carefully refraining from giving her anything resembling a ballad or love song. Take "A Hundred Easy Ways," her first big

Cast (in order of appearance)

Guide Patrick Quinn
Appopolous Lewis J. Stadlen
Lonigan Steve Ryan
Wreck Raymond Jaramillo McLeod
Helen Jenny Hill
Violet Alix Korey
Speedy Valenti Stephen DeRosa
Eileen Laura Benanti
Ruth Donna Murphy
A Strange Man Ray Wills
Frank Lippencott David Aaron Baker
Robert Baker Richard Muenz
Associate Editors Patrick Quinn, Ray Wills
Mrs. Wade Becky Ann Baker
Chick Clark Gregory Jbara
Ruth's Escort Ray Wills
The Dancers Michael Arnold, Joyce Chittick, Jeffrey Hankinson, Michelle Kittrell, Cynthia Onrubia, Tina Ou, Vince Pesce, Alex Sanchez
The Singers Christopher Eaton Bailey, Carson Church, Rachel Coloff, Susan Derry, David Engel, Colm Fitzmaurice, John Halmi, Ann Kittredge, Ian Knauer, Laurie Williamson

comedy number and a marvel in construction for a nonsinger. The leisurely paced setups were sung to a rolling melody, after which the music broke down and stopped—allowing Russell to deliver the jokes in the rapid-fire, acid-dripping manner she was famous for. After an explosion of laughter, the music (and Russell) started up once more. Leonard Bernstein, Betty Comden, and Adolph Green gave her four socko comedy numbers in all, with Russell's outsize personality making her Ruth Sherwood invincibly delectable. Brooks Atkinson, in the *Times*, suggested that she might as well run for president, because "she can sing and dance better than any president we have had. She is also better looking and has a more infectious sense of humor."

Russell was followed in the role by Carol Channing; other successful

Ruths included Nancy Walker and Kaye Ballard. The role depends not on traditional musical theatre skills but on a larger-than-life, cartoonlike persona cloaking keen comic sense. Donna Murphy seemed not to fit on this list; her Tony Award–winning performances in Stephen Sondheim's *Passion* (1994) and Rodgers and Hammerstein's *The King and I* (1996) were not, exactly, strong on comedy. That Murphy does indeed have a comic sensibility was displayed in the off-Broadway spoof *Song of Singapore* (1991), in which she chewed up all the scenery in sight. So casting her in *Wonderful Town* was not as much a stretch as supposed. She simply had to remember not to "sing" the songs but to lob them across like fat, juicy gopher balls. Which she did, and how.

Writer Ruth McKenney and her kid sister Eileen came to New York in the midst of the Depression to pursue life and love. Ruth finally found success writing stories for the *New Yorker* about the pair's struggles in Greenwich Village. (In the stage version, she is trying to peddle stories to "The Manhatter." A friendly editor tells her to write about what she knows.) The stories were successfully reprinted in book form in 1938, which led to Broadway. *My Sister Eileen* opened on December 26, 1940, the night after *Pal Joey*—another Encores! entry originally directed and produced (and doctored) by Mr. Abbott. I've just now read *Eileen*'s original overnight reviews, seven raves out of seven, and I find that six of them specifically indicate that director George S. Kaufman wrote the best jokes. Burns Mantle, the dean of drama critics of the day, bluntly states that the play had six authors: first Ms. McKenney and Leslie Reade, whose unusable version was replaced by a script by Joseph Fields and Jerome Chodorov, which was doctored by Kaufman and Moss Hart. (This very public acknowledgment, perhaps, was the root of Fields's and Chodorov's sensitivity to what occurred when Comden, Green, Bernstein, and Abbott started rewriting their baby twelve years later.) *My Sister Eileen*, starring Shirley Booth, ran for a rollicking 864 performances in wartime New York. Ruth McKenney's sister Eileen married another *New Yorker* writer, Nathanael West (aka Nathan Weinstein), best known for the novels *Miss Lonelyhearts* and *The Day of*

> The role depends not on traditional musical theatre skills but on a larger-than-life, cartoon-like persona cloaking keen comic sense. Donna Murphy simply had to remember not to "sing" the songs, but lob them across like fat, juicy gopher balls. Which she did, and how.

the Locust. Four days before the Broadway opening of My *Sister Eileen,* Eileen and her husband were killed in a car crash.

In 1952, George Abbott signed on to direct the musicalization, which easily ranks as one of the most troubled Broadway musicals ever to turn up a winner. A mere lad of sixty-seven at the time, Abbott liked the idea of working with untried Broadway writers. (To give them a chance? Or because they were more likely to do what he told them than more established hands?) Mr. A. shepherded the first Broadway shows of Bernstein, Comden and Green, Hugh Martin and Ralph Blane, Jule Styne, Frank Loesser, Richard Adler and Jerry Ross, Bob Merrill, Stephen Sondheim (as a composer), and John Kander and Fred Ebb. He also favored "new" choreographers like George Balanchine, Gene Kelly, Jerome Robbins, Herb Ross, Donald Saddler, Bob Fosse, Peter Gennaro, and Joe Layton.

For My *Sister Eileen,* Abbott settled on more newcomers. Joseph Fields originally intended to write the show with his vastly experienced brother, Herbie, and his sister Dorothy; when they withdrew, he turned to his My *Sister Eileen* partner, Chodorov. (Joe Fields had one musical to his credit, as colibrettist of *Gentlemen Prefer Blondes;* Chodorov had none.) Composer Leroy Anderson was known for orchestral showpieces like "Sleigh Ride" and "The Syncopated Clock." Arnold Horwitt had written sketches for the 1948 Bea Lillie revue, *Inside U.S.A.,* but had limited experience as a lyricist. Donald Saddler, a Ballet Theatre dancer who had served as a cast replacement in Abbott's *High Button Shoes,* was given the choreography assignment. Hollywood star Rosalind Russell, who had last appeared on Broadway in a minor role in a one-week flop in 1931, was signed to star on the strength of her performance in the 1942 film version of My *Sister Eileen.*

When Anderson and Horwitt played their score for Russell in early

November 1952, it was immediately clear that it would not do. With rehearsals set for December and a tryout booked for January, Abbott called
in his *On the Town* team of Bernstein, Comden, and Green. They wrote
a full, new score in about four weeks (and continued to write new songs
during the tryout). As the show continued to be refashioned, the material
began to drift further and further away from Fields and Chodorov's original vision. Even then Comden and Green were known for satire, and
Bernstein happily obliged them. Abbott also inserted Comden and Green
material into the book itself. This came in two highly noticeable places:
the humorous mock-heroic "Story Vignettes," which could easily have
come from Betty and Adolph's days at the Village Vanguard; and in the
musical scene called "Conversation Piece." ("I was rereading *Moby Dick*
the other day," Ruth contributes to the awkward silence. "It's about this
. . . whale.")

Wonderful Town continued to be cobbled on the road, with Jerome
Robbins stepping in to give things a further fix. The third attempt at an
opening number, "Christopher Street," was written at Robbins's insistence; it is continually interrupted to introduce each of the featured characters with a joke, serving as a blueprint for "Tradition," the opening
number later crafted for Robbins's *Fiddler on the Roof*. (Shortly after stepping in to help his friends, Robbins went down to the House Un-American
Activities Committee as a friendly witness and named names — including librettist Chodorov, who was
thereafter blacklisted.) The show
finally reached Broadway on February 25, 1953, and became the
smash hit of the season, but a
happy hit it was not. Abbott reported that "there was more hysterical debate, more acrimony,
more tension and more screaming connected with this play than with any
other show I was ever involved with."

Despite it all, *Wonderful Town* emerged as a reasonably well-made musical. It racked up a then-respectable run of 559 performances, cut short
by the star's departure. But that's not to say the show is a lead-pipe cinch
to revive. The most recent productions — in London in 1986, at the New
York City Opera in 1994, and a 1997 concert version by Reprise!, the Los
Angeles equivalent of Encores! — have all been less than exhilarating.
Part of this is due to the flaws in the piece, including some holes in the

Rob Fisher, who more or less seems to
have been the sparkplug behind
Encores! since its inception, was a
marvel to watch on the podium.
Every choice he made seemed to be
exactly right.

Wonderful Town
Opened: May 4, 2000
Closed: May 7, 2000
5 performances (and 0 previews)
Profit/Loss: Nonprofit
Wonderful Town ($65 top) played the 2,753-seat City Center.
Box office figures not available.

Critical Scorecard

Rave 7
Favorable 0
Mixed 0
Unfavorable 0
Pan 0

score. You almost feel like the songwriters—in their initial rush to write the show in a month—quickly dashed off ballads like "A Little Bit in Love," "A Quiet Girl," and "It's Love" before rolling up their collective sleeves to concentrate on Roz's showstoppers. The songs are not bad; they are just pretty generic, by Bernstein's standards.

But the Encores! folks—that is, director-choreographer Kathleen Marshall and music director Rob Fisher—had the show well in hand. In fact, the show started working right from the clarion call opening of the overture. Fisher, who more or less seems to have been the sparkplug behind Encores! since its inception, was a marvel to watch on the podium; every choice he made seemed to be exactly right. This was quite an overture to view, actually, with the melody switching from trumpets to trombones to saxes and back, with the poor strings just sitting there underemployed. Bernstein, under extreme time constraints, was unable to participate in the orchestration as he usually did. Bernstein inherited the already hired Don Walker, the orchestrator of choice for George Abbott (and, until *Company* in 1970, Harold Prince). Walker did a fine job, taking the songwriters' lead to provide satirically swingy charts.

Marshall had a busy time of it in 1999–2000. She started the season choreographing *Kiss Me, Kate*; directed and choreographed *Saturday Night*; and supervised—but did not direct or choreograph—the Encores! productions of *On a Clear Day* and *Tenderloin*. Her work in *Wonderful Town*, though, stood out; it was delightful, refreshing, and humor filled. At one point, she slyly set her Irish cops step dancing, having them outriver *Riverdance*. Careful readers of these pages will recall a choreographic move used, repeatedly, in *Saturday Night Fever* and elsewhere, in which everybody forms a line and rushes down to the footlights. Ms. Marshall drolly slipped that one in, too. The final numbers of the show—the "Ballet at the Village Vortex" and the deliciously off-key "Wrong Note Rag"—lacked the polish of what came before, but I suppose that Ms. Marshall ran out of rehearsal time and had to quickly throw something together. Her entire *Wonderful Town* cast demonstrated a good-natured verve, something I found lacking in the more fully-realized *Kiss Me, Kate*.

All in all, this was an impressive showing by someone who until recently had been known mainly as choreographer Rob (*Cabaret*) Marshall's sister. With commitments to the 2000–2001 *Seussical* and *Follies*—plus a possible *Wonderful Town* transfer in the works—Marshall had no choice but to resign her post, right after Encores! received a special 2000 Tony Award for Excellence in the Theatre.

Donna Murphy received glowing reviews, and she was indeed marvelous. After the first-act job-hunting ballet, you could see the pain in her feet; as she prepared to launch into "One Hundred Easy Ways," she was so deflated that she looked like a walking question mark. Most important, she displayed the survival instinct that Ruth Sherwood needed as she was buffeted about by life's hard knocks, thrown about the stage by Brazilian chorus boys, pressed into a hillbilly duet like a lost Duncan sister, and forced to scat like a square hepcat who miraculously and unexpectedly finds the beat. She was ably supported by Laura Benanti, on leave from her post at the St. James in *Swing!* (The show, not the "solid, groovy, jivy" song of the same title in *Wonderful Town*.) Earlier in these pages I ventured that Ms. Benanti might well be musical comedy star material, and her performance here certainly supported that statement. "Darlin' Eileen," they call her in the second-act opening number, and "darlin'" well describes the performance. She is a Broadway baby, a real one; when she was a toddler, her father, Martin Vidnovic, was starring in the fondly recalled Maltby-Shire musical *Baby*.

Richard Muenz was sturdy in the underwritten part of Bob Baker, the man from the Manhatter. The songwriters have him pine away for "a quiet girl"; he ends up with Ruth, who does not seem to be the answer to his dreams. Oh, well, that can happen when you write a show in a month. Muenz, however, was responsible for the one false note of the evening. In accordance with a convention of the time, the chorus suddenly appeared in the midst of "It's Love" to join in the final refrain. Mr. Muenz reacted as if this was the stupidest thing he'd ever been forced to do on a stage, which was totally jarring. Whether this was at the direction of Ms. Marshall or on the actor's own cognizance, I don't know. Granted, this was a hard moment to stage effectively, as it is indeed dated; but the answer is not to wink at the audience as if to say, "Look at how bad the writing is, but what can we do?"

That moment aside, this *Wonderful Town* was pretty wonderful. A Broadway transfer was broached but proved financially unfeasible—leaving *Wonderful Town* yet another Encores! memory.

Curtain Calls

Honorable Mention
for noteworthy contributions to the season

There follows a highly personal list of people whose contributions, one way or another, made the season of theatregoing brighter.

Aida
Heather Headley
Sherie René Scott
Bob Crowley (as scenic and costume
  designer)
Natasha Katz (lighting designer)

Amadeus
Michael Sheen
William Dudley (costume designer)

Contact
Boyd Gaines
Karen Ziemba
Deborah Yates
Jason Antoon
Susan Stroman (as director and
  choreographer)
John Weidman (author)

Copenhagen
Philip Bosco
Michael Cumpsty
Blair Brown
Michael Frayn (author)
Michael Blakemore (director)

Dame Edna: The Royal Tour
Barry Humphries (as actor and
  author)

Dinner with Friends
Matthew Arkin
Donald Margulies (author)
Daniel Sullivan (director)

Dirty Blonde
Claudia Shear (as actor and
  author)
Kevin Chamberlin
Bob Stillman
James Lapine

The Green Bird
Derek Smith
Edward Hibbert

James Joyce's The Dead
Stephen Bogardus
  (replacement)
Faith Prince (replacement)
Stephen Spinella
Sally Ann Howes

Kiss Me, Kate
Brian Stokes Mitchell
Marin Mazzie
Lee Wilkof
Michael Mulheren
Michael Blakemore (director)
Paul Gemignani (musical director)
David Chase (dance arranger)

Marie Christine
Audra McDonald
Mary Testa
Shawn Elliott
David Pleasant (onstage musician)
Jules Fisher and Peggy Eisenhauer
    (lighting designers)
Jonathan Tunick (orchestrator)

A Moon for the Misbegotten
Cherry Jones
Gabriel Byrne

Morning, Noon, and Night
Spalding Gray (as actor and author)

The Music Man
Craig Bierko
Rebecca Luker
Ruth Williamson
Clyde Alves
Susan Stroman (as director and
    choreographer)
William Ivey Long (costume
    designer)
David Chase (musical director)
David Krane (dance arranger)

On a Clear Day
Kristin Chenoweth
Brent Barrett
Roger Bart
Rob Fisher (musical director)

Porgy and Bess
Dwayne Clark

The Price
Bob Dishy

Putting It Together
Ruthie Henshall

The Rainmaker
Jayne Atkinson

The Real Thing
Stephen Dillane
Jennifer Ehle
Sarah Woodward
David Leveaux (director)

The Ride Down Mt. Morgan
Patrick Stewart
Frances Conroy
Arthur Miller (author)
David Esbjornson (director)

Riverdance on Broadway
Pat Roddy
Tsidii Le Loka
Athena Tergis (onstage musician)

Sail Away
Elaine Stritch

Saturday Night
David Campbell
Lauren Ward
Andrea Burns
Christopher Fitzgerald
Stephen Sondheim (as composer and
    lyricist)
Jonathan Tunick (orchestrator)

Swing!
Ann Hampton Callaway
Everett Bradley
Laura Benanti
Casey MacGill
Caitlin Carter
Lynne Taylor-Corbett (principal
choreographer)
William Ivey Long (costume
designer)
Harold Wheeler (orchestrator)

Tenderloin
Debbie Gravitte
Rob Fisher (musical director)

True West
Philip Seymour Hoffman
John C. Reilly
Matthew Warchus (director)

Waiting in the Wings
Rosemary Harris
Rosemary Murphy
Helen Stenborg
Elizabeth Wilson

Wild Party (Lippa)
Julia Murney
Brian D'Arcy James
Taye Diggs
Alix Korey
Andrew Lippa (as composer and
lyricist)
Mark Dendy (choreographer)
David Gallo (set designer)
Kenneth Posner (lighting designer)
Michael Gibson (orchestrator)
Stephen Oremus (musical director)

Wild Party (LaChiusa)
Toni Collette
Tonya Pinkins
Eartha Kitt
Michael John LaChiusa (as composer
and lyricist)
Bruce Coughlin (orchestrator)
Todd Ellison (musical director)

Wise Guys
Nathan Lane
Michael Hall
Stephen Sondheim (as composer and
lyricist)

Wonderful Town
Donna Murphy
Laura Benanti
Kathleen Marshall (as director and
choreographer)
Rob Fisher (musical director)

Wrong Mountain
Daniel Davis
David Hirson (author)

Tony Wrap-Up
(and Other Awards)

TONY AWARDS

The 1999–2000 season's Tony Award nominations are listed below, with asterisks denoting the winners. Overlooked shows and people who—for various reasons —might have been expected to receive nominations are also mentioned.

Best Play

Copenhagen* (Author: Michael Frayn)
Dirty Blonde (Author: Claudia Shear)
The Ride Down Mt. Morgan (Author: Arthur Miller)
True West (Author: Sam Shepard)

The Tony administration committee ruled both *The Ride Down Mt. Morgan* (originally produced in London in 1991 and New York in 1998) and *True West* (produced in New York in 1980) eligible for this category. Enough voters disagreed to turn this into a two-way race between the impeccably written but dense British comedy and a last-minute, underdog sleeper with an American twang.

Best Musical

Contact*
James Joyce's The Dead
Swing!
The Wild Party (LaChiusa)

Overlooked

Aida

There was a certain amount of controversy over the nomination of *Contact*, which some believed should be ineligible because the preexisting music was not written for the stage. (The same could be said for previous Best Musical Tony winners *Ain't Misbehavin'*, *42nd Street*, *Jerome Robbins' Broadway*, and *Fosse*.) The whole discussion was slightly absurd, as critics and audiences roundly disliked *The Wild Party* and were generally mixed on *The Dead* and *Swing!* Lots of talk, but no contest.

Best Revival of a Play

Amadeus
A Moon for the Misbegotten
The Price
The Real Thing*

Amadeus and the overpraised *The Price* both failed, and not without reason. *A Moon for the Misbegotten* was better than average, but it was clearly inferior to the 1973 revival with Jason Robards and Colleen Dewhurst—which a good portion of the Tony voters were old enough to have seen. That left *The Real Thing*, which was better than the original production and a sure thing. Unless, that is, the voters had opted for a pro-American ticket.

Best Revival of a Musical

Jesus Christ Superstar
Kiss Me, Kate*
The Music Man
Tango Argentino

The Tony Awards' insistence on four nominees in most categories—which gives more shows the opportunity to advertise their nominations—resulted in nominations for two shows which I can't imagine any of the nominators liked. The contest—in this and several other categories—was between *Kiss Me, Kate* and *The Music Man*. The scales tipped toward the former, knocking the latter out of the race in every category.

Best Book of a Musical

John Weidman, *Contact*
Richard Nelson, *James Joyce's The Dead**
Michael John LaChiusa, *Marie Christine*
Michael John LaChiusa and George C. Wolfe, *The Wild Party*

Overlooked

Linda Woolverton, Robert Falls, and David Henry Hwang, *Aida*

The nomination of *Contact*, again, raised eyebrows due to the lack of dialogue in the mostly danced show. (In actuality, the show was carefully scripted.) This left two LaChiusa musicals, which few people liked, and *The Dead*. The latter had at least some fans, and I suppose that many voters who didn't actually see *The Dead* felt that it was a safe choice.

Best Original Score (Music and Lyrics) Written for the Theatre

Elton John (Music), Tim Rice (Lyrics), *Aida**
Shaun Davey (Music), Richard Nelson and Shaun Davey (Lyrics), *James Joyce's The Dead*
Michael John LaChiusa (Music and Lyrics), *Marie Christine*
Michael John LaChiusa (Music and Lyrics), *The Wild Party*

Marie Christine and—even more so—*The Wild Party* had interesting scores. Both were buried by problematic productions; if voters had received *The Wild Party* compact disc in time—and had bothered to listen to it—it might well have won. *The Dead* was constructed like a play with incidental songs, rather than an integrated score; this was a novel way of doing things, but it hurt the show's effectiveness as musical theatre. That left *Aida*, which was also built on incidental—or at least extraneous—songs. But melodic, at least.

Best Direction of a Play

Michael Blakemore, *Copenhagen**
James Lapine, *Dirty Blonde*
David Leveaux, *The Real Thing*
Matthew Warchus, *True West*

Overlooked

Scott Ellis, *The Rainmaker*
Michael Mayer, *Uncle Vanya*
James Naughton, *The Price*
Julie Taymor, *The Green Bird*
Jerry Zaks, *Epic Proportions*

The four nominees were equally matched; you could find a good reason each deserved to win, and I couldn't argue against any of them. Michael Blakemore did the most traditional work of the four, on perhaps the most complicated play. According to one theory, some voters assumed that he would lose the Best Direction of a Musical award to Susan Stroman and therefore gave him the Best Direction of a Play award as a consolation.

Best Direction of a Musical

Michael Blakemore, *Kiss Me, Kate**
Susan Stroman, *Contact*
Susan Stroman, *The Music Man*
Lynne Taylor-Corbett, *Swing!*

Overlooked

Graciela Daniele, *Marie Christine*
Robert Falls, *Aida*
Eric D. Schaeffer, *Putting It Together*
George C. Wolfe, *The Wild Party* (LaChiusa)

How do you direct a show without dialogue? If everyone is dancing all the time, isn't that choreography? These questions knocked the directors of *Contact* and *Swing!* out of contention. Stroman's supporters presumably split their votes between the favorite *Contact* and the more "directable" *Music Man*, allowing Blakemore to come out ahead. Did anyone notice that three of the director nominees and all four choreographer nominees were women? And that seven of eight nominations were split between three women?

Best Choreography

Kathleen Marshall, *Kiss Me, Kate*
Susan Stroman, *Contact**
Susan Stroman, *The Music Man*
Lynne Taylor-Corbett, *Swing!*

Overlooked

Bob Avian, *Putting It Together*
Wayne Cilento, *Aida*
Graciela Daniele, *Marie Christine*

1999–2000 was Susan Stroman's season, professionally anyway. (Offstage, she watched her husband and frequent collaborator, Mike Ockrent, die of leukemia.) Her choreography for *Contact* was a sure winner.

Best Performance by a Leading Actor in a Play

Gabriel Byrne, *A Moon for the Misbegotten*
Stephen Dillane, *The Real Thing**
Philip Seymour Hoffman, *True West*
John C. Reilly, *True West*
David Suchet, *Amadeus*

Overlooked

Matthew Broderick, *Taller Than a Dwarf*
Bob Dishy, *The Price*
Woody Harrelson, *The Rainmaker*
Derek Jacobi, *Uncle Vanya*
Roger Rees, *Uncle Vanya*
Michael Sheen, *Amadeus*
Patrick Stewart, *The Ride Down Mt. Morgan*

True West knocked itself out of the running on this award. The producer unsuccessfully tried to persuade the administration committee to allow the two stars a joint nomination, as they alternated their roles. The determination was that they could only be nominated separately, and in the roles they played on the official opening night (which saw Hoffman as the mild brother and Reilly as the wild brother). Instead of restricting Tony voters to performances with the correct cast lineup, *True West* invited them to see *either* combination. (The producers offered the traditional two tickets—with the voter to choose between two tickets to any one performance, or one ticket to a performance by each cast.) Thus, a portion of the voters saw the nominated actors in their nonnominated roles. With voter confusion dimming *True West*'s prospects, we were left with three actors re-creating roles that won Tony Awards the last time around. Neither Gabriel Byrne nor David Suchet erased memories of Jason Robards or Ian McKellen, while Stephen Dillane was even more effective than Jeremy Irons.

Best Performance by a Leading Actress in a Play

Jayne Atkinson, *The Rainmaker*
Jennifer Ehle, *The Real Thing**
Rosemary Harris, *Waiting in the Wings*
Cherry Jones, *A Moon for the Misbegotten*
Claudia Shear, *Dirty Blonde*

Overlooked

Lauren Bacall, *Waiting in the Wings*
Kristin Chenoweth, *Epic Proportions*
Olympia Dukakis, *Rose*

Cherry Jones, similarly, was fighting the ghost of Colleen Dewhurst. Veteran Rosemary Harris had sentiment on her side, and an out-and-out rave in the *New York Times*; but her role consisted mostly of sitting around passively and watching character actresses steal scenes. And she was running against her daughter Jennifer Ehle, who was making a dazzling Broadway debut. Ehle deserved the award; like her costar Stephen Dillane, she handily topped a performance that won a Tony Award the last time around. But it was hard to count out underdog Claudia Shear, the performance artist–writer who conjured a popularly received play out of scraps of Mae West's life. Had *Dirty Blonde* won best play, Ms. Shear would quite possibly have taken the acting award as well.

Best Performance by a Leading Actor in a Musical

Craig Bierko, *The Music Man*
George Hearn, *Putting It Together*
Brian Stokes Mitchell, *Kiss Me, Kate**
Mandy Patinkin, *The Wild Party* (LaChiusa)
Christopher Walken, *James Joyce's The Dead*

Overlooked

Anthony Crivello, *Marie Christine*
Adam Pascal, *Aida*

The number of nominees for the acting Tonys was increased to five this year. This made sense in some categories, due to the number of excellent performances. Here it resulted in three nominees who received ambivalent-to-poor notices and who presumably garnered few votes. The contest was between the stars of the two big revivals. Newcomer Craig Bierko was thought by some to be too close a copy of Robert Preston, so Brian Stokes Mitchell—who almost won a Tony last time out, for *Ragtime*—rode the *Kiss Me, Kate* bandwagon.

Best Performance by a Leading Actress in a Musical

Toni Collette, *The Wild Party* (LaChiusa)
Heather Headley, *Aida**
Rebecca Luker, *The Music Man*
Marin Mazzie, *Kiss Me, Kate*
Audra McDonald, *Marie Christine*

Overlooked

Blair Brown, *James Joyce's The Dead*
Carol Burnett, *Putting It Together*
Liza Minnelli, *Minnelli on Minnelli*

Five slots were necessary in this category, with the competition narrowing between two highly accomplished leading ladies—Marin Mazzie and Rebecca Luker—and the newcomer Heather Headley. (Toni Collette was hidden away in the unlikable *Wild Party*, and Audra

McDonald—who had already won three out of three Tonys—could breathe a sigh of relief at finally proving mortal.) Mazzie and Luker were very good in entertaining musicals (in which the male leads had better roles), while Headley had to make do with poor material and no support. She was able to pull it off, but the award could have easily gone to Mazzie or Luker.

Best Performance by a Featured Actor in a Play

Kevin Chamberlin, *Dirty Blonde*
Daniel Davis, *Wrong Mountain*
Roy Dotrice, *A Moon for the Misbegotten**
Derek Smith, *The Green Bird*
Bob Stillman, *Dirty Blonde*

Derek Smith and Daniel Davis were both extremely memorable in dire circumstances. Kevin Chamberlin and Roy Dotrice were both more visible, being in hits. I suppose that Chamberlin lost some votes to his castmate Bob Stillman, allowing veteran Dotrice to squeak by. Like Leading Actor Stephen Dillane and Leading Actress Jennifer Ehle, Dotrice won for a role that also rewarded his predecessor, Ed Flanders.

Best Performance by a Featured Actress in a Play

Blair Brown, *Copenhagen**
Frances Conroy, *The Ride Down Mt. Morgan*
Amy Ryan, *Uncle Vanya*
Helen Stenborg, *Waiting in the Wings*
Sarah Woodward, *The Real Thing*

Blair Brown started the season as a replacement in *Cabaret*, moved on to play the female lead in *James Joyce's The Dead*, and ended up in *Copenhagen*. This trifecta seemed to earn her the award; she gave sturdy support to her costars in the latter play (neither of whom were nominated), but this was perhaps the least interesting of her three performances. Frances Conroy was very good in *The Ride Down Mt. Morgan*; so was Helen Stenborg in *Waiting in the Wings*, with one of those juicy roles that tend to get you a nomination. But Ms. Brown had a season's worth of momentum and publicity going for her.

Best Performance by a Featured Actor in a Musical

Michael Berresse, *Kiss Me, Kate*
Boyd Gaines, *Contact**
Michael Mulheren, *Kiss Me, Kate*

Stephen Spinella, *James Joyce's The Dead*
Lee Wilkof, *Kiss Me, Kate*

Overlooked

Jason Antoon, *Contact*
Max Casella, *The Music Man*
Tony Vincent, *Jesus Christ Superstar*

As with *True West*, the producers of *Kiss Me, Kate* lobbied to get Michael Mulheren and Lee Wilkof a joint nomination; otherwise, they feared, the two would knock each other out of the running (which is quite possibly what happened). The third *Kiss Me, Kate* nominee similarly suffered from the split vote. Stephen Spinella—who won Tonys for both parts of *Angels in America*—was perhaps most deserving, but Boyd Gaines benefited from being in the more widely seen and immensely popular *Contact*.

Best Performance by a Featured Actress in a Musical

Laura Benanti, *Swing!*
Ann Hampton Callaway, *Swing!*
Eartha Kitt, *The Wild Party* (LaChiusa)
Deborah Yates, *Contact*
Karen Ziemba, *Contact**

Overlooked

Ruthie Henshall, *Putting It Together*
Sherie René Scott, *Aida*
Amy Spanger, *Kiss Me, Kate*
Mary Testa, *Marie Christine*

Five noteworthy performances. Laura Benanti and Ann Hampton Callaway hadn't a chance, as *Swing!* was destined to be overlooked in the balloting. Eartha Kitt gave what was perhaps the most spectacular performance; Deborah Yates—as *Contact*'s Girl in the Yellow Dress—was the most striking. But Karen Ziemba, who has been working her heart out along Broadway for a decade, managed to edge out the others.

Best Scenic Design

Bob Crowley, *Aida**
Thomas Lynch, *The Music Man*
Robin Wagner, *Kiss Me, Kate*
Tony Walton, *Uncle Vanya*

Overlooked

Robin Wagner, *The Wild Party* (LaChiusa)

Breathtaking scenery will always overtake just about anything else. Bob Crowley had three or four stage pictures in *Aida* that made you gasp, and made the voters vote for him.

Best Costume Design

Bob Crowley, *Aida*
Constance Hoffman, *The Green Bird*
William Ivey Long, *The Music Man*
Martin Pakledinaz, *Kiss Me, Kate**

Overlooked

William Dudley, *Amadeus*
Toni-Leslie James, *The Wild Party* (LaChiusa)

All four nominees provided some wonderful work. *Aida* and *The Green Bird* both contained some distracting costumes as well, while *The Music Man* and *Kiss Me, Kate* were highly proficient and equally worthy. Pakledinaz's colorful Italianate costumes—including those gangsters in bicolored tights with pockets—tipped the scales.

Best Lighting Design

Jules Fisher and Peggy Eisenhauer, *Marie Christine*
Jules Fisher and Peggy Eisenhauer, *The Wild Party*
Peter Kaczorowski, *Kiss Me, Kate*
Natasha Katz, *Aida**

Overlooked

Andrew Bridge, *Saturday Night Fever*
Peter Kaczorowski, *Contact*

Breathtaking lighting will always overtake just about anything else. (I said that above, didn't I?) Natasha Katz did some marvelous things in *Aida*, and her award was well deserved. Jules Fisher and Peggy Eisenhauer always seem to do striking work; their *Marie Christine* was quite impressive, although to little overall effect.

Best Orchestrations

Doug Besterman, *The Music Man*
Don Sebesky, *Kiss Me, Kate**
Jonathan Tunick, *Marie Christine*
Harold Wheeler, *Swing!*

The Tonys added a Best Orchestrations category in 1998, which was about time. (It is time they reinstate the musical director award, which was given from 1949 to 1964.) But how well can Tony voters judge orchestrations? While good costumes in a bad musical can and have been rewarded, it is hard to imagine the average voter recognizing excellent orchestrations on poor music. The tendency, I fear, is to vote for the musical that wins the most awards—which is what happened this year. Harold Wheeler's fine work in *Swing!* didn't have a chance.

SPECIAL TONY AWARDS

For a live theatrical event
Dame Edna, the Royal Tour

For lifetime achievement in the theatre
T. Edward Hambleton, founder of the Phoenix Theater

For excellence in theatre
veteran actress Eileen Heckart
theatrical agent and manager Sylvia Herscher
Encores! Great American Musicals in Concert

Regional Theatre
The Utah Shakespearean Festival, Cedar City, Utah

PULITZER PRIZE FOR DRAMA

Donald Margulies, *Dinner with Friends**
Suzan-Lori Parks, *In the Blood*
August Wilson, *King Hedley II*

NEW YORK DRAMA CRITICS CIRCLE AWARDS

Best Play
Jitney (Author: August Wilson)

Best Foreign Play
Copenhagen (Author: Michael Frayn)

Best Musical

James Joyce's The Dead

DRAMA DESK AWARDS

Best Play

Copenhagen (Tony Award winner) (Author: Michael Frayn)

Best Musical

Contact (Tony Award winner)

Best Music

Andrew Lippa, *The Wild Party* (off-Broadway)

Best Lyrics

Stephen Sondheim, *Saturday Night* (off-Broadway)

Best Revival of a Play

The Real Thing (Tony Award winner)

Best Revival of a Musical

Kiss Me, Kate (Tony Award winner)

Best Performance by a Leading Actor in a Play

Stephen Dillane, *The Real Thing* (Tony Award winner)

Best Performance by a Leading Actress in a Play

Eileen Heckart, *The Waverly Gallery* (off-Broadway)

Best Performance by a Leading Actor in a Musical

Brian Stokes Mitchell, *Kiss Me, Kate* (Tony Award winner)

Best Performance by a Leading Actress in a Musical

Heather Headley, *Aida* (Tony Award winner)

Solo Performance

Barry Humphries, *Dame Edna: The Royal Tour*

Best Performance by a Featured Actor in a Play

Roy Dotrice, *A Moon for the Misbegotten* (Tony Award winner)

Best Performance by a Featured Actress in a Play

Marylouise Burke, *Fuddy Meers* (off-Broadway)

Best Performance by a Featured Actor in a Musical

Stephen Spinella, *James Joyce's The Dead*

Best Performance by a Featured Actress in a Musical

Karen Ziemba, *Contact* (Tony Award winner)

Best Direction of a Play

Michael Blakemore, *Copenhagen* (Tony Award winner)

Best Direction of a Musical

Michael Blakemore, *Kiss Me, Kate* (Tony Award winner)

Best Choreography

Susan Stroman, *Contact* (Tony Award winner)

Best Scenic Design (Musical)

Robin Wagner, *Kiss Me, Kate*

Best Scenic Design (Play)

David Gallo, *Jitney* (off-Broadway)

Best Costume Design

Martin Pakledinaz, *Kiss Me, Kate* (Tony Award winner)

Best Lighting Design

Peter Kaczorowski, *Contact*

Best Orchestrations

Don Sebesky, *Kiss Me, Kate* (Tony Award winner)

Holdovers

As the 1999–2000 season began on May 31, 1999, the following shows were playing on Broadway.

Amy's View   Play. Opened April 15, 1999, at the Ethel Barrymore. By David Hare; directed by Richard Eyre. 1999 Tony Award: Leading Actress (Judi Dench). Closed July 18, 1999, after 103 performances (and 12 previews). Profit/loss: profit.

Annie Get Your Gun   Musical revival. Opened March 4, 1999, at the Marquis. Music and lyrics by Irving Berlin; book by Herbert and Dorothy Fields (revised by Peter Stone); directed and choreographed by Graciela Daniele. 1999 Tony Awards: Musical Revival; Leading Actress (Bernadette Peters). Still playing May 29, 2000. To date: 518 performances (and 35 previews). Profit/loss: profit.

Art   Play. Opened March 1, 1998, at the Royale. By Yasmina Reza; translated by Christopher Hampton; directed by Matthew Warchus. 1998 Tony Awards: Play. Drama Critics Circle Award for Best Foreign Play. Closed August 8, 1999, after 600 performances (and 20 previews). Profit/loss: profit.

Beauty and the Beast   Musical. Opened April 18, 1994, at the Palace; closed September 5, 1999. Reopened November 12, 1999, at the Lunt-Fontanne. Music by Alan Menken; lyrics by Howard Ashman and Tim Rice; book by Linda Woolverton; directed by Robert Jess Roth; choreographed by Matt West. 1994 Tony Award: Costume Design (Ann Hould-Ward). Still playing May 29, 2000. To date: 2,480 performances (and 46 previews). Profit/loss: profit.

Cabaret   Musical revival. Opened March 19, 1998, at the Kit Kat Klub (Henry Miller's Theatre); transferred November 14, 1998, to Studio 54. Music by John Kander; lyrics by Fred Ebb; book by Joe Masteroff; directed by Sam Mendes and Rob Marshall; choreographed by Rob Marshall. 1998 Tony Awards: Musical Revival; Leading Actress (Natasha Richardson); Leading Actor (Alan Cumming); Featured Actor (Ron Rifkin). Still playing May 29, 2000. To date: 879 performances (and 37 previews). Profit/loss: profit.

Cats   Musical. Opened October 7, 1982, at the Winter Garden. Music by Andrew Lloyd Webber; lyrics by T. S. Eliot; directed by Trevor Nunn; choreographed by Gillian Lynne. 1983 Tony Awards: Musical; Score; Book; Direction; Featured Actress (Betty Buckley); Costume Design (John Napier); and Lighting Design (David Hersey). Closed September 10, 2000, after 7,485 performances (and 16 previews). Profit/loss: profit.

Chicago   Musical revival. Opened November 14, 1996, at the Richard Rodgers; transferred February 12, 1997, to the Shubert. Music by John Kander; lyrics by Fred Ebb; book by Fred Ebb and Bob Fosse (adaptation by David Thompson); directed by Walter Bobbie; choreographed by Ann Reinking in the style of Bob Fosse. 1997 Tony Awards: Musical Revival; Director; Choreographer; Leading Actress (Bebe Neuwirth); Leading Actor (James Naughton); Lighting Design (Ken Billington). Still playing May 29, 2000. To date: 1,474 performances (and 22 previews). Profit/loss: profit.

The Civil War   Musical revue. Opened April 22, 1999, at the St. James. Music by Frank Wildhorn; "by" Frank Wildhorn, Gregory Boyd, and Jack Murphy; directed by Jerry Zaks; choreographed by Luis Perez. Closed June 13, 1999, after 61 performances (and 35 previews). Profit/loss: loss.

Closer   Play. Opened March 25, 1999, at the Music Box. By Patrick Marber; directed by Patrick Marber. Closed August 22, 1999, after 173 performances (and 17 previews). Profit/loss: loss.

Death of a Salesman   Play revival. Opened February 10, 1999, at the Eugene O'Neill. By Arthur Miller; directed by Robert Falls. 1999 Tony Awards: Play Revival; Director; Leading Actor (Brian Dennehy); Featured Actress (Elizabeth Franz). Closed November 7, 1999, after 274 performances (and 22 previews). Profit/loss: profit.

Footloose   Musical. Opened October 22, 1998, at the Richard Rodgers. Music by Tom Snow (and others); lyrics by Dean Pitchford (and others); book by Dean Pitchford and Walter Bobbie; directed by Walter Bobbie; choreographed by A. C. Ciulla. Closed July 2, 2000, after 737 performances (and 21 previews). Profit/loss: loss.

Fosse   Musical revue. Opened January 14, 1999, at the Broadhurst. Conceived by Richard Maltby Jr., Chet Walker, and Ann Reinking; choreography by Bob Fosse; directed by Richard Maltby Jr.; choreography re-created by Chet Walker; codirected and cochoreographed by Ann Reinking. 1999 Tony Awards: Musical; Orchestration (Ralph Burns and Doug Besterman); Lighting Design (Andrew Bridge). Still playing May 29, 2000. To date: 581 performances (and 21 previews). Profit/loss: profit.

It Ain't Nothing but the Blues   Musical revue. Opened April 26, 1999, at the Vivian Beaumont; transferred September 9, 1999, to the Ambassador. Book by Charles Bevel, Lita Gaithers, Randal Myler, Ron Taylor, and Dan Wheetman; directed by Randal Myler. Closed January 9, 2000, after 276 performances (and 5 previews). Profit/loss: loss.

Jekyll & Hyde   Musical. Opened April 28, 1997, at the Plymouth. Music by Frank Wildhorn; book and lyrics by Leslie Bricusse; directed by Robin Phillips; choreographed by Joey Pizzi. Closed January 7, 2001, after 1,543 performances (and 42 previews). Profit/loss: loss.

Les Misérables   Musical. Opened March 12, 1987, at the Broadway; moved October 16, 1990, to the Imperial. By Alain Boublil and Claude-Michel Schönberg; music by Claude-Michel Schönberg; lyrics by Herbert Kretzmer; adapted and directed by Trevor Nunn and John Caird. 1987 Tony Awards: Musical; Score; Book; Featured Actor (Michael Maguire); Featured Actress (Frances Ruffelle). Still playing May 29, 2000. To date: 5,439 performances. Profit/loss: profit.

Miss Saigon   Musical. Opened April 11, 1991, at the Broadway. Music by Claude-Michel Schönberg; lyrics by Richard Maltby Jr. and Alain Boublil; book by Alain Boublil and Claude-Michel Schönberg; directed by Nicholas Hytner; choreographed by Bob Avian. 1991 Tony Awards: Leading Actor (Jonathan Pryce); Leading Actress (Lea Salonga); Featured Actor (Hinton Battle). Closed January 28, 2001, after 4,097 performances (and 19 previews). Profit/loss: profit.

Night Must Fall   Play revival. Opened March 8, 1999, at the Lyceum; transferred April 20, 1999, to the Helen Hayes. Play by Emlyn Williams; directed by John Tillinger. Closed June 27, 1999, after 127 performances (and 40 previews). Profit/loss: nonprofit [loss].

Not About Nightingales   Play. Opened February 25, 1999, at Circle in the Square. By Tennessee Williams; directed by Trevor Nunn. 1999 Tony Award: Scenic Design (Richard Hoover). Closed June 13, 1999, after 124 performances (and 13 previews). Profit/loss: loss.

Peter Pan   Musical revival. Opened November 23, 1998, at the Marquis; closed January 3, 1999 (48 performances, 5 previews). Reopened April 7, 1999, at the Gershwin. Music by Mark (Moose) Charlap; lyrics by Carolyn Leigh; additional music by Jule Styne; additional lyrics by Betty Comden and Adolph Green; directed by Glenn Casale; choreographed by Patti Colombo. Closed August 29, 1999, after 166 performances (and no previews). Profit/loss: profit.

Ragtime   Musical. Opened January 18, 1998, at the Ford Center. Music by Stephen Flaherty; lyrics by Lynn Ahrens; book by Terrence McNally; directed by Frank Galati; choreographed by Graciela Daniele. 1998 Tony Awards: Score; Book; Orchestration (William David Brohn). Closed January 16, 2000, after 861 performances (and 26 previews). Profit/loss: loss.

Rent   Musical. Opened April 29, 1996, at the Nederlander. Book, music, and lyrics by Jonathan Larson; directed by Michael Greif; choreographed by Marlies Yearby. 1996 Tony Awards: Musical; Score; Book; Featured Actor (Wilson Jermaine Heredia). Drama Critics Circle Award for Best Musical. Pulitzer Prize for Drama. Still playing May 29, 2000. To date: 1,705 performances (and 16 previews). Profit/loss: profit.

Ring Round the Moon   Play revival. Opened April 28, 1999, at the Belasco. By Jean Anouilh; translated by Christopher Fry; directed by Gerald Gutierrez. Closed June 27, 1999, after 66 performances (and 31 previews). Profit/loss: nonprofit [loss].

Side Man   Play. Opened June 25, 1998, at the Roundabout Stage Right; closed September 13, 1998 (93 performances, 27 previews). Reopened November 8, 1998, at the John Golden. By Warren Leight; directed by Michael Mayer. 1999 Tony Awards: Play; Featured Actor (Frank Wood). Closed October 31, 1999, after 409 performances (and 23 previews). Profit/loss: loss.

Smokey Joe's Cafe   Musical revue. Opened March 2, 1995, at the Virginia. Music and lyrics by Jerry Leiber and Mike Stoller; directed by Jerry Zaks; choreographed by Joey McKneely. Closed January 16, 2000, after 2,036 performances (and 25 previews). Profit/loss: profit.

The Iceman Cometh Play revival. Opened April 8, 1999, at the Brooks Atkinson. By Eugene O'Neill; directed by Howard Davies. Closed July 17, 1999, after 102 performances (and 10 previews). Profit/loss: profit.

The Lion in Winter Play revival. Opened March 11, 1999, at the Roundabout Stage Right. By James Goldman; directed by Michael Mayer. Closed May 30, 1999, after 99 performances (and 22 previews). Profit/loss: nonprofit [loss].

The Lion King Musical. Opened November 13, 1997, at the New Amsterdam Theatre. Music by Elton John and others; lyrics by Tim Rice and others; book by Roger Allers and Irene Mecchia; directed by Julie Taymor; choreographed by Garth Fagan. 1998 Tony Awards: Musical; Director; Choreographer; Scenic Design (Richard Hudson); Costume Design (Taymor); and Lighting Design (Donald Holder). Drama Critics Circle Award for Best Musical. Still playing May 29, 2000. To date: 1,062 performances (and 33 previews). Profit/loss: to be determined.

The Lonesome West Play. Opened April 27, 1999, at the Lyceum Theatre. By Martin McDonagh; directed by Garry Hynes. Closed June 13, 1999, after 55 performances (and 9 previews). Profit/loss: loss.

The Phantom of the Opera Musical. Opened January 26, 1988, at the Majestic. Music by Andrew Lloyd Webber; lyrics by Charles Hart; book and additional lyrics by Richard Stilgoe; directed by Harold Prince; choreographed by Gillian Lynne. 1988 Tony Awards: Musical; Director; Scenic Design (Maria Bjornson); Lighting Design (Andrew Bridge); Leading Actor (Michael Crawford); and Featured Actress (Judy Kaye). Still playing May 29, 2000. To date: 5,150 performances (and 16 previews). Profit/loss: profit.

The Sound of Music Musical revival. Opened March 12, 1998, at the Martin Beck. Music by Richard Rodgers; lyrics by Oscar Hammerstein 2d; book by Howard Lindsay and Russel Crouse; directed by Susan H. Schulman; choreographed by Michael Lichtefeld. Closed June 20, 1999, after 532 performances (and 39 previews). Profit/loss: loss.

Via Dolorosa Solo play. Opened March 18, 1999, at the Booth. By David Hare; directed by Stephen Daldry. Closed June 13, 1999, after 99 performances (and 15 previews). Profit/loss: nonprofit [profit].

The Weir Play. Opened April 1, 1999, at the Walter Kerr. By Conor McPherson; directed by Ian Rickson. Closed November 28, 1999, after 273 performances (and 11 previews). Profit/loss: loss.

You're a Good Man, Charlie Brown   Musical revival. Opened February 4, 1999, at the Ambassador. Music, book, and lyrics by Clark Gesner; additional material by Andrew Lippa; directed by Michael Mayer; choreographed by Jerry Mitchell. 1999 Tony Awards: Featured Actress (Kristen Chenoweth); Featured Actor (Roger Bart). Closed June 13, 1999, after 150 performances (and 13 previews). Profit/loss: loss.

Shows That Never Reached Town

Every season, numerous productions are announced for Broadway that for any number of reasons never arrive. Some of these are typically more wishful than realistic; others succumb to financial woes or tryout blues. The following shows, though, were announced and at one point reasonably expected to arrive on Broadway during the 1999–2000 season. Credits are as announced, and might well have changed over these shows' bumpy journeys. Some, though not all, remain likely prospects for production.

Birdy   Play, adapted from the novel by William Wharton about two boys from Philadelphia who fought in World War II. By Naomi Wallace; directed by Kevin Knight; produced by Spring Sirkin and Ben Mordecai. Tried out in March 2000 at Duke University in Durham, North Carolina. Plans for an April 2000 Broadway opening were postponed.

Enigma Variations   French drama, about a Nobel Prize–winning novelist and a journalist. By Eric-Emmanuel Schmitt (translated by Jeremy Sams); directed by Anthony Page; produced by Emanuel Azenberg and others. With Donald Sutherland and John Rubinstein. Tried out in February 2000 at the Royal Alexandra Theatre in Toronto. Plans for a late April 2000 opening at the Brooks Atkinson were canceled due to poor Toronto reviews. Sutherland and Rubinstein went to London instead, where the play opened May 31, 2000 under the title *Enigmatic Variations* to even worse reviews and a two-month run.

Finian's Rainbow   Revival of the 1947 musical comedy satire. Music by Burton Lane; lyrics by E. Y. Harburg; book by E. Y. Harburg and Fred Saidy; revised book by Peter Stone; directed by Lonny Price; choreographed by Marguerite Derricks; produced by Rodger Hess. With Brian Murray, Denis O'Hare, and Austin Pendleton. Tried out at the Coconut Grove Playhouse in Miami and Playhouse Square in Cleveland. Plans for a February 2000 Broadway opening were postponed. A revised version, scheduled for a July 2000 tryout at the Ahmanson Theatre in Los Angeles, was canceled in April due to lack of financing.

It's Good to Be Alive (formerly entitled *Ostrovsky*)   Musical comedy, about a star of the Yiddish theatre on lower Second Avenue. Music by Cy Coleman; book by Avery Corman; lyrics by Coleman and Corman; directed by Gene Saks; choreographed by Pat Birch. Alan King was mentioned to star. Announced for spring 2000.

Jane Eyre   Musical, based on the Charlotte Brontë novel. Music and lyrics by Paul Gordon; book and additional lyrics by John Caird; directed by John Caird and Scott Schwartz. With Marla Schaffel and James Barbour. Played tryouts in Wichita, Kansas, in 1995, Toronto in 1996, and La Jolla in 1999. The announced February 2000 opening was canceled, but finally opened on December 10, 2000, at the Brooks Atkinson.

Martin Guerre   Musical, based on the sixteenth-century French legend. By Alain Boublil and Claude-Michel Schönberg; directed by Conall Morrison; choreographed by David Bolger; produced by Cameron Mackintosh. With Erin Dilly, Hugh Panaro, and Stephen R. Buntrock. Much-revised 1996 London musical played a U.S. tryout tour beginning September 1999 at the Guthrie Theatre in Minneapolis. After playing Detroit, Washington, and Seattle, the tour closed in Los Angeles on April 8. Plans for an April 26, 2000, Broadway opening were canceled.

Oklahoma!   Revival of the 1943 musical comedy. Music by Richard Rodgers, book and lyrics by Oscar Hammerstein 2d; directed by Trevor Nunn; choreographed by Susan Stroman; produced by Cameron Mackintosh. The 1998 Royal National Theatre revival was initially scheduled for a fall 1999 Broadway opening but was postponed in February when American Actors' Equity rejected Mackintosh's request to import the London cast. In April 2000 the show was announced for a December 7, 2000, opening at the Ford Center (with an American cast). The show was once again postponed in July 2000, due to scheduling conflicts.

Scent of the Roses   Drama, about a South African woman who owns a valuable painting. By Lisette Lecat Ross; directed by Gordon Edelstein; produced by Arthur Cantor and others. With Julie Harris. Tried out in July 1998 at ACT (A Contemporary Theatre) in Seattle, and played a pre-Broadway engagement in October 1999 at the Helen Hayes Center in Nyack, New York. Plans for a December 1, 1999, opening at the Belasco were canceled.

Sweet Deliverance   Comedy, about a woman who becomes famous in the "suicide industry." By Eric Houston; produced by Alexander H. Cohen and others.
Fran Drescher was mentioned to star. Announced for early April 2000.

Wise Guys   Musical about the brothers Addison and Wilson Mizner. Music and
lyrics by Stephen Sondheim; book by John Weidman; directed by Sam
Mendes; produced by Roger Berlind, Dodger Theatricals, Scott Rudin, and
Kennedy Center. With Nathan Lane and Victor Garber. Played a developmental workshop in November 1999 at New York Theatre Workshop (see
page 41). Plans for an April 27, 2000, Broadway opening were canceled.

Long-Run Leaders

The following shows, separated into plays and musicals, have run more than 1,000 performances on Broadway. The productions are listed in order of their all-time ranking. Because yesterday's record-breaking run might pale in comparison to a moderate hit of today, an additional column indicates productions that were at one time among the top ten, showing the highest level achieved.

The assumption that shows are running longer today than ever before holds true—but only for musicals. Five of the ten longest-running musicals opened since 1979, with another two likely to work their way onto the list. However, all but three of the twenty-six plays to exceed 1,000 performances opened prior to 1980. The last play to exceed 1,000 performances opened in 1983, and it climbed only to fourteenth place on the list. Performance totals are current through May 28, 2000. Shows marked with an asterisk were still running at press time.

Musicals				
All-time Ranking	Title	Opening Date	Number of Performances	Highest Ranking
1	Cats	October 7, 1982	7,485	1
2	A Chorus Line	July 25, 1975	6,137	1
3	Oh! Calcutta!! (revival)	September 24, 1976	5,852	2
4	*Les Misérables	March 12, 1987	5,439*	4*
5	*The Phantom of the Opera	January 26, 1988	5,150*	5*
6	Miss Saigon	April 11, 1991	4,097	6
7	42nd Street	August 25, 1980	3,486	3
8	Grease	February 14, 1972	3,388	1
9	Fiddler on the Roof	September 22, 1964	3,242	1

(continued)

All-time Ranking	Title	Opening Date	Number of Performances	Highest Ranking
10	Hello, Dolly!	January 16, 1964	2,844	1
11	My Fair Lady	March 15, 1956	2,717	1
12	*Beauty and the Beast	April 18, 1994	2,480*	
13	Annie	April 21, 1977	2,377	7
14	Man of La Mancha	November 22, 1965	2,328	4
15	Oklahoma!	March 31, 1943	2,212	1
16	Smokey Joe's Cafe	March 2, 1995	2,036	
17	Pippin	October 23, 1972	1,944	7
18	South Pacific	April 7, 1949	1,925	2
19	The Magic Show	May 28, 1974	1,920	9
20	Dancin'	March 27, 1978	1,774	
21	La Cage Aux Folles	August 21, 1983	1,761	
22	Hair	April 29, 1968	1,750	7
23	*Rent	April 29, 1996	1,705*	
24	The Wiz	January 5, 1975	1,672	
25	Crazy for You	February 19, 1992	1,622	
26	Ain't Misbehavin'	May 8, 1978	1,604	
27	The Best Little Whorehouse in Texas	April 17, 1978	1,584	
28	Evita	September 25, 1979	1,567	
29	Dreamgirls	December 20, 1981	1,521	
30	Mame	May 24, 1966	1,508	7
31	Grease! (revival)	May 11, 1994	1,503	
32	*Chicago (revival)	November 14, 1996	1,474*	
33	The Sound of Music	November 16, 1959	1,443	4
34	Me and My Girl	August 10, 1986	1,420	
35	How To Succeed in Business . . .	October 14, 1961	1,417	5
36	Hellzapoppin'	November 22, 1938	1,404	1
37	The Music Man	December 19, 1957	1,375	5
38	Funny Girl	March 26, 1964	1,348	9
39	*Jekyll & Hyde	April 28, 1997	1,287*	
40	Promises, Promises	December 1, 1968	1,281	
41	The King and I	March 29, 1951	1,246	4
42	1776	March 16, 1969	1,217	
43	Sugar Babies	October 8, 1979	1,208	
44	Guys and Dolls	November 24, 1950	1,200	4
45	Cabaret	November 20, 1966	1,165	
46	Annie Get Your Gun	May 16, 1946	1,147	3
47	Guys and Dolls (revival)	April 14, 1992	1,143	

All-time Ranking	Title	Opening Date	Number of Performances	Highest Ranking
48	Bring in 'Da Noise, Bring in 'Da Funk	April 25, 1996	1,130	
49	Pins and Needles	November 27, 1937	1,108	1
50	They're Playing Our Song	February 11, 1979	1,082	
51	Kiss Me, Kate	December 30, 1948	1,070	5
52	Don't Bother Me, I Can't Cope	April 19, 1972	1,065	
53	The Pajama Game	May 13, 1954	1,063	9
54	The Lion King	November 13, 1997	1,062*	
55	Shenandoah	January 7, 1975	1,050	
56	Damn Yankees	May 5, 1955	1,019	10
57	Grand Hotel	November 12, 1989	1,018	
58	Big River	April 25, 1985	1,005	

Plays

All-time Ranking	Title	Opening Date	Number of Performances	Highest Ranking
1	Life with Father	November 8, 1939	3,224	1
2	Tobacco Road	December 4, 1933	3,182	1
3	Abie's Irish Rose	May 23, 1922	2,327	1
4	Deathtrap	February 26, 1978	1,792	4
5	Gemini	May 21, 1977	1,788	4
6	Harvey	November 1, 1944	1,775	4
7	Born Yesterday	February 4, 1946	1,642	5
8	Mary, Mary	March 8, 1961	1,572	6
9	The Voice of the Turtle	December 8, 1943	1,557	4
10	Barefoot in the Park	October 23, 1963	1,530	8
11	Same Time, Next Year	March 13, 1975	1,453	10
12	Arsenic and Old Lace	January 10, 1941	1,444	4
13	Mummenschanz	March 30, 1977	1,326	
14	Brighton Beach Memoirs	March 27, 1983	1,299	
15	Angel Street	December 5, 1941	1,295	5
15	Lightnin'	August 26, 1918	1,291	1

(continued)

All-time Ranking	Title	Opening Date	Number of Performances	Highest Ranking
16	Cactus Flower	December 8, 1965	1,234	
17	Sleuth	November 12, 1970	1,222	
17	Torch Song Trilogy	June 10, 1982	1,222	
19	Equus	October 24, 1974	1,209	
20	Amadeus	December 17, 1980	1,181	
21	Mister Roberts	February 18, 1948	1,157	10
22	The Seven Year Itch	November 20, 1952	1,141	
23	Butterflies Are Free	October 21, 1969	1,128	
24	Plaza Suite	February 14, 1968	1,097	
25	Teahouse of the August Moon	October 15, 1953	1,027	
26	Never Too Late	November 27, 1962	1,007	

The Season's Toll

The following people, who worked on Broadway or made an important contribution to the legitimate theatre, died between May 31, 1999, and May 28, 2000.

Patrick Bedford, 67; died November 20, 1999, of cancer, in Manhattan. Irish actor whose Broadway credits included Brian Friel's *Philadelphia, Here I Come!* and *The Mundy Scheme*, as well as playing the role of John Adams in the national company of *1776*.

John Berry, 82; died November 29, 1999, of pleurisy, in Paris. Blacklisted stage and screen director, whose New York credits included Athol Fugard's *The Blood Knot* and *Boesman and Lena*, Lorraine Hansberry's *Les Blancs*, and the tryout of the musical comedy *The Baker's Wife*.

Paul Bowles, 89; died November 18, 1999, of a heart attack, in Tangiers. Composer of incidental music for Lillian Hellman's *Watch on the Rhine* and Tennessee Williams's *The Glass Menagerie* and *Sweet Bird of Youth*. Author of the English-language Broadway translation of Jean-Paul Sartre's *No Exit*.

Robert Burr, 78; died May 13, 2000, of emphysema, in Los Angeles. Actor best known for Shakespearean roles at the New York Shakespeare Festival. He covered for the indisposed Richard Burton in the 1964 *Hamlet*, appeared in the musical *Bajour*, and replaced Christopher Plummer in *The Royal Hunt of the Sun*.

Allan Carr, 62; died June 29, 1999, of cancer, in Los Angeles. Producer of the Broadway musical *La Cage aux Folles* and the screen version of *Grease*.

Alexander H. Cohen, 79; died April 22, 2000, of respiratory failure, in Manhattan. Producer of approximately one hundred shows, including intimate revues like

Beyond the Fringe and *An Evening with Mike Nichols and Elaine May*; imports such as Harold Pinter's *The Homecoming*; and big-budget musical failures like *Baker Street, Dear World, Prettybelle, I Remember Mama*, and two separate productions of *Hellzapoppin'* (starring Soupy Sales and Jerry Lewis). *Waiting in the Wings*, his final production, closed five weeks after his death.

Quentin Crisp, 90; died November 21, 1999, in Manchester, England. Author of the autobiography *The Naked Civil Servant* and star of the one-man show *An Evening with Quentin Crisp*.

Marguerite Cullman, 94; died July 25, 1999, in Manhattan. Well-known investor in plays and musicals, including *Life with Father, South Pacific*, and *Death of a Salesman*. Author of *Occupation: Angel*, a book about her experiences as a Broadway backer.

Anthony Duquette, 85; died September 9, 1999, of a heart attack, in Los Angeles. Hollywood designer and interior decorator. He won a Tony Award for his costume designs (with Adrian) for *Camelot*.

William J. Eckart, 80; January 24, 2000, in Dallas. Broadway designer of sets and costumes for popular musicals (in collaboration with his late wife, Jean Eckart). Credits included *Damn Yankees, The Golden Apple, Li'l Abner, Mame*, and designer-coproducer of *Once upon a Mattress*.

Charles Elson, 90; on March 30, 2000, in Armonk, New York. Lighting designer, whose credits included the 1948 revival of *Private Lives* (with Tallulah Bankhead), Marc Blitzstein's *Regina, La Plume De Ma Tante*, and *Wildcat*.

Robert Emmett, 78; on April 8, 2000, after surgery for acute appendicitis, in Manhattan. Actor and writer. He appeared in *Midsummer* with Geraldine Page and *Madam, Will You Walk* with Hume Cronyn and Jessica Tandy. Husband of actress Kim Hunter (since 1951).

Rex Everhart, 79; died March 13, 2000, of lung cancer in Branford, Connecticut. Musical comedy character man. Credits included *Skyscraper, 1776, Working*, and the 1987 Lincoln Center Theater revival of *Anything Goes*.

George Forrest, 84; died October 10, 1999, after a stroke, in Miami, Florida. Co-composer-lyricist, with partner Robert Wright, of numerous Broadway operettas, including *Song of Norway, Kismet*, and (with Wright and Maury Yeston) *Grand Hotel: The Musical*.

Anne Francine, 82; died December 3, 1999, after a stroke, in New London, Connecticut. Cabaret singer and actress, whose Broadway credits included *By the*

Beautiful Sea, Mame, the 1983 Broadway revival of *Mame*, and the 1987 Lincoln Center Theater revival of *Anything Goes*.

Martin Fried, 62; died March 28, 2000, of an aneurysm, in Manhattan. Director and longtime associate of Lee Strasberg. Credits included the 1975 production of *Hughie* (with Ben Gazzara) and the 1978 revival of *Diary of Anne Frank* (with Eli Wallach and Anne Jackson).

Robert Fryer, 79; died May 28, 2000, of complications from Parkinson's disease, in Los Angeles. Stage and screen producer, best known for musicals like *Wonderful Town, Redhead, Sweet Charity, Mame, On the Twentieth Century*, and *Sweeney Todd*.

Sir John Gielgud, 96; died May 22, 2000, in London. Legendary British actor-director-producer, whose stage career lasted from 1921 through 1988. He made his mark on plays ranging from Shakespeare, Wilde, and Shaw to Coward, Albee, and Pinter. Influential critic James Agate called his Hamlet "the high water mark of English Shakespearean acting in our time"—and that was back in 1930. Screen work included Hitchcock's *Secret Agent*, the 1953 version of *Julius Caesar*, and as the butler in the 1981 comedy *Arthur*—which won him an Oscar and made him *really* famous.

Byron Goldman, 78; died March 28, 2000, of cancer, in Manhattan. Producer and early backer of David Merrick, he was associated with almost 150 shows. Credits included *Butterflies Are Free, Minnie's Boys, Jerome Robbins' Broadway*, and *Copenhagen*, which opened fourteen days after his death.

William Goodhart, 74; died October 20, 1999, of heart disease, on Shelter Island, New York. Author of the comedy *Generation*, which starred Henry Fonda.

Edward Gorey, 75; died April 15, 2000, of a heart attack, in Hyannis, Massachusetts. Macabre illustrator and writer. His theatre work included the sets and costumes for the 1977 revival of *Dracula* (starring Frank Langella). He also provided source material for the revues *Gorey Stories* and *Amphigorey*.

Ronny Graham, 79; died July 4, 1999, of liver disease, in Los Angeles. Writer-actor and nightclub performer, best known as comedian-writer of *New Faces of 1952*. He was costar of the musical *Annie 2* and lyricist of the Broadway musical *Bravo, Giovanni*.

Milton Greene, 87; died May 27, 2000, from complications of a stroke, in Los Angeles. Musical director and vocal arranger of *Fiddler on the Roof* and other Bock and Harnick musicals, including *The Body Beautiful* and *The Rothschilds*.

Margaret Harris, 95; died May 10, 2000, in London. British set and costume designer who worked extensively in London and New York under the name "Motley" (in partnership with her sister Audrey Harris and Elizabeth Montgomery). Broadway credits included costumes for *South Pacific*; both the Jean Arthur and Mary Martin versions of *Peter Pan*; and sets and costumes for *A Man for All Seasons*.

Dorothy Hart, 94; died April 11, 2000, in Ontario, California. Wife of comedian Teddy Hart and sister-in-law of lyricist Lorenz Hart. She oversaw the rights to the latter's work and coedited *The Complete Lyrics of Lorenz Hart*.

Doug Henning, 52; died February 7, 2000, of liver cancer, in Los Angeles. Magician and actor. He created magic for and starred in the musicals *The Magic Show* and *Merlin*.

Derek Anson Jones, 38; died January 17, 2000, of complications from AIDS, in Manhattan. Director of Margaret Edson's Pulitzer Prize–winning drama, *Wit*.

Madeline Kahn, 57; died December 3, 1999, of ovarian cancer, in Manhattan. Stage and screen comedienne, whose Broadway credits included *Two by Two*, *On the 20th Century*, the 1989 revival of *Born Yesterday*, and *The Sisters Rosensweig* (for which she won a Tony Award). Films included *Paper Moon*, *Blazing Saddles*, and *Young Frankenstein*.

Lila Kedrova, 82; died February 16, 2000, of heart failure, in Sault Sainte Marie, Ontario. Russian-born film actress won a Tony Award for her performance in the 1983 revival of *Zorbá*, a reprise of her Oscar-winning role in the film *Zorba the Greek*.

Mabel King, 66; died November 9, 1999, of complications from diabetes, in Woodland Hills, California. Comedienne. Her credits included the original Broadway company of *The Wiz* and the sitcom *What's Happening!*

Bethel Leslie, 70; died November 28, 1999, of cancer, in Manhattan. Actress best known for her Tony-nominated performance opposite Jack Lemmon in the 1986 revival of *Long Day's Journey into Night*.

Samuel Leve, 91; died December 6, 1999, in Manhattan. Set designer (and sometime lighting designer) for over forty shows, including Orson Welles's *Julius Caesar* for the Mercury Theatre and the comedy *The Fifth Season*.

Charles Lowe, 87; died September 2, 1999, in Beverly Hills. Television producer and estranged husband–manager of Carol Channing.

Helen Martin, 90; died March 25, 2000, in Monterey, California. Character comedienne who made her Broadway debut in 1941 in the Orson Welles production of *Native Son*. Credits included *Purlie Victorious* and the musicals *Purlie* and *Raisin*.

Victor Mature, 86; died August 4, 1999, of cancer, in Rancho Santa Fe, California. Virile movie star of epics such as *Samson and Delilah* and *Demetrius and the Gladiators*, who appeared on Broadway opposite Gertrude Lawrence in *Lady in the Dark*.

Michael McAloney, 72; died May 16, 2000, at the Actor's Fund Home in Englewood, New Jersey. Producer of *Borstal Boy*, the 1970 Tony Award–winning Best Play, and the musical tryout *Say Hello to Harvey*. Ex-husband of singer-actress Julie Wilson.

Morley Meredith, 77; died February 3, 2000, in Palm Beach Gardens, Florida. Singer who starred opposite Maureen O'Hara in *Christine* and played Joey in the pre-Broadway tryout of *The Most Happy Fella*, prior to a thirty-year career as a baritone at the Metropolitan Opera.

David Merrick, 88; died April 25, 2000, in London. Producer of approximately one hundred Broadway shows, including influential musicals (*Hello, Dolly!*, *Oliver!*, *Promises! Promises!*, and *42nd Street*); hit comedies (*Cactus Flower*, *Forty Carats*, and Woody Allen's *Don't Drink the Water* and *Play It Again, Sam*); influential European imports (*Look Back in Anger*, *A Taste of Honey*, *Marat/Sade*, and Tom Stoppard's *Rosencrantz and Guildenstern Are Dead* and *Travesties*); and legendary revivals (Peter Brook's *A Midsummer Night's Dream*).

Hobe Morrison, 95; died January 22, 2000, in Manhattan. Drama critic for *Variety* for four decades.

Anthony Newley, 67; died April 14, 2000, of cancer, in Jensen Beach, Florida. Songwriter-performer best known in America as star and coauthor of the musicals *Stop the World—I Want to Get Off* and *The Roar of the Greasepaint—The Smell of the Crowd*.

Alan North, 79; died January 19, 2000, of lung cancer, in Port Jefferson, New York. Actor, whose stage credits included *Plain and Fancy*, *Dylan*, *Spofford*, and *Lake Hollywood*.

Mike Ockrent, 53; died December 2, 1999, of leukemia, in Manhattan. British director of such musicals as *Me and My Girl*, *Crazy for You*, and the Madison Square Garden production of *A Christmas Carol*. Husband of director-choreographer Susan Stroman.

Dick Patterson, 70; died September 22, 1999, in Los Angeles. Comic actor. His Broadway credits included the musicals *Vintage '60*, *Smile*, and as Carol Burnett's love interest in *Fade Out—Fade In*.

Irra Petina, 93; died January 20, 2000, in Austin, Texas. Russian-born mezzo-soprano who created the role of the Old Lady in Leonard Bernstein's *Candide*, as well as starring in *Song of Norway* and other Wright and Forrest operettas.

Janet Reed, 83; February 28, 2000, of a stroke, in Seattle. Comedic ballerina who was featured in Jerome Robbins's *Look Ma, I'm Dancin'!* Created many roles for Robbins (and Balanchine) at American Ballet Theatre and City Ballet, including the original production of Robbins and Bernstein's *Fancy Free*.

Lee Richardson, 73; died October 2, 1999, of cardiac arrest, in Manhattan. Character actor whose credits included *Vivat! Vivat Regina!*, *Find Your Way Home*, and *A Texas Trilogy*.

Norman Rothstein, 63; died December 23, 1999, of cancer, in Manhattan. General manager and producer of more than one hundred Broadway and off-Broadway shows.

Charles Schulz, 77; February 12, 2000, of colon cancer, in Santa Rosa, California. Cartoonist created and wrote the comic strip *Peanuts*, which served as source material for the musicals *You're a Good Man, Charlie Brown* and *Snoopy!!!*

George C. Scott, 71; died September 23, 1999, in Westlake Village, California. Stage and screen actor. Broadway credits included *The Andersonville Trial*, *Plaza Suite*, *Sly Fox*, and the 1996 revival of *Inherit the Wind*. Film credits included *Dr. Strangelove*, *The Hospital*, and *Patton* (for which he won, but did not accept, an Oscar).

Arthur Seelen, 76; February 7, 2000, in Manhattan. Owner of Broadway's Drama Book Shop.

Richard B. Shull, 70; died October 14, 1999, of a heart attack, in Manhattan. Character comedian. His credits included *Minnie's Boys* and *Goodtime Charley*. At the time of his death he was appearing in this season's *Epic Proportions*.

Sylvia Sidney, 88; died July 1, 1999, of throat cancer, in Manhattan. Stage and screen actress. Her Broadway credits included Carl Reiner's *Enter Laughing* and Tennessee Williams's *Vieux Carre*. Film credits included *Street Scene*, *Dead End*, and Hitchcock's *Sabotage*.

Stanley Simmonds, 92; died December 19, 1999, in Manhattan. Musical comedy character man. His credits included *Li'l Abner, Fiorello!, Let It Ride,* and *Mack and Mabel.*

Stanley Simmons, 71; died September 4, 1999, of heart failure, in Los Angeles. Costume designer specializing in ballet and revivals of musicals. His Broadway credits included the original production of *Waiting for Godot* and *Lena Horne: The Lady and Her Music.*

Stanley Soble, 59; died July 6, 1999, in Los Angeles. Casting director for many regional theatres, including the New York Shakespeare Festival and the Center Theatre Group in Los Angeles.

Anna Sokolow, 90; died March 29, 2000, in Manhattan. Modern dance choreographer. Her Broadway credits included the original productions of Kurt Weill's *Street Scene,* Marc Blitzstein's *Regina,* and Leonard Bernstein's *Candide.*

Craig Stevens, 81; died May 10, 2000, of cancer, in Los Angeles. Actor best known for the TV series *Mr. Lucky.* He starred on Broadway in the 1963 musical *Here's Love* (based on *Miracle on 34th Street*) and appeared in stock opposite his wife, Alexis Smith, who died in 1993.

Maggie Task, 76; January 20, 2000, of cancer, in Manhattan. Musical comedy character actress. Her credits included *Coco, Sweeney Todd,* and *Annie.*

Samuel Taylor, 87; died May 26, 2000, in Blue Hill, Maine. Playwright and screenwriter, best known on Broadway for the comedies *The Happy Time* and *Sabrina Fair,* and the libretto for the Richard Rodgers musical *No Strings.* Screenplays included *Sabrina* and Alfred Hitchcock's *Vertigo.*

Carl Toms, 72; died August 4, 1999, of emphysema, in Hertfordshire, England. British set designer, whose Broadway credits included *Sleuth, Sherlock Holmes* (for which he won a Tony Award), *Travesties,* and *The Real Thing.*

Sasha Von Scherler, 65; on April 15, 2000, of lung disease, in Manhattan. Actress who appeared in dozens of off-Broadway plays from the 1950s to 1970s, including the 1959 production of O'Neill's *Great God Brown* and Joe Papp's 1969 Shakespeare in the Park production of *Twelfth Night.*

Frank Wagner, 77; died September 12, 1999, in Fort Myers, Florida. Choreographer and dance teacher. His Broadway credits included the *Ziegfeld Follies of 1957* (starring Beatrice Lillie) and Leonard Sillman's *New Faces of 1968* (which introduced Madeline Kahn and Robert Klein).

Randolph Walker, 71; died May 22, 2000, in a traffic accident, in Manhattan. Little-known character actor. His only Broadway appearance was as a replacement in the 1977 revival of *The King and I*. After he was struck by an illegally operated double-decker tour bus on a theatre district side street, Walker's death caused a front-page uproar.

Miles White, 85; February 17, 2000, in Manhattan. Two-time Tony Award–winning costume designer of such musicals as *Oklahoma!*, *Carousel*, *Gentlemen Prefer Blondes*, and *Bye, Bye Birdie*. He also designed for films and the circus.

Patricia Zipprodt, 75; died July 17, 1999, of cancer, in Manhattan. Three-time Tony Award–winning costume designer. Her credits included *Fiddler on the Roof*, *Cabaret*, *Pippin*, *Chicago*, and many other musicals.

Index

All people, titles, and organizations mentioned in the text have been indexed. For reference purposes, selected people who are billed on the theatre program title pages but not specifically discussed in the text have also been included.

Abbott, George, 28, 195–97, 281–85
ABC, Inc., 210, 276
Abie's Irish Rose, 319
Abraham, F. Murray, 115, 210
Adaptation-Next, 257
Adler, Jerry, 258
Adler, Richard, 155
Agnes of God, 9, 10
Ahrens, Lynn, 310
Aida, 188–94, 291, 296, 297, 298, , 300–3, 305
Ain't Misbehavin', 318
Albee, Edward, 211
Alice in Wonderland, 252–55
"All for You," 154, 156
Allegro, 281
Allen, Woody, 127
Allers, Roger, 311
Alves, Clyde, 264, 292
"Always True to You (In My Fashion)," 81, 83
Amadeus, 114–18, 291, 296, 298–99, 303, 320
Amanzi Singers, 178

The American Clock, 209
American Conservatory Theater, 140
An American in Paris (film), 105
Amy's View, 307
"And I Am Telling You I'm Not Going," 98
Anderson, Carl, 239
Anderson, Leroy, 284–85
Andersson, Bibi, 209
Andrews, Julie, 92
Angel Street, 10, 319
Angels in America, 52, 182
Annie, 318
Annie Get Your Gun, 24, 83, 307, 318
Anouilh, Jean, 310
Antigravity, Inc., 111
Antoon, Jason, 202, 207, 291, 302
Anything Goes, 25, 201–3
Appleton, William W., 168
The Archbishop's Ceiling, 209
Arias, Yancey, 229
Arkin, Alan, 256–58
Arkin, Matthew, 54, 56, 291
Armour, Steve, 111

"Army of the Just," 199

Arsenic and Old Lace, 319

Art, 307

Arthur, Beatrice, 259

"Artificial Flowers," 199

Artist Descending a Staircase, 220

Ashford, Rob, 196

Ashley, Christopher, 6

Ashley, Elizabeth, 9

Ashman, Howard, 307

Ashmanskas, Brooks, 42, 146

Aspects of Love, 237

Atkinson, Brooks, 282

Atkinson, Jayne, 64, 66–67, 292, 299

Augellin Belverde (fable), 251

Avian, Bob, 88, 298, 309

Ayers, Lemuel, 151–52

Azenberg, Emanuel, 313

Babes in Arms, 281

Baby, 287

Bacall, Lauren, 120, 123, 299

Baker, David Aaron, 64, 282

Ball, Lucille, 64

Ballard, Kaye, 252, 283

"Ballet at the Village Vortex," 287

Ballet Ballads, 204

Ballroom, 207

Bankhead, Tallulah, 262, 263

Barbour, James, 314

Bardill, Mandisa, 15

Barefoot in the Park, 260, 319

Barnes, Clive, 142

Barre, Gabriel, 228, 232

Barrett, Brent, 146, 149, 292

Barrowman, John, 88, 92

Barry, Julian, 239

Bart, Lionel, 145

Bart, Roger, 146, 148–49, 292, 312

Bartlett, Peter, 6

Baruch, Steven, 110

Bates, Alan, 247

Batt, Bryan, 36

Battle, Hinton, 309

Beatty, John Lee, 146, 196, 253, 282

Beaumont, Ralph, 252

Beauty and the Beast, 191–92, 250, 307, 318

The Beauty Queen of Leenane, 14

Becket, 170

Bedford, Patrick, 321

The Bee Gees, 36

Behrman, Sam, 44

Benanti, Laura, 109–13, 282, 287, 293, 302

Benedict, Paul, 264

Benefactors, 215–16

Bennett, Michael, 207, 208

Bent, 223

Bentley, Carol, 113

Berlin, Irving, 44, 48, 307

Berlind, Roger, 42, 82, 210, 315

Bermel, Albert, 250, 251

Bernstein, Leonard, 43, 97–98, 282–86

Berrese, Michael, 80–82, 301–2

Berry, John, 321

Berry, Sarah Uriarte, 196

The Best Little Whorehouse in Texas, 318

Best Plays (book), xi

Besterman, Doug, 303–4, 309

Bevel, Charles, 309

Bierko, Craig, 264, 266, 292, 300

Big River, 319

Billington, Ken, 120, 308

"Bill's Bounce," 111

Birch, Patricia, 314

"Bird Inside the House," 97

The Birdcage (film), 257

Birdy, 313

Bishop, André, 58, 95, 96, 98, 202, 203, 207, 224, 278

Bitter Sweet, 49

Bjornson, Maria, 311

Black and Blue, 75

Blakemore, Michael, 80, 82, 85, 209, 216, 217, 291, 292, 297, 298, 306

"Blame It on a Summer Night," 111

"Bli-Blip," 109–10

Blithe Spirit, 119, 121

Blitzstein, Marc, 97–98

Bloomgarden, Kermit, 263

Blown Sideways Through Life, 275

"Blues in the Night," 111, 113

Bobbie, Walter, 195, 196, 308–9

Bock, Jerry, 195–97, 199

Bogardus, Stephen, 137–38, 291

Bohmer, Ron, 18, 22

Bohr, Niels, 216–18

Bolger, David, 314

Booth, Shirley, 120, 198–99, 283

Born Yesterday, 319

Bosco, Philip, 216, 219–20, 291

Boublil, Alain, 309, 314

"Bounce Me Brother (With a Solid Four)," 108

"A Bowler Hat," 45

Bowles, Paul, 321

The Boy Friend, 254

Boy Meets Girl, 28

"The Boy Next Door," 104

Boyd, Gregory, 308

The Boys from Syracuse, 281

The Boys of Winter, 9

Bradley, Everett, 109, 110, 112, 113, 293

Brantley, Ben, 17, 123, 160–61, 174, 205, 275

Bricusse, Leslie, 309

Bridge, Andrew, 303, 309, 311

Brigadoon, 144, 145

Brighton Beach Memoirs, 260, 319

Bring in 'Da noise, Bring in 'Da Funk, 319

Broadway Alliance, 181–82

Broderick, Matthew, 256–58, 299

Brohn, William David, 310

Brokaw, Mark, 196

Broken Glass, 68, 209–10, 213

Brolin, Josh, 174

Brown, Anne Wiggins, 166, 168

Brown, Blair, 134, 136, 137, 216, 220, 291, 300, 301

Brown, Jason Robert, 231

"Brush Up Your Shakespeare," 83

Buckley, Betty, 308

Buckley, Candy, 42

Buntrock, Stephen R., 314

Buried Child, 169

Burke, Marylouise, 306

Burnett, Carol, 28, 88, 90–92, 301

Burns, Andrea, 48, 152, 156, 292

Burns, David, 69–71

Burns, Ralph, 309

Burr, Robert, 321

Burrows, Abe, 193

Burton, Kate, 253

Burton, Richard, 120

Bury, John, 115

Bussert, Meg, 265–66

Butterflies Are Free, 320

Byers, Ralph, 264

Byrne, Gabriel, 182, 185, 292, 298–99

Cabaret, 231, 235–36, 308, 318

Cabin in the Sky, 103

Cablevision Systems Corp., 17

Cactus Flower, 319

Caird, John, 309, 314

Caldwell, Zoe, 209

Call Me Madam, 281

Callaway, Ann Hampton, 108, 109–10, 111, 112, 293, 302

Camelot, 144, 145

Cameron, J. Smith, 182

Campbell, David, 152, 156, 292

Cannon, Alice, 137

Cantor, Arthur, 314

The Capeman, 25–26, 189

Carmello, Carolee, 18

Carmichael, Hoagy, 110

Caron, Leslie, 105

Carpinello, James, 36, 38

Carr, Allan, 321

Carrafa, John, 196, 276

Carroll, Helena, 120, 124

Carter, Caitlin, 110–11, 113, 293

Carter, Glenn, 238

Casale, Glenn, 310

Casella, Max, 264, 302

Castree, Paul, 39–40

Cats, 92, 237, 308, 317

Caylor, Rose, 271

Center Theatre Group, 116

Chamberlain, Richard, 120–21

Chamberlin, Kevin, 42, 276–77, 291, 301

Champion, Gower, 145

Channing, Carol, 282–83

Charlap, Mark (Moose), 310

Charnin, Martin, 261

Chase, David, 84, 267, 292

Chekhov, Anton, 270–271, 272

Chenoweth, Kristen, 23–25, 146, 148, 149, 231, 292, 299, 312

Chicago, 231, 235–36, 281, 308, 318

Chodorov, Jerome, 282–85

A Chorus Line, 317

Christiansen, Richard, 193

Christie, Julie, 271

"Christopher Street," 285

Cilento, Wayne, 190, 192, 298

"Cincinnati," 98

Circle in the Square, 173

City Center Encores!, 47, 146, 195, 197, 199, 281, 282, 283, 286, 304

City Opera Company, 162

Ciulla, A. C., 308–9

The Civil War, 26, 308

Clark, Dwayne, 164, 166, 292

Close, Glenn, 215–16, 245, 247

Closer, 308

Clurman, Harold, 271

Coco, James, 257

Coe, Fred, 259

Coen, David, 24, 26

Cohen, Alexander H., 120, 121, 125, 315, 321–22

Cole, Jack, 252

Coleman, Cy, 314

Collected Stories, 53

Collette, Toni, 229, 234, 293, 300–301

Collins, Joan, 120

Collins, Pat, 182, 185

Colombo, Patti, 310

Colt, Alvin, 120

Comden, Betty, 282–85, 310

"Come Back to Me," 105, 147

Company, 90

Connell, Jane, 49

Connell, Gordon, 49

Conolly, Patricia, 120, 124

Conroy, Frances, 210–11, 213, 292, 301

Contact, 53, 95, 160, **201–8**, 291, 295, 296–97, 298, 301–2, 302, 303, 305, 306

"Conversation Piece," 285

Conway, Kevin, 196

Cook, Barbara, 266

Cooper, Max, 120, 182

Copenhagen, 52, **215–21**, 276, 291, 295, 297, 301, 304–06

Coriolanus, 219

Corman, Avery, 314

Cosette, Pierre, 17

Coughlin, Bruce, 229, 293

"Could I Leave You?," 90

"Country House," 91

Courtenay, Tom, 271

Coward, Noël, 47–51, 119–122

Crane, David, 23, 24, 26–27

Crawford, Michael, 311

Crazy for You, 318

Creation of the World, 209

Crisp, Quentin, 322

Crivello, Anthony, 98–99, 300

Croft, Paddy, 134

Cronyn, Hume, 119

Crouse, Russel, 311

Crowley, Bob, 88, 189–90, 192, 291, 302–3

"Cry Me a River," 111

Cuillo, Bob, 24

Cullen, Sean, 137

Cullman, Marguerite, 322

Cullum, John, 149, 209, 210

Cumming, Alan, 247, 308

Cummings, Anthony, 120

Cumpsty, Michael, 216, 220, 291

Cunningham, John, 219

Curran, Seán, 174

Daldry, Stephen, 311

Dame Edna: The Royal Tour, 29–34, 131, 291, 304, 305

Damn Yankees, 319

"Dancers in Love," 113

Dancin', 318

"Dancing in the Dark," 104

Daniele, Graciela, 94, 95, 96, 298, 307, 310

Daniels, Salie "Kat," 14–15

Daniels, William, 149

D'Arcy James, Brian, 228, 232, 293

Davey, Shaun, 134, 135, 297

Davidson, Gordon, 88

Davidson, Jeremy, 24

Davies, Brian, 134, 136

Davies, Howard, 311

Davis, Daniel, 140, 141, 293, 301

Davis, Kishna, 164, 165–66

Davis, Sammy, Jr., 16

Dawson, Mark, 259

Daykin, Judith E., 146, 196, 282

Days, Maya, 238

The Days of Wine and Roses (teleplay), 63

The Dead, 132–38, 208, 291, 295–97, 300–2, 304, 306

The Dead (film), 133

"The Dead" (short story), 133

Death Defying Acts, 258

Death of a Salesman, 68, 72, 169, 308

Deathtrap, 10, 319

Del Corso, Geralyn, 113

DeLuca, John, 102

DeMain, John, 164, 165

Dempsey, Jackie, 158, 159

DeMunn, Jeffrey, 70, 72

Dench, Judi, 307

Dendy, Mark, 228, 231–32, 293

Dennehy, Brian, 61, 308

Derricks, Marguerite, 313

Design for Living, 119

Dewhurst, Colleen, 184, 186–87, 299

Diamond, Tom, 158

The Diary of Anne Frank, 278

"Did You Move?," 205, 207–9

Dietrich, Marlene, 50

Dietz, Howard, 104

Diggs, Taye, 228, 232, 293

Dillane, Stephen, 244, 247, 292, 298, 300, 305

Dilly, Erin, 314

Dinner with Friends, 52–56, 291, 308

Dirty Blonde, 52, 275–80, 291, 295, 297, 299–300, 301

"Disco Duck," 39

Dishy, Bob, 70, 72, 209, 292, 299

Disney Corporation, 188–94, 250–51

Do-Re-Mi, 281

Dodger Theatricals, 140, 264, 315

Doherty, Moya, 176, 179–80

A Doll's House, 271

Donmar Warehouse, 171, 244–45

Don't Bother Me, I Can't Cope, 319

Dotrice, Roy, 182, 301, 306

Douglas, Kirk, 221

Drake, Alfred, 81

Dreamgirls, 13, 318

Drescher, Fran, 315

Driving Miss Daisy, 52

Dudley, Richard, 115–16, 291

Dudley, William, 116, 303

Dukakis, Olympia, 223, 224, 225, 299

Dukes, David, 116–17

Duncan, Todd, 166, 168

Duquette, Anthony, 322

Durand, Beverly, 113

Eagan, Daisy, 134, 136

Ebb, Fred, 102, 105, 106, 308

Eckart, William J., 322

Edelstein, Gordon, 314

Edwards, Ben, 186

Edwards, Gale, 238, 241–42

Ehle, Jennifer, 244–45, 247, 292, 299–300

Eisenhauer, Peggy, 96, 97, 229, 292, 303

Elaborate Lives: the Story of Aida, 191–92

Electra, 271

Elizondo, Hector, 71

Elliman, Yvonne, 240

Ellington, Duke, 108, 109, 111, 113

Elliott, Shawn, 96, 292

Ellis, Scott, 64, 65, 210, 297

Ellison, Todd, 229, 293

Elson, Charles, 322

Emery, Lisa, 54

Emery, Ted, 250, 251

Emmett, Robert, 322

Enigma Variations, 313

Epic Proportions, 23–28, 53, 256, 267, 297, 299

Epstein, Julius J., 151–52

Epstein, Philip G., 151–52

Equus, 118, 217–18, 320

Esbjornson, David, 210, 213, 292

Evans, David, 96

Evans, Maurice, 198–99

Everhart, Rex, 219, 259, 322

"Every Day a Little Death," 91

"Everybody Ought to Have a Maid," 90

"Everything's Alright," 237–38, 239

Evita, 40, 318

"Exhibit A," 154–55

Experimental Theater, 204

Eyre, Richard, 307

Face Value, 25

Fagan, Garth, 311

Falk, Peter, 210

Falls, Robert, 190–93, 297, 298, 308

Farrell, Matthew, 24

Fascinating Rhythm, 39

Fenholt, Jeff, 240

Fenn, Jean, 50

Fiddler on the Roof, 259, 285, 317

Fields, Dorothy, 284, 307

Fields, Herbert, 284, 307

Fields, Joseph, 282–85

Finian's Rainbow, 313–14

Finn, William, 23, 278

Fiorello!, 195

Fisher, Jules, 96, 97, 229, 303

Fisher, Rob, 48, 146, 149, 152, 196, 282, 286, 292, 293

Fitzgerald, Christopher, 42, 152, 154–56, 292

Five Guys Named Moe, 237

Flaherty, Stephen, 310

Flanders, Ed, 301
Flatley, Michael, 180
Follies, 89–90, 94, 95
Footloose, 37, 39, 40, 109, **308–9**
Forrest, George, 322
Forrest Hump, 9
Forstmann, Ted, 18
42nd Street, 317
Fosse, 109, **309**
Fosse, Bob, 142, 145, 153, 239, 309
Fox, Robert, 224
Foy, Eddie, 252
Fragonard, Jean-Honoré, 204
Francine, Anne, 322–23
Francois, Ryan, 113
Frankel, Richard, 12, 110
Franz, Elizabeth, 308
Fraser, Alison, 49
Frayn, Michael, 215–217, 218, 219,
    271, 291, 295, 304, 305
Freeman, Jonathan, 49
Fried, Martin, 323
Friedman, Peter, 146, 149
Friel, Brian, 271
Friends (TV show), 23
"From This Moment On," 85
Front Porch in Flatbush, 151
Fry, Christopher, 310
Fryer, Robert, 323
Fuddy Meers, 306
Fuller, Lorenzo, 86
Funny Girl, 318
A *Funny Thing Happened on the Way
    to the Forum*, 25, 27, 153

Gaines, Boyd, 202, 206, 291, 301–2
Gaithers, Lita, 309
Galati, Frank, 310
Gallo, David, 24, 228, 293, 306
Garber, Victor, 42, 315
Garland, Judy, 106
Garnett, Constance, 270–71

Gary, Harold, 71
"Gary, Indiana," 266
Gastineau, Mark, 39
Gaver, Jack, xi
Gelbart, Larry, 72
Gemignani, Paul, 82, 84, 292
Gemini, 319
Gems, Pam, 173, 271
Gershwin, George, 97–98, 162, 163,
    168, 196
Gershwin, Ira 101, 196, 162–64
Gersten, Bernard, 58, 95, 96, 98, 202,
    207, 208, 224
Gesner, Clark, 312
"Getting Married Today," 90
Gibson, Michael, 228, 293
Gielgud, Sir John, 323
Gifford, Kathie Lee, 88, 92
Gigi (film), 37
Gilbert, Willie, 193
"The Girl in the Yellow Dress," 203,
    205, 206–7, 208–9
The Girl Who Came to Supper, 49
Gish, Lillian, 271
Giuliani, Rudolph, 127–29, 131
Glyndebourne Festival, 168
"The Gods Love Nubia," 189
The Golden Apple, 204
Golden Child, 278
Goldenthal, Elliot, 250, 251
Goldman, Byron, 216, 323
Goldman, James, 196, 311
Goldman, Sherwin, 163
Goldman, William, xi, 196, 200
"Good Clean Fun," 199
"Good Looking Woman," 98
"Good Thing Going," 91
Goodhart, William, 323
Goodman Theatre, 182
"Goodnight, My Someone," 265
Gordon, Ricky Ian, 231
Gordon, Ruth, 271

Gorey, Edward, 323
Got Tu Go Disco, 39
Gotham City Gates, 111, 113
Gottfried, Martin, 142
Gozzi, Count Carlo, 250, 251
Graham, Ronny, 323
Grand Hotel, 319
Gravitte, Debbie, 196, 199, 293
Gray, Spalding, 57–62, 292
Gray's Anatomy, 57
Grease, 39, 317, 318
The Great Dictator (film), 262
Green, Adolph, 282–85, 310
Green, Martyn, 252
The Green Bird, **249–55**, 267, 291, 297, 301, 303
Greenwood, Jane, 18, 174, 182
Greene, Herbert, 263
Greene, Milton, 323
Greif, Michael, 310
Grenier, Zach, 6
Griffith, Robert E., 195
Grizzard, George, 209
Grossbard, Ulu, 71
Gruber, Michael, 110
Grupper, Adam, 229, 235
Guare, John, 25, 83
Guettel, Adam, 148, 231
Gutierrez, Gerald, 48, 186, 310
Guys and Dolls, 25, 193, 318

Hague, Albert, 155–56
Haimes, Todd, 64, 272
Hair, 239, 318
Hall, Michael, 42, 46, 293
Hall, Peter, 116, 117
Hambleton, T. Edward, 304
Hammerstein, Oscar, 2nd, 37, 144, 152, 311, 314
Hampton, Christopher, 307
Hans Christian Andersen (film), 37
The Happy Time, 64

Harburg, E. Y., 313
Hare, David, 225, 273, 307, 311
"Harlem Nocturne," 110
Harnick, Sheldon, 195–97, 200, 259
Harrelson, Woody, 64–66, 299
Harris, Barbara, 148
Harris, Dede, 264
Harris, Jed, 183–84, 271
Harris, Julie, 314
Harris, Margaret, 324
Harris, Rosemary, 120–21, 123, 244, 293, 299–300
Hart, Charles, 311
Hart, Dorothy, 324
Hart, Moss, 28, 145, 283
Harvey, 319
Havoc, June, 252
Hawley, Martha, 267
Hay Fever, 120
Headley, Heather, 189, 190, 192, 194, 291, 300–301, 305
Hearn, George, 88, 92, 300
The Heartbreak Kid (film), 257
Heckart, Eileen, 304, 305
Hector, Terry, 12, 14–15
The Heidi Chronicles, 52, 56
The Heiress, 183
Heisenberg, Werner, 216–18
Hello, Dolly!, 318
Hellzapoppin', 318
Henning, Doug, 324
Henritze, Betty, 120, 124
Henshall, Ruthie, 88, 90–92, 292, 302
Hepburn, Katharine, 63–64
Heredia, Wilson Jermaine, 310
Here's Love, 262
Herscher, Sylvia, 304
Hersey, David, 308
Hess, Rodger, 313
Heyward, DuBose, 162, 164
Hibbert, Edward, 250, 254, 291
Hickok, John, 190

High Society (film), 37

Hilferty, Susan, 276, 279

Hill, Annabelle, 86

Hiller, Wendy, 184

Hingle, Pat, 70

Hingston, Seán Martin, 202

Hirson, David, 139, 140, 141–143, 293

Hirson, Roger O., 143

"Hit Me with a Hot Note and Watch Me Bounce," 109

Hobson, Richard, 164, 166

Hoffman, Constance, 303

Hoffman, Philip Seymour, 170, 174, 293, 298–99

Holder, Donald, 311

Holgate, Ron, 82, 85

Holiday, Jennifer, 189

Holliday, Judy, 50

Holm, Hanya, 204

Hoover, Richard, 310

Horchow, Roger, 82

Horwitt, Arnold, 284–85

Hould-Ward, Ann, 192, 307

The House of Blue Leaves, 25

House Un-American Activities Committee, 73–74

Houston, Eric, 315

Houston Grand Opera, 163

How I Learned to Drive, 52

How to Succeed in Business . . . , 193, 318

Howes, Sally Ann, 134, 136, 137, 291

Hudson, Richard, 311

Hughes, Barnard, 120, 124, 271

Hunchback of Notre Dame, 191

"A Hundred Easy Ways," 281–82

"Hurry! It's Lovely Up Here!," 147, 148

Hurt, Mary Beth, 215–16

Hwang, David Henry, 25, 190, 193, 297

Hynes, Garry, 311

Hyperion Theatricals, 188, 190, 193

Hytner, Nicholas, 273, 309

"I Don't Know How to Love Him," 239

"I Got Plenty o' Nuttin'," 163

"I Got Rhythm," 105

"I Guess I'll Have to Change My Plan," 104

"I Hate Men," 81

I Picked a Daisy, 145

"I Thank You," 106

"I Will Love You," 98

Ibsen, Henrik, 270, 271

The Iceman Cometh, 72, 311

"If I Can't Have You," 39

"If I Had You," 103

"I'll Be Seeing You," 113

"I'll See You Again," 49

"I'm Glad I'm Not Young Anymore," 105

In the Blood, 53, 304

"In the Movies," 154

The Inlaws (film), 257

Into the Woods, 278

"Iowa Stubborn," 263–64

Irma La Douce, 200

Irons, Jeremy, 245, 247, 299

Ishtar (film), 257

"It Ain't Necessarily So," 163

It Ain't Nothing but the Blues, 309

"It Don't Mean a Thing (If It Ain't Got That Swing)," 108

Itallie, Jean-Claude van, 271

It's a Slippery Slope, 57, 58

"It's Beginning to Look a Lot Like Christmas," 262

It's Good to Be Alive, 314

"It's Love," 286, 287–88

"It's My Neighborhood," 39

"I've Come to Wive It Wealthily in Padua," 81
Ives, David, 146, 282
Ivey, Dana, 120, 124
Ivey, Judith, 6, 9, 119–20

Jackie Mason: Much Ado about Everything, 126–31
Jackness, Andrew, 18
Jacobi, Derek, 271–73, 299
James, Toni-Leslie, 303
James Joyce's The Dead, 132–38, 208, 291, 295–97, 300–02, 304, 306
Jane Eyre, 314
"Jasbo Brown," 166
Jbara, Gregory, 282
Jeffrey, 254
Jekyll & Hyde, 309, 318
Jelly's Last Jam, 234
Jenkins, Daniel, 140
Jesus Christ Superstar, 40, 237–42, 296, 302
Jitney, 304, 306
John, Elton, 190–92, 297, 311
Johnston, Alva, 44
Jones, Cherry, 181–187, 291, 299–300
Jones, Derek Anson, 324
Jones, Richard, 140, 141
Jones, Robert Edmond, 186
Jones, Simon, 120, 124
Jones, Tom, 66
Jourdan, Louis, 149
Joyce, James, 132–38
Juan Darién: A Carnival Mass, 249–50
Judgment at Nuremberg (teleplay), 63
Jujamcyn Theaters, 110, 182

Kaczorowski, Peter, 64, 82, 202, 264, 282, 303, 306
Kahn, Madeline, 324

Kander, John, 106, 284, 308
"Kansas Morning," 239
Kardana-Swinsky Productions, 12, 264
Kastner, Ron, 170, 244
Kat and the Kings, 11–16
Katsaros, Doug, 273
Katz, Cindy, 116
Katz, Natasha, 18, 190–92, 291, 303
Kaufman, George S., 28, 44, 196, 283
Kaye, Judy, 311
Kedrova, Lila, 324
Kelly, David Patrick, 272, 273
Kelly, Gene, 105
Kendall, Felicity, 245
Kennedy, Arthur, 69
Kennedy, Brian, 176
John F. Kennedy Center for the Performing Arts, 43–44, 140, 264, 315
The Kentucky Cycle, 52, 53
Kern, Jerome, 37
Kerr, Walter, 142
Kidd, Michael, 265
Kilgarriff, Patricia, 137
Kilner, Kevin, 54
King, Alan, 314
King, Mabel, 324
The King and I, 135, 153, 318
King Hedley II, 53, 304
Kiss Me, Kate, 80–86, 151, 204, 217, 287, 292, 296, 298, 300–306, 319
Kitt, Eartha, 229, 234–35, 293, 302
Kladitis, Manny, 36
Knight, Kevin, 313
Knighton, Nan, 18, 36
Koch, Howard, 152
Korey, Alix, 228, 232–33, 235, 293
Korsch, Conrad, 110
Kostal, Irwin, 195, 199
Koteas, Elias, 174
Kramer, David, 12

Kramer, Terry Allen, 238
Krane, David, 292
Kravis Center (Palm Beach), 59
Kretzmer, Herbert, 309
Krohn, Fred, 128
Kudisch, Marc, 18, 229, 235

La Bête, 139, 143, 220
La Cage Aux Folles, 318
LaChiusa, Michael John, 94–100,
    229–31 233–36, 293, 296–97
Lacey, Franklin, 264
"The Ladies Who Lunch," 90
Lancaster, Burt, 63–64, 65
Lander, David, 279
Lane, Burton, 145–47, 149, 313
Lane, Nathan, 27, 42, 46, 293, 315
Lane, Stewart F., 102
Langella, Frank, 116–17, 120–21
Langham, Michael, 120
Lannan, Nina, 250
Lanning, Jerry, 49, 51
Lapine, James, 276, 278–79, 291, 297
Larsen, Ray, 216
Larson, Jonathan, 310
The Last Yankee, 210, 213
"Later Than Spring," 51
Latouche, John, 204
Laughter on the 23rd Floor, 25
Lawrence, Gertrude, 119
Le Gallienne, Eva, 254
Le Loka, Tsidii, 176, 178, 292
Learned, Michael, 210
Lee, Eugene, 182, 186
The Legendary Mizners (biography),
    44
Leiber, Jerry, 310
Leigh, Carolyn, 310
Leight, Warren, 310
Lend Me a Tenor, 219
Lenny, 239
Lenox, Adriane, 82, 86

Lerner, Alan Jay, 37, 144–48
Les Misérables, 237, 309, 317
Leslie, Bethel, 324
Leve, Harriet Newman, 12
Leve, Samuel, 324
Leveaux, David, 244, 245, 292, 297
Levering, Kate, 264
Levy, Lorie Cowen, 110, 264
Levy, Steven M., 30, 120
Lewis, Norm, 229
Lichtefeld, Michael, 311
Life with Father, 319
Lightnin', 319
"Limehouse Blues," 104
Lincoln Center Theater, 95–97, 202,
    203, 223, 224, 249
Lindsay, Howard, 311
Lindsay, Nigel, 244
Linney, Laura, 272, 273
The Lion in Winter, 311
The Lion King, 24, 191, 250–51, 311,
    319
Lippa, Andrew, 228, 230–33, 236,
    293, 305, 312
"A Little Bit in Love," 286
The Little Foxes, 262
Little Me, 267
Lloyd Webber, Andrew, 40, 237–241,
    308, 311
LM Concerts, 102, 107
Loesser, Frank, 25, 263, 284
Loewe, Frederick, 37, 144
The Lonesome West, 311
Long, William Ivey, 24, 109–10, 202,
    264, 267, 282, 292, 293, 303
Longbottom, Robert, 17–18, 21–22
Lord of the Dance, 180
Lost in Yonkers, 52
Louisiana Purchase, 48
"Love," 103
"Lovely," 90
Love's Old Sweet Song, 260

Lowe, Charles, 324
Luftig, Hal, 258
Luker, Rebecca, 264, 266, 292, 300–301
LuPone, Robert, 170
Lynch, Thomas, 202, 264, 302–3
Lynne, Gillian, 308, 311

MacGill, Casey, 108–10, 113, 293
Mackay, Lizbeth, 70, 72
Mackie, Bob, 102
Mackintosh, Cameron, 88, 91, 92, 237, 314
"Madame Guillotine," 19
"Mad Dogs and Englishmen," 49
The Magic Show, 318
Maguire, Michael, 309
The Male Animal, 261
Maltby, Richard, Jr., 309
Mame, 318
Mamet, David, 271
Mamoulian, Rouben, 165
Man of La Mancha, 63, 97, 98, 135, 318
Manhattan Theatre Club, 56, 92, 230
Mann, Terrence, 19
Mantle, Burns, xi, 283
Marber, Patrick, 308
March, Joseph Moncure, 137, 228–29
March of the Falsettos, 278
Margulies, Donald, 53–56, 291, 304
"Marian the Librarian," 266
Marie Christine, 94–100, 201, 292, 296–98, 300–4
Mark Taper Forum, 88
Marshall, Kathleen, 80, 82, 146, 152, 156, 195, 196, 282, 286–87, 293, 298
Marshall, Rob, 308
Martin, Eileen, 176, 178
Martin, Elliot, 182

Martin, Helen, 325
Martin, Hugh, 103, 104
Martin, Nicholas, 254–55
Martin Guerre, 237, 314
Marty (teleplay), 63
Mary, Mary, 319
Mason, Jackie, 126–31
Masteroff, Joe, 308
Masterson, Mary Stuart, 254
Mathis, Stanley Wayne, 82, 86
A Matter of Position, 258–60
Mature, Victor, 325
Maxwell, Mitchell, 54
Maxwell, Victoria, 54
May, Elaine, 256–59
"May the Good Lord Bless and Keep You," 262
Mayer, Michael, 272, 297, 310, 311, 312
Mazzie, Marin, 80–83 85–86, 292, 300–01
McAloney, Michael, 325
McArdle, Andrea, 189
McCallum, David, 117
McCann, Elizabeth Ireland, 216
McColgan, John, 176
McCollum, Kevin, 233
McDonagh, Martin, 14, 311
McDonald, Audra, 95, 96, 98–99, 292, 300–301
McDonald, Kirk, 18, 152, 156
McGavin, Darren, 65
McGlinn, John, 48
McGrath, Kathryn, 264
McKellan, Ian, 115, 116, 117, 299
McKenney, Eileen, 283–84
McKenney, Ruth, 283
McKenzie, Julia, 92
McKneely, Joey, 229, 310
McMartin, John, 259
McNally, Terrence, 257, 310
McPherson, Conor, 13–14, 311

Me and My Girl, 318

Mecchia, Irene, 311

Meckler, Nancy, 224

Medea, 95, 99

Meet Me in St. Louis (film), 37

"Melinda," 147

Mendes, Sam, 42, 44, 46, 308, 315

Menken, Alan, 307

Menzel, Idina, 228, 232

Meredith, Morley, 325

Merman, Ethel, 50

Merrick, David, 44, 188, 325

Merrily We Roll Along, 43, 94

Metropolitan Opera, 163

Meyer, Stanley A., 192

"Mi Noche Triste," 77

Michels, Stephanie, 202

Millenium Approaches, 52

Miller, Arthur, 68–74, 169, 209–11, 213–214, 271, 292, 295, 308

Mills, Hayley, 119–20

Minnelli, Liza, 101, 102–3, 105, 300

Minnelli, Vincente, 101–102, 103, 106

Minnelli on Minnelli, 101–7, 300

The Miracle Worker (teleplay), 63

Miramax Films, 244, 247

Mishkin, Chase, 30, 120, 182, 264, 276

Miss Saigon, 237, 309, 317

Mr. Peters' Connections, 210

Mister Roberts, 320

Mitchell, Brian Stokes, 80–82, 85, 86, 292, 300, 305

Mitchell, Jerry, 312

Mitchell, Lauren, 140

Mizner, Addison, 44, 46, 315

Mizner, Wilson, 44, 315

Molaskey, Jessica, 42

Monster in a Box, 57, 58

"Montana Chem," 154

A Moon for the Misbegotten, 56, 181–87, 292, 296, 298–99, 299–300, 301, 306

Moon over Buffalo, 219

Moore, Crista, 120, 124

Mordecai, Ben, 313

More to Love, 261

Moriber, Brooke Sunny, 134, 229

Morning, Noon, and Night, 57–62, 292

Moross, Jerome, 204

Morris, Anita, 111

Morrison, Conall, 314

Morrison, Hobe, 325

Moscow Folk Ballet, 178

Mosher, Gregory, 134, 137, 173

The Most Happy Fella, 263

Muenz, Richard, 282, 287–88

Mulheren, Michael, 80–83, 85, 292, 301–02

Mummenschanz, 319

Murder at the Howard Johnson's, 260

Murney, Julia, 228, 232, 293

Murphy, Donna, 281–83, 287, 293

Murphy, Jack, 308

Murphy, Rosemary, 120, 124, 293

Murray, Brian, 272, 273, 313

Musante, Tony, 209

The Music Man, 262–69, 292, 296, 298, 300–04, 318

"My Darlin' Eileen," 287

My Fair Lady, 144, 145, 318

"My Gentle Young Johnny," 199

"My Husband, the Pig," 90

"My Miss Mary," 199

"My New Philosophy," 231

My Sister Eileen, 283, 284

Myler, Randal, 309

Nadel, Norman, 47

Napier, John, 308

Nash, N. Richard, 63–65

Nathan, George Jean, xi–xii

Naughton, James, 70, 297, 308
"Naughty Girls," 132
Nederlander Organization, 20, 238
Nederlander, James M., 216
Nederlander, Scott, 102, 216
Neeson, Liam, 177
Nelson, Kenneth, 252
Nelson, Richard, 134, 135, 296–97
Neuwirth, Bebe, 308
Never Too Late, 320
A New Brain, 23, 95, 278
A New Leaf (film), 257
Newley, Anthony, 325
New York City Opera, 65, 163
New York Drama Critics Circle
    Awards, 304–5
New York Shakespeare Festival,
    209–11, 229, 230
New York Times, 14, 17, 123, 142,
    160–61, 174, 205, 225, 275, 282,
    299
Nichols, Mike, 245, 247, 257,
    259–60, 271
Night Must Fall, 309
"Night on Bald Mountain," 40
Nine, 111
Nixon, Marni, 134, 136, 137
Noël Coward in Two Keys, 119–20
Noises Off, 215–16, 245
North, Alan, 325
Not About Nightingales, 310
Nugent, Elliott, 261
Nunn, Trevor, 308, 309, 310, 314

O'Brien, Jack, 165
"An Occurrence at Owl Creek
    Bridge" (short story), 203
Ockrent, Mike, 325
The Office, 258
"Oh, There's Somebody Knockin' at
    the Door," 167
Oh! Calcutta!!, 317

O'Hara, Jill, 252
O'Hare, Denis, 313
O'Hearn, Steve, 158
O'Horgan, Tom, 237–38, 239
Oklahoma!, 203, 314, 318
"An Old-Fashioned Love Story,"
    232–33
Olivier, Laurence, 119, 141, 170
On a Clear Day You Can See Forever,
    144–50, 197, 281, 292
"On a Clear Day You Can See
    Forever," 147
"On the S. S. Bernard Cohn," 147
Once in a Lifetime, 28
"One Hundred Easy Ways," 287
110 in the Shade, 64, 65
One Touch of Venus, 281
"One Wonderful Day," 155
O'Neill, Eugene, 182–87, 311
Oremus, Stephen, 228, 293
Orezzoli, Hector, 75, 76
Orfeh, 36, 39
Ostar Enterprises, 250, 276
Ostrovsky, 314
Ostrow, Stuart, 262
Our Country's Good, 181–82
Out of This World, 151
Overmyer, Eric, 250, 251

PACE Theatrical Group, 110
Pacific Overtures, 45–46, 94
Page, Anthony, 313
Page, Geraldine, 9, 63, 67, 120–21
Pagés, Maria, 176, 178
The Pajama Game, 155, 319
Pakledinaz, Martin, 82, 228, 258,
    303, 306
Pal Joey, 283
Panaro, Hugh, 314
Papermill Playhouse, 143
Parade, 94, 95, 201
"Paradise Is Burning Down," 98

Paramount Pictures, 229
Parks, Suzan-Lori, 53, 304
Parry, William, 42
Pascal, Adam, 190, 300
Passion, 41–45, 278
Patinkin, Mandy, 229, 233–34, 300
Patterson, Dick, 326
Peek, Brent, 24
Pendleton, Austin, 313
Perez, Luis, 308
Perkins, Osgood, 271
Perkins, Tony, 271
Peter Pan, **310**
Peters, Bernadette, 24, 83, 307
Petersen, Taliep, 12
Petina, Irra, 326
The Phantom of the Opera, 237, **311**, 317
Phelan, Michael, 264, 266
Phillips, Arlene, 36
Phillips, Robin, 309
"Phone Call to the Vatican," 111
The Piano Lesson, 52
"Pick-a-Little, Talk-a-Little" 267
Picnic, 63
Picon, Molly, 225
"The Picture of Happiness," 199
Pielmeier, John, 6–9
Pinchot, Bronson, 88, 92
Pinkins, Tonya, 229, 234, 293
Pins and Needles, 319
Pippin, 142–43, 239, 318
Pitchford, Dean, 308
Pitoniak, Anne, 273
Pizzi, Joey, 309
Plain and Fancy, 155–56
Platt, Jon B., 216, 258
Play It Again Sam, 126–27
Play On!, 234
Playwrights Horizons, 134, 136, 278
Plaza Suite, 320
Pleasant, David, 97, 292

Plummer, Amanda, 9
"Poor Little Rich Girl," 49
Porgy and Bess, **162–68**, 292
Porter, Cole, 25, 81, 82, 85, 151
Posey, Parker, 256, 258
Posner, Kenneth, 110, 228, 232, 272, 293
Poster, Kim, 116
Poulton, Mike, 271–72
Power Plays, 258
Present Laughter, 120–21
Preston, Robert, 262
"Pretty Women," 91
Price, Leontyne, 163, 168
Price, Lonny, 313
The Price, **68–74**, 169, 209, 213, 292, 296, 297, 299
Primary Colors (film), 257
Prince, Faith, 137, 291
Prince, Hal, 46, 152, 155, 195–96, 259, 311
Private Lives, 119, 120, 124
Promises, Promises, 318
Proof, 56
Pryce, Jonathan, 309
Pulitzer Prize, 52–53, 304
Putting It Together, **87–93**, 237, 292, 298, 300, 302

"Quejas de Bandoneón," 76
"A Quiet Girl," 286
Quintero, José, 184, 185

Rabb, Ellis, 254
Racing Demon, 220, 273
Radio City Entertainment, 18, 20–22, 102
Rags, 111
Ragtime, **310**
The Rainmaker, **63–67**, 292, 297, 299
The Rainmaker (film), 63–64, 72

The Real Thing, 136, **243–48**, 292, 296, 297, 298–99, 301, 305
The Red Shoes (film), 37
Reed, Janet, 326
Reed, Vivian, 96
Rees, Roger, 245, 247, 272, 273, 299
Reilly, John C., 170, 174, 293, 298–99
Reinis, Jonathan, 30
Reinking, Ann, 308, 309
Rent, 24, 52, 233, **310**, 318
Repici, William, 158
Reprise!, 285
Requiem (by Mozart), 114
Requiem for a Heavyweight (teleplay), 63
Reza, Yasmina, 307
Rice, Tim, 40, 190–92, 237–240, 297, 307, 311
Richardson, Lee, 326
Richardson, Natasha, 308
Rickson, Ian, 311
The Ride Down Mt. Morgan, **209–14**, 292, 295, 299, 301
Rifkin, Ron, 140, 141, 308
Rigg, Diana, 92
Ring Round the Moon, **310**
Ripken, Cal, Jr., 39
Ripley, Alice, 134, 136
Riverdance on Broadway, **175–80**, 292
Rizzuto, Phil, 130
Robards, Jason, 184, 185, 186–87, 299
Robbins, Jerome, 100, 258, 285
Robbins, Tom Alan, 196
"Rock Island," 263
The Rockets, 14–15
Roddy, Pat, 176–78, 292
Rodgers, Richard, 100, 144–45, 308, 311, 314
Rose, **222–26**, 299
Rosenbauer, Judith and David, 12

Rosenfeld, Jyll, 128
Ross, Andrew, 30
Ross, Jerry, 155
Ross, Lisette Lecat, 314
Roth, Robert Jess, 192, 307
Rothman, Carole, 152
Rothstein, Norman, 326
Roundabout Theatre Company, 64, 71, 271–72
Routh, Marc, 12, 110
Royal Flush, 252
Royal National Theatre, 203, 216, 224
Rubinstein, John, 313
Rudin, Scott, 42, 210, 216, 224, 229, 315
Rudko, Mark, 171
Ruffelle, Frances, 309
Russell, Rosalind, 50, 281–82, 284–85
Russo, Kathy, 58, 60
Ryan, Amy, 273, 301
Rylance, Mark, 171
Ryskind, Morrie, 196

Saddler, Donald, 284
Saidy, Fred, 313
Sail Away, **47–51**, 292
"Sail Away," 50
St. Louis Woman, 197, 199, 281
Saks, Gene, 314
Salieri, Antonio, 114–18
Salonga, Lea, 309
Same Time, Next Year, 319
Sams, Jeremy, 120, 122, 313
Sarava, 64
Saturday Night, **151–56**, 292, 305
Saturday Night Fever, 20, 35–40, 109, 121, 241, 303
Sbarge, Raphael, 6
The Scarlet Pimpernel, **17–22**
Scent of the Roses, **314**

Schaeffer, Eric D., 88, 92, 298
Schaffel, Marla, 314
Schlossberg, Julian, 258
Schmidt, Harvey, 65
Schmitt, Eric-Emmanuel, 313
Schneider, Peter, 190
Schönberg, Claude-Michel, 309, 314
Schulman, Susan H., 311
Schulz, Charles, 326
Schumacher, Thomas, 190
Schwartz, Arthur, 104
Schwartz, Scott, 314
Schwartz, Stephen, 143
Scofield, Paul, 117
Scott, George C., 271, 326
Scott, Sherie René, 190, 192, 194, 291, 302
The Season (book), xi, 200
Season In—Season Out (book), xi
Sebesky, Don, 82, 84, 303–4, 306
Second Stage Theatre, 152–53
Seelen, Arthur, 326
Segovia, Claudio, 75–76
Seinfeld, Jerry, 130
Seldes, Marian, 49
Sellers, Jeffrey, 233
Selverstone, Katy, 210, 213
Seven Brides for Seven Brothers (film), 37
The Seven Year Itch, 320
1776, 318
"Seventy-six Trombones," 265
Sex and Death to Age 14, 57
SFX Theatrical Group, 110, 116
Shaffer, Peter, 114, 116–18
Shaw, George Bernard, 270, 271
"She Wasn't You," 147, 149
Shear, Claudia, 275–79, 291, 295, 299–300
Sheen, Michael, 115, 116, 291, 299
Shenandoah, 319
Shepard, Sam, 169–71, 173, 295

Sherman, Martin, 222, 224–226
"A Shine on Your Shoes," 104
Show Boat, 37
Shubert Organization, 210, 214, 224, 276
Shull, Richard B., 24, 326
Side by Side by Sondheim, 91–92
Side Man, 272, 310
Side Show, 17
Sidney, Sylvia, 326
Sight Unseen, 53
Sills, Douglas, 19
The Silver Triangle, 263
Simmonds, Stanley, 327
Simmons, Stanley, 327
Simon, Neil, 21, 25–26, 52, 260
Simon, Paul, 25–26
Singin' in the Rain (film), 37
Sirkin, Spring, 210, 313
Six Degrees of Separation, 25, 201–3
Skinner, Emily, 134, 136
Slater, Christian, 265–66
Sleight of Hand, 9
Sleuth, 10, 320
Sly Fox, 72
Smallens, Alexander, 165
Smith, Derek, 250, 253–54, 291, 301
Smith, Jonathan, 113
Smith, Maggie, 120
Smith, Rex, 19
Smokey Joe's Cafe, 14, 25, 113, 310
"So in Love," 81
"So Many People," 154, 156
Soble, Stanley, 327
Sokolow, Anna, 327
Soloway, Leonard, 30, 120
"Someday I'll Find You," 49
"Something Very Strange," 49
Sondheim, Stephen, 41–46, 87–93, 135, 145, 152–56, 204, 278, 284, 292, 293, 305, 315
Song of Singapore, 283

The Sound of Music, 311, 318
South Pacific, 318
Spanger, Amy, 80–83, 85, 302
Sperling, Ted, 42
Spewack, Bella, 28, 80
Spewack, Sam, 28, 80
Spiegelman, Art, 229–30
Spinella, Stephen, 134, 136, 137, 291, 301–2, 306
Sprecher, Ben, 6
Squonk, **157–61**, 256
Stadlen, Lewis J., 282
Stanley, 173
Starlight Express, 237
Steel Pier, 23
Stein, Douglas, 276, 279
Stenborg, Helen, 120, 124, 293, 301
Stevens, Craig, 327
Stewart, Patrick, 210–11, 213–14, 292, 299
Stiers, David Ogden, 196
Stigwood, Robert, 36, 40, 237–241
Stilgoe, Richard, 311
Stillman, Bob, 276, 277, 291, 301
Stoller, Mike, 310
Stomp, 14
Stone, Peter, 307, 313
Stoppard, Tom, 244–47
"Story Vignettes," 285
Stratas, Teresa, 111
Stritch, Elaine, 48–50, 292
Stroman, Susan, 95, 202–4, 207, 208, 263, 264, 266–67, 291, 292, 297, 298, 306, 314
Stupid Kids, 272
Styne, Jule, 153, 310
Suchet, David, 115, 116, 298–99
Sugar Babies, 318
Sullivan, Daniel, 54, 56, 182, 186, 291
Sullivan, Ed, 126–27
Summerhays, Jane, 229, 235

"Summertime," 167
Sunday in the Park with George, 278
Sunset Boulevard, 237
Sutherland, Donald, 313
Sweet Deliverance, 315
"Sweet Polly Plunkett," 135
Swerling, Jo, 193
Swimming to Cambodia, 57, 58
Swing!, **108–13**, 293, 295–96, 298, 302, 303–4
The Swing (painting), 204
"Swinging," 204

Table Settings, 278
Taller Than a Dwarf, 53, **256–61**, 299
Tandy, Jessica, 119–20
Tango Argentino, **75–79**, 296
Task, Maggie, 327
Taylor, Elizabeth, 120
Taylor, Ron, 309
Taylor, Samuel, 327
Taylor-Corbett, Lynne, 110, 112, 293, 298
Taymor, Julie, 191, 249–53, 255, 297, 311
Teahouse of the August Moon, 320
A Teaspoon Every Four Hours, 126–27
Tenderloin, **195–200**, 281, 293
Tepper, Arielle, 134, 137
Tergis, Athena, 179, 292
Testa, Mary, 96, 292, 302
"That Kind of a Neighborhood," 155
"That's Entertainment," 104
Theatre Book of the Year (book), xi
Theatre for a New Audience, 250
Theatre World (book), xi
"There's a Boat Dat's Leavin' Soon for New York," 97, 163
They're Playing Our Song, 319
Thomas, Jenny, 113
Thompson, David, 308

Thompson, Jay, 252
Thompson, Tazewell, 165
Three Tall Women, 52
"Throw That Girl Around," 109, 113
"Till I Met You" ("Till There Was You"), 262
Tillinger, John, 309
Tipton, Jennifer, 140, 174
Titanic, 129, 232
Titus Andronicus (film), 251
Tobacco Road, 319
Todd, Albert, 271
"Tommy, Tommy," 199
Tomorrow the World, 260–61
Toms, Carl, 327
Tonight at 8:30, 119
Torch Song Trilogy, 276, 320
"The Tower of Bray," 135
"Tradition," 285
"Tragedy," 39
A Tree Grows in Brooklyn, 198–99
"Trouble," 264
True West, **169–74**, 293, 295, 297, 298–99
Tudyk, Alan, 24
Tune, Tommy, 39
Tunick, Jonathan, 88, 96, 152, 156, 252, 292, 303–4
Twelfth Night, 273
Twelve Angry Men (teleplay), 63
Twelve Dreams, 278

Uncle Vanya, **270–74**, 297, 299, 301, 302
"Under the Bamboo Tree," 104
Undergrowth with Two Figures (painting), 5
"Unworthy of Your Love," 89
Up in Paradise, 210

Van Dyke, Dick, 265, 266
van Itallie, Jean-Claude, 271

Van Laast, Anthony, 238
Van Patten, Joyce, 258, 260–61
Vennema, John C., 213
Vereen, Ben, 239–40
Via Dolorosa, 225, 311
Vidnovic, Martin, 287
Viertel, Tom, 110
Vietnam War, 72–73
View from the Bridge, 213
Vincent, Tony, 238, 302
Vineyard Theatre (Mass.), 275
The Voice of the Turtle, 319
Voices in the Dark, **5–10**, 53, 143, 256
Von Scherler, Sasha, 327

Wagner, Frank, 327
Wagner, Robin, 36, 82, 229, 240, 302–3
"Wait Till We're Sixty-Five," 147, 149
Waiting in the Wings, 52, **119–25**, 293, 299–300, 301
"Wake the Dead," 133, 135, 136
Walken, Christopher, 134, 136–38, 300
Walker, Chet, 309
Walker, Don, 263, 286
Walker, Nancy, 283
Walker, Randolph, 328
Wallace, Naomi, 313
Walton, Tony, 258, 272, 302–3
Warchus, Matthew, 170, 171, 293, 297, 307
Ward, Lauren, 42, 152, 156, 292
Warden, Jack, 70
Warfield, William, 168
Waterston, Sam, 215–16
The Waverly Gallery, 305
Waxman, Anita, 182, 229, 244, 264
"Way Back to Paradise," 97

Webber, Andrew Lloyd. See Lloyd
   Webber, Andrew
Weber, Bruce, 225
Weidman, Jerome, 195, 196
Weidman, John, 42, 44, 95, 195, 196,
   202–4, 207, 208, 291, 296, 315
Weinstock, Jack, 193
The Weir, 13–14, 311
Weitzman, Ira, 98, 202
"We're Gonna Go to Chicago," 97
"Were Thine That Special Face," 81
West, Mae, 275–79
West, Matt, 192, 307
West, Nathanael, 283–84
West Side Story, 98, 99–100, 165–66,
   262
Weston, Celia, 170
Wharton, William, 313
"What Did I Have That I Don't
   Have?," 147
"What More Do I Need?," 154
What's Wrong with This Picture,
   53–54
Wheeler, Harold, 110, 113, 293,
   303–4
Wheetman, Dan, 309
Whelan, Bill, 176, 180
"When It Ends," 234–35
"Where Have You Been All My
   Life?," 45
"Where Is the Life That Late I Led,"
   81
Whistle Down the Wind, 237
White, Jane, 49
White, Julie, 54
White, Miles, 328
Whitehead, Paxton, 119–20
Whiteley, Ben, 48
Who's Afraid of Virginia Woolf?, 53,
   91
"Why Can't You Behave?," 81

"Why Do the Wrong People Travel,"
   49
The Wild Party (LaChiusa), 227–236
The Wild Party (Lippa), 227–236
The Wild Party (film), 229
The Wild Party (literary work),
   228–29
Wildcat, 64
Wilder, Thornton, 271
Wildhorn, Frank, 18, 21, 26, 308,
   309
Wilkof, Lee, 80–81, 83, 84, 85, 292,
   301–02
Williams, Elizabeth, 182, 229, 244,
   264
Williams, Emlyn, 309
Williams, Tennessee, 310
Williamson, Nicol, 271
Williamson, Ruth, 24, 264, 267,
   292
Williamstown Theatre Festival, 65,
   72, 210
Will Mastin Trio, 12–13, 15
Willson, Meredith, 262–64
Wilson, August, 53, 304
Wilson, Elizabeth, 120, 124, 293
Wilson, Mary Louise, 254
Wilson, Patrick, 196
Wise Guys, **41–46**, 203–4, 293,
   315
Wit, 52, 157–58
The Wiz, 318
Wolfe, George C., 210, 229, 230,
   235–36, 298
Wonderful Town, **281–88**, 293
Wood, Frank, 310
Wood, John, 116
Wood, Peter, 245
Woodward, Sarah, 244, 292, 301
Woolverton, Linda, 190–93, 297,
   307

The World According to Me, 127
Wrong Mountain, 53, 139–43, 256,
    293, 301
"Wrong Note Rag," 287

Yates, Deborah, 202, 207, 291,
    302
Yearby, Marlies, 310
York, Rachel, 19
The Young Man from Atlanta, 52
You're a Good Man, Charlie Brown,
    23, 25, 149, 231, **312**

"You're Looking at the Man," 98
Yulin, Harris, 70, 72

Zagnit, Stuart, 229, 235
Zaks, Jerry, 24–27. 110, 112–13, 297,
    308, 310
The Ziegfeld Follies (film), 103
Ziemba, Karen, 202, 205–6, 291,
    302, 306
Zipprodt, Patricia, 253, 328
Zorich, Louis, 146